Information Literacy Instruction That Works

A Guide to Teaching by Discipline and Student Population

Edited by Patrick Ragains

Neal-Schuman Publishers, Inc.
New York   *London*

Information Literacy Sourcebooks
1. Information Literacy Instruction: Theory and Practice
2. Learning to Lead and Manage Information Literacy Instruction
3. Information Literacy Instruction That Works: A Guide to Teaching by
   Discipline and Student Population

Published by Neal-Schuman Publishers, Inc.
100 William St., Suite 2004
New York, NY 10038

Printed and bound in the United States of America.

The paper used in this publication meets the minimum requirements of American National Standard for Information Sciences—Permanence of Paper for Printed Library Materials, ANSI Z39.48-1992.

Library of Congress Cataloging-in-Publication Data

Information literacy instruction that works : a guide to teaching by discipline
      and student population / edited by Patrick Ragains.
         p.   cm.—(Information literacy sourcebooks; no. 3)
      Includes bibliographical references and index.
      ISBN 1–55570–573–1 (alk. paper)
      1. Information literacy—Study and teaching (Higher) 2. Electronic information resource literacy—Study and teaching (Higher) 3. Academic libraries—Relations with faculty and curriculum. I. Ragains, Patrick. II. Series.
   ZA3075.I537 2006
      028.7071'1—dc22   2006013765

This book is dedicated to my parents, Rees and Leta Ragains, who have always given me their love, encouraged my skepticism, and supported my education.

—Patrick Ragains

Contents

Figures

Instructional Resources
on the CD-ROM

Note: Resources on the CD are numbered according to the corresponding number in this book.

Preface

The goal of making students information literate through effective library instruction sits at the core of our mission as academic librarians. How do we go about accomplishing this challenge? We plan. We perform outreach. We build collections. We craft lessons. We develop tools. We focus.

Helping learners acquire and then hone the skills necessary to fully utilize the information resources available today is among the most demanding and time-consuming tasks in our day-to-day work lives. It is made all the more difficult when we consider the diversity of students we must reach, the specific requirements of individual disciplines, and the challenge of special topics.

I developed *Information Literacy Instruction That Works* to offer well-tested strategies and successful methods to teach today's college and university student. The individual chapter authors present practical ways to plan, develop, market, deliver, and assess training. They balance theory and research with sensible suggestions, time-saving tips, and useful materials. You will find sample assignments, brochures, lesson plans, tutorials, evaluation forms, bibliographies, and more. It was my hope that this text would provide my busy colleagues with a starting point to springboard new ideas, help develop fresh lessons, or refine existing teaching plans.

It is likely that you are responsible for improving the information literacy (IL) abilities of an increasingly diverse student body, many with distinct needs. In such a climate, finding effective teaching methods that work with a myriad of subjects and special topics can be daunting. *Information Literacy Instruction That Works* is intended to make this easier. You should leave this text with a newfound confidence in your ability to teach students of all types to find the information they need with an ease and grace of their own.

Organization

Information Literacy Instruction That Works is divided into four parts addressing the questions raised in key areas:

- What are the best ways to teach IL skills in colleges and universities?
- How do we teach an increasingly diverse student body, which has many students in special circumstances with specific needs?
- What are the best ways to teach information literacy in numerous subject areas, each with distinctive features?
- How do we educate students to research special topics, many requiring legal and governmental research?

All of these major parts open with an introductory overview in which I discuss the contents of the subsequent chapters. Each chapter illuminates a certain area, though all also cover a number of essential common issues—knowing the audience, determining what needs to be taught, delivering instruction, and assessing the process.

The two chapters in Part I, "Planning to Teach Information Literacy in Colleges and Universities," offer a current lay-of-the-land and address basic matters of instructional design and delivery. I wrote Chapter 1, with the support of many other colleagues, to offer a broad range of advice on ways to build relationships with faculty, prepare and provide instruction, and teach with technology. In Chapter 2, Jean Caspers discusses ideas for how to collaborate with faculty. She gives sound advice on how to build good working relationships for the benefit of students, presents and analyzes different kinds of faculty-librarian interactions, and provides a sample assignment to use in shared teaching situations.

Part II, "Teaching Information Literacy to Individual Audiences," focuses on developing teaching techniques and strategies for the unique needs of wide-ranging students. In Chapter 3, Mark Emmons presents a compelling case for information literacy instruction and offers many samples of lessons to use in freshman-level instruction and ways to assess success. The community college environment is Ann Roselle's focus in Chapter 4. Alexander Gyamfi, author of Chapter 5, covers classroom instruction for students with disabilities. Finally, Tina Adams and Sean Evans recommend best practices for teaching IL skills and furnishing library support for remote education students in Chapter 6.

The next two parts are designed to broaden content-related knowledge. Part III, "Teaching Information Literacy in Specific Disciplines," addresses the need to shape instruction to nine curricular areas:

- English literature
- art and art history
- film studies
- history
- psychology
- science
- agricultural science and natural resources
- hospitality and gaming
- international marketing

In Chapter 7, Janelle M. Zauha considers the surprising complexities of providing information literacy instruction to literary studies. Peggy Keeran, in Chapter 8, shows how to guide students toward a fuller understanding of both art's past and how to shape its future. Chapter 9 by Neal Baker provides recommendations to help use cinema to both support academic teaching in other disciplines and facilitate student's understanding of the forms and functions of film. Chapter 10 by Joel D. Kitchens discusses how to teach students to respect the complexities of historical scholarship. Nonny Schlotzhauer's Chapter 11 analyzes some of the best strategies to help students navigate the increasingly multifaceted and varied body of academic psychological literature.

In Chapter 12, Gregg Sapp explores the intricacies of increasing the scientific literacy of our students and library patrons. In Chapter 13, Allison V. Level tackles a broad range of agricultural topics—from biotechnology to rural development and beyond. Chapter 14 by Cory Tucker delves into best information literacy practices for the growing industry of hospitality and gaming, a business sector that already has an annual take of $10 trillion worldwide. I wrote Chapter 15 to outline ways to support international marketing courses for students at both the undergraduate and graduate level.

"Teaching Special Topics in Information Literacy" is Part IV, the final part of *Information Literacy Instruction That Works*. It will help you teach these important research skills to students and coworkers. Such research is often a major component in business, public administration, education, and nursing. Students often lack convenient access to a good law library but still need court decisions, statutes, administrative rules and regulations, executive orders, and other legal information related to their area of study.

In Chapter 16, Duncan Aldrich shows how students can be taught to retrieve legal information from free Web-based sources. Chapter 17 by Susie A. Skarl takes advantage of the ways in which the Internet has eased access to everything from census data to legislation. Chapter 18 by Brian B. Carpenter closes the book by describing how to aid students in navigating the complex world of the U.S. Patent and Trademark Office and the assorted ancillary information depositories related to it.

In addition to the chapters previously described, this book features a CD-ROM that expands the content of many of the chapters with sample assignments, tips for evaluating electronic documents, topical lists of journals, hyperlinks to some suggested sites, and much more. All of these tools are designed to support the text, taking the content of many of the chapters beyond the confines of the page.

I hope *Information Literacy Instruction That Works*, with its double-pronged focus on both "the who" and "the what" of learning, fills an important need. Few responsibilities in the library are more important than helping an increasingly wide audience of users take advantage of the countless resources that we make available. I hope this book will help foster our goal to make all our students information literate—one unique learner at a time.

Acknowledgments

I acknowledge the efforts of the contributors to this book, each of whom has devoted much of his or her career to teaching and supporting information literacy. Without exception, they brought their best ideas to this book. I will always be grateful for the opportunity to have worked with them in this capacity.

PART I

Planning to Teach Information Literacy in Colleges and Universities

The two chapters in Part I of this manual address general matters related to information literacy instruction (ILI) and will help you plan and deliver that instruction in college and university settings. Chapter 1 offers a broad range of advice concerning building relationships with faculty, preparing and delivering instruction, and teaching with technology. This chapter also looks at the implications of link resolvers and *Google Scholar* for students and researchers and identifies essential points to cover with your users. In Chapter 2, Jean Caspers discusses collaborating with instructional faculty in library and ILI, giving sound advice on how to build good working relationships for the benefit of students. She presents and analyzes different kinds of faculty-librarian interactions and offers a sample assignment to use in a collaborative teaching situation.

Once you have considered the foundational information in Part I, you will be ready to use the rest of the information in this book to raise your own teaching, assessment, and overall library service to new levels of excellence.

1

Setting the Stage for Information Literacy Education

Patrick Ragains, assisted by Tina M. Adams, Duncan Aldrich, R. Sean Evans, Peggy Keeran, Joel D. Kitchens, Nonny Schlotzhauer, and Cory Tucker

Introduction

Librarianship and teaching are strongly practice-oriented professions. Individuals in these occupations gain mastery on the job. Teaching is not a focus in professional library education at large, and most literature on library and information literacy instruction (ILI) is written by practitioners who have gained substantial experience in and insight into teaching. The Instruction Section of the Association of College and Research Libraries (ACRL) maintains a bibliography related to library and information literacy instruction that lists case studies and theoretical and editorial literature (ACRL, 2003). Grassian and Kaplowitz's book *Information Literacy Instruction: Theory and Practice* effectively describes the range of skills librarians need to become effective teachers today (Grassian and Kaplowitz, 2001). Both sources are very useful to instruction librarians who want to review ILI-related literature and improve their skills. While avoiding unnecessary redundancy with earlier work, this book provides in-depth exposure to the perspectives of librarians who teach in particular settings. This chapter is applicable to information literacy instruction in a college or university setting, regardless of the student group served or the subject matter taught. It includes a definition of information literacy, describes students' need for information literacy skills, gives tips on getting to know faculty and preparing for and delivering instructional sessions (including a baseline orientation to a modern library), considers the possible effects of *Google Scholar* on academic library users, and provides overviews on assessment practices. Subsequent chapters build on the concepts introduced here by addressing the needs of particular kinds of students or their needs in specific disciplines.

What Is Information Literacy?

Previous authors have competently reviewed the development of information literacy as a concept (Behrens, 1994). We suggest a succinct and widely accepted definition: information literacy is the ability to identify, locate, and use information effectively. This definition combines critical thinking and facility with information technology. Further, ACRL's *Information Literacy Competency Standards for Higher Education* describes the technical and intellectual skills possessed by an information-literate individual. According to the standards in that document, such a person can:

- Determine the extent of information needed
- Access the needed information effectively and efficiently
- Evaluate information and its sources critically
- Incorporate selected information into one's knowledge base and use information effectively to accomplish a specific purpose
- Understand the economic, legal, and social issues surrounding the use of information
- Access and use information ethically and legally (ACRL, 2000)

Framed in this manner, information literacy is considerably wider in scope than the aims of a single instructional unit, assignment, or project. For instance, when students evaluate Web sites they may be considering aesthetics, the soundness of arguments presented on the sites, authorship, and currency, but may not concern themselves with whether the sites present information ethically or legally. Students who carry on course-related discussions using a Web-based forum may be gaining technical skills and analyzing arguments, but they may not be engaged in any of the aforementioned activities. When considering such examples we can profitably refer to Christine Bruce's phenomenological perspective, that is, that information literacy is defined in a variety of specific and limited ways, without necessarily encompassing the full scope of the ACRL standards (1997).

College and University Students' Need for Information Literacy Skills

In Chapter 3 of this book, Mark Emmons reviews recent studies of students' information-seeking practices. Among these is the Online Computer Library Center's (OCLC) *White Paper on the Information Habits of College Students*, which confirms that students use the free and open Web quite heavily for course-related research, often to the exclusion of resources owned or licensed by libraries (OCLC, 2002). Faculty are concerned about this trend because they often find students relying on information that has no scholarly or professional imprimatur and no editorial review, that is, essentially, informal communication. Academic librarians should clearly understand the implications of this situation. It charges us, first, to put quality information within easy reach of students and, second, to help give them the skills to choose and retrieve it. This affirms the long-standing mission of academic libraries to collect and provide students and faculty with the information they need. Libraries increasingly approach this goal with online collections, so that users experience their library on the Web and at some distance from library buildings. Consequently, most examples in this book refer to Web-based information.

Building Relationships with Faculty

There is no single way to reach faculty and students, so you should look for opportunities to meet people and become visible in the academic community. Normally, you will be able to work on campus committees and attend lectures, performances, and exhibit openings. You will meet people and be introduced as a librarian who specializes in particular subjects. As you become integrated into your college or university community, you can address questions about the library and its collections and resources. The following are some suggestions for reaching faculty, students, and staff, many focusing on academic librarians' roles as subject liaisons or specialists:

- Liaison activities:
    - Attend college meetings and departmental meetings.
    - Visit academic departments. This is an excellent way to meet students and faculty and to find out their questions and concerns (Atkins, 2001). You may wish to hold office hours in the departments you serve, so that faculty and students can drop by easily.
    - Learn about faculty's research and teaching activities.
    - Contact faculty at the beginning of each academic year to schedule orientation, tours, and instruction and remind them of the services the library offers. Send e-mail or flyers describing some of the available services.
    - Describe your library's instructional services—faculty must know that there is an instruction program in order to utilize it.
    - Inform faculty of new initiatives, pilot projects, services, or products that may interest them.
    - Post messages to departmental listservs. If a listserv is not restricted, ask to be added. If you cannot join the listserv, ask if you can periodically send messages for the department's administrative staff to post to the list. You will want faculty to see value in your messages, so keep them short and to the point. Customize the e-mail to let each faculty group know what might be of special interest to them.

- Communication on your campus and at distance education sites:
  - Send brochures that publicize the library to computer labs and interactive instructional television (IITV) labs, both on campus and at remote sites where classes are held.
  - Attend orientations for IITV and computer lab technicians to give a brief synopsis of what the library can do for students and all the services available. This is especially important, since students working in remote labs will often approach the lab technicians to ask research-oriented questions. You should give the lab techs a basic understanding of the library Web site, but also emphasize the many ways they can direct students to library service points for assistance.
  - Include library brochures in direct mailings from the graduate college to all new graduate students.

Whatever outreach techniques you use, remember that one faculty member impressed by library support can, through their communication with colleagues, lead to more interaction between librarians and faculty. You should not become discouraged at the onset of your outreach efforts if they seem unproductive. Building relationships with faculty and getting invited to campus events or department meetings can take time. If you are new to the campus, it may help to enlist the aid of fellow librarians to introduce you to some faculty.

Teaching faculty have a primary relationship with students, one that differs from typical librarian-student relationships. Faculty "own" the courses they teach, define expectations for student performance, and hold responsibility for grading. Unless you teach your own credit-bearing courses, your instructional contact depends at least indirectly on the faculty. For example, will they contact you to request course-related sessions? Are they willing to devote one or more class sessions to you for information literacy instruction? Are they receptive to your input concerning student assignments? Will they refer students to you for reference consultations? If you believe you and your instructional program have something worthwhile to offer students, then you must get to know faculty on their terms and promote information literacy instruction with tact and in appropriate contexts.

Preparation

This section refers primarily to preparation for course-related instruction, as opposed to semester-long involvement in a course. Typically, a professor will contact the library (or may contact you directly) to request an instruction session for a course. Before you prepare a lesson plan and decide which concepts to cover, it pays to meet with the professor requesting the session and hammer out some important details. To the extent possible, you should work with instructors to make your presentation pertinent to students' coursework. Several points to clarify are:

- The course topic and materials to cover.
- The level of the course. For example, students in a graduate class usually have information needs that are very different from those of freshmen.

- Whether the students have an associated assignment, such as a term paper or short writing exercise. What is the range of possible topics for student papers?
- The amount of class time available—will it be half a class period, a full class, or multiple class sessions?
- The class location—will the session take place in the assigned classroom or do you need to reserve a room?
- What equipment is needed—is a computer lab necessary or are an instructor-operated computer and projector sufficient?
- Whether the instructor wants you to design a follow-up assignment.
- The course instructor's expectations for student use of Internet sources. Some instructors, in an effort to curb easy plagiarism, prohibit the use of any materials found on the Web. Such blanket statements usually have unintended consequences when students, especially freshmen, interpret the prohibition to extend to all licensed library databases using a Web interface. It helps to clarify with the instructor what relevant electronic library resources are now available via a Web browser and to distinguish between these and the free Web.
- Whether you will be team teaching or on your own. Will the course instructor be present?
- Your class presentation format and style—faculty may have particular preferences.

Preparing Your Remarks and Students' Activities

The baseline orientation outlined in the section of this chapter titled "Methods of Instruction" covers library catalogs and common elements of an academic library Web site. Some form of this orientation will benefit students in most classes. There are some situations in which a baseline orientation may be omitted, such as when you need to cover information outside the scope of the catalog and multidisciplinary aggregator databases linked from your library Web site. Such instances would involve using comprehensive online databases such as *LION, STAT-USA*, an image library, a database of company information, or a source for case law. Subsequent chapters in this book cover many such scenarios.

If you are preparing a one-shot session, avoid crowding too many topics or sources into your presentation. Presenting two subject-related resources and pertinent search concepts, in addition to the baseline information, can easily take up an entire fifty- or seventy-five-minute class period. If you are presenting in a hands-on computer lab, each topic or resource will take more time than if you simply demonstrate from the instructor's workstation. Students in a lab setting need more time to follow your instructions and may have difficulties or raise questions as they work. When teaching in a lab you may need to limit the number of topics or the amount of time you spend on each point you cover.

As you introduce students to each database or resource, it helps to use a conceptual framework that leads from simple identification to more detailed examination. We suggest the following five-point framework:

1   Identify the database or resource—*What is it?*
2   Identify its scope—*What sort of information is in it?*
3   Learn the applicable search and retrieval techniques—*How does it work?*
4   Assess its content for both general and specific purposes—*Is it any good?*
5   Evaluate the resource, making comparisons with other sources—*How well does it meet my needs? What other sources might tell me more about my topic or answer my question?*

Another good way to structure a presentation is to use specific research topics. The instructor may provide you with one assigned topic or a greater number of topics from individual students. While this usually works best when you know the topics in advance and have taken time to search for information on them before the class session, you may decide to ask for volunteers to explain their topics in class. However you gather this information, it is helpful to demonstrate some research in front of the class. Doing so allows you to show students how the databases and other tools work, usually revealing some important points about the nature of their topics and the available information. This strategy also allows you to show students how an experienced searcher works, acting and reacting in real time, doing such things as:

• Formulating a search using keywords, proper nouns, dates, and other significant information taken from a topic statement
• Executing the search and examining the results
• Modifying the search with broader, narrower, or related terms
• Limiting the search results by date, language, format, and other parameters
• Evaluating a modified or limited search
• Exporting the search results
• Determining the comprehensiveness of the resource for the topic and identifying other resources to search

These recommendations will help you engage students in the context of their assignments and demonstrate value in the resources that you present and thinking strategies you model.

Preparing Instructional Materials

The following list contains a few guidelines for creating good instructional materials, including printed guides, PowerPoint presentations, and Web pages. Chapter 15 includes a detailed discussion on creating Web-based instructional guides. Keep the following points in mind when creating any media to use in group instruction:

• Be sure that any instructional materials are uncluttered, that they use clear, everyday language, and that they present information succinctly.
• Use terms and formats consistently as they appear on your library Web site

and in the catalog; that is, use accepted names for buildings, collections, and service points.

- Display call numbers using the conventions, spacing, and punctuation used in your library catalog.
- Be sure that any information you display in a classroom is legible from the back of the room. If it is not, then change or eliminate it.
- If you save a PowerPoint presentation to the Web, make sure any hyperlinks open in a new window. Doing so will allow you to return easily to your presentation after displaying a linked page.

Using Computer Technology

Instructional computer labs and fully equipped podiums are common today in colleges and universities. Working in such settings is immeasurably better than transporting portable computers and projection equipment to classrooms, a situation that was quite common through the late 1990s. Still, there are a number of things to check in wired classrooms:

- Is the room available when you need it?
- Is all of the necessary equipment present and in good working condition?
- Does the instructor's computer monitor still display while the projector is working?
- Is the projected image in focus and large enough to view from all student seating?
- Can you operate all other equipment at the instructor's podium, including the overhead projector, video players, microphone, and any other components?
- Do you have CD or DVD backups for any Web pages or other networked files you plan to use? Full backups are not always possible, but you should consider how you will teach if the computing network or remote sites are unavailable.
- Are the student computers ready to use and will students have the necessary login information?
- Can you control the student workstations?
- Is lighting in the room adequate for your session and do you know how to adjust it?
- Whom can you contact during the class session for technical assistance?

Methods of Instruction

There are several approaches to teaching library research skills to students. Generally the best scenario is the fully integrated information literacy program, in which students learn these valuable skills in many courses throughout the curriculum. In Chapter 12, Gregg Sapp discusses information literacy requirements at the University of Albany, where students may take either a general information literacy course or another option focusing on science literacy. Comparatively few colleges and universities have either type of information literacy program, so the next best and most common method of instruction is the fifty-minute "one-shot" session, delivered in a single class period. If used wisely, such sessions can be quite effective. If faculty cannot spare fifty minutes from class lecture time, then instruction librarians may consider developing in-service workshops. These could target teaching faculty and graduate assistants, but could be open to anyone who wants to come and learn or refresh their search skills. Weekly drop-in workshops highlighting a different discipline each week can also have some impact. You should be prepared to try any of these techniques, but also be willing to abandon any that do not prove successful.

If time permits, it is always beneficial to engage students in hands-on learning. Facilitating learning through activities rather than simply lecturing to students creates a dynamic classroom environment that attracts students' attention and produces greater interaction. Recent literature on the virtues of problem-based learning (PBL) shows that it can be an effective teaching and learning strategy for introducing information literacy to students. John M. Keller's ARCS Model (Attention, Relevance, Confidence, Satisfaction) complements many kinds of active learning and is a good basis for conducting a successful class session (Keller, 1987). Keller synthesized existing research on psychological motivation to create the ARCS model. Although not intended to stand apart as a separate system for instructional design, the model suggests the four criteria to motivate student learning and recommends how to meet these conditions. Trudi Jacobson and Lijuan Xu have described their use of the ARCS model in information literacy courses, a setting in which librarians have more time to engage students by motivating and rewarding them (Jacobson and Xu, 2004).

Keep in mind that the content you teach and the Web-based guides and tutorials you make available can create favorable conditions for learning but will not, by themselves, teach students how to find and use information competently. Students gain both critical habits of mind and technical skills through practice. The educational theorist John Dewey believed that practical experience gives learners the raw material they need to develop well-integrated intellectual constructs on a given subject. Educators, especially those involved in adult education, have increasingly accepted David Kolb's sequencing of educational experiences, leading from concrete experience to acquisition of skills, reflective observation, abstract conceptualization, and active experimentation (i.e., the testing of concepts) (Kolb, 1984). Students must gain experience by practicing some relevant examples before they can form generalizations about concept mapping and search strategies and competently evaluate the information they retrieve (Ragains, 1995). This brings us to another constant of student-faculty relationships: course assignments are key to practicing and acquiring new knowledge. Student learning depends more upon required, graded assignments than on the exhortations of instruction librarians.

A Baseline Orientation

What do students need to know about gathering and using information? Research among undergraduates and graduates differs, and it is important to understand these differences when teaching students how to use a library. Undergraduates tend to come to their research topics driven by the content of their class; that is, instructors assign or suggest topics for research. For graduate students, the research process is more multifaceted, ranging from class-specific assignments to literature reviews for theses and dissertations. Undergraduates are less likely than graduate students to have explored the catalog and pertinent databases on their own. Graduate students are also more apt to follow citations to works and other items listed in bibliographies.

Students at all levels usually benefit from some instruction in using the catalog and library Web site, so try to include these in each orientation you offer. Students and others often presume they can search library catalogs adequately but are often unaware of how they can fully exploit a catalog's functionality to find more information. Concepts and techniques to cover include:

- Institutional scope. Describe the catalog's coverage of specific libraries in your institution or in other colleges or universities or, for sources like *RLIN* and *WorldCat*, a wider range of libraries.
- Scope of library holdings described in the catalog. The catalog may list books, films, videos, audio recordings, journal titles, government publications, microform collections (by collection title only versus individual records describing collection contents), course reserves, manuscript collections, archives, maps, photographs, and images.
- Accessible Web-based materials. Tell students about pertinent sources linked from the catalog, including electronic journals and books, scanned reserve readings, art and photographic images, manuscript guides, and other sources. Be sure to give them any special instructions for retrieving these materials outside the library or from off campus.
- Library holdings excluded from the catalog. These may include journal articles, some books and periodicals, government publications, and other nonbook materials.
- Search functionality. Show students how keyword searches function. Do these searches work with implied Boolean operators? Also cover user-defined operators, author and subject heading searches, and searching by material format or location.
- Limiting and sorting by availability and publication date.
- Functionality of hyperlinks in catalog records (e.g., authors, subject headings, series).
- Links to other catalogs.
- Request/hold functions.
- Viewing one's circulation record.

Similarly, give students an overview of your library Web site as it relates to their course and research. Points to cover include:

- Services and information linked from the library home page. These may include library hours, the online catalog, interlibrary loan services, course-related reserves, metasearch (i.e., federated search), subject-related lists of databases and other lists of licensed resources, online reference sources, and department and staff directories.

- Site search. Most library Web sites are complex, so many users can benefit from a site search tool. Be sure to tell students what is covered by the site search and what is excluded (e.g., it may search Web pages on the library site, but not the catalog or licensed sources).
- Site map. A site map provides easy access to the titles of Web pages on the site. It shows how the Web site is structured and can serve as an advance organizer for users.

Covering the preceding points will expose students to the most prominent parts of your library Web space and promote a basic familiarity with information they are likely to need. Always emphasize librarians' availability to meet with students one-on-one or in groups to help them with topics discussed in the session or other research questions. Depending on the scope of your presentation, the instructor's preferences, and the amount of time available, you may also wish to orient students to the following:

- The library building
- Specific collections or call number ranges in the circulating and reference collections
- Equipment, including photocopiers, computer workstations, and microform equipment
- Service points for reference assistance, circulation, special departments, or branches

Users' discovery processes can vary greatly, ranging from the undergraduate who is gaining knowledge and learning how to find it to the seasoned faculty member who acquires information via a wide-ranging but efficient network of scholarly interaction. A baseline orientation will set the stage for teaching more sophisticated strategies or demonstrating specific databases.

Teaching Students to Use Information Technology

While the current generation of college students has grown up in a world in which technology and the Internet are mainstays, many of them have misconceptions about what the Internet is and what the Internet can do for them, especially as a research tool. Students are often ill-equipped to harness the immense amount of information that confronts them. However, we must acknowledge that the Internet is the medium of choice for information gathering, and we must structure much of our instructional effort within that framework (Jones et al., 2002; OCLC, 2002).

It is important for you to point out the pros and cons of doing research over the Internet. Explain and show examples of how open Web searching is fundamentally different from searching library resources. Academic library collections have been screened to maximize reliability, since librarians generally discriminate about what they purchase in order to build a quality collection. Admittedly, questionable or poor information still slips in, but collection development activities are intended to promote quality in a library's print and online holdings. The Internet has information on thousands of topics, but much of it is unedited and unregulated.

Online tutorials can complement the information you present during an instructional session by encouraging students to review the points you make in class. Tutorials can reinforce key elements of research or library use and are most effective if they provide opportunities for the viewer to interact with the tutorial. Faculty can use Web-based tutorials on their own in wired classrooms or with individual students. The University of Denver's Penrose Library has some excellent tutorials on its Web site, including information on using the catalog, finding articles, full-text sources, evaluating information, and more (University of Denver). Not coincidentally, Penrose Library's assessment efforts show the benefit of tutorials after being introduced and used in library instruction sessions.

Link resolvers such as *SFX* search across an institution's licensed sources and library catalog for full-text or other means of locating a publication. Reference and instruction librarians must now teach students and faculty how to use resolvers successfully. The following are some points to make about link resolvers:

- A link resolver is designed to allow a user to retrieve a publication or information about it while the user is online. Saved search results normally do not include data from link resolvers. Students needing to export resolver data can do so by copying the basic resolver link of each desired item (e.g., right click the computer mouse on the link and choose Copy Shortcut), then pasting the URL into a document for use at a later time. This URL should open the resolver's menu of services related to the original citation.
- If a resolver does not go directly to the target online article, book, or other source, it may go to a journal's Web site or an analogous destination, such as a vendor or publisher's site. The user must then navigate to the desired article or other source (if, indeed, the desired item is within the range of licensed online content available through the user's institution).

Link resolvers often work in tandem with a federated search system (also known as metasearch), which allows users to search multiple databases simultaneously, rather than selecting individual databases and searching each in its native interface. If your library uses a federated search tool, you should demonstrate it prominently in baseline orientations. Show its range of functions, including capturing results, moving them to folders, creating personalized lists, and setting up search alerts. Also compare federated search results with those obtained from the native interfaces of individual databases. Stress the differences between the metasearch and individual databases' interfaces and tell students what these differences mean in terms of ease of use versus precision (Helfer and Wakimoto, 2005).

Google Scholar: *An Emerging Tool Affecting Researchers*

Users increasingly encounter link resolvers and federated search tools on their library's Web site. *Google Scholar* aims to offer similar utility in the familiar *Google* environment. Due to *Google Scholar*'s popularity and ease of use, we must presume that students will use it. When teaching, you may wish to compare *Google Scholar* and other available sources in the context of your students' needs. Some points to make about *Google Scholar* are:

- *Google Scholar* will retrieve articles and other content that are within its current scope (although Google does not fully disclose its coverage) and licensed by your college or university.
- In order to get the licensed content from a *Google Scholar* search, either you must be working online within your campus computing network or, if you are remote from campus, you must use your library's means of access for licensed sources. This may require users to rewrite URLs when an "easy proxy" method is used for remote access.
- *Google Scholar* may fail to retrieve some content that is licensed by your library. One reason for this is that Google may not have completed arrangements with some of your library's licensed online vendors. Further, Google's re-indexing may lag behind your library's latest licenses.
- *Google Scholar* provides useful scholarly information on a wide range of topics. However, it cannot ensure comprehensive coverage of scholarly or professional literature on any topic. Perhaps more important, it is currently insufficient to support medical research and practice, review of legal precedents, searching of prior art for intellectual property, and any number of other information-gathering activities where health, economic advantage, and other tangible benefits are at stake.
- *Google Scholar* is not adequately sophisticated to meet precise searching needs, such as reliable citation searching or searches expressed as complex Boolean statements.
- *Google Scholar* searches documents, while licensed databases can search fields, including those that describe a publication's subject matter, authors, and dates, thereby allowing more precision in their results. Tagging in hypertext documents can lend prominence to titles, author names, and keywords and can make Web search results more relevant (i.e., resembling the results of database searches). Based on these points, you may ask students to consider *Google Scholar*'s functionality versus the index/database model.

Google Scholar may fundamentally change researchers' skeptical attitudes toward the open Web. This will be more likely if *Google Scholar* can encompass critical amounts of licensed scholarly information and make it available through the *Google* interface. For now, *Google Scholar* may have advantages for undergraduates whose information needs are less precise than those of upper-division undergraduates, graduate students, and faculty. Online journal aggregators such as EBSCO and ProQuest are monitoring the progress of *Google Scholar*, since *Google Scholar*'s arrangements with publishers may significantly undercut their market share. *Google Scholar* has not yet replaced any disciplinary database or widely accepted multidisciplinary databases. Instead, *Google Scholar* provides access to a growing collection of scholarly journal literature (provided the user is affiliated with a college or university that licenses the online journals) and an assortment of other scholarly and professional literature, including some otherwise unpublished theses and conference papers. As such, *Google Scholar* can supplement existing scholarly databases, but it cannot replace them.

Assessment

Assessment is another factor vital to success in information literacy instruction. Assessment data provide you with feedback, encourage you to reflect upon and improve your teaching, and allow you to report more objectively to your administration concerning your instructional activities. You have at least two opportunities to assess an instruction session. Your first opportunity is at the end of the session, when you can distribute a survey or questionnaire to students to measure their satisfaction. A sample satisfaction survey is available on the CD-ROM accompanying this book (file 1-1.doc on the CD-ROM). Librarians can also distribute pre- and post-test surveys, which Mark Emmons covers in Chapter 3. Such tests are relatively time consuming and require more involvement from the course instructor, but they can yield more useful information about what students have learned than one can glean from satisfaction surveys.

You can also conduct useful assessment more informally. After your session, contact the course instructor and ask what changes he or she would like you to implement in your next session. The instructor may ask you to cover a new topic or resource in your presentation. In any case, asking for feedback demonstrates your commitment to providing the best possible instructional service. In addition to the discussion of assessment in Chapter 3, we refer you to the ACRL/Instruction Section Bibliography (ACRL, 2003) and Chapter 12 in *Information Literacy Instruction: Theory and Practice* by Grassian and Kaplowitz (2001).

A recent noteworthy development is the ICT Literacy Assessment, a test from the Educational Testing Service (ETS) specifically designed for use in higher education. This test seeks to measure how students find, use, manage, evaluate, and convey information in today's academic and work environments. As of mid-2005, several thousand students in the California State University system had taken this test, in addition to students at Portland State University and Purdue University (ETS, 2005). The involvement of ETS, one of the world's largest test developers, is significant for lending prominence to information literacy–related skills. Librarians should monitor the continuing development and use of this assessment instrument.

Conclusion

Teaching can be very satisfying, but it is time consuming. This can be particularly true early in your career when you are just starting to make contact with faculty and develop programs and tools to serve their students. While your instructional workload can change once you have gained more experience and have more tools and techniques ready to use, even good tools normally do not substitute for your own continuing involvement. Students and your public service colleagues in the library will ask you questions, and faculty will suggest changes and may ask for similar instructional support for other courses. New faculty take on existing courses, which will require you to build new relationships and perhaps abandon old practices. In short, successful instruction often results in more demands on your time. Our future role involves meeting those demands in ways that are pedagogically sound, in traditional, time-tested ways (i.e., face time with students) and incorporating advances in information technology—primarily Web-based functions that make it easier for students to discover and retrieve relevant information. To the extent that you do both of these things (and do them well), your instructional work will benefit students and support faculty's teaching, both of which are central to the purpose of an academic library.

Bibliography

Association of College and Research Libraries (ACRL). 2000. *Information Literacy Competency Standards for Higher Education.* Chicago: ACRL. www.ala.org/ala/acrl/acrlstandards/standards.pdf (accessed September 2, 2005).

———. Instruction Section. Research and Scholarship Committee. 2003. *Bibliography of Citations Related to the Research Agenda for Library Instruction and Information Literacy.* www.ala.org/ala/acrlbucket/is/iscommittees/webpages/research/bibcitations.htm (accessed August 29, 2005).

Atkins, Priscilla. 2001. "Information Literacy and the Arts: Be There—or Miss It!" *College and Research Libraries News* 62, no. 11 (December): 1086–1088, 1092.

Behrens, Shirley J. 1994. "A Conceptual, Analytical and Historical Overview of Information Literacy." *College and Research Libraries* 55: 307–322.

Bruce, Christine Susan. 1997. *The Seven Faces of Information Literacy.* Adelaide: Auslib Press.

Educational Testing Service (ETS). 2005. *ICT-ETS News and Events.* www.ets.org/ictliteracy/news.html (accessed August 30, 2005).

Grassian, Esther S., and Joan R. Kaplowitz. 2001. *Information Literacy Instruction: Theory and Practice.* New York: Neal-Schuman.

Helfer, Doris Small, and Jina Choi Wakimoto. 2005. "Metasearching: The Good, the Bad, and the Ugly of Making It Work in Your Library." *Searcher* 13, no. 2 (February): 40–41.

Jacobson, Trudi E., and Lijuan Xu. 2004. *Motivating Students in Information Literacy Classes.* New York: Neal-Schuman.

Jones, Steve, Mary A. Madden, Lisa N. Clarke, and Pew Internet and American Life Project. 2002. *The Internet Goes to College: How Students Are Living in the Future with Today's Technology.* Pew Internet and American Life Project. www.pewinternet.org/PPF/r/71/report_display.asp (accessed April 30, 2005).

Keller, John M. 1987. "Strategies for Stimulating the Motivation to Learn." *Performance and Instruction* 26, no. 8 (October): 1–7.

Kolb, David. 1984. *Experiential Learning: Experience as the Source of Learning and Development.* Englewood Cliffs, NJ: Prentice Hall.

Online Computer Library Center (OCLC). 2002. *How Academic Librarians Can Influence Students' Web-Based Information Choices: OCLC White Paper on the Information Habits of College Students.* www5.oclc.org/downloads/community/informationhabits.pdf (accessed April 2005).

Ragains, Patrick. 1995. "Four Variations on Druecke's Active Learning Paradigm." *Research Strategies* 13: 40–50.

University of Denver, Penrose Library. 2005. *Help with Research—Tutorials and Assessment Quizzes.* http://library.du.edu/findit/HelpWithResearch/index.cfm (accessed August 30, 2005).

2

Building Strong Relationships with Faculty-Librarian Collaboration

Jean S. Caspers

Introduction

Librarians interact as teachers with students in a variety of settings, including at the reference desk, in consultations, as instructors of record for credit-bearing courses focusing on information literacy, and as guest lecturers in other professors' classes. As a guest lecturer, the librarian's involvement with the students is limited, but when the cooperation needed to set up a guest spot is replaced with a collaborative relationship designed to integrate the librarian's knowledge with the course instructor's content specialization, more meaningful learning can occur. In this chapter I discuss differences between cooperation and collaboration, present some case study scenarios, and offer suggestions for building collaborative teaching relationships.

What Is Collaboration?

Let us say you grab the first dictionary at hand to find a definition of *collaboration*. The dictionary might be a battered old volume left over from your student days now kept on your office shelf, such as the *Webster's Ninth New Collegiate* (1983). From the Latin *collaborare*, the dictionary entry reads: "to labor together."

Webster's defines labor as an "expenditure of physical or mental effort esp. when difficult or compulsory." The first definition for *collaboration* in the *Oxford English Dictionary* (*OED*) emphasizes labor, as being particularly concerned with cultivation and tilling of the earth. The secondary meaning in both dictionaries implies working with an enemy. One might conclude that collaboration is dirty, hard work and sometimes downright treacherous at that.

But wait—this is not how collaboration has been depicted in the library literature recently. In *The Collaborative Imperative*, Dick Raspa and Dane Ward write about collaboration as if it is fun! "Are you willing to play?" they ask, and then continue: "Being playful does not mean not taking work seriously or trivializing our enterprise. Rather, playfulness is the capacity to engage an enterprise deeply—mind, heart, and spirit—all parts of us brought into the action of the moment." Evoking Mihaly Csikszentmihali's "flow" and Abraham Maslow's "peak experience," they evoke an ideal of a true collaborative teaching experience as something wonderful (Raspa and Ward, 2000).

Your own experience collaborating with teaching faculty will probably lie somewhere between the *OED*'s image of natural antagonists laboring together to furrow an endless field and Raspa and Ward's joyously shared experience of reveling "in states of wonder" (Raspa and Ward, 2000). Pennsylvania State University political scientist Larry Spence's reflections on how he and librarian Debra Cheney began working together may better capture the heart of the matter. "She had to learn more about my courses," Spence writes, "and I had to learn more about her approach to information literacy. We began to collaborate, which meant that she participated in the design and management of the course" (Spence, 2004).

Although the *OED* offers *cooperation* as a synonym for *collaboration*, librarians often distinguish between the two. Raspa and Ward describe coordination as a situation wherein "individuals have identified a common goal, but are working toward it independently, completing their parts of the process without any overlapping responsibility. This kind of working relationship remains common in the realm of library-related instruction: the faculty member and the librarian schedule a session that fits into the syllabus, and the librarian teaches a one-hour session on finding information in the subject area." They emphasize that collaboration is a "more pervasive, long-term relationship in which participants recognize common goals and objectives, share more tasks, and participate in extensive planning and implementation" (Raspa and Ward, 2000). Leo Denise defines *collaboration* as the creation of a project "to solve problems, develop new understandings, [or] design new products" (Denise, 1999). He characterizes collaborators as individuals, each employing his or her own strengths in pursuit of an outcome, rather than to build a long-term relationship. By definition, the process is limited to the completion of their objective. This fits well into the culture of the academy where the faculty tend to be independently creative by habit and training but may work together with someone else as long as their individual goals are satisfied by the partnership.

Why Collaborative Teaching?

Collaboration between teaching faculty and librarians and the integration of information literacy into disciplinary coursework are acknowledged as best practices for the teaching of information literacy concepts and skills (ALA, 2005). When we librarians teach, we are usually working with an instructor of record who "owns" the class and who is the gatekeeper of access to the students. In this sense, our ability to engage with the students depends on our relationship with the instructor. Our ability to engage in a meaningful way, relevant to the students' immediate perceived needs, depends on the quality of our communication with the instructor. If we have access to the students in a class but they do not see what we provide as being of immediate relevance to their coursework, then no matter what techniques and strategies we use as teachers, they will not accept much of what we offer.

I have simplified the continuum of potential librarian-faculty relationships around teaching into a three-stage model. Each of the examples I will use in this chapter fall somewhere on this continuum:

Parallel Work ——————▶ Cooperative Work ◀——————▶ Collaborative Work

The first stage, which is furthest from being collaborative in nature, I have termed *parallel*. Here the instructor has goals and the librarian has goals but there is a loose connection between the two. An extreme but common parallel situation would be when a librarian is asked to give the class a library tour while the instructor is out of town at a conference. The students may have a valid need to learn about using the library, although the situation places library instruction as only marginally relevant and outside the core components of their course. In such a situation the librarian's teaching is parallel to that of the instructor. The middle ground on the continuum is cooperative work. Most of our teaching will fall into this area, and much of the cooperative work we do with instructors has good and worthwhile results. When we discuss course goals with an instructor, design lessons which help meet the course goals, appear as a guest or visiting teacher (or provide online units), evaluate our assignments, provide feedback to the students about their work, and obtain feedback from the instructor or students in order to improve our teaching, we may define all these elements as cooperative or collaborative, depending on the degree of interaction between the librarian and instructor.

The diagram shows a larger gap between parallel and cooperative work than between cooperative and collaborative work because, although the step from parallel to cooperative is a big one, the relationship between cooperative and collaborative work is closer, and the interplay may shift back and forth (thus the double-ended arrow between cooperative and collaborative).

Moving from Parallel to Cooperative and Collaborative Interactions

If you want to form working partnerships with faculty, you may find it helpful to start with two basic questions. Do you and the person with whom you plan to work have common goals and objectives related to student learning? How might collaboration help students in the course? You can probe these questions during an initial meeting with the professor to discuss information literacy instruction for the class.

Consider the following three scenarios. The first describes a course that included six units which were fully collaborative in design, implementation, and evaluation. Although it is true that "course-integrated instruction *generally* [emphasis mine] grows out of course-related instruction and develops in those classes where an ongoing relationship has already been established," if the conditions are right, a new relationship can jump directly into collaboration (Ormondroyd, 1988).

Scenario 1: A Free Speech Course

A new Communications faculty member was teaching a freshman intensive writing course with a focus on free speech. Upon meeting, she and the librarian began energetic discussions about First Amendment rights as they involved libraries. They agreed on most points and each was strong in her understanding of the issues. The librarian knew details of the Communications Decency Act (CDA) and the Childen's Internet Protection Act (CIPA) and was articulate about the American Library Association's stance on censorship. She had worked with the Amnesty International student group on campus to extend the library's display on banned books to feature censored journalists and authors. The faculty member knew more about current and recent cases involving broadcasting and businesses. She had experience teaching First Amendment issues, was a published author on freedom of the press (Cornwell, 2004), and had worked with the American Civil Liberties Union (ACLU). The librarian was aware of her library's full range of resources. The faculty member was an expert at legal research and used LexisNexis regularly for her own research. They were both excited about working together on this course. The instructor had already begun developing a course Web page. She and the librarian collaborated to create research assignments to integrate into the online syllabus.

The collaborative sessions covered an orientation to the library building, demonstrations about the use of library catalogs and periodical indexes, a mini-lecture with examples about citing sources using APA (American Psychological Association) style, and a discussion about the evaluation of resources including print, online, or information in any other format. Students were given class time to begin the assignments linked to each session with the librarian and professor both present. Both the librarian and the professor received copies of each assignment. Since the course was writing intensive and included both informal and formal writing requirements, guided "process journals" were required of students to report on their experiences of searching and making decisions about the resources they would retrieve from their searches. Figure 2-1 shows this "process journals" assignment.

Figure 2-1   Sample Assignment: Guidelines for Process Journals (2-1 on CD-ROM)

Process journals serve a purpose that is, in part, similar to reflection papers. Part of the goal of process journal entries is to encourage you to reflect consciously on the research process. These process journals serve an additional purpose. They are intended to become a research map for you as you progress through your major research paper. The following guidelines will assist you in preparing process journals:

1   State your topic and indicate one or more key questions about your topic you hope to answer in your research paper.

2   Indicate what type of material you are seeking, that is, books, magazines, journal articles, news articles, and so on (while these may be determined by a particular assignment, list them anyway).

3   Indicate what search tools you used (while these may be determined by a particular assignment, list them anyway).

4   Make a preliminary set of keywords you expect to use for searching.

5   Perform your searches on the selected databases, using your chosen keyword searches.

6   List any new keywords you picked up during the search process.

7   Note which keywords provided the best results (quality, more than quantity).

8   Note which keywords performed poorly.

9   Explain the process by which you came up with additional keywords, for example, from the records of search results, from articles, from Web pages you found during your search, or from conversations with other people.

10   Explain the difference between effective and ineffective keywords.

11   For assignments involving more than one database, reflect on the differences and similarities you see between each of the databases you explore.

12   You most likely will reject more resources than you will select. Reflect on how you made some of those decisions. Give at least one example. What criteria did you use?

13   Indicate what, anything if, frustrated you about your search process or results?

14   Identify what you need to know more about.

15   List any other questions would you like to ask about the research process.

After the librarian presented the library catalogs and introduced the students to the concept and basic approaches to periodical indexes, the professor taught the students her own approaches to searching LexisNexis for law reviews, how to cite them, and some fine points of the database that she found particularly useful. Since the appeal of the case under discussion was on its way to the Supreme Court while the class was in progress, the librarian chose the Children's Internet Protection Act (about library filtering of pornographic material) for sessions about evaluating online and news content for bias. The students analyzed the arguments and authority of the creators of a half dozen preselected Web sites to represent the various factions actively involved in the debate over library filtering. Their individual follow-up assignments required them to apply evaluation criteria they had learned in the exercise to Web content related to their own research topics.

The librarian graded the papers for these sessions. After completion of six library sessions and related assignments, the course continued, but the librarian and professor's structured collaboration was finished for the term. Some of the students contacted the librarian formally or informally (by appointment or dropping by the reference desk or her office) for research assistance during the following weeks. The students' final projects included poster sessions about free speech issues. When the professor invited the librarian to attend these sessions, the two spontaneously decided to move the poster sessions from the privacy of the classroom into the public space of the library. The librarian arranged for the students to present them in the library's highly trafficked lobby. The professor was the final evaluator of these projects. Librarians, the students' classmates, and other attendees of the poster session also filled out feedback forms provided at the poster sessions, but the librarian did not formally grade these final projects. Such an assessment, perhaps with emphasis on the sources cited and the integration of source information into the presentations, certainly would have deepened the collaborative nature of the partnership and is a situation the librarian intends to seek in future collaborations.

Although the class belonged to the instructor of record and she was the acknowledged leader, the information literacy component of the course was a collaborative effort between the librarian and the professor. Both agreed that the students' experience was enhanced by their partnership.

Lessons from Scenario 1

When you have an opportunity for open collaboration:

- Have some fun: Rejoice if you find a teaching partner who shares common intellectual interests!
- Integrate information literacy into the course to support assignments.
- Be flexible:
  - Use the delivery modes the teacher is using (in this case, a Web-based syllabus).
  - Do not be afraid to teach what you know even if it extends you beyond your usual on-the-job role.
  - Be willing to step aside and allow your faculty partner to teach a "library" resource (LexisNexis in this case) if he or she is the expert. Do not jealously hold onto your turf.

Scenario 2: An English 300-Level Course

This scenario focuses on the need for collaborators to be flexible in their approaches. The librarian takes the lead in moving the interaction into a collaborative mode. The result is collaborative in design and implementation, but not collaborative in evaluation. Although the course instructor saw value in the librarian's idea, the pair did not converge upon the same goals. The design was cooperative, but the implementation fell solely to the librarian. Their goals were parallel, at best. The instructor fully met her own goals, whereas it was not clear that the librarian had achieved her purpose.

The librarian shook her head as she walked to her office from the reference desk, fresh from an encounter with a student from an upper-division English course, for which she had done three library sessions. Her class presentations had been supported by a small suite of linked Web pages, which she had designed specifically for the course. Included with other resources were a bibliography of reference books and links to background sources appropriate for the students' research. A few days after the last session, the student had asked for help to get started with research for the class. The student wondered where she might find background information to define some terms. The librarian asked whether she had checked any of the resources she had been shown in class. The student looked bewildered. The librarian asked, "Did you check the library Web page for the class?" The student shrugged her shoulders. When the librarian sat down next to the student and displayed the page, the student said, "Oh yeah, I remember this now!" Together they identified the resources she needed. It turned out to be a good reference encounter, but the librarian was unsettled because the student had forgotten about the Web page she had so carefully created.

Later that day when a professor called about setting up a class for the next term, the librarian asked whether there was a class Web page for the syllabus and other information. There was not. The professor said she had not learned to do that because she was not sure whether the class would benefit enough to justify the time required. The librarian had a stroke of brilliance. She said, "How about if we work together to set up a Web page for your class? You could find out whether you like it, and I could integrate the library resource pages right into it. If the students have to go there to see the syllabus they'll also become familiar with the library resources!" The librarian was certain the library resources would be more memorable to the students if linked into a class Web page they would use regularly for other class purposes as well.

Once they had conceived their plan, the professor left it to the librarian to create the Web page. After the librarian drafted an initial plan based on the syllabus and showed it to the professor, the professor smiled and said, "Looks good." The two things most important to the professor were to have the syllabus available from the Web page and to have a section where student papers could be posted for peer review. Failing to find a work-study student capable of uploading the papers, the librarian decided to do it herself. Given the librarian's other work commitments, the amount of time it took felt staggering. She felt like a slave to the process.

The professor was happy with the experience and eager to do it again, but the librarian had to tell her that it was impossible for her to participate again in a similar endeavor. The time commitment was too intensive, she explained, and when she had asked students whether having the library resources linked to the class page made them more likely to use those resources, their responses were lukewarm. Although they said the link from the class page to the library resources was a nice idea, most of them indicated they were not any more likely to use that link than simply to start at the library's home page.

Because the librarian fulfilled her commitment to the class, her relationship with the professor was enhanced (despite telling the faculty member why she could not continue uploading the papers). If this professor ever learns to build Web pages (or begins to use courseware such as WebCT) to support her classes, she and the librarian may have an opportunity to collaborate on a similar project in the future. As it is, the professor continues to call the librarian each term to work with one or more classes, but their working relationship—happily maintained a half dozen years hence—is cooperative, rather than collaborative.

Lessons from Scenario 2

Beyond the initial query to establish shared goals for student outcomes, it is important to consider some additional questions before making commitments to a creative venture:

- Do not become so enamored of your own idea that you fail to listen for an interest in collaboration (or lack thereof) from your intended teaching partner.
- Be sure you have the time and resources available to support your commitment.
- Maintain a clear vision of your purposes and boundaries.

Scenario 3: Foundations of Education

The third scenario illustrates a situation that resulted in a collaboratively designed and collaboratively delivered information literacy instruction unit. Previously, the course instructor had regularly given students a library assignment she had prepared without consulting a librarian.

The librarian noticed that students were frustrated by a scavenger hunt, assigned by a professor in the Education department. Many of the resources listed were no longer available in print format, but the assignment referred to the older print versions. One of the students complained that she felt the assignment was busy-work. The librarian decided to contact the professor.

The librarian thought about how to approach the professor tactfully. Clearly, the instructor needed to know that some of the library resources had changed format. She composed a carefully worded e-mail message to that effect. She considered attaching a revised copy of the scavenger hunt, but decided against it since she did not feel that would contribute to the best possible outcome. Instead, she asked whether the students had a research project for which they used library resources and if she could help integrate library instruction into that assignment. The professor replied that she had no such research project and thanked the librarian for the tips to revise the scavenger hunt. She indicated she would make the revisions.

The librarian was disappointed but let the matter drop until the next semester when students reappeared with the same outdated scavenger hunt assignment. She called the professor again and asked for an appointment to discuss the assignment. She told the professor that students had complained about it, and she offered to brainstorm some alternative approaches to a library orientation. The professor was a bit embarrassed that she had forgotten to make the revisions, but she accepted the librarian's offer and they agreed to meet over lunch.

At the lunch meeting, the librarian asked the professor to share her desired student outcomes for the class. The librarian listened carefully to the professor, thinking about ways the library might support the class. Although the professor wanted students to know about library resources for education majors, she had not yet developed an assignment to support this. The professor taught about professional associations and government agencies that would be important to the students in their education careers, however. She had been an officer in a professional association and an advisor to a government agency, and she was particularly attuned to these resources in her teaching.

This was an opening, so the librarian pounced on it. She said, "How about if we design an assignment where students would review the publications and Web sites of different educational associations and government agencies and learn about their missions and goals? Then we can ask the students to report their findings back to the class." The professor was excited about the idea, and the pair immediately drafted an outline on a paper napkin.

The professor abandoned the scavenger hunt. In its place, two class sessions in the library framed an assignment that fully supported the professor's goals for the course and achieved more of the librarian's desired outcomes for education majors. It took a bit more time for this pair to begin working collaboratively, but the end result was more satisfying to each of them—and more beneficial to the students—than what either had conceived alone.

Lessons from Scenario 3

The scenarios in this chapter can be summarized as follows:

- Be respectfully persistent.
- Listen actively, looking for common ground and authentic connections.
- Be ready to spring into action if you evoke an enthusiastic response.

Teaching faculty range in their technological skills across the board from Luddite to expert. Even the most savvy, however, may not be keeping up with the library's changes. In Scenario 1 the professor was a whiz at using LexisNexis for legal research. The professor in Scenario 3 was sending students to use print reference materials that had been replaced by electronic resources years before. Assess the situation as you talk with the faculty with whom you plan to work. You have an important role to play on campus in terms of sharing your knowledge about information technologies as well as library resources, and that role will shift, depending on the relative strengths and weaknesses of each of your partners.

Persuading the Reluctant Professor

What can you do if you are not able to meet with a faculty member to discuss a class, perhaps because she or he just does not see the need? A professor who wants library instruction for a class yet does not make time to meet with you may seem an unlikely collaborative partner. Perhaps this person just has not encountered the right approach. As was the case in Scenario 3, he or she may think that library instruction is a good thing or may simply be filling in space in the syllabus with an exercise designed to get students into the library building. Sometimes a professor with a similar motivation will simply ask for a library tour for his or her class. Delivering exactly what the professor requests may seem the best you can do, but are you willing to suggest an approach that may be more meaningful to the students? If you are asked to teach a library research session but realize the timing is pedagogically poor (e.g., too long before the instructor assigns a research paper), are you willing to suggest a future date that might be more helpful for the students? Sometimes this seems risky (will you alienate the professor?), but soundly asserting your goals for student success may open a conversation that ultimately leads to a better learning experience for students. Since both you and the professor want the students to succeed, you may find the professor a receptive audience. So, take the risk. Make that call.

Once you make contact, ask, "What would you like your students to be able to do?" Then listen for ways in which the professor's goals align with your own. Point out these commonalities. Also listen for areas where your own strengths can dovetail with those of the professor. For instance, a professor may bemoan students' poor judgment in utilizing information from the Web. Tell the professor that you have experience with techniques to evaluate information sources and that you should collaborate to teach students how to evaluate information pertinent to the subject matter of the course. If the professor is interested, then the two of you are already working together toward a common goal. To paraphrase Spence, by listening, you have learned more about the professor's concerns. In turn, the professor has learned more about your approach to information literacy.

Analyzing the Scenarios

The Institute for Information Literacy's document *Characteristics of Programs of Information Literacy that Illustrate Best Practices: A Guideline* [Category 6] specifies that successful collaborations involve partners working closely together "at the planning stages, delivery, assessment of student learning, and evaluation and refinement of the program." As we have seen, collaboration at all four levels was not achieved in two of our three scenarios.

Although the first scenario was relatively limited in duration, it represented a fully collaborative relationship. The faculty member and librarian were both fully involved in the design, implementation, and evaluation phases of an instructional unit. The librarian was not involved in all aspects of the course. Scenario 2 showed the results of a creative idea sprung unawares upon a receptive instructor. This instructor was willing to allow the librarian to implement her idea, but it was, at most, a coordinated effort rather than collaboration. The idea did not reflect a shared enthusiasm, since the professor merely accommodated the librarian's suggestion. Although the instructor was able to use the librarian's idea (and labor) to support her own purposes, their purposes were parallel. The instructor did not hamper the librarian's purpose, but she did not incorporate it to the degree the librarian had hoped (i.e., increasing students' use of library collections and licensed resources). Instead, the instructor used the Web platform created by the librarian to mount the syllabus for the course in a convenient way and showcase the students' work for peer review.

The third scenario highlighted the importance of being flexible. Through gentle persistence, the librarian moved the interaction into a collaborative mode. The result was collaborative in design and implementation, but not in assessment. Again, the librarian's role was tied to a subset of outcomes within the course. The instructor was enthused about the idea of introducing the students to professional association and government Web sites and the library's education periodicals in order to achieve a goal she had pursued earlier by other means. She and the librarian planned and delivered the class sessions together. By grading the presentations and papers alone, however, the instructor retained control of the evaluation of the students' work.

The scenarios described in this chapter illustrate the elements necessary for collaborative success in addition to some pitfalls which may or may not be avoidable. Because collaboration means working together, a mutual intention must be either in place or evoked. If this does not happen, it is beyond the librarian's control, and a coordinated or parallel effort may be the best possible situation.

Summing Up: Strategies for Successful Collaboration

The lessons learned in this chapter can be summarized as follows:

- Know what you want to teach. Clearly articulate your goals for student information literacy to people outside the library profession and unaccustomed to our jargon.
- Be respectful but persistent. If you see that students are confused or floundering with an assignment involving information literacy concepts and skills, let the instructor know and offer to work together to address the students' needs.
- Listen purposefully. Understand that the faculty member is the sole owner of the course. Unless he or she believes what you have to offer will enhance the course goals, there will be little chance of working together. Therefore, learn what the instructor wants students to achieve. Try to identify and acknowledge useful information literacy–related elements of the existing lesson plan. Then determine how your goals for students' information literacy competencies can support the instructor's goals for the course.

- Direct the conversation to two questions: What common goals do you and the instructor have for students in this course? How can your collaboration enhance student success in this course?
- Be flexible in your approach, but do not lose sight of your own goals for students. When you begin collaborating it is wonderful to get swept up in the fun of co-creation. Be sure to monitor your developing plans for units, activities, assignments, and supporting materials to be sure they support your own educational values.
- Be realistic about the amount of time and the resources you can offer to support each course. Do not promise more than you can deliver—it is often better to underpromise and then overperform.
- Assess the relative strengths and weaknesses in each partnership.

Conclusion

Elizabeth Burge, a librarian-turned-education-professor, emphasized the need for proactive outreach by librarians. "There is a real limit to the energy and time I am prepared to spend on checking out how responsive and connected the library staff want to be. If my initial expectations of them are low, then I have to decide how I will deal with that result; some days I am too weary even to think about the problem, so . . . I take the path of easiest action and don't call the librarian" (Burge, 1991).

We have much to offer to students, and our most effective path to meaningful instructional time with them is through the teaching faculty. It is up to us to build high expectations about what we can do in the classroom. Doing so will encourage faculty to be receptive when we offer our energy in support of their course goals.

Bibliography

American Library Association (ALA). 2005. *Characteristics of Programs of Information Literacy That Illustrate Best Practices: A Guideline*. www.ala.org/ala/acrl/acrlstandards/characteristics.htm (accessed September 1, 2005).

Burge, Elizabeth J. 1991. "Relationships and Responsibilities: Librarians and Distance Educators Working Together." In *The Off Campus Library Services Conference. Albuquerque, New Mexico, October 30–November 1, 1991*. ERIC ED 339383.

Caspers, Jean. 2004. *IQS: Freedom of Speech*. Linfield College. http://calvin.linfield.edu/~jcaspers/freedom.htm (accessed October 12, 2005).

Cornwell, Nancy C. 2004. *Freedom of the Press: Rights and Liberties Under the Law*. Santa Barbara, CA: ABC-CLIO.

Denise, Leo. 1999. "Collaboration vs. C-Three (Cooperation, Coordination, and Communication)." *Innovating* 7, no. 3: 25ff. Academic Search Premier, EBSCOhost. http://search.epnet.com (accessed December 17, 2004).

Ormondroyd, Joan. 1988. *Course Integrated Library Instruction. ERIC Digest*. Syracuse, NY: ERIC Clearinghouse on Information Resources. ERIC ED 306960.

Raspa, Dick, and Dane Ward. 2000. "Listening for Collaboration: Faculty and Librarians Working Together." In *The Collaborative Imperative: Librarians and Faculty Working Together in the Information Universe*, pp. 1–18, edited by Dick Raspa and Dane Ward. Chicago: Association of College and Research Libraries.

Spence, Larry. 2004. "The Usual Doesn't Work: We Need Problem-Based Learning." *portal: Libraries and the Academy* 4, no. 4: 485–493.

PART II

Teaching Information Literacy to Individual Audiences

The essays in Part II focus on teaching techniques and programmatic strategies for information literacy instruction (ILI). Mark Emmons presents a compelling case for ILI, offers a smorgasbord of lessons to use in freshman-level instruction, and discusses assessment in Chapter 3. The community college environment is Ann Roselle's focus in Chapter 4, as she views societal needs through the lens of an astute library director. In Chapter 5, Alexander Gyamfi covers classroom instruction for students with disabilities. Concluding this portion of the book, Sean Evans and Tina Adams recommend best practices for ILI and library support for remote students.

The information in Part II is applicable to ILI in any subject. As such, you can use it in tandem with Parts III and IV of this book, which cover discipline-specific instruction and special topics, respectively. Put another way, the discussions in Part II will impart savvy as you plan and deliver ILI, while Parts III and IV will broaden your content-related knowledge. Both effective skills and subject knowledge are essential to good teaching, which is the aim of this book.

3

Tailoring Instruction for College and University Freshmen

Mark Emmons

Introduction

This chapter is a practical resource for librarians and classroom instructors who teach basic information literacy concepts and skills to students in their first year of college. It describes how traditional freshmen gather information, their learning environment, and the information literacy competencies they are expected to master. After an overview of the instructional design process and learning styles, a series of sample exercises illustrates the full range of information literacy competencies. The chapter concludes with examples of assessment techniques that can help improve teaching and measure success.

The Context for Information Literacy in Higher Education

As the twentieth century closed amid celebrations and worries about Y2K and the current century dawned to hopes of a new era, instruction librarians were at a crossroads. Millennials were the first cohort of traditional, incoming freshmen who had grown up around computers their entire lives and spent all of their teen years searching the Web. They were armed with superior technical skills, but classroom faculty and librarians observed that they often lacked the skills to find, evaluate, and use information in an academic setting. Students were using more Web resources as evidence and citing fewer scholarly books and articles. Fewer students were visiting the library and asking questions of reference librarians. Plagiarism increased due to the ease with which electronic information can be copied.

With much of the evidence anecdotal in nature, librarians began to conduct local studies on how the typical college student gathers information. They presented their results at conferences and in journal articles. In 2002, three national organizations took notice and attempted to answer the question, How do typical college students gather information to support their studies?

OCLC's White Paper on the Information Habits of College Students

In June 2002, OCLC (the Online Computer Library Center) published the *White Paper on the Information Habits of College Students* (2002). Observing that fewer students were visiting libraries in person at the same time that use of library Web-based resources was dramatically increasing, OCLC commissioned Harris Interactive to examine how a sample of more than 1,000 college students actually used the Web.

They discovered that students were confident Web users, with the majority finding what they seek most of the time. Students value accurate and up-to-date information but question the reliability of the information found on Web sites and are aware that the Web cannot answer all of their questions. Students continued to use their library's Web and print resources but preferred easier access to information.

Based on the study, OCLC made several recommendations to librarians. Among these are placing an "emphasis on students' and librarians' common preferences for accuracy, authority, timeliness, and privacy" and providing "relentless promotion, instruction, and customer service."

The Internet Goes to College

In September 2002, the researchers at the Pew Internet and American Life Project published *The Internet Goes to College* (Jones et al., 2002). They were curious about how the Internet had affected the social and academic lives of college students. The project surveyed over 2,000 students and later used ethnographic research methods to observe students using the Internet.

They found students were very familiar with the Internet, using it for social, entertainment, and communication purposes as well as academic research. Seventy-three percent of the students surveyed used the Internet more than the library for research. As in the OCLC study, students commented that it was easier to find information on the Web than in the library. In fact, "college students seemed to rely on information seeking habits formed prior to arriving at college, where the vast majority of students used the Internet as their major source for school projects."

Noting that students needed help finding "credible, academic sources," the researchers at Pew recommend teaching students "search techniques that will get them to the information they want and how to evaluate it."

Dimensions and Use of the Scholarly Information Environment

In November 2002, the Digital Library Federation (DLF) and the Council on Library and Information Resources (CLIR) published the *Dimensions and Use of the Scholarly Information Environment* (Friedlander, 2002). In order to help libraries plan new services, they commissioned Outsell to see how "patterns of information use for teaching, learning, and research" have changed because of the Internet.

Interviewing over 3,000 undergraduate students, graduate students, and faculty members, they found that undergraduates were "more willing to rely on electronic sources," although the split was approximately 50/50 between print and electronic. When they searched online, they were frustrated with getting access, finding information, determining credibility, and analyzing information, with nearly 40 percent seeing "insufficient training on how to search for information as an impediment" as at least a minor problem. Interestingly, 98 percent found information taken from the library credible and 75 percent found information from the Internet credible—but of these last, 46 percent would only use Internet information after obtaining additional verification.

Most of the recommendations made by DLF and CLIR involve areas of further study, but they do note that undergraduates are far more likely to ask librarians for help, "adding to the function of the librarian as teacher" and that "integrating librarians' functions and services into the undergraduate learning experience may prove a fertile area for future growth."

While these studies contradict each other in some ways (due partially to methodological differences), they tell us that building information literacy programs for undergraduate students is important. Further, they tell us important things about students. In high school, the majority of research assignments are now completed using Web resources. Students can and do find what they need on the Web. They are skeptical that the resources on the Web can actually answer all of their questions and are not confident about the reliability of the information they find. They are frustrated at times with searching the Web, but they value the ease of searching that it offers. Students find information made available through libraries more credible but would prefer easier access than libraries provide. All of the studies recommend teaching students how to find, evaluate, and use information.

These findings should not surprise any experienced librarian, but they do provide formal evidence of student skills and attitudes that was heretofore anecdotal and scattered. Most important, the results from the studies can be used to help design library services and library instruction programs.

The First-Year Experience

Statistics from the National Information Center for Higher Education Policymaking and Analysis (HigherEdInfo.org) confirm the widely held notion that "students are more likely to drop out of postsecondary education during the first year than any other time." In response to the ongoing problem of retaining students, many campuses offer courses specially designed to help students make the transition from high school to college. These courses are collectively known as freshman or first-year experience (FYE) programs.

Although courses designed specifically for freshmen have been offered for over 100 years, they experienced a renaissance in the 1980s in response to the difficulty of retaining students and to a series of scathing reports on higher education published in the wake of the publication of *A Nation at Risk* (NCEE, 1983) and given new momentum with the launch of the Boyer Report (Kenny, 1998), which argued for new models to educate the often overlooked and underserved undergraduates at universities.

John N. Gardner, Debra Decker, and Francine G. McNairy describe the earlier reports and the history and nature of FYE courses in an article illustrating two examples of librarian involvement (Gardner, Decker, and McNairy, 1986). Cindy Pierard and Kathryn Graves expand on this early study with their review of the literature on the history of FYE programs and library outreach (Pierard and Graves, 2002). They find that FYE courses improve student retention and promote greater use of libraries.

In 2002, Colleen Boff and Kristin Johnson collaborated with the National Resource Center (NRC) to conduct a nationwide survey determining the extent of library involvement in FYE courses (Boff and Johnson, 2002). They found that 86 percent of FYE courses involved the library, with the majority giving tours, offering instruction on article indexes and databases, the catalog, and the Web, and providing guidance for research assignments.

FYE courses come in many forms and are an ideal means to reach freshmen. The two previously mentioned surveys divide FYE courses into courses that are primarily focused on either orientation to college or university life or on subject content. Some FYE courses blend these two approaches. Whatever the approach, FYE programs offer an excellent place to integrate information literacy into the curriculum.

If your own campus offers FYE courses, contact the program coordinators to share your common interest in student success and ask to integrate information literacy into the curriculum. If there are no FYE courses on your campus, the next best alternative is to scour the general education requirements in your institution's undergraduate catalog for courses required of all students. Read your college or university general catalog and talk to faculty to find out if the curriculum calls for information literacy skills. English classes are usually required, but a full range of arts, humanities, social science, and science courses may also be needed.

Information Literacy Competency Standards for Higher Education

In 2000, the Association of College and Research Libraries (ACRL) developed the *Information Literacy Competency Standards for Higher Education* (ACRL, 2000). The standards are listed in Chapter 1, in the section titled "What Is Information

Literacy?" Designed to provide a framework for student learning and assessment, each of the five competency standards is subdivided into performance indicators and outcomes. These standards have become a crucial point of reference for instruction librarians and the programs they offer.

Instructional Design

Instructional design is a systematic approach to developing instruction. It involves analyzing learning needs, setting goals and objectives, developing and implementing a lesson plan, and assessing the results based on the goals. When using an instructional design approach, it is necessary to treat each class visiting the library as a new class. One standard lesson does not fit all needs, although it is possible to create reusable modules that work from class to class.

During the analysis phase of instructional design, you should consult with faculty to determine their expectations. Ask them to answer questions designed to answer who, what, where, when, and why, for example, who are the students, what do you want them to learn, why is it important, when and where is the class. Let them know what types of information resources are available and required to accomplish their goals. If your current information literacy program has standard expectations of FYE students, communicate these to faculty and then find a way to meet both the information literacy–related goals and the instructors' goals for their students.

During the design phase of instructional design, you will identify student learning needs in terms of knowledge, attitudes, and motivation. Find out what students already know. If you are teaching your own credit-bearing class, you can accomplish this with formal or informal measures, either by asking pertinent questions of your students or by pretesting them. If you are not teaching the class but are a guest lecturer, then you should raise these questions with faculty when planning your sessions.

Once you have identified student needs and knowledge, it is time to develop goals and objectives. Goals are broad statements that set the fundamental direction of the class and explain what the faculty member wishes to accomplish. The ACRL's information literacy competency standards serve as an excellent starting point for developing your own instructional goals. Objectives are based on goals and are specific statements that explain what the students will learn or accomplish. Objectives might cover concepts, processes, skills, or even attitudes. Objectives set measurable levels of achievement and provide the basis for assessment. The mnemonic SMART reminds us that objectives must be Specific, Measurable, Attainable, Results-focused, and Timely.

In the next part of the development phase, the instruction librarian develops a lesson plan based on previously defined goals and objectives. By breaking an assignment into a logical progression of smaller tasks, it is possible to choose appropriate learning experiences. A lesson plan structured according to David Kolb's learning theories will give students an opportunity to reflect on experience (why?), conceptualize (what?), experiment (how?), and plan for application (what if?) (Kolb, 1984).

Lesson plans should address not only the processes described by Kolb but also learning styles. To summarize the best way to address the needs of students with various learning styles, I recommend following five simple guidelines:

- Base the lesson on student needs and tie assignments to course objectives.
- Tell why, explain what, show how, and ask what if.
- Teach to the eye and to the ear.
- Give plenty of hands-on practice time.
- Engage higher-level critical thinking skills such as analysis, synthesis, and evaluation.

During the implementation phase of instructional design, the instruction librarian prepares materials, practices, and teaches the class. It is beyond the scope of this chapter to describe the speaking, directing, and facilitation skills necessary for effective teaching, except to note that good teaching will help students learn. Poor teaching can disrupt the entire process, not to mention losing both the students' attention and the faculty's confidence.

During the evaluation phase of instructional design, the instruction librarian and the faculty member find out if they have accomplished their goals and objectives for student learning. There are two types of evaluation. Formative evaluation provides feedback that will help improve instruction the next time. Summative evaluation assesses the effects or outcomes of instruction, including the measurement of learning. I will discuss various assessment techniques in the section of this chapter titled "Evaluation of Library and Information Literacy Instruction."

What to Teach

Although there are no shortcuts in instructional design, this section describes assignments, activities, and exercises that you can easily adapt to meet information literacy goals and objectives as well as the needs of FYE students. These activities and exercises are designed to take the typical needs and knowledge of a first-year student making the transition to college and match them to information literacy standards. They can be taught to individuals, small groups, or the whole class. They are broadly organized into ACRL's five information literacy competency standards, but many of the assignments fulfill multiple standards. Standards 1 and 3, in particular, overlap quite a bit and the tasks in Standard 4 often cover the entire range of information literacy. The examples are numbered according to the pertinent ACRL standard (i.e., examples 1.1 through 1.21 refer to ACRL IL Competency Standard 1). My examples are by no means exhaustive. They are only a sample of what is possible, with the range of tasks limited only by student needs and the imagination of the instruction librarian and classroom faculty. I have included only a brief description of each activity. If an activity intrigues you, then you should be able to find related literature in print and on the Web.

Standard 1: The Information-Literate Student Determines the Nature and Extent of the Information Needed

A typical first-year student is familiar with the Web and resources in school and public libraries. Up to this point in time most of their papers have been reports on a topic using these resources. The activities and exercises in this section familiarize students with formulating a search statement and the range of information available, including the scholarly literature. The following exercises are multidisciplinary in nature. You can use them effectively in general education as well as in discipline-specific courses.

- **1.1. Identifying one's information needs.** Ask students to list everything they already know about their topic, using either an outline or a concept map. Ask them to examine the list in order to identify gaps in their knowledge. They should write questions they need to answer in order to fill the gaps.

- **1.2. Teaching about the information cycle.** You, the instructor, chart and discuss the stages of scientific information flow from its inception as an idea through its description in an encyclopedia. Cover both unpublished and published stages.

- **1.3. Getting background information.** Have students read several articles on the same topic in different subject encyclopedias. Ask them to record who, what, where, when, and why and note each article's differences in content and emphasis from the others.

- **1.4. Reading critically. Part 1: Comprehension.** Assign your students to read a scholarly journal article. Ask them to identify the thesis or research question, the research methods, the results, and the conclusions.

- **1.5. Reading critically. Part 2: Analysis and evaluation.** After students complete the preceding comprehension-related exercise, have them evaluate the article's methods, looking for strengths and weaknesses. Ask them to evaluate the article's results and conclusions, looking for logic and bias.

- **1.6. Reading critically. Part 3: Variation on analysis and evaluation.** Have students read scholarly journal articles on the same topic that reach different conclusions. Ask them to explain the differences by examining each article's thesis or research question and research methods.

- **1.7. Identifying bias.** Have your students compare coverage of a controversial issue in different sources, including a Web site, encyclopedia article, book chapter, newspaper article, popular magazine article, and/or scholarly journal article. Ask them to compare the different sources by identifying and discussing biases they find in each.

- **1.8. Identifying suitability of information by its source.** Have students read about a topic in different sources, including a Web site, encyclopedia article, book chapter, newspaper article, popular magazine article, and/or scholarly journal article. Ask them to compare and contrast content in each source. Finally, have them list types of information needs each source would address (e.g., informing nonspecialized readers versus a group with specialized prior knowledge, training, or viewpoints).

- **1.9. Identifying the suitability of a source for an assignment.** Ask students to determine the suitability of a Web site, encyclopedia article, book chapter, newspaper article, popular magazine article, and/or scholarly journal article to answer a sample research question (you supply the question).

- **1.10. Comparing popular magazines with scholarly journals.** Have students compare a popular magazine to a scholarly journal. Ask them to note similarities and differences, comparing content, style, purpose, bias, audience, authority, scope, accuracy, and style of presentation.

- **1.11. Comparing articles in popular magazines and scholarly journals.** Have students compare articles on the same topic published in a popular magazine and a scholarly journal. Ask them to compare the two articles' content, style, purpose, bias, audience, authority, scope, accuracy, and style of presentation.

- **1.12. Comparing the Web to a full-text multidisciplinary database.** Have your students search both the Web and a full-text multidisciplinary database using identical search statements. Ask them to compare the quantity and quality of results from each source. For quality, ask students to compare the first three results from each list. Ask them which source gave the better search results for their paper and to explain why.

- **1.13. Comparing a full-text multidisciplinary database to a subject-specific database.** Have your students search both a full-text multidisciplinary database and a subject-specific database using identical search statements. Ask them to compare the quantity and quality of search results from each. For quality, ask students to compare the first three results from each list. Ask them which source gave the better search results and to explain why.

In some FYE courses, students become acculturated to college life by taking an intensive course in a discipline, such as nursing, engineering, or agriculture. The following exercises address beginning steps in learning about a discipline and its literature.

- **1.14. Browsing the stacks.** Send your students to browse the library stacks in an area devoted to one discipline. Ask them to identify the major areas of emphasis, some of the subdisciplines, and the major contributors to the discipline.

- **1.15. Reading classic works.** Have students read and criticize a book or article that is considered a classic in its discipline. Provide reviews and criticism for them to read. Ask them why the work became a classic and to identify the work's impact on the discipline.

- **1.16. Compiling an anthology.** Assign your students to develop an anthology of seminal works in the discipline and to justify their selections.

- **1.17. Preparing for a mock interview with a scholar.** Ask students to prepare to interview a major scholar in their discipline (living or dead). They should write interview questions and anticipate answers. Have students identify and read some of the scholar's works, locate and read reviews and criticisms of the works, and find and read biographies. Ask students to identify the scholar's impact on the discipline and explain why this person is considered a key figure.

- **1.18. Analyzing core journals.** Have students compare and contrast three core journals from the discipline (you can preselect the journals for them). Ask them to discuss the content and scope of each journal and to identify its audience.
- **1.19. Identifying research trends in journals.** Have your students peruse recent issues of an assigned core journal (published during the last three years) and identify three current research trends.
- **1.20. Examining coverage of research trends in a subject database.** Assign students to search a subject database, using two or three key concepts. They should read titles and abstracts of the most current twenty to thirty items in the search results and identify three current research trends.
- **1.21. Completing authentic work projects.** Assign a project that someone who graduates from a discipline will be expected to complete when they get a job related to their field of study. These projects will vary greatly depending on the discipline, but might include writing a research proposal, planning a project, solving a problem, or investigating an individual or an organization.

Standard 2: The Information-Literate Student Accesses Needed Information Effectively and Efficiently

Typical first-year students find answers to questions by searching the Web. They know the library has quality resources, but they find searching difficult. The following activities and exercises guide students through the most appropriate and effective search strategies and techniques.

- **2.1. Finding evidence for a social issue.** Have students read a newspaper or popular magazine editorial on a social issue and locate evidence in scholarly journals to support or refute points made in the editorial.
- **2.2. Finding evidence for a science-related issue.** Assign students to read a newspaper or popular magazine editorial on a science-related issue and locate evidence in scholarly journals to support or refute points made in the editorial.
- **2.3. Finding evidence for consumers.** Have students investigate something they believe is a "best" product or service. Have them list evidence from sources including Web sites, newspaper and magazine articles, and scholarly articles.
- **2.4. Developing vocabulary to use in search statements.** Have students read an article in an encyclopedia related to their thesis statement or research question. Ask them to identify keywords to use in search statements. A variation on this is to conduct the same exercise using a scholarly journal article.

- **2.5. Comparing keyword searching to use of controlled vocabulary.** Have your students perform a keyword search in a database that uses controlled vocabulary. Point out the controlled vocabulary terms in the record (i.e., subject headings or descriptors). Have them search again using subject headings or descriptors, then compare these results with those of their keyword searches.
- **2.6. Comparing free text searching to Boolean searching.** Select a database that uses Boolean search operators. Tell students to search it just as they would a Web search engine such as Google (i.e., they should use keywords or natural language in their searches, not Boolean operators). Ask them to analyze the quantity and quality of results. Use either Venn diagrams or human subjects to explain Boolean logic (e.g., stand up if you are wearing shorts OR skirts AND sneakers, but NOT if you are wearing glasses). Next, have them combine two keywords they previously used with OR, AND, or NOT. Ask them to analyze these search results and compare them with their earlier results.
- **2.7. Developing concept maps to use in search statements.** Give your students a thesis or research question and tell them to break it down into two to four key concepts. Have them list synonyms and related, broader, and narrower terms for each concept. Ask them to identify the appropriate historical and geographical scope. Finally, ask them to write a search statement based on the terms and scope they listed.
- **2.8. Demonstrating search techniques.** After students perform one or more of the preceding exercises, perform one or more searches in a local database (catalog, index, etc.). Search for, locate, and, if time permits, retrieve an item (book, full-text article, etc.).
- **2.9. Using call numbers to browse.** Have students identify relevant call numbers for their research topics, and then send them to browse the stacks in each area. After they return, ask them to report their findings to the class.

Standard 3: The Information-Literate Student Evaluates Information and Its Sources Critically and Incorporates Selected Information into His or Her Knowledge Base and Value System

Typical first-year students are confident Web users, but they question the reliability of the information they find there. The following activities and exercises give students the tools to evaluate information sources, not only on the Web, but from virtually any information source.

- **3.1. Identifying main ideas.** Assign students to read a scholarly journal article that you have selected for them. Tell them to highlight clues from the content and structure of the article that may indicate its main idea. Ask them to write one sentence describing the main idea.
- **3.2. Identifying an author's credentials.** Have your students identify the credentials and qualifications of an author of a Web site or scholarly journal

article. They should consult sources other than the site or article, such as the Internet and biographical resources in the library. Ask them to decide if the author is qualified to write on the topic and justify their conclusions.

- **3.3. Showing relationships between primary and secondary sources.** Use a primary source available in your library and describe how it was used in a secondary source such as a scholarly article or book. Congressional hearings or U.S. Supreme Court opinions are good primary sources to use for this type of exercise, since they cover many topics of public interest and are selectively available online on *GPO Access* (www.gpoaccess.gov) and in print in many federal depository libraries.
- **3.4. Analyzing references.** Have students read a scholarly journal article and then locate and read some of the articles cited. Ask them to describe how the author of the original article used the sources. Were the articles quoted, paraphrased, or summarized? How were they used as evidence?
- **3.5. Analyzing critical reception of a work.** Have students read and compare three book reviews or criticisms of a work and identify differences in the reviews' content, bias, and reception.

Standard 4: The Information-Literate Student, Individually or as a Member of a Group, Uses Information Effectively to Accomplish a Specific Purpose

Most first-year students wrote reports and gave presentations when they were in high school. In college they begin to write research papers and incorporate scholarly information into their assignments. The activities and exercises in this section help students incorporate the information they find into a wide range of assignments.

Preparing Students to Write a Research Paper

One of the most common assignments faculty give to students is the research paper, which is a substantial, formal essay, written over the course of a term. In it, students answer a question, solve a problem, or argue a thesis, using outside research findings as evidence. While research papers give students an opportunity to showcase their critical thinking, library research, and writing skills, they are not necessarily the best assignment to give to a student in the first year of college or university. They will have used the Web, rather than scholarly literature, as a resource. In other words, they will most likely have no prior experience writing a research paper. Understanding this situation leaves faculty with two options: either helping students build the skills needed to complete a research paper or providing an alternative assignment.

Faculty who assign research papers can help prepare their students by breaking the research process down into components. They can begin with exercises to help students develop a research question or problem or thesis statement. This can be a very difficult process for a new student, involving understanding a discipline, gaining enough background information to focus, and reading enough pertinent literature to be able to revise one's original questions or statements.

Once students develop a research question or problem or thesis statement, they will need to find sources they can use as evidence. In this area librarians have traditionally excelled, teaching students the intricacies of selecting the appropriate tools and deliberately crafting appropriate search strategies to find supporting information. Students also need to learn how to evaluate information sources. They tend to identify relevant studies fairly easily, but they find it more challenging to determine which are of the best quality. The activities and exercises related to ACRL Information Literacy Competency Standards 2 and 3, presented earlier, will help students learn to analyze and evaluate information sources.

Once students have gathered, read, and analyzed sources related to their topics, they are ready to organize them into a literature review. An annotated bibliography is a useful preliminary assignment. One way to prepare for this before committing thoughts to writing is for students to share one- or two-minute oral summaries with classmates in small groups or in front of the entire class. Also, students will most likely need to learn how to quote, paraphrase, and summarize outside sources in their paper. Finally, students need to learn the conventions of citing other works. You may cover quoting, paraphrasing, and proper citation as part of an annotated bibliography assignment or discuss these points separately.

Alternatives to the Research Paper

There are many alternatives to research paper assignments that will give students worthwhile experience with the processes of selecting, analyzing, and using information. Instead of assigning a research paper, instructors can ask students to write in another format, which will vary according to the purpose of the assignment. For an overview of a topic, students might write encyclopedia entries, each complete with a bibliography. To give a concise overview of a current event, students can write newspaper-style articles. If the instructor wants students to identify main ideas, then the students might be asked to produce outlines or PowerPoint presentations, poster sessions, or Web pages.

Of course, students are not limited to writing. Oral presentations are just as useful in developing critical thinking and information literacy skills. Students can be asked to give informative, persuasive, or instructional speeches or demonstrations. Students can participate in panel presentations or conduct debates. They can join roundtable discussions. You can structure and assign a whole class project to produce a mini-conference that mixes different types of speaking and writing, such as poster sessions, speeches, panel presentations, and roundtable discussions.

Students can also create pathfinders for future researchers to use. Such guides can focus on the full range of published works on a subject or can focus on one format, such as books, articles, multimedia, or Web sources. Pathfinders come in many forms, including printed handouts, Web guides, a course syllabus with reading list, or the annotated bibliography and literature review that follow.

The following activities and exercises are a wide range of alternatives to research papers, including those previously discussed:

- **4.1. Write a book or article report.** Students read a chapter in a book or a scholarly journal article, and then write a descriptive and evaluative summary.
- **4.2. Compile an annotated bibliography.** Students select a predetermined number of scholarly books and journal articles. Assign them to cite each source using a standard citation style and write an annotation for each, describing the main and supporting ideas. They should evaluate each work and explain why it helps prove a thesis, solve a problem, or answer a research question.
- **4.3. Write a literature review.** Students write a literature review, focusing on works published during a given time period. They should explain parameters for items included in the literature search. Students may begin from scratch or build on a previously assigned annotated bibliography. The review must tie together ideas from the various sources.
- **4.4. Update an existing literature review.** Students can update a literature review that was written five to ten years previously. They should explain parameters for items included in the literature search, which should be based on the original review. As previously, the review must tie together ideas from the various sources.
- **4.5. Write a research proposal.** Students write a mock research proposal for a funding agency. They should include a literature review of comparable studies, a proposed methodology, and funding needs.
- **4.6. Evaluate a research proposal.** Students judge a preselected research proposal based on its originality and quality against a set of criteria. Students should explain their evaluative criteria. An alternative is to look at several preselected research proposals and approve just one for funding. In either case, students must justify their response.
- **4.7. Prepare and deliver a poster session.** Students present a topic on a poster, combining text and graphics. The poster must emphasize main ideas and include supporting evidence.
- **4.8. Write program or liner notes.** Students write program notes for a theatrical or musical performance or liner notes for a music or film recording. They should investigate the work's history, including people who wrote, composed, directed, and performed the work and its critical reception.
- **4.9. Criticize a book or film.** After the instruction librarian or faculty distinguishes between a review and criticism of a work (i.e., a review is for consumers deciding how to spend their time and money, while criticism is an argument made about a work, based on theory and evidence), students write a criticism. They should identify the work's themes and main ideas, compare it to similar pieces, and develop an argument about it.
- **4.10. Develop a syllabus.** Students write a syllabus for an imaginary class on their topic. They should include key concepts and people, a reading list, and

three assignments. Ask students to defend their choices in a separate document.

- **4.11. Compile a nonfiction reading list.** Students compile a nonfiction reading list on their topic. They should include sources that provide an overview as well as seminal works. Ask students to defend their choices in a separate document.

- **4.12. Compile a fiction anthology.** Students compile an anthology of fictional readings that includes short stories, novellas, or excerpts from novels. Students may also include poems that are germane to the scope of their anthologies. Whether the anthology focuses on a theme or a single author, students should include both "best" works and a representative range of works. Ask students to defend their choices in a separate document.

Standard 5: The Information-Literate Student Understands Many of the Economic, Legal, and Social Issues Surrounding the Use of Information and Accesses and Uses Information Ethically and Legally

First-year students may already have dealt with issues of citation, censorship, copyright, and plagiarism throughout their education. All of this becomes more complex in college. The activities and exercises in the following list give students an opportunity to reflect on the economic, legal, and social issues related to information.

- **5.1. Identify formats.** Students examine citations for a variety of works, including a book, a book chapter, an article, and a Web site. Ask them to identify the format of each source.

- **5.2. Write citations.** Have your students refer to a standard citation style and use it to construct citations for a variety of works, including a book, a book chapter, an article, and a Web site.

- **5.3. Analyze citations.** Using the bibliography in a scholarly journal article, have your students determine the format of each item. Ask them to describe whether each work was quoted, paraphrased, or summarized and to analyze how each work cited was used as evidence.

- **5.4. Discuss censorship.** Display some controversial Web sites and debate the merits of censorship. Students should defend their responses with arguments that include rational, ethical, and emotional reasoning.

- **5.5. Discuss copyright.** Have students debate the merits of copyright, using books, television, film, or music as examples. Students should defend their responses with arguments that include rational, ethical, and emotional reasoning.

- **5.6. Discuss plagiarism.** Assign students to debate whether professors should use online plagiarism detection services. Students should defend their responses with arguments that include rational, ethical, and emotional reasoning.

Evaluation of Library and Information Literacy Instruction

The final step of instructional design is to evaluate whether you have met your goals and objectives. By determining the impact a program has on student learning, evaluations can prove the worth of the program to instruction librarians, library and campus administrators, faculty, and funding agencies. It is also useful to ask students to evaluate their own learning by reflecting both on the process and what they have learned. The self-reflection exercises described in the following section can be used as formative assessment, if students share their impressions with the instructor.

Student Self-Reflection

The self-reflection exercises described below can be used as formative assessment if students share their impressions with the instructor. Likewise, most of the formative evaluation exercises can be used for self-reflection.

- **Planning.** Students break their assignment down into parts, create a flowchart and calendar, and explain each step of the process in their own words.
- **Use advance organizers.** At the beginning of class, pose a question. Tell the students to keep the question in mind, as you will bring it up for discussion before the end of class. For example, before starting an activity comparing scholarly journals to popular magazines, ask, "Why would professors ask you to use scholarly journals instead of popular magazines?"
- **Have students keep a research log.** Have your students keep a research log describing their research process, sources consulted, keywords and headings, and search techniques. Tell them to emphasize what worked and what did not but that they can write about their feelings related to the process, too.
- **Use a checklist or rubric.** Develop a checklist or rubric, and then have students use it to monitor their own progress and make sure they have completed all assigned tasks.
- **Have students design their own rubric.** Have students develop scoring criteria and use them in a rubric.

Formative Evaluation

Formative evaluation provides feedback that will help improve instruction the next time. Time is often at a premium when conducting library instruction, so I focus here on quick and simple techniques of formative evaluation:

- **Gather informal feedback.** While students are engaged in hands-on activities, observe and ask questions of individuals and groups to get informal feedback.
- **Gather formal feedback:**
  - **Use $+\Delta$ (*Plus Delta*).** Write two columns on the board in front of the class. Ask the class for feedback in order to improve the lesson. Under a

column labeled +, record aspects of the lesson that they thought went well and should be kept as is. Under a column labeled Δ, record the aspects of the lesson that they thought should be changed, added, or removed.

- **Have students write a one-minute paper.** Ask students to take one minute to write a brief paper, summarizing your session's main idea, recording one thing they learned, and listing one thing that still confuses them.
- **Have students write and share.** Ask the class a question related to your presentation. Have students write down their answer on paper. Ask students to share their responses with the entire class.
- **Use "think, pair, share."** Ask a question related to your presentation. Have students form pairs or small groups to discuss and answer the question. Ask students from different pairs or groups to share responses with the entire class.
- **Give pre- and post-tests.** Give a simple two- to four-question quiz at the beginning of the class period. Repeat the quiz before the students leave and compare the results.
- **Conduct focus group interviews with students.** While more time consuming, gathering a cross-section of students together to answer specific questions and discuss their library instruction experiences can bring a wealth of information that will improve the program.

Summative Evaluation

Summative evaluation assesses the outcomes of an instruction program in the realms of knowledge, skills, attitudes, and behaviors. Summative evaluation measures how well students met goals and objectives. The best summative evaluation will most likely take place well after the instruction has ended in order to have time for the lessons to be applied and integrated into the student's world view.

Summative evaluations may use any of the techniques described under self-reflection or formative evaluation, in addition to the following forms:

- **Give pre- and post-tests.** Give a valid and reliable instrument to students before they begin the class and again after they have completed the class. Compare results. Tests may be for knowledge, skills, attitudes, or behaviors. Unlike a formative pre- and post-test that focuses on improving individual teaching skills or lesson plans, summative pre- and post-tests are given before and after the implementation of an entire program and focus on improving the program.
- **Give a standardized test.** There are two national standardized tests for information literacy. Project SAILS (Standardized Assessment of Information Literacy Skills) has just piloted three years of testing, and ETS (Educational Testing Service) is in the early phases of determining validity and reliability of its new ICT (Information and Communications

Technology) test. The main drawback of standardized tests is that they fall outside your own instructional design process. These tests do not measure goals and objectives set specifically for the class, but instead measure general information literacy competencies. Still, they can provide useful general data as well as data for making easy comparisons with other information literacy programs.

- **Administer a survey.** Question students and/or faculty with multiple choice, multiple multiple choice, or short essay. The CD-ROM accompanying this book includes two post-instruction surveys, each using a Likert scale.
- **Look at search activity in a transaction log.** Analyze search statements in an automatically produced transaction log.
- **Analyze student portfolios.** Use a rubric to assess the work in student portfolios. Bibliographies and research papers are particularly useful for assessing information literacy instruction.

Conclusion

I have offered both a representative sample of activities available to teach information literacy skills to first-year students and suggestions to allow you to improve your teaching and measure student learning. It would be impossible to include every possible assignment and assessment activity here, but you should find it easy to develop your own learning activities if you first survey your students' skills, using sound instructional design principles and accepted information literacy standards as you plan and using these suggestions as models.

Bibliography

Association of College and Research Libraries (ACRL). 2000. *Information Literacy Competency Standards for Higher Education.* www.ala.org/ala/acrl/acrlstandards/information literacycompetency.htm (accessed April 30, 2005).

Boff, Colleen, and Kristin Johnson. 2002. "The Library and First-Year Experience Courses: A Nationwide Study." *Reference Services Review* 30, no. 4: 277–287.

Friedlander, Amy. 2002. *Dimensions and Use of the Scholarly Information Environment Introduction to a Data Set.* Digital Library Federation: Council on Library and Information Resources. www.clir.org/pubs/reports/pub110/contents.html. Tables listed separately on www.diglib.org/pubs/scholinfo/ (accessed April 30, 2005).

Gardner, John N., Debra Decker, and Francine G. McNairy. 1986. "Taking the Library to Freshmen Students via the Freshman Seminar Concept." In *Advances in Library Administration and Organization. Volume 6: A Research Annual*, pp. 153–171, edited by Gerard B. McCabe and Bernard Kreissman. Greenwich, CT: JAI Press.

HigherEdInfo.org. National Center for Higher Education Management Systems. www.higheredinfo.org (accessed April 30, 2005).

Jones, Steve, Mary A. Madden, Lisa N. Clarke, and Pew Internet and American Life Project. 2002. *The Internet Goes to College: How Students Are Living in the Future with Today's Technology.* Pew Internet and American Life Project. www.pewinternet.org/PPF/r/71/report_display.asp (accessed April 30, 2005).

Kenny, Robert W. 1998. *Reinventing Undergraduate Education: A Blueprint for America's Research Universities*. The Boyer Commission on Educating Undergraduates in the Research. naples.cc.sunysb.edu/Pres/boyer.nsf/ (accessed April 30, 2005).

Kolb, David A. 1984. *Experiential Learning: Experience as the Source of Learning and Development*. Englewood Cliffs, NJ: Prentice Hall.

National Commission on Excellence in Education (NCEE). 1983. *A Nation at Risk: The Imperative for Educational Reform*. U.S. Department of Education. www.ed.gov/pubs/NatAtRisk/index.html (accessed April 30, 2005).

OCLC. 2002. *How Academic Librarians Can Influence Students' Web-Based Information Choices: OCLC White Paper on the Information Habits of College Students*. www5.oclc.org/downloads/community/informationhabits.pdf (accessed April 30, 2005).

Pierard, Cindy, and Kathryn Graves. 2002. "The Greatest Problem with Which the Library Is Confronted: A Survey of Academic Library Outreach to the Freshman Course." In *Making the Grade: Academic Libraries and Student Success*, pp. 71–89, edited by Maurie Caitlin Kelly and Andrea Kross. Chicago: Association of College and Research Libraries.

4

Tailoring Instruction for Community College Students

Ann Roselle

Introduction

Numbers tell the story. Community colleges are the largest, fastest growing sector of higher education and currently serve close to one-half of all undergraduates.[1] For over 100 years, community colleges have offered an inclusive comprehensive education through open admissions, affordable tuition and fees, and responsiveness to diverse populations.[2] Their name, "community," reflects both their origins and their principal sources of strength.

Role of Phoenix College

Phoenix College, an urban community college founded in 1920, serves as a case study throughout this chapter. Phoenix College is one of ten community colleges in Arizona's Maricopa Community College District (MCCCD). Its mission is to be a "comprehensive community college responsive to the changing needs of the community and individuals pursuing academic, occupational, developmental and personal enrichment goals."

Student Characteristics

Community college students are diverse in their backgrounds and their reasons for attending college. Minority students make up 30 percent of community college enrollments. Nationwide, 47 percent of black undergraduate students, 56 percent of Hispanic, 48 percent of Asian or Pacific Islander, and 57 percent of Native American undergraduates attend community colleges. Fifty-two percent of community college students are first-generation college students, and 58 percent are women. Forty-six percent of community college students are twenty-five years or older and 32 percent are thirty years or older, thereby creating a multigenerational classroom environment. Community colleges serve immigrants and international students, and English as a Second Language (ESL) classes are frequently offered. Likewise, due to community colleges' commitment to open access, some students who enroll are not prepared for college work, so developmental courses are offered regularly in subject areas such as mathematics, reading, and writing.

Community college students are more likely to need to balance work and family responsibilities with their studies. Over 80 percent of community college students work in either full-time or part-time positions, and 30 percent of the students who work full time also attend community college full time. Overall, 63 percent of community college students are part-time students.

Community colleges offer an array of programs, including certificates and associate degrees, to meet academic, occupational, developmental, and lifelong learning needs of students. It is not surprising, then, that the educational goals for students attending community colleges vary as much as their demographic characteristics.

Twenty-three percent of community college students transfer to a four-year institution to earn a bachelor's degree. On the other hand, many students immediately enter the workforce after completing an associate's degree. This is especially the case with students in occupational programs. In 2003, for example, 62 percent of applicants taking the national registered nurse examination graduated with associate degrees. In addition, students who already have a degree often select certificate programs or workforce training classes in order to keep up with the latest developments in technology or other changes in their fields.

Phoenix College Students

The students at Phoenix College, approximately 5,800 Full Time Student Equivalent (FTSE), possess many of the same characteristics as community college students across the country in terms of age, gender, and being the first generation to attend college. However, Phoenix College is more diverse than the national averages. Minority students make up the majority of the student body, which includes 30 percent Hispanic students. Phoenix College enrolls students from over 100 countries, and these students speak more than thirty different languages. Many of Phoenix College's students are considered to be at risk of academic failure.

Seventy-five percent of the students attend part time, and over 25 percent of the students work sixteen or more hours per week. Phoenix College has a disproportionately high number of ESL students. In addition, students are increasingly entering Phoenix College at a developmental level, with approximately 70 percent of students showing in testing a deficiency in English, mathematics, or reading skills.

Providing information literacy instruction to a growing population of diverse students is a challenge because these students differ widely in their English language proficiencies, computer competencies, and library experiences. Effective information literacy instruction to community college students, therefore, needs to be flexible so as to adjust to students' capabilities and not to lose students' interest. In the section of this chapter titled "Integrating Information Literacy," I recommend some specific program strategies to reach such students.

Student Information Literacy Competencies

Challenges in designing an information literacy program and establishing information literacy competencies arise in a community college learning environment, like Phoenix College, where educational goals vary broadly among the students. Information literacy needs may vary for the student whose community college degree will be the terminal degree compared to the student who will be transferring to a four-year institution. At Phoenix College, campus-wide information literacy competency standards were specifically designed for the associate degree student as part of the general education experience across the curriculum. To address students' varying educational goals more fully, librarians, faculty, and administrators could profitably explore the development of competency standards designed specifically for other scenarios, such as the certificate degree or occupational education programs.

The Association of College and Research Libraries' (ACRL) *Information Literacy Competency Standards for Higher Education* is an extremely useful document as a base for developing competencies, and was indeed used by Phoenix College, but constituents should recognize that the performance indicators and learning outcomes for the five standards were written for *all* levels of higher education. Therefore, some of the performance indicators and learning outcomes are less appropriate for community college students. When developing competencies, one can use the ACRL standards as a starting point, but would be less effective to apply the statement in its entirety without some restructuring or rewriting of content. Creating an understandable, suitable set of information literacy competency standards and learning outcomes is an extremely important step, since everything else—classroom content, teaching strategies, and assessment methods—stems from these standards.

Faculty Characteristics

The student-to-faculty ratio at community colleges in the United States is twenty to one. The master's degree is the most commonly attained degree for full-time and part-time faculty.[3] Faculty spend the majority of their time (68 percent) on teaching, rather than research.

Adjunct faculty have historically played a major role in community colleges, not only for the economic benefits to the colleges but also because these faculty-practitioners often have unique skills and up-to-date knowledge of their field. Sixty-six percent of faculty are part-time.

In this chapter I use the terms *librarians* and *instructors* to distinguish between these two groups of faculty. However, since librarians and instructors at community colleges share similar characteristics, including the level of terminal degree, faculty status, and learning-centeredness, there is an opportunity for collaboration that may not be as readily available in four-year colleges or research universities. On the other hand, the presence of a large population of adjunct faculty, who are often less accessible and may not be hired on a regular returning basis, can be a challenge to collaborative efforts.

Phoenix College Faculty

Faculty characteristics at Phoenix College are generally similar to the national averages. Unequivocally, the focus of instructors and librarians is on student learning. Phoenix College instructors and librarians have a genuine interest in pedagogical issues, new teaching techniques, and innovations in technology. Allocations of time and finances for professional development to learn and apply new skills and knowledge in these areas are readily available, including many grants directly from the community college district. Workshops and training sessions that advance teaching and learning are provided by the district's Maricopa Center for Learning and Instruction and the Phoenix College Learning Technologies and Development Department. Travel funds for professional growth outside the district are also readily available.

Librarian-Instructor Collaboration

Collaboration among librarians and instructors takes place in meaningful ways at community colleges where there is a campus-wide commitment to developing information-literate students. Community colleges that are dedicated to promoting lifelong learning are well situated to support collaborative information literacy efforts. Instructors who recognize that the world of information is too complex and changes too rapidly to focus only on student learning of discipline content help create an environment conducive to information literacy collaboration. Likewise, librarians who recognize that information literacy instruction is not the sole responsibility of the library help set the grounds for collaboration.

First, a recommended step toward collaboration is to develop a curriculum map of courses where information literacy is introduced or reinforced by instructors or librarians. Openly developing such a map demonstrates to the campus at large that librarians recognize that they are not the exclusive owners of information literacy. Librarians are excellent leaders of information literacy initiatives, but they will be less effective if working in isolation from the instructors and the rest of the campus.

Second, capitalizing on already established grounds of collaboration can help promote information literacy skills across the curriculum. Historically, librarians and instructors have worked collaboratively to develop collections. This existing relationship can be expanded to impact information literacy instruction. Due to limited budgets for community college libraries and the fact that these libraries do not serve as warehouses of research, the actual use of resources is one of the major factors when deciding to order new resources or keep existing ones. When building collections, therefore, librarians can collaborate with instructors to create assignments and exercises that will ensure the use of the resources while developing student information literacy skills. This is a particularly effective strategy to use when instructors request new resources. Librarians can use this opportunity to review with instructors existing class assignments and promote instruction by librarians to help ensure that students learn how to access the collections and, especially in the case of electronic resources, how to apply effective search strategies.

Third, co-teaching can be a setting for effective collaboration. Collaborative teaching enables the librarian to provide input into the course content to make certain that information literacy is adequately and effectively integrated. Faculty in community colleges can focus more of their time on course development, which provides the opportunity for both the instructor and the librarian to experiment with new instructional models. One of the best environments for collaborative teaching is within curricular learning communities in which classes are linked or clustered during a term, focusing on a particular theme (Fogarty, Dunlap, and Dolan, 2003). Community college libraries that offer classes for credit can initiate the building of learning communities, particularly with those instructors who have already incorporated library instruction into their classes. Information literacy instruction should be able to link successfully with courses across a broad spectrum of disciplines.

In a learning community, information literacy skills and knowledge are applied in a meaningful way because they are linked to a subject discipline. Likewise, participating in learning communities ensures integration of these skills and knowledge. Even without credit-bearing courses, librarians can still participate in a very significant way in learning communities where they share their expertise, skills, and knowledge to help develop course content, as well as to schedule and provide instruction at the most suitable times for the linked classes. While librarians at four-year colleges or universities often have the opportunity to co-teach in first-year experience (FYE) programs, these programs often cannot work in the community college environment where there are so many part-time students who enroll in courses off and on, depending on their personal and work-related responsibilities. Therefore, the formation of learning communities is one of the only real viable options for collaborative teaching at community colleges.

Fourth, collaboration between instructors and librarians also needs to flourish in distributed learning environments. As more and more courses are developed for online delivery, collaboration must be supported to ensure the integration of information literacy. Fortunately, libraries are so technology based that maintaining linkages in this environment is quite natural. Librarians can work with instructors to redesign assignments that fully utilize electronic resources where students learn information literacy competencies in the areas of retrieval and evaluation of information. Librarians and instructors can collaboratively develop online tutorials that would mirror the library instruction offered in a traditional classroom setting. There are also new avenues for librarians to participate in online courses that utilize course delivery software such as WebCT or BlackBoard. Librarians can participate in online threaded discussions and synchronous classroom chats or build resource pages for inclusion into the online course content.

Librarian-instructor collaboration takes time. Librarians may need time to learn more about a discipline in order to participate in a learning community or may need to become proficient in new technologies in order to participate in online classes. For instructors, time may be required to understand components of information literacy or to revise assignments that connect these skills with their discipline content. Since community college librarians and instructors usually are not required to research and publish, more time may be devoted to instructional collaborative efforts than perhaps at a four-year college or university.

One other challenge to collaboration is the large number of adjunct instructors employed by community colleges. Often, adjuncts are hired to support evening and weekend courses. Since flexibility of instructional delivery is what attracts many to community colleges, evening and weekend classes often make up a major part of the course offerings. Therefore, to ensure integration of information literacy instruction, collaboration must occur with adjunct instructors. This can be difficult because adjunct instructors are often harder to contact and may be unavailable for consultations with librarians outside their class time. Adjuncts also generally do not stay as long at one institution. One strategy to developing collaboration with adjuncts is through close cooperation with department chairpersons, who, in turn, can encourage or even require adjuncts to work with librarians.

When developing strategies to use new ways to enhance collaboration, community college librarians should review all of their current activities that they perceive to be signs of collaboration. A reevaluation of these activities may, in fact, lead to the discovery that some of them are not collaborative at all in the sense of being mutually beneficial activities that help meet the goal of greater student information literacy competency. For instance, how collaborative is the relationship with the instructor who invites you to teach a fifty-minute "Introduction to the Library" session when he has to go out of town? How beneficial is collaborating on a scavenger hunt exercise for the instructor who never integrates information literacy into her class? Is giving the same library tour every year to the same course the highest level of collaboration that can take place with that instructor? There is no harm in stopping activities that do not or only minimally help students to become information literate. Removing these tasks will free up time for librarians to initiate and engage in more complete collaborative efforts that impact student learning positively. Fortunately, much has been written on how librarians can develop collaborative relationships with instructors for promoting information literacy (ACRL, 2001; Ellison, 2004; Raspa and Ward, 2000). Jean Caspers' discussion in this book of the interpersonal dynamics of librarian-instructor collaboration provides excellent practical advice.

Collaboration at Phoenix College

At Phoenix College, librarian-instructor collaboration occurs at varying levels. Librarians review assignments and exercises designed by instructors as often as possible, including WebCT-based English classes. However, collaboratively designing assignments is primarily done only with instructors who have an ongoing, close professional relationship with the librarians. When instructors request a new library resource, such as an online database or a new periodical, the librarians strive to work with instructors to ensure that the resources will be used in assignments that develop students' skills and knowledge in information literacy. Individual instruction sessions are specifically tailored to meet the needs of classes, with particular attention to the needs of ESL students.

Learning communities are just beginning to be piloted on campus, and librarians have taken a leadership role with this initiative, including cowriting grants to support development of learning communities and attending a summer institute (with instructors and administrators) on learning communities. The librarians' activities have included (1) assisting with the organization of course content to link the classes successfully, (2) helping to design class assignments that integrate technology and information literacy, and (3) providing more extensive information literacy classroom instruction. Often, instructors permit only one class period for library instruction. In a learning community, where students are enrolled in at least two similar classes, the librarian can easily meet with the same group of students more than once without taking away any additional time from the instructors. Instruction sessions can, in this way, build upon each other. Students in these learning communities build better bonds with the participating librarians that can help with retention, which is a major interest of Phoenix College.

Integrating Information Literacy

Collaboration among librarians and instructors is only one necessary component for integrating information literacy across the curriculum. The other is administrative support. For community colleges, demonstrating how an information literacy program or strategies for instruction are directly aligned with the colleges' mission and goals is extraordinarily important to ensure administrative support for the activities. Administrative support may materialize in the form of financial or human resources to help achieve the goals of the information literacy program, including reassigning time or extra contracts for collaborative activities by librarians and instructors. Many community colleges use national surveys, such as the *Community College Survey of Student Engagement* or the *Noel-Levitz Student Satisfaction Inventory*, to help assess the quality of their community college education and whether or not they are meeting their mission and goals. Fortunately, these surveys include some questions that begin to focus on information literacy, including the extent to which students use and integrate information and their use of various technologies. Librarians can use results from these surveys to leverage administrative support for a more fully integrated information literacy program.

Along with connecting information literacy to the college mission and goals, administrative support for information literacy programs can be built by connecting to the accreditation process. The U.S. Department of Education recognizes six private educational associations—Middle States, New England, North Central, Northwest, Southern, and Western—to serve as accrediting agencies to ensure that higher education institutions meet acceptable levels of quality. All of these accrediting agencies include assessment of student learning, which fits with information literacy, in the accreditation process and have developed standards to reflect the importance of this criterion (see Figure 4-1). In addition, several of the agencies include information literacy in their accreditation requirements. The accrediting documents from the Middle States Commission on Higher Education serve as excellent examples. Along with requiring information literacy as part of Standard 12 (General Education), the commission incorporates information literacy into Standard 11 (Educational Offerings). The commission writes, "Information literacy is vital to all disciplines and to effective teaching and learning in any institution." According to the commission, evidence of sound educational offerings include "collaboration between professional library staff and faculty in teaching and fostering information literacy skills relevant to the curriculum" and "information literacy incorporated in the curriculum with syllabi, or other material appropriate to the mode of teaching and learning."

Integration at Phoenix College

Phoenix College was last accredited in 1996 by the North Central Association of Colleges and Schools. During the accreditation visit, the site team recommended that the college establish a more institutionalized program for assessment of student learning. In response, Phoenix College has established eight college-wide assessment committees charged with drafting outcome statements, developing mechanisms for measuring student learning in their respective areas, and sharing results and recommendations with the campus at large. In 2003 the librarians presented a plan to create an Information Literacy Assessment Committee to the college administrators. The college administration supported the plan because the librarians demonstrated the relationship between information literacy to the college's vision of promoting lifelong learning, the college's general education mission, and the accreditation standards for the college's next site visit in 2006. Along with administrative backing for the plan, support has included release time for the librarian who serves as chair of the committee and funding for supplies and assessment tools. The college-wide Information Literacy Assessment Committee, which consists of librarians and instructors across various disciplines, began analyzing assessment results in September 2005. The outcomes

Figure 4-1   Accrediting Agencies and Information Literacy Standards

Accrediting Agency	*Standard*	*Information Literacy Statement*
Middle States Commission on Higher Education	**Standard 12: General Education**	The institution's curricula are designed so that students acquire and demonstrate college-level proficiency in general education and essential skills, including . . . information literacy.
New England Commission on Institutions of Higher Education	**Standard 7: Library and Information Resources**	Professionally qualified and numerically adequate staff administer the institution's library, information resources, and services. The institution provides appropriate orientation and training for use of these resources, as well as instruction in basic information literacy. [7.4]
The Higher Learning Commission, North Central Association of Colleges and Schools	**Criterion 4: Acquisition, Discovery, and Application of Knowledge**	The organization promotes a life of learning for its faculty, administration, staff, and students by fostering and supporting inquiry, creativity, practice, and social responsibility in ways consistent with its mission.
Northwest Commission on Colleges and Universities	**Standard 2: Educational Program and Its Effectiveness**	Degree and certificate programs demonstrate a coherent design; are characterized by appropriate breadth, depth, sequencing of courses, synthesis of learning, and the assessment of learning outcomes; and require the use of library and other information sources. [2.A.3] Faculty, in partnership with library and information resources personnel, ensure that the use of library and information resources is integrated into the learning process. [2.A.8]
Commission on Colleges, Southern Association of Colleges and Schools	**Standard 3: Institutional Mission, Governance and Effectiveness**	The institution ensures that users have access to regular and timely instruction in the use of the library and other learning/information resources. [3.8.2]
The Accrediting Commission for Community and Junior Colleges, Western Association of Schools and Colleges	**Standard 2: Student Learning Programs and Services**	A capability to be a productive individual and lifelong learner: skills include oral and written communication, information competency, computer literacy, scientific and quantitative reasoning, critical analysis/logical thinking, and the ability to acquire knowledge through a variety of means. [II.3.b]

from the assessment activities are expected to improve teaching of information literacy, increase instructors' awareness of the role that librarians play in instructional design, and strengthen collaboration between librarians and instructors. Establishing information literacy as part of Phoenix College's institutionalized assessment program has already greatly raised awareness of the importance of information literacy across the campus and has improved the visibility of the librarians.

Information Literacy Programs

The Association of College and Research Libraries (ACRL) has identified core elements of best practices in information literacy programming (ACRL, 2003). Of these, I have already discussed Mission, Goals and Objectives, Administrative and Institutional Support, and Collaboration. A few of the other elements—Articulation with the Curriculum, Pedagogy, and Outreach—are particularly challenging for information literacy instruction at community colleges.

Teaching credit-bearing courses can be one of the most effective ways to integrate information literacy instruction into the curriculum and build an information literacy program. Credit-bearing courses provide students with the opportunity to learn skills and develop knowledge at an in-depth level that is generally unattainable from a single information literacy session. Credit courses also enable librarians to participate more fully in learning communities. However, a major challenge to attracting community college students to these credit courses occurs when the courses do not transfer as general education requirements to four-year institutions. Credit courses that can only be advertised to potential students as "good for you" electives often fail to attract sufficient enrollment, which is imperative to course offerings.

Pedagogy is also challenging at community colleges, where the diversity of students is so broad. Instructors and librarians have to consider more than just multiple learning styles. They must also incorporate strategies to facilitate learning among populations of ESL and developmental students. The benefits of active and collaborative learning have been well documented and extensively discussed within the library profession, so I will not reiterate them here. However, the library profession needs to recognize the advances in brain research on long-term memory and how students learn (Erlauer, 2003; Scherer, 2000; Wolfe, 2001). Brain research and its impact on pedagogy are rarely mentioned in the library literature. Brain-congruent or brain-compatible activities for teaching information literacy can improve student retention of content, which is particularly important to students who may be unprepared for community college work. Patricia Wolfe's *Brain Matters: Translating Research into Classroom Practice* (Wolfe, 2001) serves as a good introductory text that librarians can use when developing brain-compatible activities to improve student learning. Activities Wolfe suggests incorporate simulations, problem-based learning, graphic organizers, music, rhyme and rhythm, writing, active engagement, and mnemonics. An increased depth of understanding and application, which occurs when applying active learning and brain stimulating techniques, is more important than the quantity of material being covered.

Pedagogical concerns are further complicated in a distributed learning environment where community college students vary greatly in terms of their computer literacy. When developing an information literacy program for a community college, librarians should review and carefully decide what can be best learned online as compared to in person. Another concern is the extent to which librarians are prepared to move into the traditional or online classroom. While librarians have many experiences with reference, instructional services, and lecture-based instruction, they may be less prepared or less comfortable in engaging students in active learning. Nevertheless, they must become proficient in stimulating student learning.

Outreach activities to instructors to market new initiatives within the information literacy program can be surprisingly challenging at community colleges where instructors and librarians already work quite closely. That is, instructors who are already comfortable with the information literacy sessions offered may be less willing to try something new. Librarians may fear alienating instructors viewed as allies when reorganizing their information literacy program in ways that require course instructors to change their own instructional planning and delivery. It is important for librarians to make the case to instructors that well-considered changes in the program will ultimately benefit their students.

One way that libraries try to meet instructors' expectations while allowing librarians to offer new types of information literacy instruction is to offer a menu of options, such as tours, walk-in workshops, one-on-one consultations, fifty-minute "one shots," classes on specific library resources, course-related instruction sessions, credit-bearing information literacy courses, learning communities, and online tutorials. On the one hand, this "something for everyone" approach can help encourage all instructors to utilize instructional services and may assist in meeting the needs of a diverse student population with varying educational goals. On the other hand, adding more and more options can put a strain on existing resources. Balancing the workload of librarians and managing classroom utilization can become overwhelming. In order to commit fully to new offerings and develop the most successful information literacy program possible, librarians may have to eliminate instructional services that are not optimally effective. A zero-based review of library activities may help in discovering activities that are no longer justified in comparison to other more pressing needs. In fact, a reprioritization of all library goals and action plans may be in order when librarians work to develop an improved information literacy program.

There is another key element that is characteristic of exemplary information literacy programs that ACRL did not include in its list. An information literacy program needs a *vision*—an ideal for the future. Developing a vision can be a liberating process whereby librarians, instructors, and administrators imagine the ultimate information literacy program, without being bogged down by the logistics of existing human, financial, and facility resources. Visions are not constrained by current realities and can vary from one community college to the next. But there is no way for an information literacy program to evolve—to get even close to an ideal—without a vision. Some possibilities are:

- A required credit-bearing course for all incoming students, which would be taught by dynamic librarians, with articulation to four-year colleges and universities
- For all academic and occupational programs to incorporate information literacy into their core classes, using assignments that are designed collaboratively by instructors and librarians
- An expanded service learning program where students apply information literacy skills during real work situations
- Utilization of proven, effective online tools for student learning of information literacy, used by all instructors who teach online courses
- Implementation of the most promising assessment tool ever designed; one that produces usable data and which, when applied to an information literacy program, has measurable, positive results

Planning and Implementing Information Literacy at Phoenix College

At Phoenix College, the library's vision for information literacy has recently changed. The ideal is to develop a wide-ranging selection of information literacy credit courses that meet the diverse needs of the students. The courses could range from those designed specifically for ESL students to students planning to transfer to a four-year college, to occupational students who will be immediately employed in the health professions. The vision is for these courses to be offered using a variety of appropriate delivery options and to enable students to be actively engaged in the learning process. In order to make the vision a reality, the library had to make some changes. The subject liaison structure was disbanded and librarians were grouped into teams. The instructional team devotes the majority of its time to collaborating with instructors, teaching courses, developing instructional tools, and serving on the campus-wide Information Literacy Assessment Committee. This team also attends pedagogy-related workshops and seminars on emerging technologies for teaching and learning. In order to balance workload, the librarians stopped promoting the fifty-minute one shot and provide classroom instruction only for those instructors who genuinely integrate information literacy into their teaching. The plan is for those previous introductory sessions taught by librarians on very basic skills, such as finding a book in the library catalog or taking tours to identify locations of collections, to be replaced by online guides and tutorials.

Starting in 2005–2006, the library will offer a three-credit course entitled "Information Skills in the Digital Age," along with a more traditional one-credit course entitled "Electronic Database Searching." The three-credit course transfers to all three state universities and carries the General Education Literacy and Critical Inquiry designation at Arizona State University. While the course does promote skills in accessing, evaluating, and using information, it also exposes students to the social and economic consequences of technology and information.

The courses are offered in a variety of delivery options, including traditional, hybrid, and online, and all employ active learning.

Assessment of Student Learning

Assessment demonstrates effectiveness and can move an information literacy program in the right directions. In addition, a campus-wide commitment to information literacy assessment can help support any initiative for improving student information literacy competencies. It is not surprising, then, that ACRL includes assessment/evaluation as one of the characteristics of best practices in information literacy programming. At the community college level, one of the biggest challenges to assessing student learning is identifying appropriate and meaningful student samples and locating suitable assessment tools.

As already noted, community college students generally are not in cohorts and many students attend only part time. Community college students frequently move in and out of college, as family and work needs temporarily take precedence. In addition, although prerequisites do exist for some community college courses, there is no typical order in which students take classes. It can be difficult, therefore, to sample a group of students who have had similar educational experiences.

Likewise, the ways in which community college students develop information literacy competencies are also unsystematic, except perhaps at those institutions with an information competency graduation requirement with required coursework. Students learn through reference interactions; individual library instruction sessions; information literacy credit courses; course-integrated information literacy assignments; one-on-one interactions with librarians, instructors, or computer lab assistants; and instructional guides and tutorials. In all of these activities, learning can take place either face-to-face or virtually. Again, it is difficult to identify and sample a population of community college students who have had similar exposure to information literacy instruction.

In addition, identifying assessment tools that are appropriate for community college students can be difficult. One popular strategy to assess student learning is the use of rubrics with student portfolios, which tracks students' performance throughout their years at college. This strategy can be more difficult at the community college because the fluctuation in student attendance makes storing traditional portfolios impractical. E-portfolios, on the other hand, might enable community colleges to follow the work done by students more easily, making this assessment technique more attractive.

Standardized tests are also popular for measuring information literacy. National tests, such as Project SAILS and the newly designed ETS ICT Assessment, have some advantages for community colleges. These testing organizations develop the instruments, conduct statistical analysis, and write final reports, all of which can be extremely helpful to those community colleges that do not have designated institutional research departments. Unfortunately, these tests were not designed specifically for community colleges, and some of the test questions can be inappropriate.

The results of the tests also allow for benchmarking, but, again, because the tests are not just for community colleges, comparisons may be inappropriate. Since the students participating in these national tests can vary so much from each other—for instance, university seniors compared to first-year ESL community college students—it is questionable if any inferences based on comparing results with educational institutions should be made. Interestingly, the Bay Area Community Colleges developed and began testing an information competency assessment instrument specifically for community colleges in 2005. Community colleges were welcome to receive copies of the assessment instrument, make adjustments to the tool if necessary, and use it with their students. As I wrote this, the instrument was still being tested for validity and reliability. Ultimately, it may have real potential for community colleges nationwide.

Along with campus-wide assessment through portfolio analysis or standardized testing, assessment of student learning can also take place at the course level. One of the more popular techniques for course-level assessment of information literacy is the use of pre-tests and post-tests. This technique can be challenging for community colleges because of attendance and retention issues with community college students. Many of the students taking a pre-test may not be around to take the post-test. Another question is the extent to which pre-tests and post-tests are applicable for fifty-minute one shots, especially in cases where testing is conducted during the same class period. In addition, rubrics, sets of guidelines for scoring, have been successfully used by colleges as a tool to evaluate performance on certain information literacy tasks taught within courses (Creel, 2004; Delaware Tech Librarians, 2004; Guarini Library, 2004; Jacobs, 2004). The collaboration between librarians and instructors in developing rubrics can be a wonderful exercise to ensure that both groups have a clear understanding of the course expectations for the information literacy competencies.

Assessment at Phoenix College

The librarians at Phoenix College use pre-tests and post-tests with credit-bearing courses as well as in single library instruction sessions for assessment of student learning. When possible, the librarians coordinate with the instructors to administer pre-tests prior to the students' coming into the library for their course-integrated instruction. In addition, student evaluation questionnaires and classroom observations by library colleagues are used to evaluate sessions.

At the campus level, the Information Literacy Assessment Committee chose to participate in Project SAILS during 2004–2005. Since benchmarking with Project SAILS can present problems for community colleges, the committee decided to test two Phoenix College subgroups to allow for some comparisons. The multiple-choice test was administered to (1) a group of students in sections of an introductory English course where they presumably had received limited information literacy instruction at Phoenix College and (2) students in courses across the curriculum where information literacy skills were taught integrally by instructors and librarians. Along with subgroup comparisons, it is expected that results from Project SAILS will help pinpoint information literacy skill sets that the campus can focus on. The committee plans on using results from Project SAILS to launch a significant information literacy instruction campaign across the campus starting in 2005–2006.

The Future of Information Literacy in Community Colleges

The American Association of Community Colleges (AACC) commissions authors to write papers on their visions of the future for community colleges in "New Expeditions Issues Papers." These papers identify many trends that have a potential impact on information literacy instruction. Likewise, ACRL conducts environmental scans and produces white papers that identify higher education trends. Three factors that have been identified by these organizations, which may have the most immediate impact on information literacy at community colleges, include accountability, technology, and economic demand.

Accountability

While community colleges must be accountable to their accrediting agencies, other constituents increasingly demand accountability. For example, community colleges have had to increase external revenue sources and private donors in order to keep tuitions and fees affordable. Therefore, community colleges must now demonstrate accountability to these external groups. Community colleges are also now competing with for-profit educational institutions, such as the University of Phoenix, and higher education companies like Devry and ITT Educational Services. Accountability to students and their families becomes even more important as competition increases. Accountability to the public at large and to local employers continues to be important to secure ongoing financial support from the community and employer placement of graduates. Finally, the federal government continues pushing for more specific accountability measures by higher education accrediting agencies.

Librarians can capitalize on the accountability trend by convincing college administrators that student information literacy is a core performance measure. In an expanding knowledge economy, the argument for graduating information-literate students is an easy one to make. Applied critical thinking and fluency with information technology (two essential components of information literacy) can improve students' academic success and retention and help prepare community college students for the workforce. Once information literacy is tied to accountability, integrating its components across the campus will become a necessity, and librarians and instructors should more readily receive administrative support for information literacy instruction.

Technology

Along with demonstrating accountability, community colleges are increasingly using emerging technologies to deliver instruction to stay competitive in the education market. Online learning provides flexibility in time, place, and pace, which are all becoming increasingly common expectations of community college students. As online learning increases, it is imperative that information literacy teaching and learning remain integrated. Librarians, now more than ever, must continually upgrade their technology skills to enable them to outreach in a virtual learning environment and to develop meaningful online instructional tools that help to meet the goals of an information literacy instruction program. Since community college students vary in their computer competencies, librarians at the same time have to devise mechanisms to ensure that less technologically capable students are not left behind.

Economic Demands

Developments in the economy demand at least some college education and training for most jobs (Sum, 1999). In addition, there are economic demands to quickly fill employment shortages in specific areas, such as nursing, fire science, emergency medicine, and teacher education. In response, community colleges are working on new ways to develop a workforce more quickly to meet societal needs. For example, occupational programs at some community colleges are redesigning their curriculum to accelerate programs, and many community colleges are striving to increase the number of students in dual enrollment or Achieving a College Education (ACE) programs. Shortening the time span for community college education will impact information literacy instruction. Information literacy credit courses that are electives may no longer be a viable option for students with fully packed program requirements. Librarians will have to develop new strategies to ensure that information literacy continues to be integrated during accelerated instruction with ample opportunities for students to apply their newfound skills and knowledge.

Conclusion

This chapter reviews challenges to library and information literacy instruction at community colleges, including:

- Extremely diverse students who need stimulating and continuing information literacy instruction
- Obstacles that interfere with librarian-instructor collaboration when implementing new instructional approaches
- Insufficient resources for information literacy planning and assessment designed specifically for community colleges

Despite these challenges, the key message of this chapter is a positive one. Trends in accountability, technology, and workforce needs make this an optimal time for fully integrating information literacy at community colleges. To successfully do so, this chapter discusses and makes recommendations for:

- Investigating how information literacy is already taught on campus; reevaluating and making changes to instruction in order to optimize efforts

- Developing a vision for an information literacy program
- New opportunities for integrating information literacy within distributed learning environments
- A campus-wide commitment to information literacy through administrative support by connecting to college assessment initiatives or accreditation activities

Community colleges will always be committed to open access. They will persist in being unconventional and flexible to meet the needs of an ever-changing economy. Rapid changes, whether economic based or student demographic based, will continue to impact community colleges. Information literacy instruction at community colleges, therefore, must continue to rapidly evolve to maximize its benefits for students.

Notes

1. Reported enrollment data are by headcount, including a large number of part-time students (American Association of Community Colleges, 2000).

2. The average annual cost of tuition and fees at public community colleges in 2004–2005 was $2,076. In the same year, the average annual cost of tuition and fees at public four-year colleges was $5,132, while the average cost at private four-year colleges was $20,082 (College Board, 2004).

3. A master's degree is possessed by 65.1 percent of the full-time and 55 percent of the part-time faculty. Sixteen percent of full-time and 7.5 percent of part-time faculty possess a PhD. A bachelor's degree is possessed by 11.9 percent of full-time and 24.8 percent of part-time faculty (American Association of Community Colleges, 2000).

Bibliography

Accrediting Commission for Community and Junior Colleges. 2002. Accreditation Standards. www.accjc.org/Core%20Documents.htm (accessed July 20, 2005).

American Association of Community Colleges. 2000. *National Profile of Community Colleges: Trends & Statistics*. 3rd ed. Washington, DC: Community College Press.

———. 2004. *New Expeditions Issues Papers*. www.aacc.nche.edu/Content/Navigation Menu/ResourceCenter/Projects_Partnerships/Current/NewExpeditions/IssuePapers/ IssuePapers.htm (accessed July 20, 2005).

Association of College and Research Libraries (ACRL). 2000. *Information Literacy Standards for Higher Education*. www.ala.org/ala/acrl/acrlstandards/informationliteracy competency.htm (accessed July 20, 2005).

———. 2002. *A Collaboration/Team Building Bibliography*. www.ala.org/ala/acrlbucket/in folit/bibliographies1/collaboration.htm (accessed July 20, 2005).

———. 2003. *Characteristics of Programs of Information Literacy That Illustrate Best Practices: A Guideline*. www.ala.org/ala/acrl/acrlstandards/characteristics.htm (accessed July 20, 2005).

———. 2005. *White Papers and Reports*. www.ala.org/ala/acrl/acrlpubs/whitepapers/ whitepapersreports.htm (accessed July 20, 2005).

Bay Area Community Colleges Information Competency Assessment Project. 2004. http:// topsy.org/ICAP/ICAProject.html (accessed July 20, 2005).

College Board. 2004. *Trends in College Pricing*. Washington, DC: Washington Office of the College Board.

Commission on Colleges. 2001. *Principles of Accreditation: Foundations for Quality Enhancement*. www.sacscoc.org/pdf/PrinciplesOfAccreditation.PDF (accessed July 20, 2005).

Creel, Diane W. 2004. *Primary Trait Analysis*. www.nvcc.edu/depts/assessment/oldsite2/Information%20Literacy.ppt (accessed July 20, 2005).

Delaware Tech Librarians (Delaware Technical and Community College). 2004. *Information Literacy Guidelines for Rubrics*. www.library.dtcc.edu/wilmlib/Infolitrubric.html (accessed July 20, 2005).

Ellison, Alicia B. 2004. "Positive Faculty/Librarian Relationships for Productive Library Assignments." *Community and Junior College Libraries* 12, no. 2: 23–28.

Erlauer, Laura. 2003. *The Brain-Compatible Classroom: Using What We Know About Learning to Improve Teaching*. Alexandria, VA: Association for Supervision and Curriculum Development.

Fogarty, Julia, Lynn Dunlap, and Edmund Dolan. 2003. *Learning Communities in Community Colleges*. Washington, DC: American Association of Community Colleges.

Guarini Library (New Jersey City University). 2004. *Information Literacy Rubrics*. www.njcu.edu/Guarini/Instructions/Rubrics.htm (accessed July 20, 2005).

Higher Learning Commission. 2003. *Handbook of Accreditation*. www.ncahigherlearningcommission.org/resources/handbook/Handbook03.pdf (accessed July 20, 2005).

ICT Literacy Assessment. www.ets.org/ictliteracy (accessed July 20, 2005).

Jacobs, Alan. 2004. "Rubric for Information Literacy/Technology Literacy." www.sc.maricopa.edu/assessment/Information%20Literacy/infoliteracy.htm (accessed July 20, 2005).

Middle States Commission on Higher Education. 2002. *Characteristics of Excellence in Higher Education: Eligibility Requirements and Standards for Accreditation*. www.msche.org/publications/Characteristicsbook050215112128.pdf (accessed July 20, 2005).

New England Commission on Institutions of Higher Education. 2001. *CIHE Standards for Accreditation*. www.neasc.org/cihe/stancihe.htm (accessed July 20, 2005).

Northwest Commission on Colleges and Universities. 2003. *Accreditation Handbook*. www.nwccu.org/Pubs%20Forms%20and%20Updates/Publications/Publications.htm (accessed July 20, 2005).

Project SAILS. http://sails.lms.kent.edu (accessed July 20, 2005).

Raspa, Dick, and Dane Ward. 2000. *The Collaborative Imperative: Librarians and Faculty Working Together in the Information Universe*. Chicago: Association of College and Research Libraries.

Scherer, Margaret M., ed. 2000. *The Science of Learning*. Special issue of *Educational Leadership* 58, no. 3 (November): 8–87.

Sum, Andrew. 1999. "Literacy in the Labor Force: Results from the National Adult Literacy Survey." http://nces.ed.gov/pubsearch/pubsinfo.asp?pubid=1999470 (accessed July 20, 2005).

Wolfe, Patricia. 2001. *Brain Matters: Translating Research into Classroom Practice*. Alexandria, VA: Association for Supervision and Curriculum Development.

5

Tailoring Instruction for Students with Disabilities

Alexander Gyamfi

Introduction

Growing numbers of people with disabilities are attending institutions of higher education in increasingly inclusive settings. This increase has been made possible by the passage of disability laws, which prohibit educational institutions from discriminating against people with disabilities. Availability of adaptive or assistive technologies has also made it possible for people with disabilities to be a part of a regular classroom. These technologies provide functional alternatives to standard operations of mainstream technologies and thus provide enhanced opportunities for learning outcomes for people with disabilities.

Information literacy has become the *zeitgeist*, or spirit of the times, for academic librarians. Mastery of its concepts and skills equips individuals with the ability to locate needed information, determine its relevance and adequacy, filter and evaluate it, and then to use it critically, creatively, responsibly, and ethically (American Library Association, 2000; Siitonen, 1996). Acquisition of these skills makes it possible for individuals to access and use information for the purposes that they desire, making them full participants in today's information society.

Research carried out in Canada and the United States identifies information literacy skills as one of the competencies that the workplace will demand of employees in the future (Eaton and Treadgold, 1999; SCANS Report, 2000). The Prague Declaration also affirmed the necessity of an information-literate society and stressed the need for all nations to address the information literacy needs of their citizens (Gibson, 2004). Therefore, the provision of information literacy skills for people with disabilities is not just a matter of right, but also one of acquiring valuable skills needed for the participation in democratic process, social programs, the labor market, and other economic opportunities.

An information literacy classroom may include students with disabilities (SWD) and those who do not have disabilities. In such a classroom with a diverse mix of students, teachers have to instruct all students to the required academic standards. The duty of a teacher as described by Dewey is "to survey the capacities and needs of the particular set of individuals with whom he/she is dealing and must at the same time arrange the conditions which provide the subject-matter or content for experiences that satisfy these needs and develop these capacities" (Dewey, 1938). A one-size-fits-all approach to instruction would not work in a diverse classroom. This chapter discusses approaches to providing information literacy instruction to SWD in an inclusive classroom.

Defining Disability

Central to any discussion of issues related to people with disabilities is the threshold question of who is considered an "individual with a disability" (Hawke, 2004). Generally, the term *disability* is used to connote some physical, mental, or other kind of incapacity that prevents people from performing some life support tasks such as seeing, hearing, walking, speaking, and processing information. Various frameworks define disability differently, however, based on their respective conceptual viewpoints. For example:

1   Functional limitations. This framework defines disability as the inability or limitation of an individual in performing socially defined roles and tasks expected of the individual within a given environment (Nagi, 1965). This definition stresses the activity limitations of the individual.

2   Medical. This framework defines disability as the inability to engage in any substantial activity by reason of any medically determinable physical or mental impairment (DeJong, Batavia, and Griss, 1989; United Kingdom, *DDA*, 1995). The identification of a disability in this framework involves an assessment of one or more medical conditions responsible for a person's limitations in performing needed tasks.

3   Sociopolitical. This framework defines disability as the loss or limitation of opportunities to take part in society on an equal level with others due to social and environmental barriers. This framework considers disability as the consequence of a "disabling environment" (Hahn, 1984), and holds that barriers in society or environments "disable" people. If these barriers are

removed or reduced, then people will be able to take a full and active part in society. According to this view the three main barriers that impede people's full and active participation in society are:

- Environment—this includes inaccessible buildings and services, inaccessible communication and language
- Attitudes—this includes stereotyping, discrimination, and prejudice
- Organizations—this includes procedures and practices, which are inflexible (Bernell, 2003)

All of these definitions take a narrow view of disability based on the concept espoused by the respective framework. A broad definition of an individual with a disability, however, is set forth in the Americans with Disabilities Act (ADA) of 1990 to mean an individual who:

1 Has a physical or mental impairment that substantially limits that person from performing one or more major life activities such as caring for one's self, performing manual tasks, walking, seeing, hearing, speaking, breathing, learning, and processing information
2 Has a record of physical impairment that substantially limits one or more life activities
3 Is regarded as having such an impairment (U.S. GAO, 1990)

Types of Disabilities

A recent report by the U.S. National Center for Education Statistics (Lewis and Farris, 1999) indicates that the number of postsecondary undergraduate students in the United States identified as having disabilities represents 9.3 percent of the total student population. Many studies have identified disabilities that students in postsecondary institutions report to include: learning disabilities, mobility impairment, health impairments, mental illness or emotional disturbance, hearing impairments, blindness and visual impairments, speech or language impairments, and other impairments (Lewis and Farris, 1999; NSF, 2000). The literature however, identifies learning, mobility, visual, and hearing disabilities as high incidence disabilities reported by students in postsecondary institutions.

Regardless of the type of disability, educators primarily have to deal with its functional result (Smith et al., 2001). The instructor needs to know the nature of disabilities to be dealt with in order to provide the necessary accommodation and teaching strategies to meet the students' needs. Identifying the types of disabilities is an important step to effective instruction and provision of accommodation. Therefore, it is necessary to explain the different types of high incidence disabilities reported by students in postsecondary institutions. These types of disabilities are:

- Learning disability. This term broadly describes a number of conditions that affect individuals in their ability to learn or to process information. Learning disabilities can interfere with a person's ability to read, write, remember, compute, or process written or spoken information (Lazzaro, 2001). A learning disability includes conditions such as dyslexia, reading difficulties, memory deficits, attention disorders, and cognitive and metacognitive deficits (Beale and Tippet, 1992; Hallahan, Kauffman, and Lloyd, 1999).

- Mobility impairment. An individual with mobility impairment has a physical condition that limits movement of hands, arms, legs, or any other voluntary muscle. Mobility impairments can be permanent or temporary. A broken bone, for example, can temporarily impact a student's ability to walk independently or write. A medical condition such as arthritis or repetitive stress injuries can also impact fine motor abilities. Permanent mobility impairments, on the other hand, include but are not limited to conditions such as paraplegia, chronic illnesses such as multiple sclerosis or chronic fatigue syndrome, cerebral palsy, spina bifida, and cystic fibrosis (Merced College, 2005; Stanford, 2005).
- Hearing impairment. This indicates individuals who have serious restrictions in their abilities to perceive sound. It includes the following conditions:
  - Deafness. A total or partial loss of hearing function so severe that it no longer serves as a major channel for information processing.
  - Hearing limitation. A functional loss in hearing which is still capable of serving as a major channel for information processing (Merced College, 2005).
- Visual impairment. A generic term that includes the following conditions:
  - Blindness. A state in which the person afflicted cannot see at all. Such a person has a visual acuity of 20/200 or less in the better eye after correction.
  - Low vision. The person afflicted has visual acuity of 20/70 or less in the better eye after correction. There is a serious restriction in the person's field of vision or the person cannot see effectively. However, some functional vision exists to be used for information processing (Smith et al., 2001).

Legislation

In the United States, various federal laws have been enacted that provide a clear and comprehensive mandate for the elimination of unfair burdens and discrimination against qualified individuals with disabilities to pursue higher education. Institutions are obligated to provide access to buildings and reasonable accommodations to SWD so that they can participate in or benefit from the services, programs, and activities that they provide. These laws include the Rehabilitation Act of 1973 and the Americans with Disabilities Act (ADA) of 1990.

The Rehabilitation Act of 1973

This law requires that programs conducted by or receiving funds from federal agencies must not discriminate against individuals with disabilities who are qualified. Section 504 of the Rehabilitation Act of 1973, as amended in 29 U.S.C. § 794, states: "No qualified individual with a disability in the United States shall be excluded from, denied the benefits of, or be subjected to any program or activity provided by an institution receiving federal financial assistance" (29 U.S.C. § 794).

Section 504 also requires institutions to provide "appropriate academic adjustment" for SWD. Section 508 of this law mandates that all electronic and information technology (EIT) developed, maintained, procured, or used by federal agencies and federally affiliated institutions and organizations are made accessible to persons with disabilities (Federal Register, 2000). All postsecondary institutions fall under the domain of the accessibility standards for technologies. These include, in part:

- Software applications and operating systems
- Web-based information or applications
- Telecommunications products
- Video or multimedia products
- Information appliances such as fax machines and kiosks
- Desktop and portable computers (Franklin Jr., Wilson, and Ebel, 2004)

The Americans with Disabilities Act (ADA) of 1990

The Americans with Disabilities Act (ADA) of 1990 significantly expanded upon the Rehabilitation Act of 1973, so that all institutions of higher education are now subject to nondiscrimination requirements. The ADA also stipulates that higher education institutions provide "reasonable accommodation" for individuals with disabilities. The law requires all higher education institutions to provide qualified individuals with disabilities:

1 Equal access to all educational programs, equipment, and buildings
2 Reasonable accommodations for every student with a disability attending higher education
3 Access to admission and entrance without respect to one's disability (Rehabilitation Act of 1973 § 504; Northeast Technical Assistance Center)

The duty to provide reasonable accommodation is a fundamental statutory requirement for higher education institutions. However, the burden is on qualified students to make known their disabilities and provide appropriate documentation that identifies and describes their needs, doing both in a timely manner (Rothstein, 2003; Tincani, 2004).

A qualified student with a disability is one who is able to meet an institution's admission, academic, and technical standards (i.e., all essential nonacademic admission criteria) with or without accommodation. Once a student establishes that he or she is disabled and qualified, the institution has a responsibility to explore alternate means to allow the student to participate in the institution's program on a nondiscriminatory basis (Stephen, 2000).

In some instances an individual with a disability may not need any accommodation to meet the eligibility criteria and standards required for inclusion. In other cases an individual with a disability may need an accommodation or academic adjustment to meet the eligibility criteria and standards required. However, if an accommodation or an academic adjustment that has been requested goes beyond what is "reasonable," it is not discriminatory to exclude that person with disability from the benefit or opportunity of the program (Jarrow, 1997).

An accommodation is not reasonable if:

1 It poses direct threat to the health or safety of others
2 Substantial change would occur in an element of a course or a given student's curriculum
3 Substantial alteration is required in the manner in which services are provided (Jarrow, 1997)

Accommodation for Students with Disabilities

Under ADA, *reasonable accommodation* means a modification or adjustment of an academic program that will enable an otherwise qualified person with disability the same rights and privileges as a similarly qualified individual who is not disabled. Accommodation usually involves procedural changes and modification in instructional strategies and academic evaluation practices, tailored to the unique needs of each student with disability (Jung, 2003).

Examples of reasonable accommodations that instructors or institutions provide or allow SWD to use include but are not limited to the following:

- Examination or homework accommodation, such as:
  - Extended time for test taking or homework
  - Modification of test taking or performance evaluations
- Tape recording of class lectures
- Mobility accommodation, such as:
  - Appropriate seating arrangement
  - Providing chairs or tables with adjustable height
- Auxiliary aids and services, such as:
  - Assistive or adaptive equipment
  - Large-print materials
  - Note takers, readers
  - Professional sign language interpreters
- Access to the Internet and Web sites

These accommodations are provided as compensatory strategies to ensure equal access in all aspects of classroom learning activities by SWD.

Instructional Delivery in an Information Literacy Classroom

Research shows that long-term personal and educational outcomes for students, especially students with disabilities, are affected by curricular content and instructional techniques, as well as teachers' skills, attitudes, and expectations (Speece and Keogh, 1996). Typically, information literacy instructors are general education teachers who have expertise in content knowledge and pedagogy. Many of these instructors do not have the expertise of special educators who are trained to tailor instruction to fit the needs of individuals with disabilities. Special educators have the knowledge and skills related to designing, making accommodations, or modifying instruction and implementing effective classroom management and motivational strategies for individuals with disabilities (Kame'enui and Simmons, 1999). In an inclusive information literacy classroom, it would be desirable for general education teachers and special education teachers to bring their individual expertise and experiences together to enhance the teaching and learning of SWD. Since information literacy instructors in many institutions would not have the luxury of team teaching with special education teachers, however, it behooves them to plan and execute their own strategies to teach individuals with disabilities in an inclusive classroom to the required academic standards.

A framework that information literacy instructors can adopt to strategize for effective instruction in an inclusive classroom is Madeline Hunter's model of Instructional Theory Into Practice (ITIP). This model identifies three categories for organizing effective instructional delivery. These are:

- Content category—what the instructor is going to teach
- Behavior category—how students can learn and let you know that they have learned the material
- Teaching behavior category—what the teacher will do to facilitate learning (Goldberg, 1990)

Successful learning of students in an inclusive information literacy classroom would depend on what the instructor does to facilitate learning. Thus, the teaching behavior category sets the tone for class activities.

How the Instructor Can Facilitate Learning

To facilitate learning in an inclusive information literacy classroom, the instructor needs to examine the following five characteristics: the curriculum (content), rules, instruction, material, and environment (CRIME) scene, in the classroom in order to accommodate the needs of students (Prater, 2003). These CRIME characteristics of the classroom have to be flexible and accessible to all students.

Content

The content of an information literacy course represents what the instructor is going to teach. The course syllabus guides the instructor of the sequence of how the content is to be taught. To the students, the syllabus directs their study in terms of the work to be accomplished in the course. The syllabus also sets the rules and regulations of the class, and thus it sets the stage for instruction and learning in the class.

Syllabus

The instructor must provide students with a detailed syllabus in both print and electronic formats the first week of class. This would give students ample time to discuss what is expected of them (rules and regulations, assignment due dates, etc.) and to seek clarification of any problems they may find in the syllabus.

Although the burden is on SWD to make their disabilities known, the instructor can facilitate this process by adding a note to the syllabus encouraging students to make appointments to discuss their accommodation needs (Tincani, 2004). The instructor may include a statement like the following on the course syllabus and repeat it during the first class meeting: "If you need course adaptations or accommodations because of a disability, if you have emergency medical information to share with me . . . please make and appointment with me as soon as possible" (Ball State University). When an instructor meets individuals with disabilities in person and talks with them, he or she gets a better understanding of the students' needs and any accommodations and modifications the students would require for the course.

Rules

Like all classrooms, rules in an information literacy classroom are the dos and don'ts of the class. Specifically, rules are a set of expectations intended to regulate forms of individual behavior, interaction, and performance in the classroom setting. Examples of posted rules in the classroom may relate to matters such as how the instructor will deal with tardiness, absences, late assignments, test and assignment make-ups, and academic misconduct (Ohio State University Office of Disability Services, 2000). However, some individuals with disabilities may require extended time for submission of assignments or homework, extended time for test taking, time off to see a doctor, and other allowances. The instructor would need to make reasonable adjustment to the posted class rules in order to accommodate SWD.

The Classroom Environment

The next characteristic the instructor has to consider is the classroom environment. The classroom is where students spend the largest part of their school time, and it is where their major social and educational experiences occur (Doyle, 1986). Federal regulations require that higher education institutions ensure the physical accessibility of the institutions' environment, such as classrooms, buildings, and other facilities that are used by students (Hawke, 2004).

William Doyle (1986) has noted that classroom management and instructional delivery are closely intertwined as some "minimal level of orderliness is necessary for instruction to occur" (p. 394). Classroom management includes the organization of physical space, arrangement of individuals in that space, and the materials and resources available. It influences the traffic pattern, the use of materials, the amount of time spent on particular learning tasks (Loughlin, 1992), and the safety of students in the classroom. An accessible environment is important to maximize the learning potential by SWD, as it provides them the opportunity to participate in all activities of the classroom. The concept of accessibility extends beyond physical accessibility of the classroom, and in an information technology context, it also includes online or Web accessibility (Smith et al., 2001).

The physical accessibility of the classroom includes but is not limited to the arrangement of furniture, seating, layout, wall space, and signage of the classroom. The classroom arrangement that is conducive would make SWD comfortable and feel welcome as part of the class. Some examples of classroom arrangements that may be required by individuals with disabilities in an information literacy class are listed in Figure 5-1.

Instructional Strategies

Teaching in a diverse classroom underscores the need for flexible methods and strategies that meet the needs of all learners. Instructors have to embrace inclusionary approaches that enable SWD to overcome barriers to learning a specific set of principles or content. This means the instructor needs to provide or ensure that auxiliary aids and alternate formats of materials are available so that the teaching provided in class is made as accessible as possible to individuals with disabilities (Hawke, 2004).

Auxiliary aids, especially adaptive/assistive technologies (AT), have been found to enhance the learning opportunities of students with disabilities. Various forms of adaptive/assistive technologies have become standard fare for individuals with disabilities to participate actively in all classroom-learning activities and are viewed as important tools for effective instruction (Hawke, 2004; Wekle and Hadadian, 2003).

An adaptive/assistive technology is a modified or customized technology that is used to increase or improve the functional capabilities of individuals with disabilities (*Technology-Related Assistance for Individuals with Disabilities Act of 1998*). Adaptive/assistive technologies encompass a range of devices from low to high technology. High-technology assistive devices consist of microcomputer components, and include hardware and software that allow for the storage and retrieval of information. Low-technology assistive devices, on the other hand, are nonelectronic or use electronic components that are not computer based (Beck, 2002).

There are adaptive/assistive technologies for each type of disability, and by using

Figure 5-1   Classroom Arrangement

Disability	Seating Arrangement	Layout
Mobility	• Provide ample floor space around table for students using wheelchair, braces, crutches, or mobility assistance devices in the front, on the side, or at the back so that they do not block the flow of movement in the classroom. • Provide adjustable table or chair that can accommodate students comfortably (e.g., tables adjusted to the height of a wheelchair).	• Arrange furniture so that instructor and students can move easily around the classroom.
Visual	• Provide ample space around table for storage of materials and other equipment. • Keep a front row seat open for a student with vision impairment. • A corner seat is convenient for a student with a guide dog (www .loyola.edu/campuslife/health services/disabilitysupportservices/ vision.html).	• Inform students of changes made to the classroom layout. • Classroom should be free of hazards; no low-hanging mobiles that could injure students. • Orient students to the physical layout and other distinguishing features of the classroom (Smith, Polloway, Patton, and Dowdy, 2001). • Maintain consistency in placement of furniture, equipment, and instructional materials (Smith, Polloway, Patton, and Dowdy, 2001).
Hearing	• Seat students near the instructor or source of orally presented information. • Seat students so that they can easily see any visual aids that are used in class (Smith, Polloway, Patton, and Dowdy, 2001). • Seat students so that they can easily see both their sign language interpreter and instructor by keeping lines of sight free for visual access to information. • Position the note taker near the student.	• Face the class when speaking so that students who read lips can read what you are saying (e.g., avoid talking when you are writing on the board).

the appropriate type, SWD can successfully participate in information literacy instructional activities. Therefore, by adopting flexible instructional methods aided by the use of adaptive/assistive computer technology by SWD in the classroom, teaching and learning in an information literacy classroom can be made accessible to all students as reasonably as possible.

Instructional Approaches in an Information Literacy Classroom

For effective instructional delivery, the instructor would need to specify the course units and class activities as well as providing accommodations and appropriate modifications for students with disabilities in the following areas of the curriculum.

- Course design
  - For the instruction to be accessible to all students the instructor may need to convert any PowerPoint presentations into HTML format and also make the content of printed materials available in an accessible Web-based format.
  - The instructor should provide an outline for study objectives.

Lecture is the most common college teaching format. However, many students have poor note-taking skills and cannot identify and write down key points in a lecture (Tincani, 2004). For students with learning disabilities, note-taking and organizing information may be especially difficult because listening to the instructor and simultaneously writing down notes can be challenging for them (Hughes and Suritsky, 1994).

To offset the difficulty students may have in note-taking in an information literacy class, the instructor may need to provide an outline of the content to be covered. First, the instructor would have to identify the title and the theme of the unit to be taught. Then the instructor would need to create an outline, which shows the unit's content and organization, as well as highlighting the relationship between concepts. For example, if the unit to be taught is "Skills Development for Information Literacy," the outline can be the following:

- Define who is an information-literate person.
- Explain the need for information literacy.
- List the cluster of skills needed to be information literate.
- Explain concepts. What is:
  - a bibliography?
  - an annotation?
  - an annotated bibliography?
- List some of the different bibliographic styles.
- Explain ethical issues related to information use:
  - citing sources
  - plagiarism
  - intellectual property
  - fair use
  - copyrighted work and works in public domain

Vision-impaired students should receive print materials in alternative formats at the same time that materials are given to the rest of the class. The instructor should also repeat aloud what is written on the chalk-board or presented on overheads and

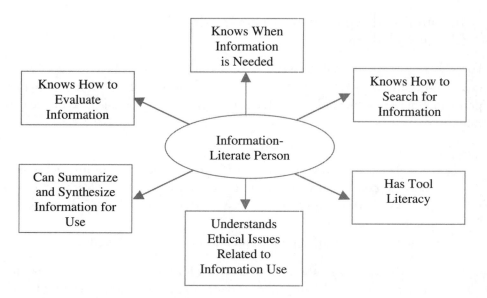

Figure 5-2   An Information-Literate Person: Skills

in handouts for the benefit of the vision-impaired students. The sign language interpreter for a student who is deaf should be allowed in class to interpret the proceedings in class to the student.

Content Enhancement

The format and density of information in a textbook or lecture notes can sometimes place great demands on students' identification of essential ideas, understanding, and integration of information into a coherent meaningful whole (Jitendra et al., 2002). Students find learning from textbooks difficult and boring and require instructional support to facilitate learning from text (Vaughn and Schumm, 1996). The instructor therefore needs to present essential content information to appeal to various learning styles. The instruction delivery formats may include charts, images, graphs, tables, sound, and other vehicles to increase students' ability to extract needed information from written text.

A chart can be used to explain the content of a lecture. For example, the discussion about skills a person must acquire in order to be considered "information literate" can be presented in a chart (see Figure 5-2). Organizing and presenting information in a different but appropriate style (e.g., in a chart or in a graphical or visual form) can promote students' understanding, especially for some students with learning disabilities who find it difficult to decode information in a written text.

Searching for Items in the Library (e.g., a Book)

Representing the essentials of the content as "gist statements or main ideas" (Kame'enui et al., 2002) is an instructional strategy that could be used to teach students how to search for a library material. This approach involves, for instance,

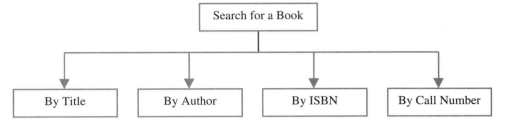

Figure 5-3   Different Ways to Search for a Book

listing different ways a book can be located. These include searching for a book by its title, author, International Standard Book Number (ISBN), and call number. Figure 5-3 is a visual representation in the form of a chart, depicting the different ways to do the search. Instructors can also use this illustration to highlight the re-lationship between the main ideas.

Searching Databases: Using Boolean Logic

The same approach can be used to teach students the search strategies to be used in accessing information from databases. The core strategies (main ideas) involve using the Boolean operators AND, OR, and NOT. The Venn diagrams in Figure 5-4 illustrate the results of performing Boolean searches. The diagrams show graphically how using the AND operator narrows a search, using the OR operator

Operator	Example search	The search will find. . .	Venn diagram results shown in grey
AND	University AND College	Items containing both "University" AND "College"	
OR	University OR College	Items containing either "University" OR "College" or both. OR broadens a search, resulting in more hits	
NOT	University NOT College	Items containing "University" NOT "College" NOT narrows a search	

Figure 5-4   Searching a Database: The Boolean Strategy

broadens a search, and using the NOT operator excludes material from a search (Oregon School Library Information System, 2002).

The graphical representations can be presented in a PowerPoint format or on overhead transparencies to explain the concepts to students. Visual representation may help students who have difficulties processing written or spoken information.

Student Learning: Using Adaptive/Assistive Computer Technology

Specialized hardware and software allow individuals with a wide range of disabilities to use computing and networking technologies in the classroom. The adaptive/ assistive software and hardware described in the following text must be integrated into the computer system. Modified monitors and keyboards should also be available for students' use in an information literacy classroom. However, this is not a one-size-fits-all prescription for providing assistive technology in the classroom. The instructor must ensure that there is a match between the user needs, the assistive technology, and the contexts in which students will use it.

Adaptive/Assistive Technologies for Students with Learning Disabilities

The educationally relevant characteristics of students with learning disabilities include memory deficits, cognitive and metacognitive deficits such as difficulty in focusing or listening, and the lack of strategies for planning, organizing, and setting priorities (Beale and Tippet, 1995; Conte, 1991; Hallahan, Kauffman, and Lloyd, 1999). Assistive technologies that can help students to participate fully in information literacy class activities are listed in Figure 5-5.

Mobility Impairment and Adaptive/Assistive Technologies

Mobility impairment may impact a student's ability to manipulate objects, write, type at a keyboard, or have endurance for longer class periods or for class assignments. Adaptive/assistive technologies that can be used in class include those listed in Figure 5-6.

Visual Impairments and Adaptive/Assistive Technologies

The student with visual impairment is unable to use visual imagery or nonverbal cues and has a distinct disadvantage in perceiving and processing spatial information in the classroom (Smith et al., 2001). For the student to participate fully in the classroom learning activities, the assistive technologies listed in Figure 5-7 can be used.

Hearing Impairment and Adaptive/Assistive Technologies

The educationally relevant characteristics of students with hearing impairments are an inability to organize auditory information either consistently or at all. Such

---

**Figure 5-5   Matching Class Activities with Adaptive/Assistive Technology
for Students with Learning Disabilities**

Class Activity	*Adaptive/Assistive Technology*
Reading/Listening to Class Lecture	• Visual aids—handouts, guidelines of lecture notes, and overheads in alternate formats • Keyboards with large-print key labels—this helps users to locate keys • Speech screen output (JAWS) with headphones—text on the computer screen is read aloud • Computer guides instruction—with this technology the lecture can be repeated as often as necessary to assist student in retaining information
Note-Taking	• Tape recorder—allows student to record lecture to transcribe later, or play tape as often as necessary to assist student in retaining information
Database/Internet Search	• Keyboards with large-print key labels—this helps student locate keys to input data • Speech screen output (JAWS) with headphones—information from the screen is read out loud • Computer guides instruction—with this technology information can be repeated as often as necessary to assist student who might require repeated practice of "search strategies" in order to build skills

---

students have difficulties with verbally based learning (Diefendorf, 1996). The adaptive technologies listed in Figure 5-8 can be used by hearing-impaired students to participate fully in classroom activities.

Information Literacy Instruction for Students with Disabilities: Emerging Trends

There are new developments in instructional delivery methods, and instructors should investigate them in order to apply the strategies to information literacy instruction in an inclusive setting. Two such approaches to instructional delivery are online long-distance education and Universal Design of Learning (UDL).

Online Long-Distance Education

Online long-distance education courses will be vital to teaching information literacy to students with disabilities. Advantages of delivering online long-distance education courses include flexibility of time and location; self-paced learning; learning according to the student's preferred learning styles; and increased self-directed learning (Cincinnati State Technical and Community College).

The World Wide Web Consortium (W3C) has developed common protocols that make the Web fully accessible to people with disabilities. Both the ADA of 1990 and Section 508 of the Rehabilitation Act of 1973 mandate the provision

---

**Figure 5-6   Matching Class Activities with Adaptive/Assistive Technology
for Students with Mobility Impairment**

Class Activity	Assistive/Adaptive Technology
Reading/Listening to Class Lecture	• Screen readers
Note-Taking	• Personal computers fitted with adaptive keyboards. Providing computers for word processing can remove the burden of handwriting. • Keyboards with large-print key labels—this helps users to locate keys. • Trackballs as mouse alternatives. • Printed materials, videotapes, overhead transparencies, and other visual materials.

Database/Internet Search	• Adapted keyboards such as:
	  • Key guards: these are metal or plastic templates that fit over standard computer keyboard with a hole for each key, and it prevents accidental keystrokes (Lazzaro, 2001)
	  • Left- or right-handed keyboards: for individuals who need to operate the keyboard with one hand
	  • Mouth stick and head pointer: devices that can be used to press the keys on a keyboard
	  • On-screen keyboard: for this type of adapted keyboard, provide sip and puff, or optical head pointer to be used by student to press the keys of an on-keyboard
	• Joysticks as functional alternatives to keyboard

Other Activities	• Dragon Naturally Speaking software—student may take tests on computers fitted with this software

---

of equal access to information technology for individuals with disabilities, although such access has often come slowly, if at all. Virtually all colleges and universities in the country fall under the compliance domain of ADA and Section 508 of the Rehabilitation Act of 1973 in the context of accessibility to information technology. This enforceable statute gives the added impetus to make all Web sites and Web information used in an institution accessible to all students. This will make online long-distance education an effective resource for people with disabilities, since it would offset accessibility problems (Santacana, 1999).

Universal Design of Learning

Universal Design of Learning (UDL) is an innovative approach to the flexible delivery of instructional programs and pertains to creating suitable learning environments for students with disabilities. UDL is based on the concept of universal design, which seeks to design products and environments to be as usable as possible by all people regardless of age, ability, or situation (UD Education Online, 2003). In the classroom, the UDL approach is about providing educational

---

Figure 5-7 Matching Class Activities with Adaptive/Assistive Technology for Students with Visual Impairment

Class Activity	Assistive/Adaptive Technology
Reading/Listening to Class Lecture	• Magnifying glass/sheet: can be used when reading text. A partially sighted student can use this optical aid to read notes, overheads, and other handouts. • Zoom Text—enlarges texts and graphics on the computer screen. With this, a partially sighted student can read online reserved readings and read and follow class lecture notes and discussion posted to the computer screen.
Note-Taking	• Braille Translation Software (e.g., Duxbury Braille Translator): converts standard text into Braille and vice versa. Class notes, assignments, and other information available via the computer terminal can be printed out in Braille, and student assignments, and other text communication and information in Braille can be translated back into text. • Braille Printer or Braille Embosser—prints out documents in Braille. • Braille Note Takers—combine Braille keyboards for input and Braille displays for output. They allow students to take notes in class. (Lazzaro, 2001) • Keyboards with large-print key labels—this helps users to locate keys. • Print (dark) copy of handouts to partially sighted students. • Tape-recorded notes.
Database/Internet Search	• Job Access with Speech (JAWS): information from the screen is read aloud, providing technology to access a wide variety of information. • JAWS outputs text to Braille displays. • Zoom Text—enlarges texts and graphics on the computer screen Using these assistive technologies, students can follow class instructions on database search.

---

programs in ways that respond to differences in learning styles and abilities of students. In the UDL model, digital technologies are incorporated into the curriculum to provide alternative ways of accessing information by all students.

The underlying principle of UDL is that curricula should include alternate formats in order to meet the diverse needs and abilities of students (Gordon, 2002). According to this principle a universally designed curriculum would offer:

1 Multiple means of representation to provide students different ways of acquiring information and knowledge
2 Multiple alternatives for allowing students to demonstrate what they know
3 Multiple means of engagement to tap into learners' interests and motivate them to learn (CAST, 2005)

According to the proponents of UDL, the flexible nature of digital technology makes it possible to provide multiple alternatives, and therefore teaching and

**Figure 5-8   Matching Class Activities with Adaptive/Assistive Technology
for Students with Hearing Impairment**

Class Activity	Assistive/Adaptive Technology
Reading/Listening to Class Lecture	• Assistive Listening Device: amplifies sound energy to allow the hearing impaired to more easily perceive the spoken word, and other sound sources (Lazzaro, 2001) • Printed materials, videotapes, overhead transparencies, and other visual materials.
Note-Taking	• Tape Recorder: allows student to tape record class lecture and assignments to be translated by a sign language interpreter
Database/Internet Search	• Most Internet resources are accessible to people with hearing impairments because these resources do not require the ability to hear. However, when Web sites include audio output, provide text captioning or transcription, for student to access information.
Viewing Films/Videotapes	Close/Open Captioning: provides literal representations of speech and action in text form on the screen

learning can be customized. Learning materials that are designed to provide universal access can increase access for students with disabilities. For example, students who have visual impairments or reading difficulties or are dyslexic may be unable independently to access information from a book in a print format. However, providing the text in a universally designed digital format can offer options for these students. It can be (a) read out loud by a computer screen reader, (b) printed on a Braille printer, or (c) presented with highlighted main points and organizational support. By providing this level of access, students with a broad range of learning needs are all able to use the same resources and have access to the same information (CAST, 2005; Netherton, 1999).

UDL Resources for Instructors

Currently there are no known applications of UDL in information literacy instruction. However, with an increasingly diverse student population in information literacy classrooms, instructional librarians should explore the use of UDL in their curricula. The following resources offer guidance for instructors who wish to know more about UDL:

- Center for Applied Special Technology (CAST). www.cast.org. This site provides extensive information about UDL.
- A Framework for Universal Design in Curriculum Development. www.cec .sped.org/osep/appendix.html. This site summarizes the principles of universal design in a practical context, to help teachers and other interested persons understand how UDL can be employed in the classroom to provide broader access to the curriculum for all students.

- Integrating Technology into the Standard Curriculum. www.cec.sped.org/osep/recn3.html /. This site provides contacts, resources, and approaches to integrating technology into the curriculum.
- Teaching Every Student. www.cast.org/teachingeverystudent. Another site providing information about UDL and its practice.

Conclusion

Students with disabilities attend higher education institutions in an inclusive setting. Federal laws require that they have equal access to all educational programs and be provided with reasonable accommodation in order to participate and benefit from all classroom activities. Research demonstrates that being educated in an inclusive classroom benefits all students, since it enhances their social growth and communication skills and increases their awareness of diversity. For students with disabilities, an inclusive classroom education increases their motivation and self esteem, gives them a chance to aim at the same goals as everyone else, and improves their academic performance (Moore and Gilbreath, 1998). It is therefore important that instructional librarians commit to inclusive strategies to help all students learn and achieve in their inclusive information literacy classroom. This means instructors would have to design and deliver their instructions in flexible ways that meet the needs of all their students, be aware of what accommodations to provide for students with disabilities, and be familiar with and know how to use available assistive technologies in the classroom.

The following recommendations will help librarians understand and provide services that meet the needs of students with disabilities:

- Include persons with disabilities as participants in planning, implementing, and evaluating library services, programs, and facilities (American Library Association, 2000).
- Consult with the office for disability services in your institution for information on specific disabilities and the needs of students who have them.
- Have information about the range of adaptive technologies that are available in the library and the school at large.
- Approach your institution's funding entities for budgetary support for the purchase of assistive technologies and other related needs for students with disabilities.
- Explore sources of external funding to enable the library to support innovations and new services for students with disabilities.
- Provide staff development programs for librarians to acquire the necessary skills and knowledge for the operation of both low and high assistive technologies. Consult with relevant professional associations and regional or state support networks to provide library-specific programs in this area.

The following professional associations and groups specialize in library services and education for students with disabilities:

International

- The International Federation of Library Associations and Institutions (IFLA) Section of Libraries for the Blind. This group promotes national and international cooperation among libraries serving blind and other print-handicapped readers.
- IFLA's Section of Libraries Serving Disadvantaged Persons. This section of IFLA provides an international forum for librarians who serve people who cannot use the conventional library services and materials, such as people who are deaf.

National (United States)

- American Association of the Deaf-Blind. www.tr.wosc.osshe.edu/dblink/aadb.htm. This association provides advocacy and makes referrals to advance the economic, educational, and social welfare of deaf-blind persons.
- The American Library Association's (ALA) Office for Literacy and Outreach Services (OLOS). This ALA office supports and promotes literacy and equity of information access initiatives for traditionally underserved populations that include people with disabilities (American Library Association).
- The Association of Specialized and Cooperative Library Agencies (ASCLA; a division of the American Library Association), Libraries Serving Special Populations (LSSPS) Section. This ASCLA section has separate forums on Library Service to People with Visual or Physical Disabilities, Library Service to the Deaf, Library Service to the Impaired Elderly, Library Service to Developmentally Disabled Persons, and Academic Librarians Assisting the Disabled.
- Learning Disabilities Association of America. www.ldanatl.org. This organization deals with legal issues, advocacy, education, research, resources, fact sheets, state chapters, and support groups for people with learning disabilities.
- National Multiple Sclerosis Society. www.nmss.org. This society promotes research, education, and advocacy on critical issues pertinent to MS victims (Disability Resources, 1999).

Bibliography

American Library Association. 2000. *Information Literacy Competency Standards for Higher Education*. www.ala.org/ala//acrl/acrlstandards/informationliteracycompetency.htm (accessed June 4, 2005).

Americans with Disabilities Act (ADA) of 1990. Public Law 101-336. *U.S. Statutes at Large* 104 (1990).

Ball State University. *Students Who Have Mobility or Dexterity Limitations*. www.bsu.edu/dsd/fac-mobility/ (accessed July 13, 2005).

Beale, I. L., and L. J. Tippet. 1992. "Remediation of Psychological Process Deficits in Learning Disabilities." In *Learning Disabilities: Nature, Theory and Treatment*, pp. 526–568, edited by N. N. Singh and I. L. Beale. New York: Springer-Verlag.

Beck, Jennifer. 2002. "Emerging Literacy through Assistive Technology." *Teaching Exceptional Children* 35, no. 2: 44–48.

Bernell, S. L. 2003. "Theoretical and Applied Issues in Defining Disability in Labor Market Research." *Journal of Disability Policy Studies* 14, no. 1: 36–45.

Center for Applied Special Technology (CAST). 2005. *What Is Universal Design for Learning?* www.cast.org/research/udl/ (accessed May 28, 2005).

Cincinnati State Technical and Community College. *Advantages of Online Learning.* cincinnatistate.edu/CurrentStudent/Academics/AcademicDivisions/About_DL.htm (accessed July 13, 2005).

Collins, Mary E., and Carol Mowbray. 2005. "Higher Education and Psychiatric Disabilities: National Survey of Campus Disability Services." *American Journal of Orthopsychiatry* 75, no. 2: 304–315.

Conte, R. 1991. "Attention Disorders." In *Learning about Learning Disabilities*, pp. 55–101, edited by B.Y.L. Wong. New York: Academic Press.

DeJong, G., A. Batavia, and R. Griss. 1989. "America's Neglected Healthy Minority: Working-Age Persons with Disabilities." *Milbank Quarterly*, 67 (suppl. 2, pt. 2): 311–351.

Dewey, J. 1938. *Experience and Education.* New York: Simon and Schuster.

Diefendorf, A. O. 1996. "Hearing Loss and Its Effect." In *Hearing Care for Children*, edited by F. N. Martin and J. G. Clarke. Boston: Allyn and Bacon.

Disability Resources. 1999. *Librarians' Connections: Professional Associations.* www.disability resources.org/DRMlibs-ala.html (accessed August 8, 2005).

Doyle, W. 1986. "Classroom Organization and Management." In *Handbook of Research on Teaching*, pp. 392–431, edited by M. C. Wittrock. New York: Macmillan.

Eaton, J., and K. Treadgold. 1999. "Why Teach Information Literacy." *School Libraries in Canada* 19, no. 2: 8–10.

Ethier, Denise. 1999. "District Technology Planning for All Students: Helping to Meet the IDEA '97 Mandate." *Leadership and the New Technologies Perspectives*, issue 9. http://www2.edc.org/LNT/news/Issue9/feature1.htm (accessed August 1, 2005).

Federal Register. December 21, 2000. *Electronic and Information Technology Accessibility Standard: Architectural and Transportation Barriers Compliance Board.* 36 CFR Part 1194 [Docket No. 2000-01] RIN 3014-AA25.

Franklin Jr., C., T. Wilson, and M. S. Ebel. 2004. "Equal Access." *Network Computing*, 61–65. www.nmc.com (accessed July 20, 2005).

Fuller, M., A. Bradley, and M. Healey. 2004. "Incorporating Disabled Students within an Inclusive Higher Education Environment." *Disability and Society* 19, no. 5: 455–468.

Gibson, Craig. 2004. "Information Literacy Develops Globally: The Role of National Forum on Information Literacy." *Knowledge Quest* 32, no. 4: 16–18.

Goldberg, Mark F. 1990. "Portrait of Madeline Hunter." *Educational Leadership* 47, no. 5: 141–143.

Gordon, David. 2002. "Increasing Access through Technology." *NEA Today* 21, no. 2: 40–41.

Hahn, H. 1984. *The Issue of Equality: European Perceptions of Employment Policy for Disabled Persons.* New York: World Rehabilitation Fund.

Hallahan, D. P., J. M. Kauffman, and J. W. Lloyd. 1999. *Introduction to Learning Disabilities*, 2nd ed. Boston: Allyn and Bacon.

Hawke, C. S. 2004. "Accommodating Students with Disabilities." *New Directions for Community Colleges* no. 125: 17–27.

Horn, L., and J. Berktold. 1999. *Students with Disabilities in Postsecondary Education: A Profile of Preparation, Participation and Outcomes*. Washington, DC: National Center for Education Statistics.

Hughes, Charles A., and Sharon K. Suritsky. 1994. "Note-Taking Skills of University Students with and without Learning Disabilities." *Journal of Learning Disabilities* 27: 20–24.

Jarrow, Jane E. 1997. *What Is a "Reasonable" Accommodation?* www.janejarrow.com/public_library/inservice-material/resnableacc.html (accessed July 13, 2005).

Jitendra, A. K., L. L. Edwards, C. M. Choutka, and P. S. Treadway. 2002. "A Collaborative Approach to Planning on the Content Areas for Students with Learning Disabilities: Accessing the General Curriculum." *Learning Disabilities Research Practice* 17, no. 4: 252–267.

Jung, Karen E. 2003. "Chronic Illness and Academic Accommodation: Meeting Disabled Students' 'Unique Needs' and Preserving the Institutional Order of the University." *Journal of Sociology and Social Welfare* 30, no. 1: 91–112.

Kame'enui, E. J., D. W. Carnine, R. C. Dixon, D. C. Simmons, and M. D. Coyne, eds. 2002. *Effective Teaching Strategies That Accommodate Diverse Learners*, 2nd ed. Upper Saddle River, NJ: Merrill/Prentice Hall.

Kame'enui, E. J., and D. Simmons. 1999. *Toward Successful Inclusion of Students with Disabilities: The Architecture of Instruction*. Arlington, VA: Council for Exceptional Children.

Lazzaro, Joseph J. 2001. *Adaptive Technologies for Learning and Work Environments*, 2nd ed. Chicago: American Library Association.

Lewis, Laurie, and Elizabeth Farris. 1999. *An Institutional Perspective on Students with Disabilities in Postsecondary Education*. Washington, DC: U.S. Department of Education, National Center for Education Statistics.

Loughlin, C. E. 1992. "Classroom Physical Environment." In *Encyclopedia of Educational Research*, 6th ed., pp. 161–164, edited by M. E. Alkin. New York: Macmillan.

Merced College. 2005. *Disabled Student Services—Types of Disabilities*. www.mccd.edu/dss/disabilities.htm (accessed July 13, 2005).

Moisey, Susan D. 2004. "SWD in Distance Education: Characteristics, Course Enrollment and Completion and Support Services." *Journal of Distance Education* 19, no. 1: 73–91.

Moore, C., and D. Gilbreath. 1998. "Educating Students with Disabilities in General Education Classrooms: A Summary of the Research." Western Regional Resource Center. http://interact.uoregon.edu/wrrc/AKInclusion.html (accessed July 30, 2005).

Nagi, S. 1965. "Some Conceptual Issues in Disability and Rehabilitation." In *Sociology and Rehabilitation*, pp. 1000–1113, edited by M. Sussman. Washington, DC: American Sociological Association.

Netherton, L. 1999. "Making Media Center Resources Available to All Students." http://www.cec.sped.org/osep/ud-sec3.html (accessed July 21, 2005).

Northeast Technical Assistance Center. www.netac.rit.edu (accessed July 13, 2005).

North East and The Islands Regional Technology in Education Consortium. http://www.neirtec.org/udl (accessed July 13, 2005).

NSF. 2000. "Women, Minorities and Persons with Disabilities in Science and Engineering." http://nsf.gov/statistics/nsf00327/access/cl/cl.htm#cls213 (accessed July 30, 2005).

Ohio State University Office of Disability Services. 2000. *Instructor Handbook: Teaching Students with Disabilities*. Columbus: Ohio State University.

Oregon School Library Information System. 2002. *Electronic Search Strategies: Boolean Operators*. www.oslis.K12.or.us/elementary/index.php?page_citeExamples (accessed June 30, 2005).

Prater, A. M. 2003. "Strategy for Success in Inclusive Classrooms." *Teaching Exceptional Children* (May/June): 58–64.

Rehabilitation Act of 1973. 1973. Public Law 93-112. *U.S. Statutes at Large* 87.

Rose, David H., and Anne Meyer. 2002. *Teaching Every Student in the Digital Age: Universal Design for Learning.* Alexandria, VA: Association for Supervision and Curriculum Development.

Rothstein, Laura. 2003. *Students with Disabilities and Higher Education: A Disconnect in Expectations and Realities.* www.heath.gwu.edu/PDFs/Disconnect.pdf (accessed July 13, 2005).

Santacana, A. P. 1999. *Providing Higher Education for Disabled University Students through Distance Learning with New Communication and Information Technologies.* Paper for the Conference on Disabled Students in Higher Education, Grenoble, March 24–26.

SCANS Report. 2000. *Secretary's Commission on Achieving Necessary Skills.* U.S. Department of Labor Employment and Training Administration. http://wdr.doleta.gov/SCANS (accessed June 15, 2005).

Siitonen, Leena. 1996. *Information Literacy: Gaps between Concept and Applications.* Conference Proceedings. 62nd IFLA General Conference, Beijing, August 25–31, 1996. www.ifla.org/IV/ifla62/62-siil.htm (accessed June 19, 2005).

Smith, T.E.C., E. A. Polloway, J. R. Patton, and C. A. Dowdy. 2001. *Teaching Students with Special Needs in Inclusive Settings,* 3rd ed. Boston: Allyn and Bacon.

Speece, D. L., and B. K. Keogh, eds. 1996. *Research on Classroom Ecologies: Implications for Inclusion of Children with Learning Disabilities.* Mahwah, NJ: Lawrence Erlbaum Associates.

Stanford, Anee. "Types of Disabilities: Definitions of Disability Commonly Used by Schools." http://www.geocities.com/aneecp/distypes.htm (accessed July 13, 2005).

Stephen, Thomas B. 2000. "College Students and Disability Law." *Journal of Special Education* 33, no. 4: 248–257.

Technology-Related Assistance for Individuals with Disabilities Act of 1998. 1988. Public Law 100-407. *U.S. Statutes at Large* 102.

Tincani, Matt. 2004. "Improving Outcomes for College Students with Disabilities." *College Teaching* 52, no. 4: 128–132.

UD Education Online. 2003. "About Universal Design." http://www.udeducation.org/about/aboutud.asp (accessed July 30, 2005).

United Kingdom. Parliament. 1995. *Disability Discrimination Act 1995 (DDA),* chap. 50. http://www.opsi.gov.uk/acts/acts1995/1995050.htm (accessed February 20, 2005).

U.S. General Accounting Office (GAO). January 1990. *Persons with Disabilities: Reports on Costs of Accommodations.* Briefing Report to Congressional Requesters. Washington, DC: U.S. Government Printing Office.

Vaughn, S., and J. S. Schumm. 1996. "Classroom Ecologies: Classroom Interactions and Implications for Inclusion of Students with Learning Disabilities." In *Research on Classroom Ecologies: Implications for Inclusion of Children with Learning Disabilities,* edited by D. L. Speece and B. K. Keogh. Mahwah, NJ: Lawrence Erlbaum Associates.

Wekle, B., and A. Hadadian. 2003. "Can Assistive Technology Help Us to Not Leave Any Child Behind?" *Preventing School Failure* 47, no. 4: 181–186.

Wray, Mike. 2003. "How to Assess Disabled Students without Breaking the Law." *Learning and Teaching in Action* 2, no. 1. www.ltu.mmu.ac.uk/ltia/issue4/wray.pdf (accessed July 14, 2005).

6

Tailoring Instruction for Students in Distance Learning Environments

Tina M. Adams and R. Sean Evans

Introduction

This chapter explores the relationships between an academic unit and a university library in regard to providing services to remote students and faculty. We discuss the need to define the off-campus population to be served by the library, philosophies and methods for providing distance service and instruction, and outreach to and collaboration with distance faculty to ensure quality service. We focus on our own experiences at Northern Arizona University (NAU) in providing support to remote College of Education students in a Native American reservation-based setting, emphasizing that it is adaptable to almost any distance program in higher education.

Needs Assessment and Student Information

When preparing to work with a group of remote library users, you should understand as much as possible about the group and their learning environment. Specific areas of concern are: student academic skill or level, computer connectivity, technology level, and even the demographic characteristics of the group. You can often obtain information about students from your institution's fact or data

Figure 6-1   Educational Attainment Data Derived from the U.S. Census Bureau's _American FactFinder_

Place	Population 25+ years	Percent high school graduate or equivalency	Percent with some college; no degree	Percent with bachelor's degree	Percent with graduate or prof. degree
United States	182,211,639	28.63	21.05	15.54	8.86
Arizona	3,256,184	24.32	26.39	15.15	8.38
New Mexico	1,134,801	26.59	22.90	13.60	9.85
Utah	1,197,892	24.58	29.11	17.86	8.26
Navajo Nation Reservation & Trust Land, AZ, NM, UT	88,662	26.32	16.97	4.66	2.63

Educational Attainment of Population 25+ years in Selected Areas, 2000 (Highest Level Attained)

book. Campus data books include useful demographic information about students, often presented at the college or major level. In addition, you may wish to consult with the academic department you are preparing the instruction for, your institution's graduate office, or the registrar. Administrative units in charge of distance education will often have information on students at remote sites. If your students are geographically concentrated, consider using U.S. Census data available from _American FactFinder_ (http://factfinder.census.gov/) for a greater understanding of the learners' environment. Figure 6-1 is based on data from _American FactFinder_ and compares educational attainment of residents of the Navajo Indian Reservation and related trust areas with that of persons in several individual states and the United States as a whole. These data were useful to our own efforts.

Literature Review

It is paramount when planning for expanding library services to consult the current research, especially when those services involve unique student populations. The professional literature can be very useful, both as a starting point for planning and as a way to augment your own experience. That said, in many cases there may be very little literature that pertains to your precise situation. In 2002, when the Cline Library's Education Team began looking for ways to improve services to the university's remote Native American students, we found only a few useful articles written in the mid-1990s that discussed public library services to this population. We found nothing in the literature regarding academic library services to Native American student populations (Patterson, 1995). We drew upon literature from outside the library field when appropriate, but relied most heavily on our own experience, experiences of our faculty, and university and personal assessment. We found Diana G. Oblinger's speech about effective instructional approaches to be most useful. Oblinger, vice president of Educause, in her 2004 speech "Educating the Net Generation," said that students remember:

- 10 percent of what we read
- 20 percent of what we hear
- 30 percent of what we see
- 50 percent of what we say and hear
- 80 percent of what we say
- 90 percent of what we say and do (Oblinger, 2004)

This point is important to consider when you are deciding how best to serve any population of users. There is a strong consensus that when learners are active and engaged they are far more likely to retain information. This concept can be applied creatively to library instruction either in person or online, as well as in traditional classroom teaching.

Preparation

The academic concerns regarding distance instruction are usually straightforward. These include: Is it a graduate or undergraduate class? Is this a cohort group, in which students advance through a program together? Is this a satellite campus in-person class, a Web-based class, a hybrid class (some instruction delivered in person, and some on the Web) or a class taught via interactive instructional television (IITV)? What is the nature of the assignment or research that the library is supporting? Will students be best served by access to electronic resources alone, print-based library resources, or some combination thereof? Is the assignment already fixed, or is the instructor open to negotiating an assignment that maximizes the role of library resources and services?

When serving some remote student populations, you may find particular challenges, such as cultural barriers and manifestations of the "digital divide," that will require you to take extra care when planning your instruction in order to bridge any skill or technology gaps. In rural or economically disadvantaged areas, you may encounter students who are less technologically savvy, owing to their limited access to computers. One example from our own experience involves Native American students who reside on the reservations in rural Arizona. The reservation areas are heavily dependent upon the university's computer labs, which are sometimes the only places for many miles where people have the opportunity to use computers. You may not encounter a situation quite like ours, but it is essential to understand such aspects of any group you intend to serve. Your group of remote students may fit more closely with either the "net generation" learners to which Oblinger refers or traditional adult returning learners, or the group may be a mixture of both (Oblinger, 2004).

Cost

The most costly and essential elements for serving distant users may already be in place and require little or no additional funding. For instance, there are costs to the college or university if it builds or supports satellite computer or IITV labs. For libraries that choose to provide in-person distance instruction, there are many other costs: use of a university fleet vehicle or rental car, perhaps an overnight stay, with additional lodging and food cost. Sending one librarian to teach a session away from campus may have broader impacts on the library's general travel budget. It also means the library does without librarians' services while they travel to and teach at remote sites. In our case, many of the sites on the reservations are a hundred miles or more from the main campus and library in Flagstaff, Arizona, so even when an overnight stay is not necessary, several hours of travel time are required.

In our experience, instruction sessions away from the library have been very well attended. Remote students are typically well motivated and want to develop their research skills, but you should be aware of the financial resources needed and plan accordingly with your library administration. Because of the direct and indirect costs of site visits, however, libraries are looking for ways to provide instruction remotely. Commercial Web-based meeting tools, online Web-based learning modules, and commercial Web course management chat and discussion tools provide ways to do this. These tools may be provided by your institution to support remote classes, and the library may be able to employ them without any added cost.

Consultation with the Course Instructor

The instructor is your primary source of information regarding the class and the goals of the instruction session, and potentially for the future research needs of these students. It is important to fully understand instructors' expectations for a relationship with the library. For instance, how will students use the library and what special support does the instructor want? With remote students, it is sometimes difficult to provide all of the materials they will need in an online environment. The library must be able to work with faculty to develop assignments that it can effectively support. This may also mean that the library will have to be flexible about *how* it can provide digital content for classes, whether it be something relatively simple (like accessing commercial databases or providing electronic reserve readings) or more sophisticated (such as creating digital resources composed of readings, archival material, photographs, streaming video and audio, etc.).

Have a thorough discussion with the instructor regarding the expected learning outcomes of the library session. Learning outcomes are statements of what a student will be expected to be able to do as a result of a learning activity (Doherty and Ketchner, 2005). It will not be helpful to come into the class without first agreeing on the goals of the instruction session. Begin by allowing the instructor to articulate what is needed. For example, an instructor might say, "I want my students to get an overview of how to do research in education." This is a good starting point, but you should probe further to identify the learning outcomes implied in the request. With your knowledge of the research process, you may interpret the actual request as, "I want students to gain an understanding of the tools and/or appropriate databases specific to education." State this clearly to the instructor. To promote a shared understanding, you might work with the instructor to write a learning outcome for the library session. Always remember to ask if there is a specific assignment or project the instructor has created that will be the product or result of the students' library research. Once you know this, tie the assignment to the learning outcome. This need not be a formal process, as some instructors may not write learning outcomes, but you can achieve the same goal just by being aware of the underlying issues when a faculty member contacts you to request library-related instruction. Either formally or informally, incorporate these techniques into your initial discussion so that you both know what is needed and expected.

Instructional Equipment

A late sixteenth-century proverb states, "What cannot be cured must be endured" (Knowles 1999, 613). This tends to be a difficult lesson for new librarians to learn. Often you must be able to adapt to the way things are, rather than insisting that conditions change to your liking. If performing an on-site distance instruction session is your only recourse, then here are a few things to keep in mind before you hit the road. First, learn about the environment in which you will teach. Will there be computers for students, or a computer and projector for you and the instructor to use? Are the computers Macs or PCs? Are there enough computers for each member of the class? Next, get in touch with the person who is in charge of the facility. Find out about access, scheduling, and any unique conditions that may affect your presentation (Adams and Evans, 2004). Many computer labs are not set up appropriately for classroom instruction. Be prepared!

Technology-related concerns can sometimes be the most difficult for instructional librarians to overcome, requiring a clear understanding of how the library's resources are accessed by students at a distance. Will students need a unique campus or library proxy setup (PIN, library ID number, username, and password), and will they have these in time for the instruction session? Does the proxy need to be configured at the remote site, or is your library using an automatic proxy utility? Will students need to download a Web browser plug-in or other software application? Will students be expected to use their own computers or computers belonging to a public library or school, or does your institution have a computer lab at the satellite location? Depending on these conditions, you will need to know how technologies such as firewalls and filters may affect access to library resources and adjust your instruction session or support accordingly.

What should you do if you find you do not have a computer for your presentation or if there are compatibility problems with equipment? You may have to conduct the instruction session by walking around, looking over students' shoulders at their computer monitors, indicating the steps they need to take: "Click here; now, click there." This may seem frustrating, but later in the session, when students participate in the hands-on aspect of the class, they will still benefit from the instruction, no matter how imperfect it seems to you. Supplement the instruction session with a written handout or an accessible Web page that includes information on library access, research strategies, and contact information. Make sure students, faculty, and lab staff all get this information.

In-person instruction is not the only way to approach distance instruction. IITV classes broadcast from the home campus to satellite locations are still popular, and you may be asked to participate in these classes to teach research skills. Teaching library skills via IITV can be uncomfortable at first, but keep in mind that it helps students when you present information in both visual and auditory formats. For instance, you should be prepared to write down all important information such as Web addresses, telephone numbers, and other contact information and broadcast it via a pad camera, since students in this environment cannot interact seamlessly with you.

In addition to getting comfortable with using a pad camera for writing notes, you must remember to speak clearly and monitor all IITV screens, showing the different IITV sites, in order to be aware of students' questions or spot problems or confusion. You may spend much of the session showing students how to navigate through your library's Web space, while you explain what you are showing on the television monitors. This may sound daunting your first time out. If possible, visit an IITV lab on your campus and familiarize yourself with the equipment prior to "going live" for the first time. Most universities that offer IITV classes will have a support unit or, at the very least, technical staff who operate the equipment for the various classes. If possible, get an orientation from the lab manager or technical support staff person. Also, if the various IITV sites are equipped as computer labs, you can set aside time for hands-on searching, just as you do when teaching face-to-face. You may need to enlist the help of the staff at the remote site to facilitate this.

Team Teaching

Do not be afraid to ask your colleagues for help. When delivering distance instruction sessions there may be a need to have more than one librarian present. One person can teach while the other one "roves" to assist students individually and help them keep up. When the hands-on part of the session begins, you will find the second person indispensable for helping with questions and consulting with students individually. An added bonus is that it really is easier to establish rapport with students if you and your colleague use appropriate humor and jokes and play off each other, to keep the class lively and show students your friendly side. Inviting a colleague along will increase costs, so consider for which classes and how often you will ask for assistance.

What and How to Teach Remote Students

Often, the students you teach in any class will be of various cultural, ethnic, and socioeconomic groups, so it is generally wise to use a variety of instructional approaches in each session you teach. In our own experience in teaching Native

American students, in-person contact is by far the most effective form of instruction. When asked, these students will usually express a preference for face-to-face instruction (Adams and Evans, 2004). We have found that Native American students are often reluctant to ask questions. Research on learning styles in Native American populations shows a preference for working in groups and a research style that is holistic, rather than linear or sequential. As is true with most students, research finds that Native American students learn best when material is presented with a visual component, like illustrations, multimedia, or other visual aids. They also prefer observational and collaborative activities to lectures and textual learning (Hilberg and Tharp, 2002). Of course, the research and our own observations are all generalizations and there are exceptions. We do not believe that all Native American students are alike, but we have found these preferences for learning generally hold true (Adams and Evans, 2004).

Earlier, we alluded to statistics about memory retention. Oblinger said that we remember 90 percent of what we say and do. This holds true regardless of one's cultural background. In addition to providing hands-on activities for students, you should create opportunities for them to interact verbally with the instructor and among themselves. A simple approach is to ask students to engage in a short small-group discussion and then "report out," or summarize their findings for the entire class. This requires a little advance preparation. Prior to your breakout sessions, give them a scenario, problem, or question to answer. The problem should be based on the assignment and goals of their research. The question or scenario can vary in difficulty, as long as you allow students enough time to finish and report. If the assignment allows the use of Web sites in their research, you might give them a short handout about evaluating Web sites. One evaluation tool you may wish to consider using is "Evaluating the Information: Applying the CRAAP Test," which refers to currency, relevance, authority, accuracy, and purpose as criteria for evaluating information sources (California State University, Chico, 2004). Ask each group to use the criteria listed on the handout to critique a Web site of their choosing and prepare to discuss their findings in front of the class. Thus, without a lot of extra effort or preparation, you can fulfill the "say and do" retention requirements and students will be more likely to remember the key points of your session.

When preparing for an instruction session (or even in your daily reference interactions) it is important to consider many different ways of teaching. Before you step into the classroom you can brainstorm about ways to accommodate challenges and different learning styles. You may want to quickly make a list of ideas. Keep in mind that what you have students see, do, and say should be in line with the learning objectives you have identified, the means of delivering instruction, and the needs of the assignment:

- What do students need to "see" to accomplish this assignment?
- What do students need to "do" to reinforce what they "see"?
- What can students "say" about what they "do"?

The preceding points are generally compatible with an interactive teaching approach. Interactive teaching is particularly valuable when you are delivering instruction at a distance, whether in-person, via IITV, or in a commercial Web-based course management environment (like WebCT or Blackboard) chat room. Activities and assignments that require students to give you feedback will, by their very nature, provide evidence of students' understanding of and engagement in what you are teaching.

Hands-on or kinesthetic activities improve student mastery by up to 30 percent (Oblinger, 2004). In the following paragraphs, we offer some methods you can use to promote interactive learning.

A technique we call "Pair and Share" is an adaptation of the teaching technique "Think, Pair, Share" described in Neil Fleming's book *55 Strategies for Better Teaching* (Fleming, 2002). This technique allows for varied learning styles and is engaging for students. It can be done in a library instruction session quite easily. Simply ask students to pair up. Then in breakout session style, allow students to work in their pairs for an allotted period of time, usually about fifteen minutes. Although this can work with almost any subject field or topic, it is best when this process incorporates the students' assignment to make the session meaningful and not contrived. For example, if education students have been assigned to write a research paper or complete a project about a particular educational theory, you can ask them to find one good article or resource about a theory they have chosen or are assigned. Next, ask students to share by reporting the results of their research. Give each group just a few minutes to report. You can ask each team to tell the larger group one thing they learned about their topic or issue that they did not know before. Once the class completes this exercise, each student will have at least one resource in hand to use for a research paper or project.

Another technique that we use is called "You're the Critic." This technique gives students the opportunity to construct their own knowledge and encourages critical thinking. According to Oblinger, "net generation" and even older learners have problems determining whether the sources they find via the Internet are of quality, so this is an important exercise (Oblinger, 2004). Its structure is similar to "Pair and Share," but the goal is different. Instead of asking students to report one thing they learned about a topic, you give them the responsibility of evaluating a resource and telling the class why the resource is good or not good. You can employ this technique in a library instruction session when students have been told to make use of free Web resources in an assignment. In one instance, the instructor and the librarian had identified a host of Web sites related to a particular aspect of journalism. We asked students to pair up and choose a Web site (which we listed for them on slips of paper) or to "Google" one. We asked each pair to review the site, using a set of criteria we had listed on a handout. Each student pair reported their critique of the Web site, including their assessment of the resource's quality and reliability or lack thereof. Either of these techniques can be incorporated into an online chat session or IITV. In the IITV environment, the technique remains the same, that is, students break out and then report back. In the chat environment, it may take a little more planning. You could prearrange pairs of students (or small groups of three or four) prior to the session by having the instructor set up group chat rooms online, where, during the breakout part of the session, each group enters its assigned chat room to conduct the exercise. After the breakout period, each group returns to the main chat room, where group representatives will report back to the entire class.

According to Oblinger, students like to work on "things that matter," or research that has an application (Oblinger, 2004). A related technique called case-based learning is often a good approach. Case-based learning tells a story, raises an issue, has elements of conflict, lacks an obvious answer, encourages students to think and take a position, and demands a decision (Davis, 1993). Any case you employ needs to be concise. Again, you will need to give students enough time to complete their work. To use this approach, you will often need to collaborate with the instructor well in advance to create an appropriate case and assignment to use in the context of the library instruction session. For instance, we asked the instructor of a Communication Sciences Disorders class to help us create a scenario that students could research. The instructor wrote up a short clinical scenario including a patient's history, symptoms, and characteristics and then asked students to research the best treatment options for the patient. The entire assignment was done online via the use of modules that progressed sequentially through the research process. Each student (or group) would, in the environment of their online class, access the scenario and complete each module, which they submitted to the instructor before starting the next module. The librarian's role was to design each module and link to appropriate resources that would move students through the research process.

Increasingly, universities are moving away from IITV classes and even in-person distance classes in favor of Web-based courses. According to Oblinger, studies show that access to information technology is increasingly prevalent across racial and socioeconomic groups (Oblinger, 2004). This may be true in general, but for some populations, as with the Native American groups whom we serve (and for many other rural or economically disadvantaged populations), computer availability and computer skills are still issues.

We now use WebQuest modules to serve on-campus and remote courses more effectively in a Web-based environment. The following is a description of a WebQuest:

> A WebQuest is an inquiry-oriented activity in which most or all of the information used by learners is drawn from the Web. WebQuests are designed to use learners' time well, to focus on using information rather than looking for it, and to support learners' thinking at the levels of analysis, synthesis and evaluation. (Dodge, 1998)

WebQuests contain five modules which include Introduction, Task, Process, Evaluation, and Conclusion. Instructors can use them to convey the research process to students through sequential modules. Instructors can include illustrations, audio, and video files to address students' varied learning styles. WebQuests can compensate for having fewer opportunities for in-class library instruction. Using WebQuest-type tools, we embed library-related content, instruction, and virtual assistance into the university's Web-based classes. These modules improve upon subject or class-specific Web pages in several ways. While course-related Web pages are very popular and address many of the needs of our distance learners for access to a librarian-vetted list of resources, they are not designed to provide instruction about the research process. WebQuests, in contrast, are designed to give research instruction, although they are just one of a myriad of tools that librarians can use to teach remote classes interactively.

Improving Library Services to Remote Users

A prerequisite to improving library services to remote students and faculty is to shed some older ideas about reference service and interlibrary loans (ILL). You and your library must strive to create an environment that permits the delivery of standard, necessary services to users regardless of where they are, and do so as equitably as possible. To achieve this a few services will need to be changed and a few old models cast off.

Many universities and their libraries have designated offices that provide some sort of support for remote users' research needs. Staff in these units often perform similar services to those in existing library units. Some distance support units answer questions regarding access and research, provide research support, acquire material, and provide instruction—the very things that libraries already do. Our recommendation is to do away with these specialized offices and to incorporate their resources into the existing library to expand and enhance services. Doing away with duplicative services frees up library staff and resources to augment existing reference and interlibrary loan services and create new services for the benefit of all students and faculty. This approach assumes that all students and faculty, regardless of location, share similar needs. The efficient functioning of any library demands doing away with redundant services.

For ILL the most important challenge in supporting distance education is to make it possible for someone to take courses from your college or university without having to rely upon a local library (if one is even present). This means that your ILL unit may have to invest in systems that permit electronic delivery of articles to students. Further, instead of running an ILL program that requires remote users to pick up and return materials to the institution's library, it is preferable to place books and other tangible library materials directly into the hands of remote students and faculty by express mailing requested materials directly to them, wherever they are.

To enhance electronic access, consider the following:

- Capture URLs for searches in your library catalog and licensed databases that are pertinent to students' information needs. Post these on a Web page or within online courseware for students to use. When necessary, be sure to rewrite any URLs to facilitate off-campus access.
- Subscribe to e-book providers like *NetLibrary* and *books 24x7*, which permit your users remote access to books they may need.
- Use free Web-based government information. The U.S. Government Printing Office (GPO) has greatly increased the number of current titles available

via the Web. Many federal government publications can support criminal justice, education, health, nursing, political science, and other majors or programs. Better yet, these titles are offered without copyright or license restrictions. Full cataloging records with hyperlinks to online documents are available from the GPO, which facilitates online retrieval of the publications. As a corollary, many federal government Web sites, including ERIC (www.eric.ed.gov) and the National Criminal Justice Reference Service (www.ncjrs.org) have excellent track records maintaining free online libraries.

- Provide Web-based access to unique, pertinent information in your library.

Since remote students have fewer opportunities to ask for help or browse your library's print collections, it is beneficial for you to recommend some search strategies or select materials for them. Many commercial databases allow users to save permanent URLs of their searches. You can capture and place these URLs on course-related Web pages. Web-based library catalogs have a similar utility, letting users save existing hyperlinks (e.g., subject heading and author links) and their own searches. Librarians at the University of Nevada, Reno, placed both catalog and proxied database links on a Web page to assist students in a remote graduate MBA class on organizational behavior. The links took students to searches in EBSCO's *Business Source Premier* and library catalog holdings for pertinent books available at the community college where the class met, at UNR's main campus library and electronic books, licensed from *books 24x7*. Students learned they could explore the existing search results and also modify the searches to suit their own interests.

An example we used involves reservation-based students. Many of these students are majors in NAU's Bilingual and Multicultural Education program, and they find our library's Special Collections and Archives materials very useful. This division of the university library collects material related to the Colorado Plateau region. Students can find a rich collection of materials related to Navajo and Hopi culture and history, including materials that are relevant for studying early "education" efforts and the related movement to assimilate Native Americans into white culture. We incorporated text and sound files of local and education-oriented oral histories into a Web page for a graduate course on the history of American education. There are probably important collections like this in your library as well. Familiarize yourself with your library's unique collections and be prepared to let students and instructors know if you think a collection is appropriate to a particular class.

You may also wish to beef up your library collection to support remote courses. In one instance we worked with an instructor who was teaching a reservation-based IITV class, to identify and provide an array of biographies of famous Native Americans. If our library did not have a requested biography, then we purchased it on rush order.

Efforts like these can take significant amounts of your time, so you should always consult with the course instructor before preparing instructional Web pages or ordering items intended for a specific course. This is simply another example of the benefits of knowing about course subject matter, assignments, and students' interests before delivering your instruction. However, do not just wait for faculty or students to ask for something. Course instructors may be unaware of unique electronic content, such as from NAU's Special Collection and Archives, or that database searches can be captured and made available to others, so you should proactively offer this kind of information when it seems appropriate. While these points apply equally to supporting on-campus and remote courses, following them will help lessen some disadvantages students experience when they are away from the main campus.

For reference services to remote users, exploit the available technologies and services your library already provides. Most libraries now offer some version of an online "Ask-a-Librarian" e-mail–based reference service. Place links to your Ask-a-Librarian service conspicuously throughout your library's Web space. Include links in any Web pages you create for remote classes and on any printed handouts. Consider adding a reference chat service or incorporating the library into course management software (like WebCT or Blackboard) that your college or university uses. Your library could offer a toll-free phone number for remote users. Whatever means your library provides users to contact the library should cover as many hours per week as possible. The reference desk is the most logical point, even if only for coverage of evening and weekend hours. Wherever these communications are received in the library, it must be a place where a user will most often encounter proficient service providers when needed. There should also be a means for users to leave messages or requests after hours. Your estimated response times should be posted, so users will know they can expect a return phone call or e-mail within a set period of time. Your library must promote these services continuously.

Promotion of your library's distance services may be challenging. Your target audiences are your institution's students, faculty, and staff. The best way to reach them is to make use of the other official communication channels your institution already has in place. If academic departments on campus have lists of e-mail or mail addresses for distance faculty, acquire those lists and use them. Another approach is to provide academic departments on campus with basic information about the library and ask that it be included in established mailings and communications. Find out if there are semester or annual orientations for distance (or onsite) faculty, and get on their agendas. For communications with students, consider having materials included in mailings from the registrar, graduate office, or academic departments. Instructions sent to remote students concerning their campus e-mail accounts or student identification usernames and passwords can also include information on how to obtain library services. For more outreach ideas, you can consult "Brainstorming Ideas for Faculty Liaison: 100 Ways to Reach Your Faculty," produced by ALA/RUSA's Business Reference in Academic Libraries Committee (BRASS).

On the topic of your library's Web site, the following considerations and decisions must be made for remote users:

- Make sure that services and contacts for remote users are prominently displayed.
- Explain how to obtain student IDs and PINs, e-mail usernames and passwords or a proxy setup, or link to campus Web sites that provide that information.
- Explain how other library services work. Have FAQ pages that answer questions like "How long will it take to get a book?" "Do you charge for these services?" or "What information do I need to complete this request?"
- Put your request forms on the Web and test them thoroughly to make sure they work. This will improve access and service to all users, regardless of their location.

Consider providing supplementary "how to" information on the library Web site. Users like self-sufficiency, and may avoid asking basic questions (and may be even less likely to do so from a distance). For example, provide information on:

- How to search your catalog and navigate your library Web site (refer to the baseline orientation outlined in Chapter 1)
- How to perform basic searches in the library's licensed databases
- Any good electronic reference tools about composition, citation guides, or dictionaries

Conclusion

This chapter is intended to provide a basic introduction to delivering library instruction and services to remote users, but most of the measures we recommend will benefit all library users, whether they are remote or onsite. We hope this discussion will encourage librarians who have not yet worked with remote users and faculty to think about users globally, rather than as on-campus or distance users. These changes will not occur overnight, nor will they occur without cost or shifting human and budgetary resources. The payoff, however, will be significant. Your users, wherever they are located, will be able to use the library's tangible materials and electronic resources more effectively. In short, they will feel a greater connection to the campus community and the library.

Bibliography

Adams, Tina M., and R. Sean Evans. 2004. "Educating the Educators: Outreach to the College of Education Distance Faculty and Native American Students." *Journal of Library Administration* 41, nos. 1–2: 3–18.

Business Reference in Academic Libraries Committee (BRASS). "Brainstorming Ideas for Faculty Liaison." www.ala.org/ala/rusa/rusaourassoc/rusasections/brass/brassprotools/brasspres/miscellaneous/liaison.htm (accessed April 27, 2005).

California State University, Chico, Meriam Library. 2004. "Evaluating Information: Applying the CRAAP Test." www.csuchico.edu/lins/handouts/eval_websites.pdf (accessed April 27, 2005).

Davis, Barbara Gross. 1993. *Tools for Teaching.* San Francisco, CA: Jossey-Bass Publishers.

Dodge, Bernie. 1998. *The WebQuest Page.* http://webquest.sdsu.edu/ (accessed April 4, 2006).

Doherty, John, and Kevin Ketchner. "Demystifying the Learning Outcome." http://jan.ucc.nau.edu/~jjd23/presentation/library/index_files/v3_document.htm (accessed February 2, 2005).

Fleming, Neil. 2002. *55 Strategies for Better Teaching.* Christchurch, NZ: Neil Fleming.

Hilberg, R. Soleste, and Roland Tharp. 2002. "Theoretical Perspectives, Research Findings and Classroom Implications of the Learning Styles of American Indian and Alaska Native Students." West Virginia: ERIC Digest ED 468 000.

Holtze, Terri. 2002. "100 Ways to Reach Your Faculty." www.ala.org/ala/pio/campaign/academicresearch/reach_faculty.pdf (accessed October 24, 2005).

Oblinger, Diana. 2004. *Educating the Net Generation.* www.educause.edu/e04/program/1663?PRODUCT_CODE=e04/FS01&MEETING=e04&HEADING=Featured%20Speaker (accessed February 2, 2005).

Patterson, Lotsee. 1995. "Information Needs and Services of Native Americans." *Rural Libraries* 15, no. 2: 37–44.

Unattributed. 1999. Proverbs. In *The Oxford Dictionary of Quotations,* p. 613, edited by Elizabeth Knowles. New York: Oxford University Press.

Wolpert, Ann. 1998. "Service to Remote Users: Marketing the Library's Role." *Library Trends* 47: 21–42.

PART III

Teaching Information Literacy in Specific Disciplines

Part III of this manual outlines information literacy instruction (ILI) in support of subjects commonly taught in modern colleges and universities. Each contributor to this section of the book is a master teacher in one or more content areas. Various humanities, science, social science, and business-related subjects are discussed in depth. Each chapter includes discussions of effective teaching techniques and user characteristics and illustrative coverage of the subject's information sources. Our intent is to show you important aspects of teaching library and information literacy concepts in each subject or discipline with as little redundancy as possible. You should refer back to Chapter 1 for ideas common to sound ILI and support, regardless of the subject matter.

Some academic librarians (but certainly not all) become subject liaisons or specialists as a result of their previous academic studies or work experience. Alternatively, a subject liaison assignment may only be a matter of filling a need in your organization. For instance, a librarian with a master's degree in English may become a business or engineering specialist. The following chapters will help you learn to teach research skills in various disciplines and provide a roadmap for your own self-directed learning in the disciplines covered. When planning this book, I wanted to cover even more subjects, including engineering, music, and anthropology. Due to space limitations, however, this was not practical. There is a need for these subjects to be covered adequately in ILI-related literature, and I hope others will help fill these gaps in the near future.

Chapter 12, Gregg Sapp's fascinating and instructive chapter on science literacy, stands apart from the other chapters in Part III. This is so for several reasons. He discusses the conceptual and practical foundations of a credit-bearing course, concentrating on the role of scientific information in today's society. This is a compelling model for content-rich ILI. I am hopeful that other librarians will adopt and extend his example, which has applicability to other disciplines outside the sciences, including language and literature, economics, media studies, psychology, art, and music.

Use the information and advice presented in Part III to jumpstart your teaching and other liaison-related work, such as collection development. Although it would have been beneficial to cover even more subjects in this part of the book, another essential resource has recently become available. The ACRL/Instruction Section Teaching Committee has launched a very worthwhile effort to disseminate discipline-related information literacy standards, curricula, and lessons via its Information in the Disciplines Web site (www.ala.org/ala/acrlbucket/is/projectsacrl/infolitdisciplines). This effort holds much promise to enable academic librarians and their institutions to enrich their ILI presence across all content areas. Armed with the advice and resources in the following chapters as well as the Instruction Section Teaching Committee site, you, too, can become a master teacher.

7

English Literature

Janelle M. Zauha

"There are many kinds of literary research, and some make scarcely any use of libraries."

(Stallybrass, 2004, p. 1351)

Introduction

At first glance, libraries and literature departments sound like a marriage made in heaven. One collects and provides access to texts; the other studies and interprets texts. What is not to like? Surprisingly, their relationship is not so simple. Literary scholars and their students do use texts, but often in nontraditional, unpredictable ways that simply bypass the library and its services entirely. As it turns out, creating a useful instruction-focused relationship between the English department and its library can be a challenging endeavor.

This chapter serves as a starting point for librarians who are responsible for providing instruction to students and faculty in English Literature departments. My discussion will provide some insights into the scholarship and pedagogy of the discipline, discuss the characteristics and needs of different learners within it, offer suggested strategies for reaching and working with learners, identify selected key resources for the study of literature in English, provide sample instructional aids and outreach materials, and locate professional literature and contacts to further develop the librarian's knowledge and skills in the discipline.

One of the challenges of writing on this topic is the number of local variables at play: educational background of the librarian, size and focus of the department, nature of the library's collection, technology infrastructure, larger institutional goals, and more. All of these factors will influence the decisions a librarian makes about developing instruction for a specific group of learners. My institution, Montana State University—Bozeman, where many of the following examples and practices are staged, is a land-grant university with a focus on agriculture, science, and technology—not on the humanities. It has a small English Department of sixteen full-time faculty, a fluctuating but significant number of adjunct instructors, ten to fifteen graduate students in a terminal master's program, and 275–300 undergraduate majors. The ways I work with this department will differ from the ways I would work with a larger, more robust department. In a sense, though, a department of this size is the perfect model for a new literature librarian whose sights are set on basic knowledge and goals.[1]

Working with Your English Department

No matter what the local environment, understanding the larger discipline of English and of the humanities in general is critical before local needs, resources, and opportunities can be put into context. As Mara Saule states, "Librarians giving instruction must understand the unique characteristics of both humanistic research and of the humanist in order for instructional programs to be most effective" (Saule, 1992). Knowing broadly how humanists view research and how their scholarship differs from the sciences and social sciences enables you to make better assumptions about how research is being defined and taught, if at all, to the students you seek to help.

Equally important is the need to understand the problems or gaps inherent in your discipline's approaches to research and its teaching. Reed Wilson's "Researching 'Undergraduate Research' in the Humanities" provides an excellent discussion of the differences between research in the humanities and the sciences and the implications of these differences. Wilson describes the humanities research tradition as one that prioritizes individual interpretation to the detriment of student research development: "Despite research in composition studies that promotes and validates a 'process-centered' approach to student writing, we continue to believe in the 'product' as the only 'proof' of student learning and achievement" (78–79). As a departure from this, Wilson advocates a "data collection" conception of humanities research, one which would more accurately reflect the "lab work" of humanists while teaching it to new undergraduates through extensive, structured mentoring (Wilson, 2003).

The study of literature as it has traditionally been defined mirrors the larger humanities practices that Wilson points out. While the concept of the text within literary studies has changed radically in the past several decades to embrace many variant formats, origins, and ways of reading, the scholarly activity of literature remains a largely noncollaborative, solitary endeavor focused on individual interpretation of texts. Of course, for every generalization there exists a deviation, but English departments may safely be characterized as eclectic groups of scholars with widely varying research interests and skills, teaching philosophies, and theoretical agendas. Despite their individual differences, however, it is most likely the case that the literature scholars in your local department usually "work alone because of the primary importance of the individual intellect operating on an intellectual problem or issue," like scholars in other humanities disciplines (Burnette, Gillis, and Cochran, 1994: 182).

Discovering Broad Trends in the Study of Literature

In 1954 Thomas Clark Pollock posed the question, "Should the English major be a cafeteria?" as the title of a paper he presented at a meeting of the College Section of the National Council of Teachers of English. The tenor of this title hints at Pollock's answer. He asserts that student choice of electives liberally allowed, "as one chooses among displayed dishes in an automat," should not supplant the English major as a "carefully planned program, designed . . . from soup to entrée to nuts by a master chef" (Pollock, 1954). Authority, order, design, unity—these were characteristics of the study of literature in Pollock's time, and generally in the first seventy-five years of its existence as an academic discipline. By now, however, many of these earlier characteristics have gone the way of the automat, and have become historical artifacts, themselves the subject of study.

Today, literary studies might be likened to a smorgasbord where scholars and students encounter a rich table of possibilities—in terms of noncanonical authors, alternative texts, literary theories, and cultural and historical contexts—and have a greater degree of freedom to build their own intellectual meal, selecting and creating new combinations outside the control of a "master chef." As Jonathan Culler points out, "Students today are more likely to be stimulated to major in literature by a course on women's writing or on postmodern fiction than by a survey of English literature from Beowulf to Virginia Woolf" (Culler, 2003). The bones of the traditional canon persist, including standard course divisions such as era, genre, or author studies, but on an individual level, literary studies are routinely changed and stretched to accommodate new ways of thinking about and contextualizing the traditional texts as well as emergent authors and literatures. Feelings about this within the discipline are mixed, with some scholars lamenting what they see as "intellectual fragmentation" of literary studies (Showalter, 2003) and others exclaiming, "I can't even figure out what 'English' is anymore" (Benton, 2005).

To better understand the multifarious world of literary study today, look at any volume in the Modern Language Association's *Approaches to Teaching World Literature* series. The table of contents for *Approaches to Teaching Austen's Emma*, for instance, fully corroborates the breadth and variety of what Rick Rylance and Judy Simons name as the most important types of context used to study literature today, including:

- Period social, historical, political, and cultural processes
- Biographical
- Relation of passages within the larger work
- Relation of the work to other publications by the author or others in the genre
- Literary contexts including genre and style
- Language contexts, including word usage, meaning, and dialect
- Critical contexts such as the reception of a work over time, including reviews, measures of popularity, position in the canon, and the application of various critical theories (Rylance and Simons, 2001)

This increased interest in contextual study is broadening English studies into a much more interdisciplinary field. As Robert Eaglestone explains, "English is already developing by analyzing a wider range of sorts of texts. Already, secondary teachers teaching pre-twentieth-century texts often show films or television adaptations to their students, which widens the category of English. The relatively new discipline of cultural studies grew from precisely this interdisciplinary understanding of English. Where English traditionally looked at 'literature,' cultural studies analyze all aspects of culture, from artworks (novels, poetry, plays, but also comics, films, television programs, music, and so on) to other sorts of 'cultural production' (the design of houses, fashion) to social habits (going to nightclubs, being part of certain groups). All these are 'texts' to be interpreted" (Eaglestone, 2002).

Discovering Local Departmental Trends and Practices

Understanding the larger trends in the field is important in establishing credibility with your department, but knowledge of local departmental offerings, focuses, and other characteristics is equally important. The basic tools for knowing your department are not surprising. They include the course catalog, the departmental Web site, and statistics gleaned from a departmental secretary. Important considerations include the demographics of the department; faculty-to-student ratios; and how thinly faculty are spread across the discipline, that is, the scope of the courses they teach. Identifying the options and degrees offered by the department is also critical. Are there large groups of students focusing on a secondary education option, creative writing, American studies, rhetoric, or linguistics? Likewise, a department offering a master's degree but no doctorate will have a different relationship with its graduate students and with the library.

More time-consuming is the important task of getting to know the intellectual focus of individual faculty. Since literature remains largely a noncollaborative, interpretation-based discipline, discovering how individual faculty read texts and define "research" is crucial. Not doing so will make marketing targeted library services for students much more difficult. It is imperative that the literature librarian be able to articulate compelling connections between faculty scholarship and pedagogy in order to sell the idea of library instruction.

Rather than ricocheting from office to office hoping to hit the jackpot of a professor who is eager to collaborate, a better method is to begin with homework. Locate and read what your faculty have written in order to understand their theoretical and pedagogical interests. Search for their works in the *Modern Language Association International Bibliography* (MLAIB)—where you will often find their dissertations as well as their more current published works. This is especially useful if the scholar publishes solidly in the field of literature, of course, in the journals and monographs indexed by the Modern Language Association.

Another important groundwork task is to locate the curriculum vitae of your faculty on the departmental Web site. These may be more current than *MLAIB* and will often list research in progress or forthcoming publications. Course syllabi may also be available online and their content and presentation will give you a feel for focus as well as level of technology or information literacy.

Employ additional nonobtrusive discovery methods as much as needed to get a feel for scholarship and priorities in the department. These might include watching for campus announcements, reading campus publications, searching for research and grants announcements, and attending departmental colloquia and public programs.

When you feel somewhat educated about the department, begin using more direct methods of discovery:

- Ask to be included in a departmental meeting where you will be introduced (but will primarily listen).
- Meet with key faculty such as the department head or chair and the directors for undergraduate and graduate studies to discuss broader research competency needs and goals within programs.
- Schedule meetings with individual faculty who seem most open to working with you or whose courses you have identified as pivotal—those who teach the research methods classes, for instance.
- Explore other ideas for connecting with faculty as presented by Terri L. Holtze in her "100 Ways to Reach Your Faculty" (Holtze, 2002).

Meeting Faculty Needs

As you learn more about your local department, you may have the feeling that your assistance is not needed, especially if faculty do not have a habit of assigning research papers and have not made the connection between contextual studies and library research. Faculty in the department may be engaged primarily in performing and teaching the kind of research that does not call on the library. The tradition of valuing individual interpretation persists, and strictly speaking, does not require contextual research. This does not make these research or teaching methods wrong, but it does make reaching students more difficult.

Persistent efforts to explore faculty research, pedagogy, and library use patterns, however, will reveal some opportunities. You may find that your English faculty lag behind their students in use of technology and would welcome one-on-one assistance in learning more about online library resources and broad Web searching. Do not assume their ignorance of all things digital or make technology the primary focus over subject matter, however. Some literature faculty have extensive knowledge of electronic texts and Web developments. Few of them have great love of technology for its own sake. Understanding that there is a certain ambivalence toward technology in this field is important. As indicated in the Report of the 2001–2002 ADE (Association of Departments in English) Ad Hoc Committee on the English Major, it may be felt that "Web sites and chat rooms can enrich literature courses and help engage students in active learning. But technology can also drain time needed for research and course preparation" (Schramm et al., 2003).

Faculty may also lag behind their students in knowledge of what the library offers, including the latest databases and services such as library instruction. Often they are experts at using traditional services such as interlibrary loan and are not aware of the dynamic nature of the library. It is critical to market your services and tout the latest library developments through brochures, e-mail updates, newsletters, or other available means (see item 7-8 on the CD-ROM, "Welcome Back"). Attractive marketing brochures remind faculty that the library is not static (see Figure 7-1).

When framing what you can do for your faculty, you may find that the term *information literacy* does not carry much meaning in English departments. Rather than belabor a vague concept, talk about the components of it that are germane to this field. Using the Association of College and Research Libraries' (ACRL) "Research Competency Guidelines for Literatures in English" as a starting point will help ground the discussion in recognizable terms such as primary resources, reviews, literary criticism, theory, and background information (LES, 2004).

Although their research may be noncollaborative, many faculty will welcome the opportunity to work with librarians to devise research projects that utilize library instruction if they can be shown to increase student competencies in meaningful ways. Once you have some course-integrated instruction in place, provide a means for faculty to routinely give you feedback. This reinforces your commitment to providing quality services to them while giving you meaningful formative as well as evaluative feedback. Use a Web form to solicit end-of-semester assessment input (Zauha, 2004).

What to Teach

As in most disciplines, students in literature want varying levels of resources and assistance at different stages in their studies. Although putting students into discrete learning categories can be misleading, it is helpful to think about how to serve the different needs of beginning (freshman and sophomore), intermediate (junior and senior), and advanced (graduate) literature students. There is never a precise cutoff point for which group should learn which resources, but inappropriate

Welcome Back,
Dept. of English,
to MSU Libraries!

Schedule your Library Instruction Session today!

Figure 7-1   Welcome Back Brochure

introduction of detailed, complex tools such as the *MLAIB* to a freshman group will usually produce dismaying results. To avoid this, work closely with faculty to understand the differences between student levels in your setting and specific course goals. For any group, providing course or program integrated instruction, collaboratively planned with teaching faculty, will be your best protection against missing the mark.

Meeting the Needs of Beginning Undergraduate Students

Close reading of texts and exploration of literary conventions are frequently the early undergraduate focus in English, rather than writing papers that research literary or other contexts. This focus on primary texts means that lower-division undergraduates are less likely to work with complex research tools such as the *MLAIB* that center on access to secondary texts. Their contact with library research during the first semesters of their study is more likely to come in writing classes where basic research papers may be assigned but where literature is not usually the subject focus. This does not mean that there is no place for library instruction in their courses, just that such instruction needs to be carefully integrated.

Freshman and sophomore students in literature studies share many characteristics with their counterparts in other disciplines when it comes to library use:

- They tend to get frustrated with research if they do not meet with success early in the process, especially in the current confusing full-text/non-full-text environment, yet they are not patient with learning technical details. This is especially so because they often do not have enough time to do whatever research they have been asked to do, despite its fairly limited scope.
- Even low levels of research can take them considerable time, because they are not familiar with library language, layout, procedures, resources, or help options, and may not be terribly interested in using new technology.
- Those who are technologically savvy tend to think most things can be found on the Web and uncritically prefer that research environment.
- Their understanding of how to evaluate print or online resources is minimal.

These characteristics coupled with the infrequency with which their professors choose to integrate library research into their syllabi make this group particularly challenging to reach.

Strategies for Working with Beginning Undergraduates

So how can you work with new English majors? Target selected courses taught by faculty who are open to collaboration to begin providing the foundation for at least some of these students. Getting your foot in the door is only the first step, of course. Carefully designing a library session that does not overwhelm these students, tax their attention span, or otherwise alienate them is the next challenge. Two things will help you succeed in selecting a content and skills focus that will help novice students: working closely with the course instructor to make sure that what they learn directly addresses an assignment that you have collaboratively designed, and designing that assignment with selected objectives from the ACRL Literatures in English Section Research Competency Guidelines in mind.

It often takes more than one try to make things work, so find an instructor who is willing to take risks and experiment. I have worked for several semesters with a faculty member who frequently teaches the survey of American literature courses to lower-division English majors. English 218 and 219 at MSU are slated for the sophomore year, but others may also enroll. Most students come to these courses with little or no experience with research. They may have never spoken to a librarian or set foot into the library. Class size is capped at forty-five and the catalog describes the class as a "[s]urvey of selected works and authors in the American literary tradition. . . . Taught within the contexts of historical, social and cultural developments."

Given the focus of the class, the instructor wants to motivate students to explore basic background and context resources for the works studied in this course. She sets the stage for this by having students routinely write reading questions for all the works they read for class. These questions may be about anything from the meaning of a work to how the religious environment at the time influenced a particular author. Students hand in their questions each day and they receive credit for them.

These questions lead up to a larger resource project assignment that is collaboratively designed by the instructor and the librarian. The stated objectives of the assignment are to:

- Develop skills to efficiently find resources to enhance understanding of literary works
- Familiarize students with library resources
- Learn about multiple information resources by working with group members and sharing findings with the class

For this project, students work in groups of three or four, researching contexts for chosen authors, and they present their findings to the class. Pooling their questions for the author they have chosen, students find library resources that will answer those questions and bring these back to the group for incorporation into their class presentation.

This assignment opens the door to library research without combining it with the stress of a lengthy formal research paper. Instead, individuals in each group turn in a write-up of their research experience that includes: (1) a statement of their question; (2) the answer; (3) a bibliographic citation for the source(s) they used to find the answer; (4) an explanation of how they found the source or the tools they used to find the source.

To prepare students for this project, the librarian is invited to their class for one session. The instructor and librarian prepare carefully, so that the session provides maximum interaction between the instructor, the librarian, and the students. The goals of this session are modest because the time is short, research is not the main focus of the class, and the students are not ready for detailed, complex levels of information. Both the instructor and librarian understand that several unstated objectives need to be fulfilled, namely, that students will:

- See that a librarian is approachable and is interested in their work
- See their instructor interacting with a librarian in a mutual discovery quest, generating ideas, sharing information, and considering options, as a

model for how they might work together and how they might use the librarian later

- Gain a very basic, conceptual understanding of what types of information they will find in various resource categories by grasping the essential differences between a reference source, the library catalog, and an online index to journal articles

To achieve these objectives, the librarian and instructor begin by focusing together on the author or work assigned for the day, bouncing questions of their own off the class and each other (the librarian has also read the work for that day) and brainstorming possible topics of inquiry with the class, drawing on student reading questions, and jotting options on the whiteboard. Next, the group talks about where the "answers" to some of these questions might be found. The librarian demonstrates some options from the library's Web site and talks about categories of information such as reference or background information, longer monographic studies, and journal articles. She also "book talks" a few print volumes she has brought over from the reference collection, such as the *Encyclopedia of the United States in the 19th Century*.

Students receive a bibliography the librarian has prepared that emphasizes these resource categories and lays out help options (see item 7-2 on the CD-ROM, "Library Session for ENGL 218"). The session does not focus on reviewing this bibliography in detail, however. Students are encouraged to use it as a starting point, as a reminder of some of the many resources they could use for their research. In addition they are encouraged to contact the librarian either individually or in their groups if they need further help. At no point in the session is lengthy attention given to technology details, baroque search methodologies, complex databases (such as the *MLAIB*), or other advanced options.

This has proven to be a successful combination of library session and research project, of collaboration between librarian and instructor, one that engages students and lays the foundation for more extensive research later in their major. To determine how well the assignment and session are working, the librarian and instructor meet after each semester to discuss student responses and final products. The instructor has observed that the results of this collaboration include presentations that incorporate appropriate library resources and that students are more motivated to explore library resources. She also finds that students themselves report improved understanding of research options in the discipline. In addition to reviewing results in a post-semester meeting with the librarian, the instructor may complete an online peer evaluation of library instruction each semester, rating elements such as the librarian's preparation, the session content and focus, observed outcomes, and overall effectiveness (Zauha, 2004).

Of course, not all faculty are open to collaborating this closely with librarians, and it is often necessary to find creative alternatives for reaching new literature students. Some things to consider include:

- Providing instruction for their required writing classes, although these classes will usually not be literature focused

- Consulting with the writing center staff to make sure tutors know to send literature students to you for further help
- Distributing print materials through the department that advertise your services and provide basic resource information
- Infiltrating the English Club and offering to provide an extracurricular session, or simply discovering more about student needs by spending time with them outside the class at club functions and other events

In whatever way you attempt contact, be sure you are enthusiastic and knowledgeable about the discipline. Even at this early stage, students in the major are often very committed to the study they have chosen and are passionate about what they are doing. They will respond to you if you are able to show a similar level of excitement and interest.

Meeting the Needs of Intermediate Undergraduate Students

Intermediate-level literature students in their junior and senior years are required to do more extensive research for papers, and their instructors often assume a knowledge of library research skills that students simply lack. These students may have some of the same needs as undergraduates, especially if they have not had any contact yet with the library. Generally, literature students at this level:

- Have varying research skills
- Are engaged in course work that calls for increasingly sophisticated understanding of literary conventions, contexts, and theories
- Have some difficulty distinguishing among categories of information in the discipline, such as how reviews differ from criticism, and where that information might be located
- Are given research assignments that require use of more complex databases and search strategies in order to locate secondary materials such as criticism, reviews, and information pertinent to social or historical contexts
- Are using a broader range of resources and must learn to compare and evaluate them critically
- Have some need for special library services, such as interlibrary loan
- May be open to extended contact with a librarian, especially in a one-on-one setting

Strategies for Working with Intermediate Undergraduates

Junior- and senior-level courses in English usually shift focus away from the broad survey courses of the early major and onto specific author, era, or genre courses. Their research assignments require more skilled use of the *MLAIB*, as well as introduction to other subject databases that will yield more complex contextual information. While earlier library instruction may have focused on introducing students to different types of scholarly resources, intermediate instruction adds an interest in teaching them the complexities of those resources. For this reason, students at this level will benefit more from instruction that involves hands-on practice in an electronic classroom.

It is appropriate to incorporate library instruction into any upper-division English course that requires a research paper, as long as the instructor is open to the idea. An example at MSU is ENGL 431, Studies in a Major Author, which is billed as "intensive study in the works, biography, and criticism of a particular author" in the course bulletin. Students who are engaged in researching Seamus Heaney for the semester, for instance, will need to move beyond general knowledge of library resources into use of specific tools such as the *MLAIB* in more depth and variety than they did in their beginning courses.

A library session for ENGL 431 is usually staged in the library's electronic classroom, which is perfectly suited for smaller, upper-division courses. Here students can participate in a session that combines group discussion with database demonstrations and hands-on work at individual computers. The librarian again distributes a bibliography of suggested resources in different categories such as background information and journal articles, reviewing key services such as Interlibrary Loan (see item 7-3 on the CD-ROM, "Bibliography for ENGL 431"). This time, however, the emphasis is on the details of using complex resources such as *MLAIB* and *WorldCat* rather than on the conceptual frameworks of research, although those concepts may be briefly reviewed.

Additional teaching materials for a course at this level may include a chart of the different types of finding aids that literature scholars typically need. This type of teaching aid can more graphically represent categories of resources for locating authors' works, reviews of those works, criticism, biographical information, background, historical or social context, and citation searching (see item 7-4 on the CD-ROM, "Finding Aid Categories for ENGL 431"). This can help sort out the many confusing research options these students face and help them identify specific types of secondary materials.

In the session itself, the librarian focuses on the use of the *MLAIB* in particular, demonstrating search strategies based on a "Tips for Searching the *MLAIB*" sheet (see item 7-7 on the CD-ROM). Because the *MLAIB* is a complex database that indexes materials that are not often held at MSU (with its nonhumanities focus), it is important for the students to have enough hands-on experience in the session to minimize frustration later, when they are working alone. In any environment, the current complexities of linking to full-text journals from the citations in the *MLAIB* require that considerable attention be paid to technological details. Fortunately, students at this level are better able to deal with this because they are more focused. Introducing students to the *MLA Directory of Periodicals* (part of the InfoTrac version of the *MLAIB*) also helps them understand the world of journals in the field, peer reviewed and otherwise, and that knowledge gives them further tools for evaluating the resources they find. If possible, students should also be introduced to the *Annual Bibliography of English Language and Literature* (*ABELL*) index as an equally important source for secondary literature in their field. At MSU, *ABELL* is held only in print format, so this requires creative and often time-consuming introduction in the library instruction session, especially since students now find print indexes more difficult to use than online.

WorldCat is another important resource for intermediate students because it opens the universe of research to them in ways that the local library catalog usually cannot do. Here they discover how large their topic could be and how necessary careful construction of search parameters is. *WorldCat*'s size and complexity make it an excellent training ground for Boolean logic and other methods of limiting and focusing searches. Students at this level also benefit from learning what *WorldCat* reveals about varying editions of works. Since their research deadlines are often longer, intermediate students can use *WorldCat* effectively if they learn to pace their research and make productive use of interlibrary loan.

A final way in which students in courses such as ENGL 431 can be served is to offer them special one-on-one consultation with the librarian after the library session. At MSU, a Research Assistance Program (RAP) is offered to all students, faculty, and staff as a means of ensuring that researchers can get undivided attention when they need it. Students at this level begin to realize the enormity of the world of literary research and are often very open to further contact with the librarian.

The problem for library instruction designed for upper-division undergraduates is that it is often forced to achieve too much in one semester. Instruction for this ENGL 431 course, for instance, strives to teach students to:

- Deepen their understanding of the different types of reference works and the information they offer
- Understand and use subject headings more effectively in databases and catalogs
- Use more effective search strategies and commands in complex databases
- Identify and obtain more materials available outside the local library catalog
- Evaluate and select appropriate resources through better understanding of publishing processes, types of journals, and literary editions

Intermediate students also need to learn about e-texts and Web resources and the problems of evaluation, access, and citation inherent in them. This in itself could constitute another library session (see item 7-5 on the CD-ROM, "Evaluating E-Texts on the Web"). You should consult with the course instructor to decide what to cover from this broad range of possibilities.

Needs of Graduate Students

Graduate students come into the department from varied backgrounds. If they are students who are continuing their studies after receiving their BA at your institution, they will obviously need less introductory information than students who are new to the program. Students in either category may not have learned good basic research skills, and they will certainly not be aware of the full range of research options in the discipline or in their particular library. Because their research is so specialized, it is usually necessary to meet with graduate students individually to determine how you can help them.

Overall, graduate students' research needs are more complex than undergraduates'. Their relationship with the library will usually test the limits of most library collections and services. Generally, graduate students:

- Want help narrowing, focusing, or pacing unwieldy research plans for their professional paper, thesis, or dissertation
- Often do not use *MLAIB* and *WorldCat* to their best advantage, in part because they have not done a comprehensive research project before this
- Need to make extensive use of interlibrary loan services
- Are expected to analyze primary texts in more sophisticated ways; they must know more about the process of literary production and the need for critical evaluation of varying editions and text formats
- Need to know more about publication venues and options from resources such as the *MLA Directory of Periodicals*
- Perform more comprehensive research and thus need access to more bibliographic tools in their subject area and more broadly (such as *Dissertation Abstracts International*)
- May be enrolled in a degree option (such as teaching) that determines a less literary focus to their research and need access to appropriate databases (such as *ERIC*)
- Need career information, such as job lists and information about professional societies

Strategies for Working with Graduate Students

Working closely with the department's director of graduate studies will help you identify trends in student preparedness and understand requirements for various student research projects, such as professional papers, theses, and dissertations. Getting a foothold in the graduate research methods course is imperative, assuming such a course is offered, which is not the case at MSU. When this is not possible, try entering their world through their teaching. If they are teaching assistants, talk with them about the research needs of their own students and make it clear that you are available to help them with their degree work as well.

Meeting with graduate students one-on-one is time consuming, but it is often the most productive way to help them. Providing them with lists of resources that your library offers for their level of research may simplify your work with them, but there really is no substitute for individual assistance. The MSU Libraries' G-RAP program (Graduate Research Assistance Program) is a consultation service targeted at graduate students in any department (see item 7-6 on the CD-ROM, "Announcing G-RAP"). Making your graduate students aware of a program like this is often an important lifeline for them.

Another service for graduate students is delivery of extracurricular research sessions focused on topics you identify with input from them and the director of the graduate program. These might include refresher sessions on the *MLAIB* or career information seminars (see item 7-1 on the CD-ROM, "Career Resources for English Students"). The important thing to remember is that you are modeling a relationship with these students that you hope will carry over into their professional lives, whether they become university faculty elsewhere or high school teachers.

Anticipated Trends and Developments

Exciting developments in the information resources available to scholars and students in this discipline make the future of library instruction for it both a pleasure and a challenge. Some of the latest online products from vendors like Gale (*Literature Resource Center*) and ProQuest (*Literature Online*), which relate, repackage, and recombine traditionally discrete literature resources such as the *MLAIB*, *ABELL*, and the *Dictionary of Literary Biography* into seamless search environments are certain to increase student access to scholarly materials. Students using Gale's *Literature Resource Center*, for instance, have access to the full text of so many kinds of secondary scholarly material in one quick search that their former frustrations with research are bound to be mitigated.

One of the biggest challenges in this new one-stop-shopping environment, however, will be helping students understand the kinds of materials they find. To unsophisticated researchers, it is often not clear what types of information are being jumbled together in one search result set. Their confusion will undoubtedly grow as federated searching becomes the norm, not just in literature databases, but across all databases and the Web simultaneously. The librarian's role as guide and critical thinking model will become more and more essential—but only if she aggressively markets her skills in that area to both faculty and students. As students become less and less aware of the boundaries and characteristics of traditional library resources (a trend that is already quite noticeable), librarians and faculty will face an uphill battle to instill into their students the values of critical thinking and ethical use of texts.

As journal publishers in the humanities make more of their full-text content available online through products such as *Project MUSE* and *JSTOR*, the English scholar's stereotypical aversion to computers will fade even further into the past. Literature resources on the Web in general will continue to grow and become an ever more important staple in the scholar's diet. E-texts will continue to become more prevalent, sophisticated, and reliable as authoritative texts. The latest developments in Web searching that include the "Googlization" of journal packages such as *Project MUSE* and the digitization of library collections will further blur the lines between traditional scholarly resources and popular culture materials that are all retrieved together in a broad Web search.

In a discipline that is trending toward ever greater contextualization of literary texts and expansion of the definition of "text" and the act of "reading," this is all good. The Web offers a veritable feast of contextuality to students and scholars in English studies, making it all the more certain that the current interest in exploration of contexts will continue. Exploding information options have created the sense, and daily deliver the actuality, of ever-widening gyres of context available for study. Easy access to resources such as full-text databases in literature and other disciplines, new ways of communicating and publishing, digital libraries of images, e-texts, and other media across all disciplines, archival access, and proliferation of Web author guides, bibliographies, and other subject resources make it increasingly crucial for students and faculty to understand research options and apply them creatively. The librarian who grounds her instruction in knowledge of the discipline, the diversity of current information options, and her local department's priorities will be positioned to work closely with all levels of learners in literary studies to fully exploit the digital future.

Note

1. I wish to thank Dr. Amy M. Thomas, Associate Professor and Coordinator of the master's program in the Department of English at Montana State University—Bozeman, and Dr. Linda K. Karell, Associate Professor and Chair of the Department of English at Montana State University—Bozeman, for their interest and input into the preliminary stages of this chapter. Without their cooperation and collaboration, my work with students in English at MSU would not be possible.

Bibliography

Altick, Richard D., and John J. Fenstermaker. 1993. *The Art of Literary Research.* 4th ed. New York: Norton.

Association of College and Research Libraries (ACRL), Literatures in English Section (LES). www.ala.org/ala/acrl/aboutacrl/acrlsections/literaturesineng/leshomepage.htm (accessed October 23, 2005).

Association of Departments of English (ADE). www.ade.org (accessed October 23, 2005).

Baker, Nancy L., and Nancy Huling. 2000. *A Research Guide for Undergraduate Students: English and American Literature.* 5th ed. New York: Modern Language Association.

Benton, Thomas H. 2005. "Life After the Death of Theory." *Chronicle of Higher Education* 51, no. 34 (April 29). http://chronicle.com (accessed October 23, 2005).

Browner, Stephanie, Stephen Pulsford, and Richard Sears. 2000. *Literature and the Internet: A Guide for Students, Teachers, and Scholars.* New York: Garland.

Burnette, Michaelyn, Christina M. Gillis, and Myrtis Cochran. 1994. "The Humanist and the Library: Promoting New Scholarship through Collaborative Interaction between Humanists and Librarians." *The Reference Librarian* no. 47: 181–191.

Coffey, Dan. May 2005. "Studies of Interest to English and American Literature Librarians." www.public.iastate.edu/~dcoffey/studies.htm (accessed October 23, 2005).

Culler, Jonathan. 2003. "Imagining the Coherence of the English Major." *ADE Bulletin* no. 133 (Winter): 6–10. www.ade.org/bulletin/ade_winter03.pdf (accessed October 23, 2005).

Day, Betty H., and William A. Wortman. 2000. *Literature in English: A Guide for Librarians in the Digital Age.* Chicago: Association of College and Research Libraries.

Eaglestone, Robert. 2002. *Doing English: A Guide for Literature Students.* 2nd ed. London: Routledge.

Gibaldi, Joseph. 2003. *MLA Handbook for Writers of Research Papers.* 6th ed. New York: Modern Language Association.

Greenblatt, Stephen, and Giles Gunn, eds. 1992. *Redrawing the Boundaries: The Transformation of English and American Literary Studies*. New York: Modern Language Association.

Hall, Donald E., ed. 2001. *Professions: Conversations on the Future of Literacy and Cultural Studies*. Urbana: University of Illinois.

Harner, James L. 2002. *Literary Research Guide: An Annotated Listing of Reference Sources in English Literary Studies*. 4th ed. New York: Modern Language Association. Updates available at www.english.tamu.edu/pubs/lrg.

Holtze, Terri L. 2002. "100 Ways to Reach Your Faculty." A presentation for "Different Voices, Common Quest: Adult Literacy and Outreach in Libraries." An Office for Literary and Outreach Services (OLOS) Preconference at the American Library Association Annual Meeting, Atlanta, GA, June 13–14, 2002. www.ala.org/ala/pio/campaign/academicresearch/reach_faculty.pdf (accessed October 23, 2005).

Marcuse, Michael J. 1990. *A Reference Guide for English Studies*. Berkeley: University of California.

———. October 2004. "Research Competency Guidelines for Literatures in English: DRAFT." www.ala.org/ala/acrl/acrlstandards/standardsguidelines.htm (accessed October 23, 2005).

Modern Humanities Research Association (MHRA). www.mhra.org.uk (accessed October 23, 2005).

Modern Language Association (MLA). www.mla.org (accessed October 23, 2005).

———. *Approaches to Teaching World Literature*. www.mla.org/store/CID39 (accessed October 23, 2005).

Pollock, Thomas Clark. 1954. "Should the English Major Be a Cafeteria?" *College English* 15, no. 6 (March): 327–331.

Rylance, Rick, and Judy Simons. 2001. "Introduction: Why Study the Contexts of Literature?" In *Literature in Context*, edited by Rick Rylance and Judy Simons, xv–xxix. New York: Palgrave.

Saule, Mara R. 1992. "User Instruction Issues for Databases in the Humanities." *Library Trends* 40, no. 4 (Spring): 596–613.

Schramm, Margaret, J. Lawrence Mitchell, Delores Stephen, and David Laurence. 2003. "The Undergraduate English Major: Report of the 2001–02 ADE Ad Hoc Committee on the English Major." *ADE Bulletin* no. 134–135 (Spring–Fall): 69–91.

Showalter, Elaine. 2003. *Teaching Literature*. Malden, MA: Blackwell.

———. 2003. "What Teaching Literature Should Really Mean." *Chronicle of Higher Education* 49, no. 19 (January 17). http://chronicle.com (accessed October 23, 2005).

Stallybrass, Peter. 2004. "The Library and Material Texts." *PMLA* 119, no. 5 (October): 1347–1352.

Vincent, C. Paul. 1984. "Bibliographic Instruction in the Humanities: The Need to Stress Imagination." *Research Strategies* 2, no. 4 (Fall): 179–184.

Wilson, Reed. 2003. "Researching 'Undergraduate Research' in the Humanities." *Modern Language Studies* 33, no. 1–2: 74–79.

Zauha, Janelle M. 2004. "Faculty Evaluation of Library Instruction." www.lib.montana.edu/instruct/feedback.html (accessed October 23, 2005).

8

Art and Art History

Peggy Keeran

Introduction

In the humanities, knowledge is cumulative. Texts hundreds of years old may be as relevant in a research project as the most current criticism. When students in art and art history programs begin to research a topic, they enter into a centuries-old conversation. The dialogue within the discipline is a visual and written history and a commentary about art. As students explore this world, they will discover the issues and concerns that are addressed in the various discussions. When first introduced to the discipline of art or art history, students learn the foundations of creating or writing about art. Once they have absorbed the visual and written vocabulary for the discipline, they create their own art or explore aspects of art history in depth. Here, both the artist and the art historian need to enter their discipline's conversation and must discover their own voices within the history of the discipline. Library research is essential in discovering that conversation, and library instruction is one key means of enabling students to do so.

Regardless of an artist's or scholar's goals, an understanding and acknowledgment of what has transpired either visually or in words gives their own work authority and credibility. Students discover the conversation in a variety of ways: through class lectures, discussions with professors and fellow students, images in books and periodicals, writings by or about art and artists, visits to galleries and museums, the Web, and library research. Of all these options, libraries offer the most authoritative and comprehensive access to words and images from the broadest range of sources. The classroom, the museum, and the art gallery are microcosms of the discipline. While the Web may provide quantity, the library provides quality. Through library instruction students can gain the skills to search for images and words to inform their work and answer their research questions. The goal of library instruction is to help them discover the tools and processes necessary to enter the conversation and find all the perspectives necessary to create a complex piece of art or critical analysis.

Academic art departments may teach a wide range of topics related to art, ranging from the practice of art and design to the study of its history, to the conservation, management, or display of art. The way sources are discovered or how art students use the library varies within the discipline. Can we make generalizations about how students use books and periodicals? Indexes? The Web? Images? What type of library instruction strategies benefit their research needs? This chapter focuses on two types of researchers, the studio artist and the art historian, and how to provide instruction that will be meaningful to them.

Institutional Setting: University of Denver

The School of Art and Art History at the University of Denver includes nearly 200 undergraduate and graduate students. A bachelor's degree program is offered in studio art, as are bachelor's and master's degree programs in art history and electronic media design. The art and anthropology departments offer a joint master's program in museum studies, and the art and business school offer a joint master's program in art museum administration. About half of the students enrolled in the classes are nonmajors.

As the liaison to the School of Art and Art History, my responsibilities include library instruction, one-on-one consultations, and collection development. Through my collection development responsibilities, I have strong professional relationships with most of the school's faculty. We work together to create a library collection that allows professors to teach creatively and students to find relevant materials. The art school has a separate slide library and a Web-based digital image database, which are not part of my responsibilities.

Research Needs of the Artist and Art Historian

The studio art and art history students may consult the same bibliographic databases, books, and periodicals, but each uses library collections differently. Both need sources that will inform their projects, however, with the outcome a unique piece of art or scholarship. Following is a general description of each group, but be aware that when studio art students take art history classes, they need to use the library as would an art historian, and vice versa.

Studio artists use the collections to inform their own artistic work. They may browse books, periodicals, and the Web for images. The periodicals they need include contemporary art, media-specific magazines and journals, and trade publications. They use the library as a laboratory, or an extension of the classroom, to practice their profession, looking for images, ideas, and inspiration for their work. Consequently, they may use the whole library collection, not only the art books. Beyond images, they often read the writings of or interviews with artists in order to understand how artists view and discuss their own work. Students need the critical analysis of art in order to understand how art is judged by critics and scholars. These sources give students the vocabulary to talk about their own art and about their own pieces in relationship with the work of others (Frank, 1999). Students also need to find sources of funding through grants and fellowships, as well as information about residency programs, competitions, and academic programs.

The art historian's research requirements are more theoretically based. He or she will formulate a question and develop a search strategy to explore it, initially using library and union catalogs, bibliographic databases, and images. As with the studio artist, the art historian requires access to a wide variety of resources beyond the art collection. Depending upon the critical methodology used to interpret an image, art historians may read books on the lives and philosophies of artists, art movements, or genres, as well as books on history, culture, and society, philosophy, psychology, religion, dance, theatre, economics, science, medicine, literature, critical theory, and other topics. They may need access to archives that hold art-related primary sources. Because of all the possible directions research may take, they need the research skills to navigate successfully through their own discipline as well as any others that might provide insight.

On a more practical level, art historians need to know how to find information to support or inform their research. They may need to find information about degree programs in art history, addresses of archives, scholarships, and fellowships. They may need to learn about grants and grant writing in order to fund research and travel to archives, museums, and galleries. Just as with studio artists, there is a practical, economic component to their research, which the library should address by building supportive collections and providing instruction.

Literature Review

Because studio artists' research needs are not as traditional as those of art historians, they may not be as visible to reference librarians. Understanding how studio artists use the library is important when developing collections and bibliographic instruction. In 1994, Sara Shatford Layne gave an overview of the known research patterns for those seeking visual art information, including searching for images by characteristics of individual pieces, by artist, by title, style, subject, date, and place. Layne states that librarians have to be advocates for artists, to help influence the development of research tools useful to their image-seeking requirements (Layne, 1994). Since then, the ability of the Web to display images and the initiatives to create Web-based image collections have gradually alleviated some of these problems, but finding art by all the characteristics artists require is still problematic. Deirdre Stam surveyed art librarians to discover how artists use their library collections. She sees the artist as someone who uses the whole library collection, not just the art library, to find images. In addition, the artist needs to find books and articles on art movements, artists, and iconography. She found that artists are not willing to use traditional indexes to locate relevant works (Stam, 1995). Susie Cobbledick interviewed four artists at an academic institution and found that the library is only one of a vast array of sources used to inform or provide inspiration for their works. They need access to the universe of knowledge for their inspiration, not just art books—everything from psychological studies to historical textiles to the history of a specific site for a piece of public art. Children's books, magazines, newspapers, advertisements, live models, the medium itself, and even the imagination of the artist are all sources of visual information (Cobbledick, 1996). Polly Frank drew attention to the presence of studio artists in the general academic library, noting that artists may be present, but not visible, because of the way they use the library. Most of the students she surveyed tended to browse for the information they needed. They may have used the library catalog to locate an area of interest in the book stacks, explored that area, then returned to it, rather than using the library catalog again. They want attractive, well-maintained books with high quality images, lots of books and exhibition catalogs on new arts and artists, narrative sources, such as the philosophical writings of artists, books on techniques, directories of art schools, and access to images that show what things look like, such as images of animals or boats or human anatomy (Frank, 1999). Sandra Cowan turned a critical eye upon the ways librarians gather information about artists and their information-seeking practices, and concluded that art librarians may not be adequately attentive to how artists develop their creative ideas. Librarians need to acknowledge that library collections are one of a vast number of sources used in the creative process, and to address the needs we can, but not negate the other avenues they choose to follow (Cowan, 2004).

Several authors address various ways to approach instruction within art and art history. Edward Teague discussed design students' research and recommended bibliographic instruction that addresses the technical, contractive (the parameters of the design project), and expansive data (the factors that stimulate an artist to create an image). To encompass all these aspects of the design project, he recommended four segments of instruction: (1) an overview of the design process, (2) an analysis of the components of the process, (3) library resources, and (4) individual consultations (Teague, 1987). Henry Pisciotta described the merits of a nontraditional, discussion-based model when teaching studio artists: discussion is more like studio work, it is persuasive and rewarding, it is similar to the reference interview (asking questions, listening, recommending possible avenues of exploration), it yields valuable information that can be used to address students' needs, and it can promote an appreciation of reference services (Pisciotta, 1989). Barbara Fister and Linnea Wren, respectively a librarian and an art historian, teamed up to generate enthusiasm for the research process by requiring students to conduct primary and secondary research as a group and then to make dramatic re-creations of historical events from the Renaissance using the materials they found. Their goal was to help students learn about research to produce a creative product. Fister, the librarian, met several times with the class and then with the groups to help with the research process (Fister and Wren, 1990).

Maya Gervits and Halina Rusak illustrated the role of instruction in an information-rich world, using their instruction program for the art and archaeology of the African Diaspora as a model. By providing guidance to the vast array of materials and, through a program of instruction that includes fundamentals of research, course-specific instruction, one-on-one consultation, and Web-based research guides, they believe librarians can help students become more effective and efficient searchers (Gervits and Rusak, 2000). Priscilla Atkins found that, by visiting classes, she became a "relationship builder": by getting to know the students and their needs through contact outside the library, she actually brought the students into the library and found, because of the personal contact, that the students more willingly sought her help. Further, by being involved with the classes and responding in the moment to questions in which the library plays a role, librarians can build bridges between the library and the classroom which then enhance interactions in the library setting (Atkins, 2001). Using the University of Virginia experience as the model, in which the strong ties between the faculty and librarians have produced a coherent program of instruction, Lucie Wall Stylianopoulos advocated integrating library skills instruction into the curriculum as the most effective method for ensuring that students learn to become effective, critical researchers (Stylianopoulos, 2003).

For a variety of strategies and ideas for library instruction in the arts, you can consult *Library Instruction for Students in Design Disciplines: Scenarios, Exercises, and Techniques*, compiled by Jeanne Brown, and *Creative Strategies for Library Instruction in the Arts, Literature, and Music*, edited by Marilyn Whitmore. Brown's volume includes a chapter on promoting the Library of Congress (LC) classification as a browsing tool, incorporating information literacy into art and art history programs, evaluating Web sources, and methods for demystifying the structure of library research—from decoding the subject heading to differentiating between a catalog and an index—for the undergraduate student (Brown, 2002). Whitmore's volume covers the arts more broadly, and contains lesson plans for topics in film, dance, studio arts, theater, and the visual arts, literature, communications, and music (Whitmore, 2001).

Instruction

At the University of Denver, all first-year, honors, and transfer students have a basic library instruction course in their first-year English course, in which they begin to learn how to write well-reasoned, well-researched papers. We use a combination of online tutorials to teach basic search strategies (e.g., keyword searching, Boolean operators, truncation), and then students come to the library for workshops where they apply what they learned in the tutorials. Our goal is to help students become familiar and more comfortable with the process. During the workshop the instructor meets with each student to discuss his or her topic and to offer suggested avenues for exploring or refining the topic. The librarian works with each student to formulate search strategies and search relevant databases to find books and articles. Students then print out the articles and go to find books. Our previous experience indicated that students, intimidated by the process, were hesitant to ask for help. The workshop environment allows us to work with students in a classroom environment and emphasizes the process as something to be learned (i.e., faculty recognize that most students do not already have these skills). These workshops tend to be successful because students get engaged in the workshop and find relevant materials. In the process, the students get to know the reference librarians as the sources for help with research.

After this introduction for first-year English classes, the reference librarians work with their liaison departments to offer instruction. Most of the art and art history classes I teach are upper-division undergraduate or graduate courses. In these classes, students must learn where they fit into the conversation about art, and they learn how to establish a voice within that dialogue. How can library instruction help these students? For example, what referential images and philosophies will they bring to their art? As scholars, what is informing the question being explored? Are they discussing the art from a specific methodological perspective? If so, what types of sources will they need to examine their question and which reference tools will help them find the evidence they need to support their position?

We do not have a formal library instruction program for the art department at the University of Denver. I participate in the graduate orientation program and am introduced by the art and art history faculty as an important resource in the research process. Then I meet with all the new art history graduate students as a class in the library to instruct them how to use the library and its resources. For both upper-division and graduate students, I teach invited, one-shot classes, tailored to the content of the course. Finally, faculty who have students with research questions and problems refer them to me for one-on-one consultation.

For one-shot art history classes, I create Web-based research guides which include both core and related sources. These guides are both a blessing and a curse: because we use a template for our research guides, they are easy to create and maintain, but all the guides look alike. Students see the same format and think they have heard what I will say. I address the problem by giving the students an overview of the resources listed on the guide, many chosen specifically for the course at hand. By combining core sources and a variety of related sources of secondary importance, I can make connections between the sources and the scope of the class, illustrating how different research tools provide different perspectives. The research guide then becomes a unique tool for a specific course.

Students can be overwhelmed by the ways that technology constantly changes the research landscape and by the ways that research tools and search interfaces can affect the research process. I firmly believe in helping students become as independent as possible, but, as any reference librarian knows, we purchase new reference books and acquire access to electronic resources regularly. To keep up, a knowledgeable researcher must learn to consult with reference librarians, who keep abreast of the changes. During instruction, I tell students about the changing world of research resources and assure them that there are professionals who do keep up and can serve as guides and teachers.

To illustrate some types of sources they may not have considered or even know exist, I introduce them to information found beyond library catalogs and art indexes. For an art history class on eighteenth- and nineteenth-century British artists in Italy, I include digital collections such as the *Times of London Digital Archive* and the *Eighteenth Century Collections Online*, the indexes to nineteenth-century periodicals, *Poole's Index to Periodical Literature* and *Wellesley Index to Victorian Periodicals*, and indexes from other disciplines, such as history.

The reference tool itself, because of its history or foibles, can play a part in the research process. This is an opportunity to make these seemingly boring volumes come alive and have personalities of their own. For example, a comparison between *Poole's* and *Art Abstracts* illustrates the progression of indexes from the nineteenth to the twentieth century. Very briefly, I explain who William Frederick Poole was and how and why he created his unique, but flawed, index. I then explain how H. W. Wilson took the idea of a periodical index and standardized the process of describing periodical articles, eventually producing the complete family of Wilson indexes, including *Art Abstracts*. Prior to *Poole's*, access to periodical literature was very limited, and after Poole and Wilson, research into the literature published in periodicals was transformed. Suddenly, scholars had access to the individual parts of a periodical.

I emphasize the core skills students need to find materials, such as how to use the library catalog and the basic art indexes and reference sources, but then I give them more: I want students to leave the class knowing where to start, but also stimulated with the possibilities of research. This is my opportunity to open their eyes to a world rich with potential sources and stress that within that world there are reference librarians who can make the sources more comprehensible. When students leave the class, they understand that I know the strengths and weaknesses of these research tools and that I will use my knowledge to help them conduct effective research. As part of library instruction, they learn that the reference librarian is their partner in research.

In their senior year, studio art majors are required to take a class called Professional Practice, in which they learn the practical aspects of being an artist. The course covers résumé and grant writing, exhibition proposals, photographic documentation of art, artist's statements, portfolio development, and professional presentation of work. I spend one class period introducing them to the sources within the library including print tools, online databases, and Web sources: library catalogs, indexes, directories to artists' communities; sources for finding grants; career guides (*The Business of Being an Artist*; *Great Jobs for Art Majors*; *The Artist's Resource Handbook*; *The Practical Handbook for Being an Artist*); and exhibition opportunities (*Art Deadlines List*; announcements in art magazines). The lesson plan in Figure 8-1 outlines the one-hour course I teach. This is a lot of information to cover in an hour, and the art faculty who teach this class plan to extend it to two hours. However, I have been able to weave together all the material within an hour by constantly bringing the discussion back to how and why the library meets the many-faceted needs of the art professional. If you find the following too much to cover in a single class, provide some of the content in the form of handouts (see Figure 8-2) and modify the class to cover less content in more depth. But be aware: even if you do not cover all the content listed in the lesson plan in Figure 8-1 in the class, these are all valuable to the professional, so try to address them somehow, through handouts, more class time, or an additional class.

Even after presenting the above lesson, locating images is still a challenge for students. Access to images is not organized in the same ways as access to textual publications. I show them how to use Library of Congress subject headings and

---

Figure 8-1   Art Lesson Plan: Professional Practice

Goal of the class: To introduce students to the practical aspects of being a professional artist. The course is intended to make the students think of themselves as professionals and to approach their chosen career in a manner which allows them to succeed.

Objectives of library instruction: To introduce materials available in libraries which would be valuable to a professional artist.

Materials covered: library catalogs, bibliographic databases, professional and scholarly journals, directories, career guides, exhibition opportunities, Web resources.

Research guides (2): *Professional Practice* and *Web Sites for Studio Artists* (see Figure 8-2).

Time: 1 hour

The lesson plan:

1. Introduction
   a. Explain the objectives of the session and how students will learn about a wide array of sources that will be valuable to them as professional artists.
   b. Give an overview of library services, including reference services.
   c. Consider questions such as the following:
      i. How can I find a book that describes different kinds of kilns?
      ii. How can I find grants to support my work?
      iii. Can I find books or videos on how to set up a studio?
      iv. Where can I find places to exhibit my work?
      v. How do I find books on watercolor techniques?
      vi. I need to learn how to write an artist's statement about myself. What do I say? What have other artists said about their own art?
   d. Tell the class: "Today we will learn to use the library to help answer these questions which arise in the life of a professional artist."

2. Development of library research practices useful to artists:
   a. Searching the library catalogs and collections.
   b. Browsing the shelves.
   c. Keeping current on periodical literature and announcements.
   d. Locating directories which list everything from grants to art galleries to artist communities to sources for equipment.
   e. Consulting reference librarians for new resources which could be useful.

3. Development of a handout listing materials students can access in the local library and which lists Web sites
   a. The handout represents the available sources; it is not comprehensive.
   b. Collections grow and change, so give students your contact information.
   c. Indicate call number areas for browsing.

4. Basic search techniques
   a. Revisiting basic search strategies, such as Boolean operators and truncation.

Figure 8-1 (continued)

5. Show and tell
   a. Demonstrate search strategies using the library catalog, bibliographic databases, and the Internet. Select from the following themes:
      i. Business practices and strategies for artists (e.g., management, marketing, business plans, promotion, exhibition techniques, pricing your artwork).
      ii. Studio practices (e.g., setting up a studio, guides to materials, safe practices, selection of equipment, organization).
      iii. Directories (e.g., artists' communities, art organizations, academic programs, grants, internships).
      iv. Artists talking about their art (e.g., statements, interviews, autobiographies, anthologies of writings by artists, letters)
      v. Illustrations in monographs, magazines, and databases.
      vi. Pertinent call number ranges to browse in the book stacks.
      vii. Web sites (e.g., artist statements, exhibition opportunities, basic HTML and authoring pages, stock images, artist-specific Web sites, commercial sites for artists, blogs on printmaking, ceramics, and design)
   b. Bring books that illustrate the types of material available in a library. Allow students to examine these books, see the table of contents, see how the various types of resources are arranged.

6. Browsing the collections
   a. Bring current issues of journals which list exhibits and allow the student to browse through them, to see the types of announcements (e.g., grants, exhibition opportunities, artists' residencies).
   b. Take the students into the book and bound periodical stacks. Explain how libraries arrange materials and how they can use that arrangement effectively to scan for images, art forms, artists, movements, and other.

7. Conclusion
   a. Restate the objectives of the class, and that library resources and strong searching techniques inform and support the work of the professional artist.

---

subdivisions such as Pictorial Works to locate books rich with images and how to read a book or article citation to determine if the materials include illustrations. The standard illustration indexes in the following source list are frustrating for students to use, especially in this age of the Web and its wealth of images, but, even so, I introduce them to these sources because these are often the only tools for finding images published in older periodicals and books. *Google Image Search* is a rich, albeit uneven, means of discovering quality images: images can come from museums and art galleries as well as from homemade digital snapshots. As with any Web search, the students need to learn to be discriminating about which images they choose, but they should learn how to use all means of finding images effectively, including the Web. Because copyright of images is important, I introduce them to Web sites with basic information they need to know about copyright and related issues.

While touring the library with these students, I pull a variety of art-related periodicals that publish articles on contemporary art and include announcements about competitions and exhibition opportunities. We search grants databases for funding opportunities. This class is always very informative and rewarding for me to teach, especially because students are surprised by the variety of ways the library

Figure 8-2   Web Sites for Studio Artists

Get Yourself Googled: Online Representation Resources. For artist registries in an area you may be moving to, Google search artist registry (state/city/province). Many local governments and galleries host artist registries that you may be able to participate in.

- ArtistsRegister.com. http://artistsregister.com/. An online service of the Western States Arts Federation (WESTAF). This fee-based service provides juried online representation for artists of all levels. Also has a good set of resources and links for artists in the West.

- White Columns. http://registry.whitecolumns.org/. An alternative space dedicated to unrepresented artists in New York City. Their online registry is curated, and while it does focus on artists in New York City, they also accept submissions from outsiders as well. If anything, this is an amazing site to look at to see what other people are making.

Stock Images: Artist-Specific Web Sites

Please note: Check the copyright information on each Web site. The following Web sites have stock images you can use for reference or ideas, but always get permission if you plan to use the image within your work and you plan to distribute or sell your work.

- Creative Commons. http://creativecommons.org/. This site is searchable and provides links to people who choose to have their works distributed under the Creative Commons license.

- morgueFile. http://www.morguefile.com/. A searchable site dedicated to providing free images to artists. All images are downloadable, printable, and nonwatermarked.

- Stock.XCHNG. http://sxc.hu/. The Stock.XCHNG is a site that is made up of stock photography for others to use for noncommercial purposes. Full-size photographs are available with free registration (you may still search the site and use smaller images without registering).

Stock Images: Commercially Geared Sites

These sites typically have watermarked images that cannot be downloaded or printed (without the big watermark). Good if you just need a little reference or ideas, but not good for use in your work.

- Freefoto.com. http://www.freefoto.com/index.jsp. Freefoto.com is a huge, comprehensive site that covers things from hippos, coal plants, cloud textures, public transit, to touristy pictures. While this site makes strong attempts to be navigable, the sheer number of images can cause one to get lost or sidetracked. Nonwatermarked printable images.

- Getty Images. http://creative.gettyimages.com/. This is the most searchable guide out there. Has an excellent "search clarification" feature that helps you get the image you want without sifting through hundreds of images. Images are watermarked.

Other Great Image Sources (Not Necessarily Stock Photography)

- Art Crimes: The Writing on the Wall. http://www.graffiti.org/. Art Crimes is a Web page devoted to graffiti around the world. Has links to images and personal Web sites of graffiti artists and crews around the world.

- Mother of all Art and Art History Links Page. http://art-design.umich.edu/mother/ A huge, expansive page with links to images, art history, art schools—all things art.

Figure 8-2   (continued)

Blogs, Blogs, Blogs . . .

- Barenforum. http://www.barenforum.org/blog/. A blog on printmaking.
- Drawn! The Illustration Blog. http://www.drawn.ca/. A collective blog for illustrators, comic artists, and cartoonists. Great imagery and frequent updates.
- Photoblogs.org. http://www.photoblogs.org/. A listing of registered photoblogs. Great place to search, see what other people are looking at. Some sites have free use; others are under copyright.
- University of Michigan's Art and Design school blog. http://www.art-design.umich .edu/plus/. Updated daily with images, links, and general wackiness.

Resources for Artists

- art-public.com. http://www.art-public.com/. A specialized resource for information and documentation dedicated exclusively to art in the public arena. They have a fee-based image library that is focused on public art.
- Ceramics Today. http://www.ceramicstoday.com/. This is a very thorough and informative collection of links about all things ceramic. Hosts articles and images of current work.
- International Sculpture Center. http://www.sculpture.org/. This site has a good links and informational section that is broken down by need: technical, educational, computers, and sculpture organizations. The site also hosts a portfolio of member work.
- Printmaking Links. http://www.mtsu.edu/~art/printmaking/. Covers all aspects and kinds of printmaking. Very easy to navigate. Compiled by Christie Nuell.
- Society of North American Goldsmiths Resource Page. http://www.snagmetalsmith .org/infocentral/. This page has links to galleries, images, schools, supplies, and more. The professional guides section has information on how to write a proper artist statement, a show checklist, and other helpful information.
- Storm King Art Center. http://www.stormking.org/. The Storm King Art Center is a museum that celebrates the relationship between sculpture and nature. This site has some images of the museum's pieces in situ.

This research guide was created, under the guidance of Peggy Keeran, by Kellie Cannon, a library student at the University of Denver. Cannon received a BFA in Fibers and Drawing from Colorado State University.

The complete guide, as well as the *Art—Professional Practice* guide, are available at: www.penlib.du.edu/findit/ResearchGuides.

can meet their needs and how librarians can provide assistance in finding sources valuable to the creation, execution, and marketing of their work.

What to Teach

As recommended in the lesson plan above, it is best to begin with an overview of the content you will cover and points they will learn. For example, if the class is about nineteenth-century cemetery sculpture, students should learn how to find books and articles on the topic, but they may also find city directories to identify artisans and local sources for materials and production, mail-order catalogs for mass-produced sculpture, archives, local newspapers to search for advertising, and other sources to explore the topic. Explain why a systematic approach to any research project allows the researcher to gather relevant resources efficiently, so that students do not expend their energy on the research process but instead get the materials, read and absorb the content, and then incorporate the material into exploring the research question. Get a list of topics on which the students are working and use these to find images, books, articles, and other resources. Then show them how to go through the whole process, from beginning to end. Continually demonstrate how effective search strategies allow them to discover relevant information and images. Make the research process a logical progression, to illustrate that the student can control the process by going through steps. Depending upon the topic, the student might go in a variety of directions. If the artist is contemporary, students may find reviews of books or exhibits or interviews in nonart publications, such as local newspapers or national news magazines. Microfilm collections, such as the *Archives of American Art*, may be useful for letters and other primary sources concerning the history of American art and artists.

Ultimately, if students do venture beyond the bounds of the library catalog and basic art databases, one-on-one consultation is the most successful way to provide instruction and relevant help. Do not encourage students to be totally dependent upon you, but reassure them that they can ask for individual help and that you expect them to do so. Consultation sessions by their nature are tailored to the specific needs of the student and the topic so that, together, the librarian and the student partner to identify keywords, databases, and, ultimately, sources relevant to the topic. Further, these sessions allow the librarian to teach students how to work beyond the confines of their own discipline. Individual consultations help illustrate to upper-division students who are working on difficult projects that the reference librarians are valuable allies in the research process who want them to succeed.

No librarian can know everything. I make it a practice to ask for help when I have exhausted my library's available resources, and I let students know that I, too, have to ask for help. I am a member of the Art Libraries Society of North America (ARLIS/NA; www.arlisna.org), a supportive professional association for art librarians. ARLIS-L, the e-mail listserve of the Art Libraries Society of North America, has been invaluable when I am stuck for a direction to take to help a student with research, or when my library cannot get the necessary information through normal channels.

To summarize, the components of successful art history bibliographic instruction include:

- Working with faculty to ensure the content of the library instruction is relevant.
- Scheduling the class when it will be most relevant to students. Generally, this will be after they have selected a topic.
- Using the course syllabus to develop a printed or Web-based research guide.
- Asking the instructor for topics students have identified to use as examples during the class. This step includes:
  - Using student topics to develop search strategies that highlight the scope of the resource under discussion.

- Following at least one topic through the various sources to illustrate the strengths and weaknesses of each source within the context of that research problem.
- When meeting with a class, giving an overview of the content of your presentation, including:
  - Mentioning their assignment and explaining why they need the information you will present in order to complete their research.
  - Telling students what they will learn to help them find relevant materials.
- Giving students an overview of the pertinent sources and how they relate to course assignments or expectations, before explaining individual resources in detail.
- Providing examples of basic search techniques and sources.
- Explaining how research can be done systematically, so that it will not be overwhelming. The following sublist outlines the steps to follow in such a systematic approach. By following these steps, students can leave the library with a collection of books and articles to read. By the time the items requested via the local union catalog and interlibrary loan arrive, the students will have read the materials they have and will be ready for more.
  - Search the library catalog and retrieve relevant materials.
  - Search the local or regional union catalog for additional materials and request those that are relevant. Students often believe that if information is not available immediately, it is not worth the effort of trying to get it. By learning how the whole process fits together, students can learn to take advantage of interlibrary loan and expand their horizons.
  - Search the online art databases for books, book chapters, and articles, then find the books, book chapters, and articles in the library collection.
- Explaining how research in art history provides evidence and context for the question being explored. A researcher may need to revise his or her question several times during the investigative process. As the student writes, additional evidence to support or refute arguments may be necessary and further research may be required. Research and writing become integrated, where one helps further the other, until the question is answered to the satisfaction of the author, or until the paper is due.
- Understanding that as an artist creates a work, more research may be necessary to solve problems related to the piece, for example, more images, historical context, or different techniques.
- Explaining the serendipitous aspect of research—often the result of browsing.
- Always giving a bit more than the students need to accomplish their assignments, to make them aware that there is much more beyond what is required for a single class assignment.
- Explaining to students that the reference librarian is an important part of the research process, someone to approach not only once, but continually as their project progresses and becomes refined.

- Giving students your contact information so they can get in touch if they need further assistance.

Constraints on Instruction and Research

In one-shot classes, my main constraints are time and, sometimes, lack of collections to support the research. Because of the limited amount of time I have to teach, I do not engage the students in discussion, and therefore the classes are more lecture than sharing of information or a hands-on workshop. I offset this by creating a picture of the research process for them, establishing a topic to be researched, and then weaving together all the sources to show how each contributes to the bigger picture. By using their topics as points of reference, students are more personally invested in the class and the process I am explaining. Other constraints actually occur beyond the library instruction class and can be frustrating for students. Because upper-division and graduate-level research can take many directions, we may not have some needed collections on hand and may need to fill student requests using document delivery services. Since the University of Denver is on the quarter system, we have limited time to fill interlibrary loan requests. We are fortunate to have access to digital collections including full-text journals, and we participate in a consortium with a shared union catalog through which students can borrow directly from other institutions. I tell students they should start their research early enough to identify and request needed materials via interlibrary loan in time to be able to use them for their project.

As I have already noted, finding images remains a challenge. At my institution, we have purchased some images from Saskia and have loaded them into our library catalog. Saskia (www.saskia.com) is a commercial vendor which sells images, including digital images, for instruction in art history. At present, we cannot afford *ARTstor*, and, because the art department has created its own image management database, commercial databases are not a priority. Commercial vendors are currently limited to images the vendors can get permissions to include, but the art and art history faculty require a customized image collection to aid in teaching. *Google Image Search* (http://images.google.com) provides access to millions of images, but their quality is not always acceptable and users must assume most images found are copyrighted. However, for students researching contemporary artists, the images found using a Google search could provide them with information about the location of a gallery that deals with the artist, so they need to learn how to follow clues. It is best to acknowledge the problems with finding relevant images and recommend that students try a variety of methods to find them. Teaching studio art students to do this type of research on their own, even if it can be fruitless, will allow them to develop strategies that best meet their visual needs. The reference librarian will still be a partner, but, because the artist needs to sift through a lot of images to find one that resonates, the process is really too personal for a reference librarian to act as mediator.

Marketing Library Instruction

Library instruction is a typical component of the services an academic library offers, and should be marketed as such. At the University of Denver Penrose Library, we have a well-established liaison program through which most communication between the departments and the library occurs. Through the liaison program we develop collections, discuss library-related issues that arise in the department or classes, and organize our instructional programs. To ensure that all new programs and majors are adequately funded, and therefore do not have a negative impact upon the moneys for established programs, the library dean has successfully advocated a mandatory library budget line for library materials to support new programs. We have an active Women's Library Association (WLA), a volunteer group which raises money for library collections to support the curriculum. This program allows us to enrich targeted sections of the collection, and it provides the faculty with opportunities to develop collections that support new and creative teaching opportunities. For example, we were able to purchase microfilm versions of some of the nineteenth-century art periodicals indexed in the *Index to Nineteenth-Century American Art Periodicals* and therefore build a collection that provides students with access to the articles identified using the index. As another example, we were able to buy *The Hours of Jeanne d'Évreux*, a limited facsimile edition, published by the Metropolitan Museum of Art using the latest in facsimile technology. A medievalist in the art history department needed such a reproduction to show students how to examine manuscripts. We house this facsimile in Special Collections, where the class of students are taken to learn some key points about manuscript research and view a demonstration on handling manuscripts properly.

Conclusion

Library instruction provides an opportunity to expand the research horizons of both studio art and art history students. By allowing researchers to search decades, and even centuries, of bibliographic records at once, by providing access to digital images of art, manuscripts, books, and articles, and by developing image collection databases, our use of technology enables students to explore, more fully than ever before, the various conversations about art. With the wealth of resources available, students need to have the skills to navigate through the standard online databases, but they also need to know they have partners in the library to help them. Instruction provides the foundation by helping students develop the necessary skills and by fostering an understanding of how information is organized. Finally, we convey an awareness that reference librarians are the experts who can provide a path through all the existing and developing resources students can use in their research.

Selected Key Sources

The following is an overview of core and related materials to help students in the research of art and art history.

Online Bibliographic Databases

- *Art Abstracts*. 1984–present. New York: H. W. Wilson. Online via various vendors. www.hwwilson.com. An index (1984–present), with abstracts (1994–present), to about 375 American and international scholarly and general art periodicals, as well as yearbooks and museum bulletins. Subjects include art, art history, antiques, architecture, fashion, graphics, photography, sculpture, and video. Also indexes images. Earlier years covered by *Art Index Retrospective* (1929–1983), also published by Wilson.

- *ARTBibliography Modern*. Late 1960s–present. Bethesda, MD: CSA. www.csa.com. This resource includes abstracts of journal articles, books, essays, exhibition catalogs, PhD dissertations, and exhibition reviews on all forms of modern and contemporary art.

- *Avery Index to Architectural Periodicals*. 1934–present, with selective coverage back to 1741. Santa Monica, CA: Getty Art History Information Program. www.csa.com. Bibliographic citations to articles on the history and practice of architecture, landscape architecture, city planning, historic preservation, and interior design and decoration in over 700 American and international scholarly, popular, and trade publications.

- *BHA: Bibliography of the History of Art*. 1973–present. Vandoeuvre-lès-Nancy, France: Centre National de la Recherche Scientifique, Institut de l'Information Scientifique et Technique; Santa Monica, CA: J. Paul Getty Trust, Getty Art History Information Program. Online via various vendors. This database covers European and American art from late antiquity to the present. Indexes and abstracts art-related books, conference proceedings, dissertations, art exhibition catalogs, and over 4,800 periodicals from around the world.

- *DAAI: Design and Applied Arts Index*. 1973–present. Burwash, England: Design Documentation. www.csa.com. Index to design and craft journals and newspapers.

- *Index to Nineteenth-Century American Art Periodicals*. 1840–1907. Mountain View, CA: Research Libraries Group. http://eureka.rlg.org. Indexes forty-two American art periodicals published in the second half of the nineteenth-century. Indexing includes articles, art notes, illustrations, stories, poems, and advertisements.

Dictionaries and Encyclopedias

There are a wide variety of art dictionaries and encyclopedias, from the general to the highly specialized. The following are some basic sources.

- Chilvers, Ian. 2004. *Oxford Dictionary of Art*. 3rd ed. New York: Oxford University Press. A one-volume reference source with short entries covering primarily Western art from antiquity to the present. Topics covered include biographies, histories of major museums, art movements, styles, materials, and techniques. This dictionary excludes architecture, design, photography, and the applied arts.

- Delahunt, Michael. 1996– . *ArtLex Art Dictionary*. www.artlex.com. A free, Web-based dictionary of short definitions for visual arts terms used when discussing art. *ArtLex* is also a portal to related sites that illustrate the meaning of terms. Its intended audience includes artists, educators, students, collectors, and dealers.
- Hall, James. 1979. *Dictionary of Subjects and Symbols in Art*. Rev. ed. New York: Harper and Row. Definitions of mainly Christian and classical themes and symbols in European art of the Renaissance and later.
- Macy, Laura, ed. 1998–present. *Grove Art Online*. Oxford, England: Oxford University Press. www.groveart.com. This is a Web-based standard art dictionary which includes the online, expanded version of *The Dictionary of Art*, 1997, edited by Jane Turner, and *The Oxford Companion to Western Art*. Coverage is international in scope and covers all aspects of the history of visual arts. Grove has approximately 45,000 articles, including lengthy, scholarly entries, and an image search database that provides links to 40,000 art images in galleries and museums around the world. Updated and revised, and new entries are listed in "What's New" section.

Guides to Research Sources

- Arntzen, Etta, and Robert Rainwater. 1980. *Guide to the Literature of Art History* (GLAH). Chicago: American Libraries Association.
- Marmor, Max, and Alex Ross. 2005. *Guide to the Literature of Art History 2* (*GLAH2*). Chicago: American Libraries Association. GLAH and GLAH2 are essential, annotated guides to reference works for art history research, including bibliographies, dictionaries, encyclopedias, histories and handbooks, architecture, sculpture, drawings, paintings, prints, photography, and decorative and applied arts (subdivided by medium). Sections include geographic subdivisions. The guides are international in scope, but with an emphasis on Western language resources. GLAH2 updates the list of periodicals listed in the earlier volume, and provides an annotated list of titles new to the guide. The latest volume by Marmor and Ross (with a cut-off date of 1998) builds upon the *Guide to Art Reference Books* (Chamberlin, 1959) and the earlier title by Arntzen and Rainwater (ending in 1977).
- Jones, Lois Swan. 1998. *Art Information and the Internet: How to Find It, How to Use It*. Phoenix, AZ: Oryx Press. Guide to art and art history Web sites and techniques for finding and evaluating art sites. Includes "Types of Web Sites and How to Find Them" (that is, art museums, academic institutions, corporations, individuals, cultural, civic, professional organizations, foundations, and buying and selling art) and "How to Use and Supplement Web Information," which covers seven basic steps of research and lists of print, electronic, and Web sources (e.g., art history, artists and art collectors, architecture, decorative arts, fashion, graphic arts, and photography).

- Jones, Lois Swan. 1990. *Art Information: Research Methods and Resources.* 3rd ed. Dubuque, IA: Kendall/Hunt. Guide to research methods in art history and bibliographies (with some annotations) of general art research tools and specialized resources by subject (e.g., architecture, prints, photography, decorative arts and crafts, fashion/costume/jewelry, film/video, commercial design, museum studies, and iconography).

Methodology

- Adams, Laurie Schneider. 1996. *The Methodologies of Art: An Introduction.* New York: IconEditions. A basic introduction to art theories, including formalism, iconography, Marxism, feminism, semiotics, and psychoanalysis.

Biographical Dictionaries

There are a wide range of biographical sources available that either broadly cover the discipline of art and art history or focus on a particular time period or geographic location. The general dictionaries and encyclopedias previously listed also contain biographical information. The following two works are the standard, scholarly biographical dictionaries.

- *Allgemeines Künstler-Lexicon: Die Bildenden Künstler aller Zeiten und Völker.* 1992– . Munich: K. G. Saur. In German. This source provides biographical data on significant artists working in any medium. Updates, expands upon, and consolidates Thieme-Becker/Vollmer. Publication in progress.
- Bénézit, Emmanuel. 1999. *Dictionnaire critique et documentaire des peintres, sculpteurs, dessinateurs et graveurs.* New ed. Paris: Gründ. In French. This is the second most comprehensive biographical dictionary of artists (after Thieme-Becker/Vollmer).

Journals

See also *GLAH* and *GLAH2,* listed in the preceding "Guides to Research Sources."

- LaGuardia, Cheryl. 2004. *Magazines for Libraries.* 13th ed. New Providence, NJ: Bowker. Lists recommended periodicals, with critical annotations, divided into chapters by discipline. Includes sections on architecture, art (general and museum publications), crafts, and printing and graphic arts.

Interdisciplinary or General Sources

- *Academic Search Premier.* 1965– . Ipswich, MA: Ebsco. http://search.epnet .com. This is an interdisciplinary index and full-text source for scholarly journals and general periodicals. It covers topics related to art across the disciplines, and includes reviews of books and art exhibits.

- Houghton, Walter E., ed. 1966–1989. *Wellesley Index to Victorian Periodicals, 1824–1900*. Toronto: University of Toronto Press. Available on CD-ROM. This index includes tables of contents for forty-two British periodicals from the nineteenth-century.
- *LexisNexis Academic*. Dayton, OH: LexisNexis. http://web.lexis-nexis.com. This database includes selected full text of newspapers from the United States and around the world. This database is valuable for finding interviews, reviews of exhibitions of emerging and regional artists reported in local newspapers, and the latest news about laws and legislation, funding, controversies, and other topics involving art.
- Poole, William Frederick. 1963. *Poole's Index to Periodical Literature*. Rev. ed. 6 vols. Gloucester, MA: P. Smith. 1802–1906. Also available online from www.paratext.com. Keyword index to nearly 480 periodicals; primarily American, and some British.

Online Bibliographic Databases in History

- *America: History and Life*. 1964–present. Santa Barbara, CA: ABC-Clio. http://serials.abc-clio.com. The United States and Canada from prehistory to the present.
- *Historical Abstracts*. 1954–present. Santa Barbara, CA: ABC-Clio. http://serials .abc-clio.com. *Historical Abstracts* covers world history (except U.S. and Canadian) from 1450 to the present.
- *International Medieval Bibliography*. 1967–present. Turnhout, Belgium: Brepolis. Online. www.brepolis.net. Bibliography covering the European Middle Ages (c. 400–1500).
- *Iter: Gateway to the Middle Ages and Renaissance*. 1784–present. Toronto, Canada: Iter. www.itergateway.org. *Iter* is an interdisciplinary index pertaining to the literature of the Middle Ages and Renaissance (400–1700).

Image Sources

Images are the mainstay of art, but they can be most difficult to locate. The Web has made access to images much easier in some ways, but it has made copyright issues more complex. The following are some traditional and nontraditional means of locating images. In addition, subscription image databases, such as *ArtStor*, *Davis-art.com*, *Scholars Resource*, or *Saskia*, may be available at your institution. The following are some basic sources for locating images in books and periodicals or on the Web.

- *Art Abstracts and Art Index Retrospective*. See the preceding list "Online Bibliographic Databases." Both provide indexing to images in art publications.
- Clapp, Jane. 1970. *Sculpture Index*. Metuchen, NJ: Scarecrow Press. Subject and artist index to images of sculptures published in about 950 books.
- *Google Image Search*. http://images.google.com. This tool searches the Web by keyword for images of any media, both copyrighted and noncopyrighted.

- *Grove Art Online.* See the preceding list "Dictionaries and Encyclopedias." Includes *Bridgeman Art Library.*
- Havlice, Patricia Pate. 1977. *World Painting Index.* Lanham, MD: Scarecrow Press. Suppl. 1, 1982. Suppl. 2, 1995. Suppl. 3, 2003. Entries are arranged by artist and title or subject matter. Indexes images in books published between 1940 and 1999.
- *Illustration Index.* 1957– . Lanham, MD: Scarecrow Press. Indexes photographs published in magazines. Arranged by subject.
- Thomas, Ruth S. 1998– . *Finding Images on the Web.* www.bu.edu/library/instruction/findimages/index.html. This is a Web gateway to image search engines, archives, image collections, and imagebases. Coverage includes advertisements, arts, clip art, maps, people and portraits, photography, sciences, and other subjects.

Digital Collections

- *Historical New York Times.* 1851–present (less a three-year moving wall). Ann Arbor, MI: ProQuest. Online http://proquest.umi.com. This database provides searchable full-text and page images of the *New York Times.*
- *JSTOR.* 1995– . New York: JSTOR. This is an online archive to backfiles to about 300 core scholarly journals in the humanities, social sciences, and sciences. Content starts with the first volume and continues to within three to five years of the present. New title backfiles are being added.
- *Project MUSE.* 1995– . Baltimore, MD: Johns Hopkins University Press. *Project MUSE* provides full text to current volumes for about 250 scholarly journals in the humanities and social sciences. New titles are being added.
- *Times of London Digital Archive, 1785–1985.* 2002– . Farmington Hills, MI: Thomson-Gale. http://infotrac.galegroup.com. This searchable, full-text database provides digital reproductions of the newspaper, both in full-page images and article images.

Electronic Books: Databases

Three digital collections provide electronic versions of books published in the English language from 1475 to 1800:

- *Early English Books Online.* 1999– . Ann Arbor, MI: ProQuest. http://eebo.chadwyck.com. Books, primarily in English, published in England and its colonies from 1475 to 1700.
- *Eighteenth Century Collections Online.* 2003– . Detroit, MI: Gale Group. http://galenet.galegroup.com. Books, primarily in English, published in England and its colonies in the eighteenth century.
- *Evans Digital Collection (1639–1800).* 2002– . Chester, VT: Readex. http://infoweb.newsbank.com. Books published in North America in the seventeenth and eighteenth centuries.

Web Sites for the Artist and Art Historian

- *Art Deadlines List.* http://artdeadlineslist.com. A monthly newsletter with 600–900 announcements listing art contests and competitions, art scholarships and grants, juried exhibitions, art jobs and internships, call for entries/proposals/papers, writing and photo contests, residencies, funding, and other artists, art educators, and art students of all ages. A free monthly e-mail subscription is available.
- *ArtSource.* www.ilpi.com/artsource/welcome.html. Begun by an art librarian, Mary Molinaro, this site has become a selective list of sites useful for research in art and art history.
- Graveline, Laura. *Free Art Resources on the Web.* Art Libraries of North America. www.arlisna.org/resources/onlinepubs/freeart.html. This list is comprised of links to key, free Web sites about art and artists.
- Maylon, John. *Artcyclopedia.* www.artcyclopedia.com/index.html. *Artcyclopedia* links to online images of works by artists whose works have been collected by museums.
- *Mother of All Art and Art History Links Page.* Ann Arbor, MI: University of Michigan, School of Art and Design. www.art-design.umich.edu/mother. This site links to art history departments, research resources, image collections and online art, art museums, and new media art.
- *SIRIS/Archives of American Art.* Washington, DC: Smithsonian Institution. www.siris.si.edu. The Smithsonian Institution Research Information System (SIRIS) provides access to the *Archives of American Art* database, which allows searches for the papers of artists, art dealers, art historians, collectors, records for galleries, museums, and art organizations. Many of the papers have been microfilmed and are available for interlibrary loan.
- *Voice of the Shuttle: Web Site for Humanities Research.* Santa Barbara: University of California Santa Barbara, English Department. http://vos.ucsb.edu. Includes links to architecture, art (modern and contemporary), art history, and photography sites.

Bibliography

Atkins, Priscilla. 2001. "Information Literacy and the Arts: Be There—or Miss It!" *College and Research Libraries News* 62, no. 11 (December): 1086–1088, 1092.

Brown, Jeanne, comp. 2002. *Library Instruction for Students in Design Disciplines: Scenarios, Exercises, and Techniques.* Kanata, Ontario, Canada: Art Libraries Society of North America.

Cobbledick, Susie. 1996. "The Information-Seeking Behavior of Artists: Exploratory Interviews." *The Library Quarterly* 66 (October): 343–372.

Cowan, Sandra. 2004. "Informing Visual Poetry: Information Needs and Sources of Artists." *Art Documentation* 23, no. 2 (Fall): 14–20.

Fister, Barbara, and Linnea Wren. 1990. "Recreating the Renaissance: Dramatic Presentations in the Art History Class." *Research Strategies* 8 (Fall): 200–203.

Frank, Polly P. 1999. "Student Artists in the Library: An Investigation of How They Use General Academic Libraries for Their Creative Needs." *The Journal of Academic Librarianship* 25, no. 6 (November): 445–455.

Gervits, Maya, and Halina Rusak. 2000. "Art and Archaeology of the African Diaspora: New Challenges in Art History Instruction." *Art Documentation* 19, no. 2 (Fall): 46–48.

Layne, Sara Shatford. 1994. "Artists, Art Historians, and Visual Art Information." *The Reference Librarian* no. 47: 23–36.

Pisciotta, Henry. 1989. "Let's Talk: An Approach to Bibliographic Instruction for the Studio Major, Part One." *Art Documentation* 8 (Spring): 24–25.

———. 2003. "Image Delivery and the Critical Masses." *Journal of Library Administration* 39, no. 2/3: 123–138.

Reed, Bonnie, and Donald R. Tanner. 2001. "Information Needs and Library Services for the Fine Arts Faculty." *The Journal of Academic Librarianship* 27, no. 3 (May): 229–233.

Stam, Deirdre C. 1995. "Artists and Art Libraries." *Art Libraries Journal* 20, no. 2: 21–24.

Stylianopoulos, Lucie Wall. 2003. "It's All in the Company You Keep: Library Skills Credit Courses in the Art Library." *Art Documentation* 22, no. 1 (Spring): 29–32.

Teague, Edward H. 1987. "A Portrait for the Librarian: Bibliographic Education for Students in Design Disciplines." In *Conceptual Frameworks for Bibliographic Education*, edited by Mary Reichel and Mary Ann Ramey, 99–108. Littleton, CO: Libraries Unlimited.

Whitmore, Marilyn P., ed. 2001. *Creative Strategies for Library Instruction in the Arts, Literature, and Music.* Pittsburgh, PA: Library Instruction Publications.

9

Film Studies

Neal Baker

Introduction

This chapter provides recommendations for library and information literacy instruction in film studies, also known as cinema studies. You may be asked to support courses in English, history, modern languages, or other disciplines that study film, as well as for the film studies curriculum, if there is such a program on your campus. Understanding any domain of knowledge, including an academic discipline, includes knowing how scholars and others working in the domain create and use information. Accordingly, I will begin this chapter with an overview of the discipline of film studies.

Establishing Shot: Becoming Familiar with Film Studies

Film studies is a relatively new discipline that has undergone radical changes in less than forty years. Dudley Andrew provides a useful survey in his article "The 'Three Ages' of Cinema Studies and the Age to Come" (Andrew, 2000). Andrew relates how film studies began in the United States after the importation of French critical theory in the 1970s. Film theory emerged as a dense conceptual alloy forged out of elements of structural linguistics, semiotics, Marxism, and psychoanalysis, from which comparative literature and foreign language faculties created a flashy new intellectual construct. Like the controversial Centre Pompidou in Paris, this construct was (and still is) scorned by some critics who attributed a faddish extravagance to film studies and its European theoreticians.

Film studies followed the theoretical turn taken by the humanities during the 1970s and 1980s. It became an example for more established disciplines like English, and to a great extent, critical theory now permeates graduate curricula and editorial agendas across the humanities. Ironically, film studies today has essentially scrapped its continental theory base in favor of a more pluralist approach to the study of cinema. In so doing, nominal film studies professors now embrace methodologies used in other academic disciplines. At the same time, other academics now commonly study history and culture through cinema.

A glance at the table of contents of the anthology *Reinventing Film Studies* indicates the various approaches to film that librarians might encounter (Gledhill and Williams, 2000). Part 1, "Really Useful Theory," outlines various theoretical ways of looking at films, including two essays titled "Why Theory?" and "Who (and What) Is It For?" Part 2, "Film as Mass Culture," includes five chapters that cover more recent sociological approaches to the study of film, such as audience research and the examination of movie stars. Part 3, "Questions of Aesthetics," deals with film style and textual analysis. Part 4, "The Return to History," illustrates how scholars now focus on the intersection of film texts and broader cultural contexts via historical research, where a historical setting is just as important to the analyst as is the film text. Part 5, "Cinema in the Age of Global Multimedia," concludes the anthology with four chapters that approach films via such disciplinary vectors as business and economics, media studies, and area studies.

Audience Analysis: Identify Your Users

Exactly where a cinema-related course appears in a given curriculum is a critical variable for instructional librarians. Although many academic institutions do not host bona fide film studies programs, just about every university, college, and community college in the United States offers courses that study films. Librarians who work with cinema-related courses must be prepared to supply instruction that spans a wide array of academic disciplines.

My situation at Earlham College is typical in this respect. Although Earlham is a small liberal arts college with approximately 1,200 undergraduate students and no film studies program at present, I regularly work with cinema-related courses throughout the curriculum. A professor of French, for example, recently offered a West African Cinema course that used films as an entry point to the cultures of Senegal, Mali, and Cameroon. When I provided instruction for this cinema-based class, it had nothing to do with film research and instead covered encyclopedias about Africa, country studies, bibliographies of African periodicals, and so on. More recently, a psychology professor consulted me about incorporating writing into a first-year course devoted exclusively to representations of madness in the cinema. Again, I contributed nothing in terms of what one might normally associate as cinema research and instead offered advice about how I integrate writing into the film courses I teach.

These examples underscore the importance of identifying your users. Librarians who work with cinema-related courses should never make assumptions about a faculty member's educational objectives. A course with a straightforward title like Mexican Cinema might focus exclusively on the medium of film, or just as easily be an area studies class that teaches Mexican culture via Mexican films. If Mexican Cinema does actually treat film as the course's primary subject matter, the professor might focus on film style and close analysis, or just as plausibly emphasize the historical and sociopolitical contexts that inform film texts. Moreover, depending on the professor's inclination, Mexican Cinema might include discussions of postcolonial or feminist theory. Librarians should realize that any of these scenarios might involve a course pitched for any level of student, ranging from first-year undergraduates to graduate students.

Key Props

Periodical Indexes

Just as approaches to cinema abound, so do film periodicals. The two best indexes to this body of literature are the *International Index to Film Periodicals* and the *Film Literature Index*. Published since 1972 by the International Federation of Film Archives (FIAF), the *International Index to Film Periodicals* contains almost 230,000 citations to articles from over 300 academic and popular film journals. Produced with institutional support from the University at Albany, State University of New York (SUNY), the *Film Literature Index* completely indexes 150 film and television periodicals from thirty countries and selectively indexes 200 other periodicals for articles on film and television. The *International Index to Film Periodicals* is available online via paid subscription from SilverPlatter, and the *Film Literature Index* is published in three quarterly issues and in one annual cumulation with a free online version containing citations from 1973 to 2001 at http://webapp1.dlib.indiana.edu/fli/index.jsp. As of now, there are no plans to update this online resource, originally produced by Indiana University with the assistance of a National Endowment for the Humanities grant. Current citations are available only via a print subscription.

A look at the list of journals covered by the *Film Literature Index* yields insights about the wide range of information relevant to film studies. The index covers scholarly titles like *Screen*, *Camera Obscura*, and *Cinema Journal*, the quarterly publication of the Society for Cinema and Media Studies (the field's dominant academic organization). Mingled with these abstruse periodicals one can find newsstand titles like *Premiere*, plus industry publications such as *Variety* and *American Cinematographer*. Enhancing the selection are highly specialized titles like *European Trash Cinema* and *Cinefex*, a journal devoted to special effects. Also present are more general "highbrow" offerings like *Film Comment* and *Sight & Sound*. Published respectively by the Film Society of Lincoln Center and the British Film Institute, these titles are written in an elevated level of discourse for educated film connoisseurs and occupy the middle ground between *Premiere* and *Cinema Journal*.

If periodicals like these comprise a "core" for film studies, it is important to stress an expanding periphery of noncinema and television publications selectively covered by the *Film Literature Index*. Many different disciplines publish film-related articles nowadays, as witnessed by articles in *American Anthropologist*, *American Historical Review*, *American Jewish History*, and *American Journalism Review*, to name just a few. Since movies are a mass medium, *Film Literature Index* also selectively covers mainstream sources including *Newsweek*, *Rolling Stone*, *Time*, and *USA Today*.

The scope of the *Film Literature Index* and the *International Index to Film Periodicals* makes them the best resources for locating information in periodicals relevant to film studies. However, the nature of academia today and the presence of cinema-based inquiry across the curriculum render it impossible for any single resource to ensure total bibliographic control over periodicals. Although the *Film Literature Index* selectively covers the *French Review*, for instance, it does not cover the articles about cinema published in *Contemporary French Civilization*. Similarly, the *Film Literature Index* covers a specialized biannual like *Asian Cinema* but not the groundbreaking cinema-related articles on anime (a Japanese animation genre) recently published in the area studies title *Japan Forum*. For that matter, the *Film Literature Index* has never indexed the numerous articles about cinema and television that appear in academic periodicals devoted to genres like science fiction (e.g. *Extrapolation*, *Journal of the Fantastic in the Arts*, *Science Fiction Studies*).

Due to film studies' interdisciplinary nature, access to its scholarly and critical literature is relatively complicated and diffuse. This situation actually has its advantages. The very prevalence of film-based inquiry across many disciplines means that many other databases and indexes cover articles related to film. Since many academic institutions do not offer full-fledged film studies programs, their libraries may not subscribe to the *Film Literature Index* or the *International Index to Film Periodicals*. Librarians can compensate by directing their researchers to the *MLA International Bibliography*, which contains over 1.5 million citations from more than 4,400 journals and 1,000 book publishers germane to literature, languages and linguistics, folklore, and dramatic arts. Despite the vastly larger scale of the *MLA International Bibliography*, it does not cover many of the titles listed in the *International Index to Film Periodicals* or the *Film Literature Index*. Other useful resources that cover film to various degrees are the companion art databases produced by H. W. Wilson, *Art Abstracts and Art Index Retrospective*, both of which cover material that tends to focus on film as "high art" (as opposed to popular culture). Finally, massive general databases like EBSCO's *Academic Search Premier* or ProQuest's *ProQuest 5000* will inevitably return useful citations and full text.

In summary, we can establish a hierarchy of film-related periodical indexes, which are in the following list. The last category, "General Full-Text Indexes," only provides several examples of its type and is not meant to be comprehensive.

Essential Film Periodical Indexes

- *Film Literature Index*. Coverage from 1973 to 2001 is available online via http://webapp1.dlib.indiana.edu/fli/index.jsp. More recent coverage is available via a print subscription from the SUNY Film and Television Documentation Center.

- *International Index to Film Periodicals.* Available online via SilverPlatter. Published by the International Federation of Film Archives (FIAF).

Interdisciplinary Periodical Indexes That Cover Film

- *Art Abstracts; Art Index Retrospective.* Available online via H. W. Wilson.
- *MLA International Bibliography.* Available online via EBSCO, Gale Group, OCLC, CSA, ProQuest. Published by the Modern Language Association.

General Full-Text Indexes

- *Academic Search Premier; Academic Search Elite.* Available online via EBSCO.
- *ProQuest 5000; ProQuest 5000 International.* Available online via ProQuest.

Reference Books

Specialized reference books of interest to film studies also abound. The ten examples that follow are some of the best resources available to librarians and their users.

- Baskin, Ellen, comp. 2003. *Enser's Filmed Books and Plays 1928–2001.* Hants, UK: Ashgate. An encyclopedic listing of film adaptations.
- Blandford, Steve, Barry Keith Grant, and Jim Hillier, eds. 2001. *The Film Studies Dictionary.* London: Arnold. This book contains approximately 1,000 entries devoted to the language of film production and film theory.
- Cowie, Peter, ed. *Variety International Film Guide.* Annual. Los Angeles: Silman-James. This guide reviews films released during a given year and provides industry surveys for filmmaking countries around the globe, along with features on important figures for the year.
- Hanson, Patricia King, and Stephen L. Hanson. 1986–1987. *Film Review Index.* Phoenix: Oryx. Volume one indexes reviews of films released between 1882 and 1949; volume two indexes reviews of films released between 1950 and 1985.
- Hayward, Susan. 2000. *Film Studies: The Key Concepts.* 2nd ed. New York: Routledge. A glossary of terms and concepts in film theory and film production.
- Hill, John, and Pamela Church Gibson. 1998. *The Oxford Guide to Film Studies.* New York: Oxford. Presents brief, content-rich chapters devoted to aspects of film analysis and theory (e.g., "Marxism and Film") and topics in film history.
- *International Motion Picture Almanac.* Annual. New York: Quigley. Arguably the best single-volume reference source to the film industry, offering analyses of the world market, listings of producers and distributors, and other information.

- Katz, Ephraim. 2001. *The Film Encyclopedia*. 4th ed. New York: Harper-Collins. A core single-volume work offering brief entries covering all aspects of film production and film history (e.g., directors, actors, movements).
- Miller, Toby, and Robert Stam, eds. 2004. *A Companion to Film Theory*. Malden, MA: Blackwell. Presents twenty chapters devoted to aspects of film theory (e.g., "Psychoanalytic Film Theory").
- Thomson, David. 2002. *The New Biographical Dictionary of Film*. 4th ed. New York: A. A. Knopf. One of the best single-volume works of biographical information on film personalities.

Plot Complication: How Students Typically Find Cinema-Related Information

Despite the prevalence of quality cinema-related resources available through libraries, undergraduate students are more likely to surf the free and visible Web for their research needs. Among other things, students rely on official film Web sites. Before we librarians collectively wring our hands in frustration and marvel again at our users' ignorance, let us give them the benefit of the doubt. Recent academic studies demonstrate both the importance and the depth of official film Web sites placed online by motion picture producers and distributors. Cinema scholar Kristin Thompson stresses the informational role played by an official film Web site in her 2003 article "Fantasy, Franchises, and Frodo Baggins: *The Lord of the Rings* and Modern Hollywood" (Thompson, 2003). The Routledge anthology *An Introduction to Film Studies* similarly devotes a case study to the information available at *The Blair Witch Project* official Web site (Nelmes, 2003). I used official film sites myself, while researching an article I wrote on the anime feature *Blood: The Last Vampire*. Similarly, at an academic workshop on Japanese cinema, I once saw an academic divulge that he carried out much of his research for a presentation using Google and anime fan Web sites. Film scholars do not disdain the Web, but the key hurdle to scale when teaching is to help students learn how to evaluate and select information based on criteria used in film studies and other disciplines incorporating it.

The free and visible Web holds other attractions for cinema-related researchers, students, and faculty alike. For example, a myriad of semiprofessional Web sites now compete with trade publications like the *Hollywood Reporter* in the provision of film industry news. The popular *Ain't It Cool News* (www.aint-it-cool-news) is typical of this kind of site. Updated daily, it gives its subscription-based competitors a run for their money with surprisingly accurate and detailed news about genre filmmaking written in spirited prose and accompanied by passionate fan reviews that are often just as insightful as those found in *Variety*'s more temperate pages.

Additionally, the free Web is home to two popular reference resources devoted to cinema. The *Internet Movie Database* (IMDb), first of all, has garnered widespread fame for its voluminous film information. Available at www.imdb.com and originally a project undertaken by international movie fans via Usenet bulletin boards and online newsgroups during the late 1980s and 1990s, this sprawling Web site became an amazon.com company in 1998. The IMDb currently stores over 6.3 million individual film and television credits, ranging from director to gaffer, and it is cross-referenced via hyperlinks and supplemented by plot summaries, memorable quotes, trivia, external reviews, box office performance data, and more. A second high-profile reference source is the *Movie Review Query Engine* (www.mrqe.com), which harvests reviews for over 40,000 films from hundreds of sources including newspapers (e.g., the *New York Times*), weeklies (e.g., the *Village Voice*), and Web sites. Users may simply type in a film title and select from a list of reviews. While recent films return links to literally hundreds of reviews, older films might only yield less than a dozen. The main challenge that users of the *Movie Review Query Engine* confront is evaluating which reviews of a film to favor in a list of results that includes sources like the authoritative *Sight & Sound* and the enthusiast *Film Monthly*.

Action Sequence: What to Teach

An Earlham professor recently asked students in his "Philosophy and Film" first-year seminar to find reviews of films shown in the course. The course screenings included recent popular films like *The Matrix* (1999) and older or less familiar ones such as Ingmar Bergman's *The Seventh Seal* (1957) and Woody Allen's *Crimes and Misdemeanors* (1989). The professor assigned a short research paper wherein students would integrate their own analysis of a film with that of previous reviewers. Additionally, students were to incorporate perspectives gained from philosophical texts paired with each film (e.g., Frantz Fanon's book, *The Wretched of the Earth* [1961], was paired with Gillo Pontecorvo's *The Battle of Algiers* [1965]). Aside from parameters specific to the paper itself, the professor established no conditions for my own instructional session with the class. That is, I was free to point the students to whatever information resources I thought best and employ any teaching methods that seemed most appropriate to me.

The Philosophy and Film assignment afforded a golden opportunity to fuse an information literacy agenda with the professor's course objectives. I had two primary goals for this thirty-five-minute session: (1) to introduce students to useful information resources related to the assignment, and (2) to promote critical reflection about different types of information. I first demonstrated how to locate film reviews via both the *Internet Movie Database* and the *Movie Review Query Engine*. Since most students were already familiar with the mechanics of searching these free and easy-to-use Web sites, I stressed the importance of evaluating the provenance and quality of the reviews found on them. The primary evaluative criterion I suggested was only to cite reviews taken from the online versions of print publications and to avoid reviews published only on the Web. I then introduced more specialized library resources like the online *MLA International Bibliography* and a print bibliography, the *Film Review Index*. By juxtaposing the strengths

So, You Want to Find Film Reviews?

Neal Baker
Earlham College

The Good News

- In general, it's relatively easy to find film reviews....
- This especially holds true for more recent films (e.g., 1990–present)

But....

- You need to figure out what type of film review you need
  - "Mainstream" press film reviews
  - "Specialized" film reviews
  - Scholarly analyses of films

"Mainstream" Film Reviews

- Intended for a general, wide readership
- Do not contain footnotes or scholarly jargon
- Examples:
  - *Time*
  - *Newsweek*
  - *USA Today* or any mainstream newspaper

"Specialized" Film Reviews 1

- Intended for specialized readerships like:
  - Film industry insiders
  - Sci-fi fans
  - Art cinema fans
- Contains jargon familiar to the specialized community

"Specialized" Film Reviews 2

- Examples of "specialized" publications:
  - Film industry insiders
    - *Variety*
  - Sci-fi fans
    - *Starlog* (also myriad blogs and newsgroups)
  - Art cinema fans
    - *Sight & Sound*

Figure 9-1   Lesson on Finding Film Reviews

Scholarly Analyses of Films

- Intended for academic readers
- Contains footnotes and scholarly jargon
- Peer-reviewed
- Examples:
  - *Cinema Journal*
  - *Screen*
  - *Camera Obscura*

Where to Find Film Reviews 1

- You might know these sources:
  - Internet Movie Database (free Web site)
  - Movie Review Query Engine (free Web site)
- Both of these sources contain "mainstream" and some "specialized" reviews

---

Where to Find Film Reviews 2

- You might not know these sources:
  - *MLA International Bibliography* (Library Web)
  - *Film Review Index* (Library Reference Section)
- *MLA International Bibliography* contains scholarly analyses of films
- *Film Review Index* contains "mainstream" and some "specialized" reviews

---

Golden Rule

- Regardless of where you find film reviews, the most important thing to determine is which ones best meet your research needs

---

Figure 9-1 (*continued*)

and weaknesses of popular Web sites with those of scholarly resources, I encouraged students to think about different kinds of information and drew attention to the importance of scope and coverage in deciding what sources to use. Figure 9-1 shows a sample lesson on finding film reviews (this is also reproduced on the accompanying CD-ROM).

Behind the Scenes

Strategies for Working with Faculty

The Philosophy and Film assignment previously outlined represents the course-integrated approach to information literacy at Earlham College. At Earlham, information literacy is never taught in a vacuum by means of stand-alone Library Skills 101 or Computing 101 co-curricular modules, Web-based tutorials, or full courses. Rather, librarians address information literacy competencies within the context of regular class offerings throughout the curriculum, holding sessions both inside and outside the walls of the college library. Earlham's librarians never give primacy to information literacy competencies per se, but instead emphasize the importance of such competencies in enabling a professor's instructional goals and, by extension, supporting the broader goals of an academic program.

Following is a brief summarization of the advantages of a course-integrated approach to information literacy. First, course integration facilitates buy-in from faculty and, as such, is politically efficacious. Individual faculty set the broad agenda for what they variously label "library instruction," "computer training," or "research skills" in their own individual courses; that is, faculty, rather than administrators, are responsible for instructional goals at this level. Librarians recognize that course goals come first—not library or computing goals. In this setting the instruction librarian's goals deliberately dovetail with the faculty member's goals. Second, a course-integrated approach to information literacy increases student engagement. Students are more receptive because the librarian focuses on their course assignments and the requirements of specific academic programs (e.g., milestones such as comprehensive exams and theses for Spanish majors). Course-integrated instruction is by definition relevant to a student's immediate information needs, and thereby becomes an enabling device for academic success in a meaningful, need-to-know situation.

At Earlham, the librarian's role in this course-integrated approach to information literacy essentially boils down to being as fully connected as possible with the college community. Although my examples reflect a small liberal arts college environment, they mirror wider patterns in colleges and universities in the United States. I act as a liaison to several academic departments and programs, including English, Japanese Studies, Languages and Literatures, and Philosophy. I assist these units with all aspects of library operations, ranging from acquisitions to instruction. My key strategy is this: *Every encounter with faculty becomes an opportunity for advocacy.* I try to take advantage of critical opportunities for networking with faculty not only in scheduled meetings, but more often over casual lunches, when our paths cross at a local grocery store, or during informal appointments like going for a walk together, having them over for dinner, or working out with them at the college's athletic center. In many ways, my attendance at a college lecture, sporting event, or social occasion is more important than a formal library meeting with departmental faculty, inasmuch as it demonstrates the library's deep commitment to and participation in the college mission. Likewise, a librarian's participation in the campus governance structure via committee work is of paramount importance to the library in terms of engaging completely with the college, not to mention image management and prestige.

Librarians' involvement in Earlham's course-integrated approach extends well beyond traditional library matters. For example, I regularly provide instruction for both students and faculty on using software programs like PowerPoint and Dreamweaver in the classroom. As is the case with library instruction, these sessions are entirely course integrated and never occur for the sake of promoting information literacy itself. They instead arise from curricular needs, be they course specific (e.g., constructing Web pages for a course on African American literature) or programmatic (e.g., preparing Psychology majors for their senior research presentations). Further, Earlham is planning to systematically support course-management software for all faculty and students, and librarians will participate as training liaisons in this respect.

My own role within this course-integrated approach to information literacy has its own complexities with respect to film studies. Since 1998 I have delivered one-shot introductory lectures on film analysis in courses throughout the Earlham curriculum that use cinema to study world cultures, aspects of psychology, literary adaptation, and other areas. Although this type of instruction does not fall within the normal purview of librarianship, it allows me to address information literacy issues more deeply and from a disciplinary perspective. Since 2003, I have also taught one film course per year at Earlham, thereby promoting discipline-specific research and inquiry in information literacy via student-centered teaching methods. I am currently coordinating several faculty members in creating a proposal for a Film Studies minor at Earlham. Again, this sort of involvement accords incalculable benefits in terms of networking and perceptions about librarians as partners in the mission of the college.

Assessment

Compared to the work I do with faculty, my efforts to evaluate my own library and information instruction are modest. I target assessment to strengthen my own teaching and can recommend several techniques to gather feedback. At the outset of a library instruction session, I occasionally ask students if they are aware of canonical information resources x, y, and z. Sometimes at the end of a session I ask students to jot down three things they learned. Neither of these tactics is systematic, but they enable me to quickly modify and improve my own teaching. Instead of formally evaluating the quality of students' bibliographies in a particular course, I simply ask the professor for his or her perceptions of the bibliographies. This inevitably leads to a discussion about how to improve future library instruction. Likewise, I do not formally evaluate the quality of student PowerPoint presentations or Web pages, but instead ask the professor about the results. Faculty always offer useful comments that I take to heart in developing future sessions. These practices and the resulting discussions about pedagogy reinforce the librarian's status as a partner in the educational process, for both library and technology-related instruction. Also, I take faculty's comments seriously as a matter of realpolitik. My interest promotes faculty buy-in, a factor necessary for any course-integrated approach.

In contrast to my own informal assessment efforts, the Earlham Libraries have begun using assessment data to strengthen the presence of information literacy in the first-year experience. Earlham College adopted radically new general education requirements in fall 2003, which led the libraries to develop a set of provisional, first-year research performance indicators that we are now discussing with faculty focus groups (see item 9-2 on the CD-ROM). This process may lead librarians to develop a cognate list of indicators that assess wider information literacy skills that move beyond research per se and shade into intellectual property issues, critical thinking, and the use of technology in student learning. While these formal activities focus on students, a sudden influx of eleven new tenure-track faculty members in fall 2004 motivated us to examine and retool how we attract and win over new professors to our information literacy efforts. Instead of resting on our laurels, we decided the libraries' outreach initiatives needed improvement. Three changes have had positive impacts. First, we sponsored and invited faculty to summer workshops on integrating research into their first-year courses, which most of the new faculty attended. Second, a librarian and a representative from either Computing Services or Instructional Technology and Media paired up and scheduled meetings with all new faculty members in their offices around campus at the beginning of the fall semester. These meetings introduced new faculty members to services of the administrative units most closely associated with information technology and literacy. Finally, a librarian delivered a forty-minute talk on plagiarism during the official orientation session required of all new faculty members.

Preview: The Future of Film Studies and Information Literacy

Technology will influence the future of both film studies and information literacy in many ways. Considering current technological developments in the industry, it is problematic even to talk about "film" when referring to contemporary cinema production. Not only is "film" increasingly recorded via digital technologies and often digitally created after the fact of principal location shooting via intensive post-production work, it is almost always edited digitally. Increasingly, "film" will be distributed to movie theaters and home markets via digital mechanisms including DVD and on-demand downloads via the Internet. The art and business of cinema continue within this framework, but film itself goes the way of vinyl phonograph records and vellum manuscripts. Cinema studies will consequently shift its analytic scope to account for such changes and the whole disciplinary language will evolve to reflect this.

Information literacy as it connects to the study of cinema likewise will evolve as technology impacts how researchers at all levels work with the medium. To give a current example, DVD technology enables the mass distribution of films accompanied by audio commentaries from both key production personnel and film scholars, and in some cases, additional footage, alternative endings, and more. Researchers now need to know how to locate such information (i.e., is it indexed anywhere?) and how to cite such para-textual material in their own papers. Professors and students now take excerpts from films—stills or entire scenes—and import them into new multimedia contexts requiring familiarity with software packages ranging from PowerPoint slide shows to locally produced DVD clip archives complete with menu systems and voice-over commentary, used to accompany class lectures. These lectures and their associated multimedia content are often hosted online in course-management systems that present their own layer of information literacy–related challenges. The required competencies include not only basic proficiency with assorted software, but also an understanding of pertinent intellectual property issues.

Suffice it to say that film studies and information literacy will continue to go hand in hand. As is true with most other academic disciplines, students' and scholars' information competencies intersect greatly with their understanding of the subject matter, including its information sources and the standards for veracity used in discourse. There will also be an elevated need for librarians and information technology (IT) professionals to assist researchers as they work with cinema in the age of digital reproduction. Just as film studies becomes more interdisciplinary in nature, so do the consequent information literacy solutions. Considering this likely future, the best solutions will probably be team based, involving students and faculty with library and IT staff in new ways. Yet this is really just a natural evolution. Cinema has always been a collaborative media endeavor that mixes intellect, artistry, and industry. Information literacy today is a similar enterprise. By way of conclusion, here is a list of five points that instructional librarians should keep in mind about film studies today:

- Expect to work with a variety of academic disciplines.
- Expect to work with a variety of critical approaches.
- Expect to work with students accustomed to finding film-related information on the Web.
- Expect to work with students unaccustomed to searching for film-related information using library resources.
- Expect to work with students and faculty who increasingly need to present their film-related information by means of technology resources beyond paper.

Bibliography

Andrew, Dudley. 2000. "The 'Three Ages' of Cinema Studies and the Age to Come." *PMLA* 115, no. 3 (May): 341–351.

Gledhill, Christine, and Linda Williams, eds. 2000. *Reinventing Film Studies*. London: Arnold.

Nelmes, Jill, ed. 2003. *An Introduction to Film Studies*. 3rd ed. London: Routledge.

Thompson, Kristin. 2003. "Fantasy, Franchises, and Frodo Baggins: *The Lord of the Rings* and Modern Hollywood." *The Velvet Light Trap* 52 (Fall): 45–63.

10

History

Joel D. Kitchens

Introduction

When I was a graduate student in history, one of my professors admonished his students to "cast your nets far and wide" in our quest for sources. As a librarian I often repeat these words to students as they begin research for their own papers. On the surface, many librarians do not see historical research as different from other literature-based assignments. Because of the interdisciplinary nature of today's scholarship, however, even seemingly basic questions such as "What caused the American Revolution?" have complicated answers. In history, there is rarely a single yes-or-no, black-or-white answer; more often than not, there are only numerous shades of gray. These nuances can be fun for historians (indeed, they are central to the discipline) but are quite challenging for the typical undergraduate. It is important for instruction librarians to understand the nature of the historical research process and the many types of sources needed. This chapter will focus on many of the more commonly available resources for most topics in American or Western Civilization courses, but the techniques are transferable to all historical research.

Changes in the Discipline of History

It is a cliché to say that the discipline of history has undergone profound changes over the past forty to fifty years. Yet these changes have been sweeping and have affected how historians research, write, and teach history, especially in higher education. For much of the early twentieth century, historical study and writing examined politics, diplomacy, militarism, and middle- to upper-class Western European values and societies, but the last half of the twentieth century witnessed the rise of more ethnically and socially inclusive, interdisciplinary topics and methodologies. History is no longer limited to the study of "dead white men"; the contributions of women and non-Western cultures to civilization are also beginning to get the attention they deserve. This affects not only historical research, writing, and teaching, but also how libraries acquire, organize, store, and present information. Historical scholarship and teaching also now challenge the geographic and chronological categories libraries have historically used to collect and classify information. Besides traditional classes on the American Revolution, new upper-division courses with titles such as Women in the Atlantic World, 1500–1800 now appear in course catalogs. Supporting such classes can create challenges in collection building and library instruction, since research topics could easily include women's legal status in colonial North America, race relations in the Caribbean, and women as portrayed in West African trickster tales. Library resources needed for these topics include specialized indexes in history as well as primary, secondary, and bibliographic works in women's studies, law, and folklore. Books to support these research topics could be classified under Library of Congress (LC) call numbers D, E, F, G, H, and K. Such wide-ranging topics within a single class can tax even the most resourceful librarian (Iggers, 1993; Kitchens et al., 2002; Novick, 1998; Ritter, 1993).

Although historical scholarship and teaching have changed radically, they remain important in college and university curricula. It is generally not possible to graduate with a bachelor's degree without taking a history class, but this does not mean all students have been exposed to historical research. Within a single history class, there are three levels of instruction. First, there is the subject matter itself: the facts, people, places, events, and dates. Second are the interpretations, which try to explain why events happened as they did and why they warrant attention. Third are the research and analytical skills the students must learn to find historical information and create their own interpretations. Students must develop effective communication skills (usually written) in order to demonstrate to their instructors an adequate understanding of the subject matter. The American Historical Association (AHA), the largest professional organization for scholarly historians in the United States, has useful essays on its Web site that help explain why history is important and how it should be taught. In one of these, Peter Stearns lists additional lessons beyond the subject matter students in history classes should take with them. Librarians preparing to teach bibliographic skills should keep these goals in mind:

- History teaches present societies about societal change and how societies came to be.

- History can provide lessons in morality, community identity, and good citizenship.
- History teaches students to assess evidence (especially conflicting evidence), to think critically, and communicate effectively (especially in written form).

Libraries are witnessing a sea change in the way materials are collected and made available to patrons. In addition to an increase in interdisciplinary materials, the transition from printed and microform materials to electronic access has had a huge impact on libraries. As more libraries replace existing print journals with electronic access, add full-text databases and "e-resources," and move toward federated searching, scholars using historical sources and methodologies, for whom the library is their laboratory, are dramatically affected. Instruction librarians must master the new technology and understand its implications for researchers and be able to explain the strengths and weaknesses of a variety of formats.

Historians' Information Needs

Primary Sources

Historians use a wide variety of information sources in different formats. Most important for historical research are primary sources sometimes called original sources or documents. Primary sources are those created at the time of the events under investigation, especially if by someone involved in those events. Historian Robin Winks defines primary sources as such: "[M]aterial that is contemporary to the events being examined. Such sources include, among other things, diaries, letters, newspapers, magazine articles, tape recordings, pictures, and maps." Other examples of primary sources include: government materials, such as congressional, parliamentary, or other legislative testimony, reports, debates, voting records, census records, or other government documents; court records, including opinions, testimony, marriage and birth certificates, and probate records; business records, including ledgers, pay books, and inventories; and church records, including minutes of business meetings, and published sermons and epistles. Depending on one's research topic, the advertisements, editorials, and obituaries in newspapers and magazines from the time period under examination can be considered primary sources. History professors now require students to use primary sources for many classes at all levels, whereas a few years ago these sources were usually required only in upper-level and graduate courses.

Identifying a primary source is not always a straightforward exercise. Doing so depends on the nature of one's research topic and the problem or issues under investigation. For example, an 1876 newspaper article on the American Revolution would not be a primary source for students of the Revolution since it was published 100 years after the event. However, for the student examining how the press portrayed the Revolution during the 1876 Centennial, the flowery prose, historical myths, or invented traditions used to describe or embellish the Revolution and deeds of the Founding Fathers, the same 1876 article is indeed considered primary. History students must also understand context in order to make sound judgments. This is why a history professor may object to students using a full-text online version of a newspaper and insist that they view the microfilm edition rather than the electronic text stripped from its original context, including advertisements and illustrations. On the other hand, history faculty may consider an electronic newspaper archive an acceptable representation of the original if it presents complete issues and full page images.

Catalogs

Depending on the research topic, your library's online catalog may provide access to a treasure trove of primary source documents and is usually the best place to begin searching. Other printed and online catalogs can also lead students to primary sources. You should ask the instructor if students will have time to wait for interlibrary requests for books and other circulating materials. Some instructors prefer students to use only materials available at the home institution rather than risk not being able to get a crucial source because it is held only in one library several states away.

Students with limited experience (e.g., freshmen, transfer students, or even graduate students who received their previous degrees from other institutions) should learn how to use the local catalog. Today's automated catalogs can make searching for primary sources much easier than in the old days of card catalogs. For instance, searching for *Wesley, John, 1703–1791* as an author will display all works the library owns by this eighteenth-century British theologian and reformer, just as in the days of card catalogs. However, by using keywords (or natural language) and date limiters, additional or more relevant sources can be found. Show students the intricacies of nested and Boolean searching for crafting more sophisticated and effective search strings. Depending on the local catalog interface, a sample query to find materials on women and the American Revolution might be crafted as:

- **woman OR women OR lady OR ladies OR girl OR girls** [in keyword **Anywhere**]
- **AND (revolution OR rebellion)** [in keyword **Anywhere**]
- Limit publication dates to 1775–1781

Keep in mind that a primary source does not have to be old and musty. Indeed, it may be represented by a recent date in the library catalog. A recently published set of edited papers of a famous person can be a legitimate primary source.

Another way to find primary sources in an online catalog is to perform a natural language search, adding the requirement that the word **sources** must appear in the subject field of the MARC record. Thus, the following search displays primary sources about the nineteenth-century Irish famine that killed so many and sent many survivors seeking a better life in America:

- **Ireland AND famine** as keywords **Anywhere**
- **sources** in the Subject field

The following multilibrary catalogs are essential sources for historical research:

- Center for Research Libraries (CRL). www.crl.edu/catalog/index.htm. Available only to member institutions, the catalog for this consortium includes manuscripts, government documents, and other primary sources.
- *National Union Catalog of Manuscript Collections* (NUCMC). www.loc.gov/coll/nucmc/. Published in print from 1959 to 1993 by the Library of Congress (LC), NUCMC was an attempt to catalog manuscript collections in special collection repositories from all over the United States. NUCMC is available by subscription on the Web as *ArchivesUSA* (ProQuest/Chadwyck-Healy: www.proquest.com/) or through LC and the Research Libraries Group (RLG); however, the LC/RLG version only contains records added since 1986.
- *WorldCat* (OCLC). www.oclc.org/firstsearch. *WorldCat* includes records for manuscripts, photographs, book reprints, and all manner of resources cataloged by member libraries. While *WorldCat* includes archival material, there is not complete overlap with *ArchivesUSA*.

Unfortunately, many rare or otherwise unique documents such as manuscripts and other unpublished material are available to researchers only in the repositories that house the desired items, so access may be impossible unless students have the time and resources to travel. Also, access to rare and fragile materials may be limited by the holding institution to established scholars only.

Indexes and Databases

Periodical indexes can also provide access to primary sources. Since the electronic versions of many of the older indexes are little more than scanned and searchable versions of the original printed versions, the information can be quite spartan. However, some electronic versions will provide links to full-text sites that have made the information available on the Web. The key indexes are the following:

- *Periodical Contents Index* (*PCI*). ProQuest/Chadwyck-Healey, http://pci.chadwyck.com/. *PCI* is another important electronic periodical index, going back to the late eighteenth century. Its deep retrospective nature is one of its strengths. It covers humanities and social science topics in magazines and journals published in several Western European languages. Newspapers and heavily illustrated titles are excluded. Some of the material is available full text.
- *Poole's Index to Periodical Literature.* Rev. ed. 1963. P. Smith. One of the earliest periodical indexes, *Poole's* provides simple access to the published sentiments of the literate, English-speaking public for most of the nineteenth century. Most periodicals indexed in *Poole's* are American, but a few major British publications are also included. *Poole's* is one of the core resources in Paratext's Web-based *19th Century Masterfile*.
- *Public Affairs Information Service* (*PAIS*). Available through OCLC's First-Search, www.oclc.org/firstsearch/ or CSA, www.csa.com/. *PAIS* is useful for

twentieth-century topics. This international index covers periodical literature, government publications, and selected book chapters on a wide variety of topics relating to public affairs (e.g., taxation in France, the Locarno Treaty in Europe, education in the United States). The FirstSearch frontfile for *PAIS* covers 1972 to the present. Both FirstSearch and CSA are releasing a companion retrospective database in segments that will eventually cover *PAIS* from its inception in 1915 into the mid-1970s.

- *Readers' Guide to Periodical Literature.* 1890–present. H. W. Wilson Company. The *Readers' Guide* is one of the most familiar indexes to American scholars. Early in the twentieth century, the *Readers' Guide* was the primary periodical index, covering scholarly literature in addition to popular magazines. Later, Wilson pulled out the scholarly material to create more specialized indexes (*Humanities Index, Social Sciences Index,* and others), which also are useful to historical researchers. The *Readers' Guide* is still the best resource to use for topics from the twentieth century that require the researcher to delve into popular magazines of the day (including magazines such as *Time, Newsweek,* and *Life*). The *Readers' Guide* has made the transition from print to the electronic *Readers' Guide Retrospective,* covering 1890 through 1982. *Readers' Guide Retrospective* provides few direct links to full text but is open-URL compliant and will work with link resolvers. Abstracting is practically nonexistent, as *Readers' Guide Retrospective* is little more than an electronic copy of the print version.

An enormous advantage to historians and students today is the amount of early printed material being digitized and made more widely available to researchers. In the twentieth century, scholars needing to consult some of the earliest printed works in English had to travel to the repositories owning them, or use microform materials (which often suffered from inconsistent reproduction quality and other problems). In the last few years, important collections of early printed materials have been digitized by ProQuest/Chadwyck-Healey, Readex/NewsBank, and GaleGroup. Some key Web-based historical collections are:

- *American Periodical Series* (*APS*). ProQuest. www.proquest.com/.
- *Early American Imprints* (*EAI*; Parts I and II). Readex. www.readex.com/.
- *Early American Newspapers* (*EAN*). Readex. www.readex.com/.
- *Early English Books Online* (*EEBO*). Chadwyck-Healey. http://eebo.chadwyck.com/.
- *Eighteenth Century Collections Online* (*ECCO*). Gale Group. www.galegroup.com/.
- *Harpweek.* John Adler. www.harpweek.com/.

Most of these Web-based collections were created by digitizing large print backfiles or existing microform masters.[1] Each publisher has its own search interface, and some have more powerful indexing than others. Researchers who use these products should realize that both language usage and printing have changed over time. Most publishers use optical character recognition (OCR) when digitizing these resources. However, because of the limitations of OCR and the nonstandard print characters, for example, using an *f*-shaped character for an *s* or a double *v* for *w*, most online vendors have reviewed and manually corrected the text to remove scanning errors. This extra labor adds to the high cost of these resources. Online Help can alert users to these eccentricities, but one must be aware that the problem exists. Also, the English language has changed over time and terms or concepts used in centuries past, even for common ideas or nouns, can frequently be completely foreign to modern readers.

Newspapers

Looking at an old newspaper is akin to time travel. Newspapers can lead researchers to valuable information for those interested in American history–related topics including women's portrayal in advertising, editorials commenting on political scandals of the day, recommended travel locations, the end of wartime rationing, and more. Newspapers portray history-making events as current events and are excellent resources to learn the tenor of the times.

The *Times* of London has a printed index going back to the 1780s, and the *New York Times* printed index goes back to the 1850s, but most indexes for the largest U.S. newspapers only cover the late twentieth century. A workaround is to suggest that students use the index for a major newspaper such as the *New York Times*, and then read smaller regional papers near the date the story ran in the *Times* to see if the small papers published stories on a desired topic either before or after the story's appearance in the *Times*. This is not a perfect solution, but in the case of major events, it can be better than spending hours aimlessly scrolling through reels of microfilms. The printed index for most newspapers also only covers news stories, so advertisements and most opinion pieces are not indexed. There are also indexes to cover microfilmed sets of early newspapers. The quality of these indexes varies greatly and some are quite arcane, especially indexes of microfilmed collections containing many different titles. Before walking into the classroom to discuss these collections, you should learn the layout of each pertinent index and how its citations refer to microfilm reel numbers. Although full-text backfiles of more major papers are becoming available on the Web from commercial vendors, these resources are very expensive and may be beyond the means of many otherwise well-equipped libraries. Another caveat to using these electronic newspapers is to what extent they are affected by the *New York Times Co. v. Tasini* case, which prevented certain bylined articles from being included in electronic databases. As time passes, this will be less of an issue, but it pays to be aware that electronic versions are not always as complete as a microfilm edition.

Government Publications

Government publications are excellent resources for primary research. Contrary to popular belief among librarians, local, state, and national government materials have much broader appeal than to just those interested in politics.

State agricultural extension agency reports on nutrition from the 1920s, U.S. Department of Labor reports on women working in the factories during World War II, and NASA reports on the development of the Apollo Space Program or subsidiary products such as Velcro are only three examples of government materials of interest to historical researchers in something other than politics and legislative affairs. A history class on the U.S. Supreme Court and constitutional interpretation would make extensive use of government publications. Depending on students' needs, you should be prepared to discuss how to find these materials in libraries and on the Web.

Finding government publications can be challenging and is covered in more detail in Chapter 17, but here I will discuss some resources pertinent to historical research. The *Monthly Catalog of U.S. Government Publications* is the main bibliography of materials published by the U.S. Government Printing Office (GPO). Many libraries participating in the U.S. Federal Depository Library Program (FDLP) have loaded MARC records from the *Monthly Catalog* into their online catalogs. However, most of these bibliographic records only date back to materials published since mid-1976. For records prior to that, a print version of the index must be used. Further, most agencies of the federal government publish some of their own materials independently and do not use the GPO. Since these fugitive items do not appear in the *Monthly Catalog*, other resources, such as the *Guide to U.S. Government Publications* (2005), which is a continuation of John Andriot's *Guide to U.S. Government Serials and Periodicals*, must be used.

Because participation in the FDLP is limited, not every library has extensive collections of government publications. In such cases, interlibrary loan can save the day. Also, the U.S. government is making more material freely available on the Web. Many publications are on the GPO Access Web site (www.gpoaccess .gov), while other material is located on the publishing agencies' Web sites. Since the 1970s, Readex/Newsbank and Congressional Information Service (now part of LexisNexis) have published extensive retrospective and current indexes and microform collections of U.S., United Nations, foreign national, and international publications. These services are commercially available. Both companies have made their indexes available on the Web, along with an increasing amount of content, comprised of scanned documents. The microfiche and digital *U.S. Serial Set* (from both Readex and LexisNexis) and other congressional collections (from LexisNexis) are often overlooked but contain rich troves of information on a wide variety of topics. The GPO is currently planning a Web-based National Bibliography, encompassing all depository and fugitive federal government publications issued from 1790 to the present, with hyperlinks to secure, authenticated electronic versions. Such a tool will hold immense benefits for all researchers of U.S. history.

State government publications are often available in libraries of the host state through a depository network mirroring that of the FDLP. State libraries often administer these programs, distributing publications to public and academic libraries within the state's boundaries. The extent of bibliographic access varies, but state library catalogs and *WorldCat* are good online sources for identifying state government publications. Also, research staff of state historical societies and government documents librarians can help researchers find these publications. Local government publications, including city council minutes, budgets, municipal codes, and special reports, are notoriously difficult to find, but they are included sporadically in state depository collections and in libraries whose staff have obtained copies from the issuing offices.

The World Wide Web

Besides the U.S. government, many other entities are making primary source material freely available on the Web. Some of these entities are sponsored by the federal government, while others are hosted by universities. Still other sources are being provided by individuals. Some collections of primary source material on the Web include:

- *American Memory*. http://memory.loc.gov/ammem. A digital museum from the collections of the Library of Congress, including photographs, sound recordings, motion pictures, and manuscripts.
- The British Library. www.bl.uk/collections/treasures/digitisation1.html. The British Library has several digitization projects including *The Lindisfarne Gospels*, an eighth-century illuminated manuscript, and selections from Leonardo da Vinci's notebooks.
- *Making of America*. http://www.hti.umich.edu/m/moagrp. A joint project between the University of Michigan and Cornell University to digitize full-text nineteenth-century books and periodicals.

Dennis A. Trinkle and Scott A. Merriman have edited a useful guide to historical information and sources on the Web, titled *History Highway 3.0: A Guide to Internet Resources*. Although it is already dated, this book gives excellent topical overviews and will help you identify and evaluate history-related sites. In 2003, the ALA Reference and User Services Association's (RUSA) History Section created an excellent Web site to assist librarians and instructors to teach students how to find and use primary source materials on the Web. This site defines primary sources, gives suggestions for finding primary sources on the Web, suggests quality sites, and (most importantly) emphasizes the need to carefully evaluate any information found on a Web site (ALA, 2003). This RUSA Web site is an excellent starting point for librarians preparing an instructional session for history students.

Evaluating Primary Sources

Historical research requires scholars to find and use primary sources but it is also imperative for scholars to demonstrate that they have critically examined the sources at hand and have tested them for relevance and legitimacy. Students will need to show their instructors that they have thought deeply and critically about what their sources reveal and what they do not. While the instructor may address evaluation of sources in another class period or with students individually, it never hurts for you to reinforce the need to rigorously analyze and evaluate all sources used for research.

Students should examine any primary source with the following criteria in mind. These considerations apply equally to print and online information:

- *Authorship.* Who is the author or creator of the document? Was this person present at the time of the event or otherwise involved? What qualifications permit this person to speak or write with authority? An example might be a letter written by a frontline soldier to those he left at home. He can speak with authority about camp life and what he witnessed on the battlefield. He is less likely, however, to have intimate knowledge of strategy and the machinations of his commanders (unless, perhaps, he is an aide-de-camp to a senior staff officer).

- *Audience.* Who is the intended audience? Was the document a letter intended only for the person to whom it was sent? Did its author intend to publish or otherwise disseminate it? Might the author have written some things for a particular audience that would never have been shared with another? In keeping with our lonely soldier, we may imagine that there are anecdotes he might not relate to the female members of his family or sweetheart that he would have fewer qualms describing to his father or brothers, such as the carousing, gambling, and seedier aspects of life at the front.

- *Rationale.* Why did the author create the document? Could there be any ulterior motives? Was our soldier simply informing his loved ones that he was still alive? Does he have future political ambitions that might cause him to embellish certain heroic deeds and cover up less noble acts?

- *Bias.* It is almost impossible to find anyone who has no biases. The question is how an author's bias influences what he or she wrote. How does our soldier view his commanders, his brothers-in-arms, members of other ethnic groups, or the opposite sex? Historians must address the question of bias in the sources both carefully and thoroughly.

You should also know that primary sources are rarely "politically correct." Students may not be prepared for this, so you or the instructor may wish to warn them that they may encounter sentiments, whether subtly implied or overt, that from the perspective of today's mores are considered objectionable or even unacceptable. This does not necessarily invalidate the source; indeed, depending on the topic, it makes the source more important. Racist or sexist ideas do not make these original sources illegitimate, but rather reinforce the need to study and rise above outdated and oppressive notions. While a newspaper critical of Radical Reconstruction and published by the local Ku Klux Klan leader may not accurately portray what the Radicals actually did, it would be an excellent source to gauge the reaction of a select population in the community (Kitchens, 2001).

It is also important for budding historians to realize that "journalistic objectivity" is a very recent concept. Newspapers have a long history of biased reporting. In some cases, the newspaper was the formal mouthpiece of a particular political party. Well into the twentieth century, stories appearing in American newspapers and magazines usually favored the political party or faction to which the editor or publisher belonged.

With more representations of primary sources and historical commentary appearing on the Web, instruction librarians should teach students to ask similar tough questions of any history-related sites found on the Internet. The main lesson students should learn about using primary source material from the Web or any other source is to carefully evaluate what they find and avoid pseudo-historical sites based on political or personal agendas rather than scholarship. Students should examine historical sites on the Web with a keen eye to the following:

- Qualifications and bias of the site's creator, for example, hate groups whose advocacy masquerades as scholarship.
- Predominant advertising on Web sites and its possible influence.
- Quality and extent of any primary source documents that are reproduced (e.g., students should be wary of the site that lists only seven amendments of the U.S. Constitution's Bill of Rights).
- The site's intended audience and users, for example, K–12 students, scholars, or partisan sympathizers.
- When the site was the last updated.
- Availability: Is this a unique document, or is it commonly reproduced in print format? Instructors and scholars often prefer that their students use fixed, tangible publications (ALA, 2003).

Finally, students must learn that there is a difference between using licensed Web-based library resources and simply casting their lots with the random results of Internet search engines. In your sessions, emphasize the quality, provenance, and editorial oversight related to licensed resources such as *Early English Books Online* (*EEBO*) and digital editions of the *U.S. Serial Set*.

Secondary Sources

Secondary information sources, for historians, are those created after an event or period in question, usually by scholars, often decades or centuries afterward. Books, scholarly journal articles, and book reviews are all important secondary sources for historians. The primary method of scholarly communication for historians is the scholarly monograph, or book. A historical monograph is the culmination of years spent reading, researching in the field, plowing through musty tomes, and poring over dusty, fragile manuscripts. In most research universities, publishing a monograph is usually one of the most important requirements for tenure and promotion. Scholarly articles are a means by which new ideas (which may be the basis of a future monograph) are initially presented to one's peers for comment and criticism. Book reviews are also important to inform historians of work done by peers. For students in history, secondary sources can help put facts and primary sources in proper context. Readers can follow citations found in secondary sources in order to find more primary sources. Therefore, library instruction sessions must include information on finding these materials in the local library (Dalton and Charnigo, 2004).

Catalogs

Researchers find secondary sources using the same library resources as for primary sources, especially in catalogs and indexes. Not every history assignment requires the use of primary sources, and in some instances students will need only secondary sources. As with primary sources, you should introduce the students to the local catalog first, since it is the best single inventory of what your library owns. For some topics, the online catalog's hyperlinked LC subject headings provide the best way to find relevant materials. One example involves searching for information on the Mexican-American War. The LC subject heading for this conflict is Mexican War, 1846–1848. Demonstrating the local catalog is also an excellent opportunity to explain the call number system the library uses as well as where the books are located in the campus libraries. As you would when showing how to find primary sources, demonstrate *WorldCat* as well as the Center for Research Libraries (CRL) or other shared catalogs, such as OhioLINK, the University of California's Melvyl, or Link+.

Indexes and Databases

ESSENTIAL SOURCES. Following are core bibliographic tools for finding historical articles, books, and related sources.

- *America: History and Life* (AHL) and *Historical Abstracts* (HA). ABC-Clio. http://serials.abc-clio.com. These companion databases cover over 2,000 scholarly and professional journals in history and related disciplines from all over the globe. *AHL* indexes literature on North American (U.S. and Canadian) topics from prehistory to the present, including articles, book reviews, dissertations, collections, and media reviews. *HA* indexes articles, books (but not reviews), collections, and dissertations on topics going back to 1450 on every part of the world except the United States and Canada. Both databases include article abstracts, work with link resolvers, and provide direct links to *JSTOR*, *Project MUSE*, History Cooperative, H-Net, Oxford University Press online journals, Taylor and Francis journals, Swets Blackwell, ingenta, and a number of free electronic journals. An option on the navigation menu in both databases allows searchers to toggle back and forth between *AHL* and *HA*.
- *International Medieval Bibliography* (IMB). Brepolis. www.brepolis.net. Beginning in 1967, the *IMB* indexes scholarly literature related to late-classical and medieval studies (ca. 400–1500 C.E.) from journals published in thirty languages. *IMB* is available either in print or online.
- *Iter*. Renaissance Society of America. www.itergateway.org. *Iter* indexes

materials published since the 1780s. It also includes other resources, such as a directory of Renaissance Society members.

Secondary Literature from Other Disciplines. Scholars in other disciplines often employ historical methods or examine time periods long past. Further, as the field of history has become increasingly interdisciplinary, literature from other social science, humanities, and scientific fields offer fresh insights of interest to historians and their students. The following selected list of related indexes or databases covers literature in fields other than mainstream history.

- *Bibliography of Asian Studies.* Association of Asian Studies and the University of Michigan. http://ets.umdl.umich.edu/b/bas/.
- *Chicano Database.* RLG. www.rlg.org/.
- *Gender Studies Database.* Biblioline/NISC. www.nisc.com/.
- *Hispanic American Periodicals Index.* UCLA Latin American Center. http://hapi.gseis.ucla.edu/.
- *Index Islamicus.* CSA. www.csa.com/.
- *The Kaiser Index to Black Resources, 1948–1986.* 1992. Brooklyn, NY: Carlson Pub. Available in print only.

Book Reviews. Because the monograph is the primary vehicle for scholarly communication among historians, book reviews in scholarly and professional journals are of great interest. Historians use book reviews to comment publicly on the quality of research done by their peers and consider writing reviews to be a valuable service to the profession. Unlike many disciplines in which material over five years old is considered obsolete and useless, the definitive study on a historical topic may be over thirty years old. Books by Marc Bloch and C. Vann Woodward are still considered canon by many historians decades after the works were first published. Keep this in mind when recommending review sources to students.

Frequently, instructors require students to read books and then write in-depth analyses and critiques that resemble the scholarly reviews that historians write for publication. You should be prepared to teach students how to find history-related reviews. In addition to *America: History and Life*, several resources specialize primarily in book reviews or index reviews:

- *Book Review Digest.* H. W. Wilson. Available in print or online at www .hwwilson.com.
- *Book Review Index.* Gale. Available in print or online at http://infotrac.gale group.com.
- *Humanities Index.* H. W. Wilson. Available in print or online at www.hwwilson .com.
- *Reviews in American History.* Johns Hopkins University Press. A journal with current articles available through *Project MUSE*: http://muse.jhu.edu/journals/ reviews_in_american_history and archived on *JSTOR* at www.jstor.org.

- *Social Sciences Index.* H. W. Wilson. Available in print or online at www .hwwilson.com.
- *Web of Science.* Thomson/ISI. Includes the *Social Sciences Citation Index* and the *Arts & Humanities Citation Index* at www.thomsonisi.com.

ELECTRONIC JOURNAL AGGREGATORS. The three e-journal resources listed below cover many historical periodicals. Each database works with link resolvers, which will allow your library users to retrieve articles from them when they find a citation in other online services configured to work with a resolver.

- *The History Cooperative.* www.historycooperative.org. *The History Cooperative* is a joint project between the two leading professional associations in history (the American Historical Association and the Organization of American Historians) and the University of Illinois Press to make available to members the full text of some leading journals in the field. There is some overlap among titles in *JSTOR* and *The History Cooperative*, but it is limited. Only the most recent issues of a title will be available through the cooperative. The database includes links to *JSTOR* for participating journals.
- *JSTOR.* www.jstor.org. The mission of *JSTOR* is to provide the full text of the top-tier journals in history as well as other arts and sciences starting with each journal's first issue. *JSTOR* covers only a few dozen history journals (whereas *America: History and Life* indexes over 2,000), and the most recent issues are not available from *JSTOR* (typically, the last 3–7 years). *JSTOR* can be searched like any other database, or a user can browse individual titles and issues. Since *JSTOR* attempts to scan complete issues, all materials, from articles to book reviews to op-ed pieces, are available.
- *Project MUSE.* http://muse.jhu.edu. *MUSE* began as a project of the Johns Hopkins University Press but quickly expanded to other scholarly publishers. It contains the full text of articles and other select features of participating titles. Coverage dates vary by title. For some, coverage begins in 1995, while for other titles, it may not be until 1999. Some presses have pulled out of *Project MUSE*, so their titles are no longer available.

What to Teach

In many ways, searching for history-related materials is not so different from searching for materials in other disciplines. History tends to have fewer Web-based indexes and reference tools than do science disciplines, but this is changing. Do not neglect print resources just to show off the latest electronic resource, which may be of marginal relevance to a given class. But do show students that computers take search strings very literally. A search on the phrase *civil war*, without further definition, brings up material on the American Civil War, the Spanish Civil War, the English Civil War, and a host of Third World conflicts in the late

---

Figure 10-1   Library Catalog Tutorial for History Instruction

Library Catalog—Basic Searching:

- Perform a Subject search in the Library Catalog
- Choose a specific location if desired (such as Main Library or Special Collections)

Library Catalog—Advanced Searching:

Go to the Advanced Search page:

- Enter words related to your research topic
- Choose a specific location
- Choose a Format (e.g., Book, Film, or Video)
- Set a date range (this refers to the year of publication)
- Click the Search button

Using [insert the name of your regional catalog here] and Interlibrary loan:

If you do not find the book or other information you need in the Library Catalog or in our online databases, you may request materials not owned by the university library.

- From the Library Catalog, click the [regional catalog] button
- Items you request from [regional catalog] usually arrive in four working days
- For materials not available through [regional catalog], click on the Interlibrary Loan link on the library home page

Or:

- From an **SFX Services** window, click on the link Request Item via *Document Delivery*

---

twentieth century. Teach students the basics of Boolean logic and nested searching if local systems support such tools. Controlled vocabulary allows users to search more precisely, so show students how it works in your catalog and licensed databases. To illustrate the use of controlled vocabulary, Figures 10-1 and 10-2 are user guides for an online library catalog and ABC-Clio's historical databases, respectively.

After you give these guides (or some that are similar) to students, demonstrate the search concepts. The following are sample searches for information on two topics. In each example I show the number of references retrieved for illustrative purposes only.

Topic 1: Glass in Venice (How it helped generate wealth and how glass making techniques were kept secret)

Library Catalog:

Keyword:	Glass and Venice (yields 33 matches)
LCSH:	Glass—History (yields 2 matches)
	Venice—Art (choose from subject subdivisions)

Figure 10-2   Tutorial on Advanced Searching in *America: History and Life* and *Historical Abstracts*

History Databases: Finding Secondary Sources

Choose one of these two databases:

America: History and Life (for historical works on North America)
or
Historical Abstracts (for historical works covering any time period from 1450 to the present, about areas other than North America)

1.   Go to the Advanced Search page.

2.   Click on the icon next to the Subject Terms field.
              Search the terms and select those related to your topic.

3.   Further limit your search in other ways, including:

                    Language
                    Time Period
                    (remember to click on the magnifying glass icon by each field)

4.   Click the Search button.

5.   Review your results.

6.   Click on the ⊘**Find It** button or full-text links where available.

              ⊘**Find It** will search the UNR Library Catalog or allow you to make an interlibrary loan request.

7.   Check the citations of interest, then click on Output Options to print or e-mail them.

Historical Abstracts:

Terms from
Subject Index: | Glass and Glassmaking. | and | Venice. | (yields 7 citations, some including link resolvers)

Topic 2: Arab-Israeli Conflict of 1967

Library Catalog:

Keyword: Arab-Israeli conflict 1967 (yields 124 matches)
LCSH: Arab-Israeli conflict (yields 207 matches; explore subdivisions and other subject headings)

Historical Abstracts:

Terms from
Subject Index: | Arab-Israeli Conflict. |
Language: | English | (yields 495 citations; check abstracts and subject
                    terms in records for additional terms of interest, then use
                    to narrow the search)

Historians are also notorious for simply browsing the stacks and trusting serendipity to find material. While this is not very efficient, it can turn up some interesting and pertinent information. Suggest to students that they expand their browsing range beyond the LC call numbers C, D, E, and F, in order to find other relevant sources. Depending on the topic, pertinent materials could be found in many other areas of the LC classification schedule (Dalton and Charnigo, 2004; Delgadillo and Lynch, 1999; Kitchens et al., 2002). Aside from the mechanical aspects of searching, tell students that language changes over time and ideas that are common to us could have been revolutionary, heretical, or simply missing from earlier lexicons.

If you have sufficient preparation time, prepare handouts and guides with lists of sources. Students can carry handouts with them and use them when they get around to working on their assignments. This can be especially welcome to students in sessions early in the morning or just after lunch, who may become drowsy during a presentation.

Follow Through: What to Do after an Instruction Session

After an initial instruction session (or your only session, in the case of "one-shots"), you still have instruction-related work to do. History research is not a linear process, where one begins with A and proceeds in a straight line to the logical conclusion of Z. Students will often run into difficulties or questions as the sources they discover open new avenues of inquiry. Instruction librarians should work in close conjunction with history subject specialists and communicate adequately with the frontline service points to give them the "heads up" that a class needing particular resources (e.g., reference desk, reserves, circulation, microforms, computer lab, interlibrary loan) may be visiting soon. Some librarians create Web pages for individual classes with lists of resources tailored primarily for the needs of the class. Course-related pages can be very useful if you have the time to build them, since students can refer to them after your class session. However, it may be more efficient for you to develop a more general history-related Web page with annotated lists of many resources that could appeal to many different historical interests (Texas A&M University Libraries, 2005).

Conclusion: Lessons for a Lifetime

Because the discipline of history is so library-dependent, advances in information access have made these exciting times for both historians and librarians.

The juggernaut of the digital information revolution will have profound effects on how future historians and their students do their work. Librarians have an educational role to play in helping these patrons find and use information, whether that information resides in libraries or elsewhere. You should work closely with course instructors to ensure that what they teach works with their assignments and approach. Whether you provide instruction as a one-shot or over the course of an entire semester, whether lecture style or with more active, hands-on assignments, encourage students to be flexible and creative and to look beyond the obvious. This can mean thinking of synonyms; broader, narrower, and related words; and different forms of proper nouns. Sometimes looking beyond the obvious means digging into more obscure print resources, including indexes and bibliographies as well as primary and secondary sources, and forgoing the easy method of trying to let the computer find everything—because it will not. On the other hand, for libraries fortunate enough to have a wide selection of electronic resources, students should be taught how to use them to their maximum advantage. Teach students to "cast their nets far and wide" and gather a wide variety of sources, both tangible and electronic. Also help them to be discriminating about all information they use. Practicing these critical habits of mind will serve students well, not only in their academic careers, but throughout life.

Note

1. *EEBO* was created from microfilm copies of Pollard and Redgrave's *Short Title Catalog, 1475–1640* and Wing's *Short Title Catalog, 1641–1700* and the Thomason Tracts. These are all classic early printed works in the English language. *ECCO* is a continuation of the *English Short Title Catalog* containing works published from 1701 to 1800. *EAI*, sort of an American version of the *Short Title Catalogs*, contained material published in North America between 1639 and 1800. Charles Evans initially compiled these works in his *American Bibliography*. Later, materials up to 1819 were added by Ralph Shaw and Richard Shoemaker. *EAN* is a collection based on *Clarence Brigham's History and Bibliography of American Newspapers, 1690–1820*, but carrying on further into the nineteenth century. *APS* is a collection of popular and professional periodicals from 1741 to 1900. Most of these resources were created by digitizing existing collections of microtext materials. The high costs of these collections have given many libraries pause before spending large amounts of money to duplicate items already in their collections.

Bibliography

American Library Association (ALA). 2003. RUSA History Section, Instruction and Research Services Committee. *Using Primary Sources on the Web*. www.lib.washington.edu/subject/History/RUSA/ (accessed April 20, 2005).

Dalton, M. S., and L. Charnigo. 2004. "Historians and Their Information Sources." *College and Research Libraries* 65: 400–425.

Delgadillo, R., and B. P. Lynch. 1999. "Future Historians: Their Quest for Information." *College and Research Libraries* 60: 245–259.

Guide to U.S. Government Publications. 2005. Farmington Hills, MI: Gale Group.

Iggers, G. G. 1993. "Historical Methodologies and Research." In *Teaching Bibliographic Skills in History: A Sourcebook for Historians and Librarians*, pp. 3–24, edited by C. A. D'Aniello. Westport, CT: Greenwood Press.

Kitchens, J. D. 2001. "Practical Help for History Instruction: Making the One-Shot Count." *Research Strategies* 18: 63–73.

Kitchens, J. D., P. A. Mosley, J. C. Marner, and A. L. Highsmith. 2002. "Defining History for Library Statistics: Or, Everything Has a History." *Journal of Academic Librarianship* 28: 211–223.

Novick, P. 1988. *That Noble Dream: The "Objectivity Question" and the American Historical Profession*. Cambridge, UK: Cambridge University Press.

Ritter, H. 1993. "History and Interdisciplinary History." In *Teaching Bibliographic Skills in History: A Sourcebook for Historians and Librarians*, pp. 25–47, edited by C. A. D'Aniello. Westport, CT: Greenwood Press.

Stearns, P. N. 1998. "Why Study History?" The American Historical Association. www.historians.org/pubs/Free/WhyStudyHistory.htm (accessed February 15, 2005).

Texas A&M University Libraries. 2005. History. Indexes and Databases; Related Links; Selected Journals; History 481: Slavery in World History. http://library.tamu.edu (accessed October 6, 2005).

Trinkle, D., and S. Merriman. 2002. *History Highway 3.0: A Guide to Internet Resources*. Armonk, NY: M. E. Sharpe.

Winks, R. W. 1968. *The Historian as Detective: Essays on Evidence*. New York: Harper & Row.

11

Psychology

Nonny Schlotzhauer

Introduction

Like the literature of most academic subjects, psychology-related information has grown increasingly complex with the advent of electronic resources and the emergence of the Internet. Students are now confronted with an abundance of resources, and sifting through this information is a daunting task for all, from the novice researcher to the well-seasoned scholar. The role of the librarian has evolved from showing users how to find books and journals to one that emphasizes teaching critical thinking and the technical skills essential to navigate today's scholarly information environment. Today's dynamic climate offers tremendous opportunities for librarians to take advantage of these developments by fostering a deep knowledge of research skills for all students of psychology.

This chapter identifies the essential practices, resources, and outcomes of information literacy instruction in the field of psychology. Drawing extensively on my experiences at the University of Denver as well as the observations of others, what follow are guidelines, recommendations, and key elements for a successful approach to teaching library research skills in psychology and associated subjects.

The Diverse Field of Psychology

Psychology is a complex and multilayered discipline. According to the American Psychological Association (APA), the largest association of psychologists worldwide, psychology is defined as:

> [T]he study of mind and behavior. The discipline embraces all aspects of the human experience—from the functions of the brain to the actions of nations, from child development to care for the aged. In every conceivable setting from scientific research centers to mental health care services, the "understanding of behavior" is the enterprise of psychologists. (APA)

This points to a diverse area of study, made up of many subfields with multiple applications. Since its emergence in the late nineteenth century, psychology has continued to evolve and enlarge in scope, taking in more and more subjects that touch upon most facets of contemporary life. A quick look at related Library of Congress subject headings shows that psychology is not one field, but many. Among the various subjects under the domain of psychology are the following:

Applied Psychology
Cognitive Psychology
Developmental Psychology
Educational Psychology
Forensic Psychology
Health Psychology
Industrial or Organizational Psychology
Social Psychology

These are but a few of the broad subjects of concern to psychologists. Recent developments show an increased effort to understand the human experience in areas such as environmental psychology, cultural psychology, biological psychology, positive psychology, and religion and spirituality. Now increasingly interdisciplinary, psychology frequently crosses over into anthropology, communication, education, law, medicine, and technology. Librarians must have a firm grasp of psychology's scope and keep abreast of developments in order to teach students how to effectively utilize the library resources and to assist faculty and other researchers.

Scholarly Information Process in Psychology

As with other social science disciplines, psychology's cycle of information relies upon a broad communication network. Information in the realm of the social sciences is fairly ubiquitous, coming to us from everyday media such as daily newspapers and news programs. Reading the *New York Times*, *Time*, or *Newsweek*, one often finds articles about psychology or mental health. The public absorbs this information on a daily basis, oftentimes without being aware that a pertinent news story is part of an information cycle that includes research proposals, grants, articles, books, and possibly other media. While there are no indexing tools designed to track the appearance of scholarly ideas throughout all media, it is beneficial for students to know that there are always more substantial information sources behind science-related coverage in mainstream news.

The *Journal Citation Reports* (JCR), a bibliometric analysis of journals included in the ISI citation indexes and databases, is a great tool for showing one element of the research process (JCR is available in print format and as a component of the Web-based version of the citation indexes). The *JCR/Social Sciences Edition* includes a listing of psychology journals, encompassing psychiatry, applied psychology, clinical psychology, educational psychology, experimental psychology, mathematical psychology, multidisciplinary psychology, psychoanalysis, and social psychology. It ranks journals by the number of articles published each year and also ranks the number of times journals are cited in the current year. JCR calculates a journal's "impact factor," or how often it is used or cited in comparison to a set of peer publications. JCR may be a bit advanced for undergraduates, but graduate students and faculty are particularly keen to know this information.

Regardless of your students' class standing, it is important that they understand their role in the scholarly process. This may be hard for undergraduates to grasp. Their output, whether a class essay or a senior thesis, is part of the intellectual environment for their discipline. Honors theses, capstone assignments, and other student projects are increasingly displayed on the Internet for others to view.

Review of the Literature

A review of the literature on library instruction in psychology reveals a great deal of agreement about effective teaching techniques. For the most part, the literature here is post-1990, or published since the advent of the computerized library, although a few earlier contributions are included for their continued relevance. To a large extent this literature mirrors the general theory and philosophy of information literacy common in the field of librarianship. Indeed, a review of earlier literature on instruction in psychology shows that while the tools and resources may have changed, the general concepts are not altogether different (Sutton et al., 1995). Library and information literacy instruction is also affected by higher education's increased emphasis on accountability and assessment (Thaxton, 2002).

Literature on library and information literacy instruction in psychology echoes the guidelines set forth by the Association of College and Research Libraries (ACRL), which establish the core competencies as "identifying an information need, accessing needed information, evaluating, managing, and applying information, and understanding the legal, social, and ethical aspects of information use" (ACRL, 2003). More specifically, the literature appears to endorse the guidelines put forth by Joyce Merriam, Ross T. LaBaugh, and Nancy E. Butterfield, and adopted by the Education and Behavioral Sciences Section (EBSS) of ACRL, which suggest basic skills as well as strategies for implementing library instruction (ACRL/EBSS, 2002; Merriam, LaBaugh, and Butterfield, 1992).

A common theme is the important role of collaboration between librarians and teaching faculty (Hutchins and Sherman, 2001; Paglia and Donahue, 2003; Thaxton, Faccioli, and Mosby, 2004). Collaborating with faculty can certainly help establish library research skills as a critical component of their students' education. In Chapter 2 of this book, Jean Caspers offers detailed advice on collaborating with faculty. Getting buy-in from departments is not always easy, but a little persistence can lead to productive relationships that contribute solidly to the overall learning objectives of universities and colleges.

The integration of information literacy into the curriculum, whether general in nature or course specific, is an objective that shows increasing promise (Rockman, 2004). Again, with faculty-librarian cooperation as the key, student practice of pertinent knowledge and skills is beneficial for successful information literacy efforts. Timothy K. Daugherty and Elizabeth W. Carter demonstrate that such partnerships, with a focus on outcomes, can be an effective approach to library instruction (Daugherty and Carter, 1997; 1998).

Tutorials can contribute effectively to information literacy programs. Assessment efforts at the University of Denver show that basic skill components in library research tutorials are valuable when used to supplement the concepts that librarians demonstrate to classes. A similarly successful undertaking is discussed by Dorothy Persson and Carlette Washington-Hoagland, whose article on the use of a *PsycINFO* tutorial points to increased retention of knowledge among students in an undergraduate psychology course (Persson and Washington-Hoagland, 2004).

The University of Denver Experience

The University of Denver provides a good example of the diversity within the field of psychology. The University of Denver is a medium-sized university with approximately 9,500 students in its undergraduate and graduate programs. Total undergraduate enrollment is about 4,500, while graduate enrollment is roughly 5,000. Penrose Library is deeply involved in instructional activities, from coordinated efforts with the First-Year Experience program, a new "writing across the disciplines" initiative, traditional subject-specific sessions, and one-on-one consultation.

The university has both a Department of Psychology and a Graduate School of Professional Psychology, in addition to an educational psychology concentration within the College of Education and psychology-related programs at the Graduate School of Social Work. The Department of Psychology's program is designed to provide students with a broad foundation in both content and hands-on experience in professional and scientific psychology. Students are encouraged to take courses across a range of content areas of psychology, including cognitive, developmental, clinical, neuroscience, social, and quantitative approaches. Students may pursue a BA, BS, MA, or PhD. The Graduate School of Professional Psychology offers the Doctor of Psychology (PsyD), an MA in Forensic Psychology, and an MA in International Disaster Psychology. University faculty also conduct research in animal behavior, gerontology, psychiatry, psychometrics, and trauma.

What to Teach

All institutions of higher education are confronted with the challenge of incorporating technology into teaching. However, in the online environment, librarians must continue to stress the core foundations of library research. While computers and technology hold tremendous appeal for today's students, content is still king. Critical thinking, with analysis and evaluation, continues to be at the heart of rigorous research.

An effective instruction program takes into account the level of knowledge of students, from novice to advanced, and will build throughout their time on campus. As their research experience and knowledge of psychology increase over time, so too can the complexity of instruction. The following lists are recommended sequences for different levels of students.

For lower-level undergraduates:

- Library catalog
- Reference books in psychology and related social sciences
- Disciplinary databases, for example, *PsycINFO* or *PsycARTICLES*
- Aggregator databases, including *Academic Search Premier* and *Expanded Academic ASAP*

Upper-level undergraduates and graduate students:

- Databases with broad coverage and in related disciplines, including *Social Sciences Citation Index* (*Web of Science*), *ERIC*, *Medline*, and *Sociological Abstracts*
- Sources for psychological tests and measures
- Dissertations
- Professional information sources, including association Web sites

When demonstrating research strategies and search techniques, it helps to have examples prepared to show students. Instruction librarians always face time limitations, and having canned examples will help ensure a smooth session. It may be instructive to ask for suggestions from the class for topics. This gives the students an opportunity to participate and provides a lesson in formulating a search strategy together by asking the class for suggested keywords, alternative words, or truncation possibilities.

Always provide clearly defined steps for a search strategy; doing so will help students to navigate through the library resources. In addition, linking the steps of the search strategy with the appropriate resource will enhance their understanding of the overall process. Thus, at the initial stage of choosing or defining a topic, suggesting reference books can provide clarity and background information that the student may lack. Students on occasion pursue research on topics with which they are unfamiliar. Dictionaries, encyclopedias, or handbooks can present information succinctly without overwhelming them. From there, the next logical steps are to explore books and articles on the topic, along with any other resource that may cover the topic more in depth, ending with tips on evaluating the resources.

When searching the library catalog and databases, it is best to have topics that are relevant to the class, preferably concepts that students can identify with. For undergraduates, I like to use the topic of "body image," and for graduates, I may use "multicultural counseling" or "attachment behavior," psychology-related topics that are widely researched at the University of Denver. From there, the class can work together to brainstorm possible search strategies for the topic by employing the Boolean operators AND, OR, and NOT, as well as truncation examples. Following is an example of concept mapping, using the concept "body image."

To begin concept mapping on the topic "body image," first identify the general concepts associated with the topic and search on one or more as keywords, for example:

- eating disorders
- anorexia nervosa
- bulimia

Point out elements of catalog or database records. Examining keywords, descriptors, and subject headings demonstrates to the student the different ways that researchers or indexers refer to a topic. For books, call students' attention to the following:

- tables of contents
- subject headings

In periodical databases, call students' attention to:

- descriptors
- words in abstracts

Next, narrow the search by focusing upon a specific population, such as:

- males
- females
- college students
- athletes

Finally, narrow the topic of your search. For example, search for information on the effects of:

- advertising
- mass media
- peer pressure

Figure 11-1 is a library catalog tutorial on the University of Denver's Penrose Library Web site that is used for group instruction. It shows concepts mapping for "attachment behavior" followed by some practical search strategies.

University of Denver
Penrose Library

Finding Books

First, select a topic

Example: **attachment behavior**

- There are many issues surrounding this topic
  – let's think of some.
- Next, we'll choose an issue or aspect to explore.

Figure 11-1   Library Catalog Tutorial in Psychology

Some issues surrounding our topic of attachment include:

- adults
- children or infants
- dependency
- family
- gender
- love

Let's focus on the subtopic
adult attachment

Now, let's look for books!

- Where do we start?

  - Start at the DU Penrose Library homepage, of course.
  - Let's go!

Figure 11-1 (*continued*)

Go to www.penlib.du.edu

Select PEAK:
The Library
Catalog

UNIVERSITY OF DENVER
PENROSE LIBRARY

PEAK Quick Search
Keyword

Go

Quick Links

View your account or
renew books on My PEAK

Ask a reference question

Search Prospector

Request items through
Interlibrary Loan

Finding What You Need / Services / A...   ...'s New

Finding What You Need
PEAK: The Library Catalog
Database & Article Search
Prospector
University of Denver Law Library
Other Libraries
Course Reserves
FAQ's
Research Guides
Help with Research

About the Library
Libraries, Collections, & Archives
Campus Maps & Parking

Services
Borrowing & Lending
Reference & Consultation
Library Instruction
Computers in the Library
Interlibrary Loan
Copy Services
Faculty Guide to Reserves
Cherrington Scholars Library Gateway

What's New
Featured Collection
Alerts & Announcements

Go to the catalog at www.penlib.du.edu/findit/peak/

We will perform 2 different kinds of searches:

- A simple search using **Boolean** (AND)

- An advanced search using **Boolean** and **Truncation**

Figure 11-1 (*continued*)

Boolean operators allow keywords to be combined:

- The word **AND** will narrow your search to retrieve records containing **all of your search terms**.
- The word **OR** broadens your search results to retrieve records containing **any of your search terms**.

A simple search [adult AND attachment] yields 47 entries

Figure 11-1   (*continued*)

Truncation

- With truncation, you omit or delete part of your search term or statement.

- Truncate by placing an asterisk (*) at the end of your root word. This will retrieve the root word and all of its variant endings.

- For example, *adopt** will retrieve *adopt, adopted, adoption*, etc.

A search using Boolean and truncation [adult* AND attachment] yields more entries: 70!

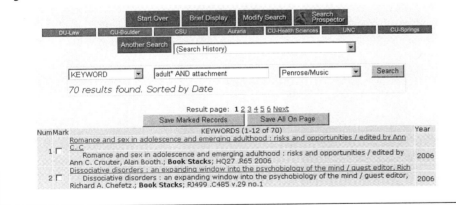

Figure 11-1 (*continued*)

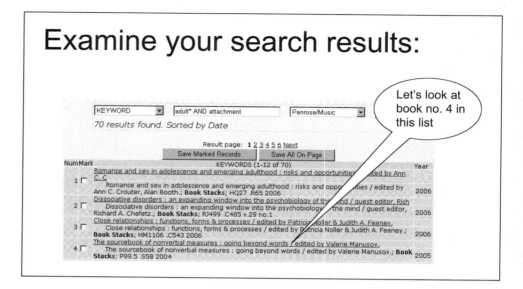

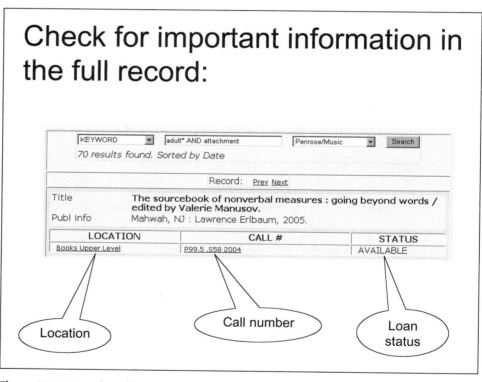

Figure 11-1   (*continued*)

Psychological Tests and Measurements

Information about psychological tests and other types of measures is available in a wide range of sources and therefore requires special attention. Teaching about tests and measurement instruments can be a daunting task, especially if your library does not have a test collection. In addition to *Mental Measurements Yearbook*, several other resources can be used to locate test information (a more complete list is included in the following section on psychology resources). Anne Cerstvik Nolan and Marilyn P. Whitmore provide a good overview on incorporating information about tests and measurement instruments in instruction (Nolan and Whitmore, 1992). A technique that I find successful is to assign a particular psychological test to a student (or group for large classes) and have the student (or group) find reviews or critiques that speak to the tests' validity. In some cases, students may be interested in trying to acquire a test. In those instances, librarians should explain to students that access to tests is limited, and in accordance with APA guidelines, tests are tightly controlled and may not be circulated, lent through interlibrary loan, photocopied, or administered. In many cases, students will have to settle for scholarly discussions of a desired test, which they can often locate via the *Mental Measurements Yearbook*, *Health and Psychosocial Instruments* (*HaPI*), and other resources listed in the section of this chapter on primary databases.

Selected Resources for Psychology

The following is a list of selected resources in psychology that you can introduce during instruction sessions. The list includes databases, print reference sources, free Web sites, and subscription databases. It also includes two general handbooks designed for students on various approaches to research in psychology and a professional journal for social science librarians. You can consult the handbooks and journal to gain a better understanding of psychology, to prepare to work as a liaison to a psychology department and provide library and information literacy instruction in the subject.

Primary Databases

- *Health and Psychosocial Instruments* (*HaPI*). www.ovid.com. 1985–present. Norwood, MA: Ovid Technologies. Produced by the Behavioral Measurement Database Services, *HaPI* indexes and abstracts measurement instruments (i.e., questionnaires, interview schedules, checklists, index measures, coding schemes and manuals, rating scales, projective techniques, vignettes and scenarios, tests) in the health fields, psychosocial sciences, organizational behavior, and library and information science.
- *Mental Measurements Yearbook*. www.unl.edu/buros. 1985–present. Lincoln: Buros Institute of Mental Measurements, University of Nebraska. *Mental Measurements Yearbook* (MMY) includes information on commercially available tests, including reviews, descriptive information, and reviewer references. The

electronic version begins with the 9th edition (1985). See the entry for *MMY* under "Print Resources" for more information.

- *PILOTS Database*. www.ncptsd.org/pilots. 1990?–present. White River Junction, VT: National Center for Post-Traumatic Stress Disorder. This database is an electronic index to the worldwide literature on post-traumatic stress disorder (PTSD) and other mental-health consequences of exposure to traumatic events. It is available free of charge to the public on computer systems maintained by Dartmouth College.

- *PsycARTICLES*. www.apa.org. 1985–present. Washington, DC: American Psychological Association. A database of full-text articles from journals published by the APA, the APA Educational Publishing Foundation, the Canadian Psychological Association, and Hogrefe & Huber. Overall, it contains fifty-three journals dating as far back as 1985.

- *PsycEXTRA*. www.apa.org. 1872–present. Washington, DC: American Psychological Association. A relatively new product from APA, it is a database of grey literature, intended to be a companion to *PsycINFO*. Most of the coverage is material written for professionals and disseminated outside peer-reviewed journals. Documents include newsletters, magazines, newspapers, technical and annual reports, government reports, consumer brochures, and more. This database includes abstracts and citations plus full text for a major portion of the records.

- *PsycINFO*. www.apa.org. 1840–present. Washington, DC: American Psychological Association. This is the preeminent database for psychological literature. It is the electronic version of *Psychological Abstracts*. It covers nearly 2,000 journals, 98 percent of which are peer reviewed, books, and dissertations. It is international in scope, covering publications from fifty countries and in twenty-five languages. The electronic version extends back to 1840, including the *Harvard Book List* (1840–1971), *Classic Books in Psychology of the 20th Century*, the *Psychological Index* (1894–1935), and *Psychological Bulletin* (1921–1926).

Interdisciplinary or General Databases Pertinent to Psychology

Multisubject databases are often good starting points for research, especially for undergraduates. Databases such as EBSCO's *Academic Search Elite* and *Academic Search Premier* and Gale's *Expanded Academic ASAP* provide a mix of scholarly journals, including many in the area of psychology, along with general interest magazines.

- *Academic Search Premier*. www.ebsco.com. 1975–present. Ipswich, MA: EBSCO. Contains indexing for over 8,000 publications, with full text for more than 4,650 of those titles. Coverage in psychology and the social sciences is quite strong. Searchable cited references are provided for more than 1,000 titles.

- *Applied Social Sciences Index and Abstracts (ASSIA)*. www.csa.com. 1987–present. Bethesda, MD: Cambridge Scientific Abstracts. An indexing and abstracting source, covering health, social services, psychology, sociology, economics, politics, race relations, and education. Updated monthly, *ASSIA* provides a comprehensive source of social science and health information for both practitioners and scholars.

- *Digital Dissertations.* www.umi.com. 1861–present. Ann Arbor: University Microfilms (UMI). The electronic version of *Dissertation Abstracts*, this database cites U.S. dissertations and some master's theses. Abstracts are available starting in 1980, with twenty-four page previews free to subscribers, beginning in 1997.

- *ERIC.* www.eric.ed.gov. 1966–present. Washington, DC: Office of Educational Research and Improvement, U.S. Department of Education: Educational Resources Information Center. *ERIC* is the world's premier database of journal and nonjournal education literature, encompassing two print sources, *Current Index to Journals in Education* (*CIJE*) and the index to "unpublished" items, *Resources in Education* (*RIE*), which includes items such as conference papers, technical reports, some doctoral dissertations, monographs, government reports, and more. More than 107,000 full-text nonjournal documents (issued 1993–2004), previously issued in microfiche and available through fee-based services only, are now freely available online in a growing database.

- *Expanded Academic ASAP.* www.gale.com. 1980–present. Farmington Hills, MI: Gale. Similar to *Academic Search Premier*, this database provides access to wide-ranging content with many social science journals indexed, with hundreds available in full-text format.

- *Linguistics and Language Behavior Abstracts* (*LLBA*). www.csa.com. 1973–present. Bethesda, MD: Cambridge Scientific Abstracts. *LLBA* provides citations and abstracts to literature on the nature, use, and teaching of language as well as linguistics, speech, communication, and related topics.

- *Medline.* www.medlineplus.gov. 1965?–present. Bethesda, MD: U.S. National Library of Medicine. Compiled by the U.S. National Library of Medicine (NLM), *Medline* is the world's most comprehensive source of life sciences and biomedical bibliographic information. *Medline* extensively covers the psychological and psychiatric literature. *PubMed* (linked from www.ncbi.nlm .nih.gov) is the publicly accessible database containing citations from *Medline* and additional journals.

- *Social Sciences Citation Index* (*SSCI*). www.thomson.com. 1956–present. Philadelphia, PA: Thomson Scientific. Initiated as a print index, this database is now part of ISI's *Web of Science* platform. It is an important tool that provides access to current and retrospective bibliographic information, author abstracts, and cited references found in over 1,700 of the world's leading scholarly social sciences journals covering more than fifty disciplines. It also covers individually selected, relevant items from approximately 3,300 of the world's leading science and technology journals. Its companion database is the *Science Citation Index* (with coverage back to 1945). A subset of the two citation indexes is the *Journal Citation Reports* (*JCR*), which presents statistical data that provide a systematic, objective way to evaluate the world's leading journals and their impact and influence in the global research community.

- *Social Services Abstracts*. www.csa.com. 1980–present. Bethesda, MD: Cambridge Scientific Abstracts. This resource provides bibliographic coverage of current research focused on social work, human services, and related areas, including social welfare, social policy, and community development. The database abstracts and indexes over 1,406 serial publications and includes abstracts of journal articles and dissertations and citations to book reviews.
- *Social Work Abstracts*. www.ovid.com. 1977–present. New York: Ovid. Produced by the National Association of Social Workers (NASW), this is the core database for literature on social work. While not extensive in its coverage of psychology, it nonetheless provides coverage of some applicable literature.
- *Sociological Abstracts*. www.csa.com. 1963–present. Bethesda, MD: Cambridge Scientific Abstracts. This database contains citations to the international literature in sociology and related disciplines in the social and behavioral sciences. The database provides abstracts of journal articles and citations to book reviews drawn from over 1,700 serial publications, and also abstracts of books, book chapters, dissertations, and conference papers. Also available in print format, which began in 1953.

Guides to Identifying Scholarly versus Popular Periodical Literature

Many libraries have developed guides highlighting the different characteristics of a magazine, a trade publication, and a peer-reviewed journal. Several good examples are listed below.

- Keeran, Peggy. *Characteristics of Scholarly, Refereed, Popular, and Trade Publications*. University of Denver. http://130.253.32.120/FindIt/HelpWithResearch/scholpop.html.
- *Popular, Scholarly or Trade?* University Libraries of Notre Dame. www.library.nd.edu/howdoi/documents/pop_schol_trade.pdf.
- Provost, Darylyne. *Identifying Scholarly Journals vs. Popular and Trade Magazines*. University of Maine. www.library.umaine.edu/general/scholarly_popular.htm.
- Torian, Regina. *Characteristics of Scholarly Journals, Trade Journals and Popular Magazines*. University Libraries—University at Albany, SUNY. http://library.albany.edu/usered/char.

Print Resources (Encyclopedias, Handbooks, etc.)

- *Annual Review of Psychology*. 1950–present. Stanford, CA: Annual Reviews. Covering all areas of psychology research and practice, the *Annual Review of Psychology* typically includes about twenty review articles written by leading experts in the field.
- Coleman, Andrew. 2001. *Dictionary of Psychology*. Oxford: Oxford University Press. This single-volume work is ideal for students of psychology and

professional psychologists, as well as the general reader. It contains over 9,000 main entries and provides clear and concise definitions of a wide range of terms and concepts in psychology, psychiatry, and psychoanalysis.

- *Diagnostic and Statistical Manual of Mental Disorders: DSM-IV-TR*, 4th ed., text revision. 2000. Washington, DC: American Psychiatric Association. The main diagnostic reference of mental health professionals in the United States. Lists diagnostic criteria for the most common mental disorders, including description, diagnosis, treatment, and research findings. A recently released online version, available by subscription, should prove popular with the academic and professional audience.

- *Directory of Unpublished Experimental Mental Measures.* 1974– . Washington, DC: American Psychological Association. This directory provides references to experimental nonstandardized mental measures currently undergoing development. Test descriptions and references to journal articles are organized into categories with an author and subject index. This directory is updated regularly with information published in new volumes.

- Kazdin, Alan E., ed. 2000. *Encyclopedia of Psychology.* Washington, DC: American Psychological Association. This eight-volume reference work is an excellent guide to every area of psychological theory, research, and practice. It is a good source to introduce students to concepts and background information on a topic.

- Keyser, Daniel J., and Richard C. Sweetland, gen. eds. 1984– . *Test Critiques.* Kansas City, MO: Test Corporation of America. This ten-volume set includes lengthy reviews of psychological, educational, and business tests.

- Koocher, Gerald P., John C. Norcross, and Sam S. Hill, III., eds. 2005. *Psychologists Desk Reference, 2nd ed.* New York: Oxford University Press. This work presents a variety of information on the entire spectrum of practice issues—from diagnostic codes, practice guidelines, treatment principles, and report checklists to insight and advice from today's most respected clinicians—providing ready access to the entire range of current knowledge. It covers assessment and diagnosis, testing and psychometrics, treatment and psychotherapy, ethical and legal issues, practice management, and professional resources.

- *Mental Measurements Yearbook* (MMY) and *Tests in Print.* Lincoln: Buros Institute of Mental Measurements, University of Nebraska. The MMY includes timely, consumer-oriented test reviews, providing evaluative information to promote and encourage informed test selection. The print version of MMY began in 1938, with its most recent volume (16th) published in 2005. *Tests in Print* serves as a companion cumulative index for locating and evaluating commercially available tests reviewed in MMY.

- *Publication Manual of the American Psychological Association.* Washington, DC: American Psychological Association. Commonly referred to as the *APA Manual*, this is a key resource used by students, faculty, and others needing information on preparing manuscripts and using proper citation style.

- Smelser, Neil J., and Paul B. Baltes, eds. 2001. *International Encyclopedia of the Social and Behavioral Sciences.* New York: Elsevier. This is an ambitious attempt to describe the state of the art in all fields within the social and behavioral sciences. Comprising twenty-six volumes, it includes 4,000 articles and includes 90,000 bibliographic references as well as comprehensive name and subject indexes. Volume 18 includes articles on psychology and related disciplines.

Association and Institutional Web Sites

- *American Psychiatric Association.* www.psych.org. The American Psychiatric Association is a medical specialty society whose members work to ensure humane care and effective treatment for all persons with mental disorders, including mental retardation and substance-related disorders.
- *American Psychological Association (APA).* www.apa.org. Official Web site of the leading professional organization for psychologists. Contains daily updates, news, publications, information on a variety of topics, and more.
- *American Psychology Society (APS).* www.psychologicalscience.org. A national organization dedicated to the advancement of scientific psychology and its representation. Founded in 1988 by a group of scientifically oriented psychologists interested in advancing scientific psychology, its mission is to promote, protect, and advance the interests of scientifically oriented psychology in research, application, teaching, and the improvement of human welfare.
- *National Institute of Mental Health (NIMH).* www.nimh.nih.gov. One of twenty-seven components of the National Institutes of Health (NIH), NIMH is the leading federal agency for research on mental and behavioral disorders. The site contains a multitude of information on the latest research, funding, agency publications, and consumer education.

Additional Resources for Librarians

- *Behavioral and Social Sciences Librarian.* 1979–present. Binghamton, NY: Haworth Press. Publishes articles on all aspects of behavioral and social sciences information, with emphasis on librarians, libraries, and the users of social science information in libraries and information centers.
- Leong, Frederick T. L., and James T. Austin, eds. 2006. *The Psychology Research Handbook: A Guide for Graduate Students and Research Assistants.* Thousand Oaks, CA: Sage. Another broad review of research strategy. Part 1 includes library use strategies.
- Reed, Jeffrey G., and Pam M. Baxter. 2003. *Library Use: Handbook for Psychology.* Washington, DC: American Psychological Association. Provides a good overview of library use for students, with possible resources to consider when teaching.

Bibliography

American Psychological Association (APA). *APA Online.* www.apa.org (accessed April 13, 2005).

Association of College and Research Libraries (ACRL). 2003. *Guidelines for Instruction Programs in Academic Libraries.* www.ala.org/ala/acrl/acrlstandards/guidelinesinstruction.htm (accessed April 12, 2005).

Association of College and Research Libraries (ACRL), Education and Behavioral Sciences Section (EBSS). 2002. *Library and Information Resource Instruction for Psychology—Guidelines.* www.lib.msu.edu/corby/ebss/psycguid.htm (accessed April 12, 2005).

Budd, John M., and Corrie Christenson. 2003. "Social Sciences Literature and Electronic Information." *portal: Libraries and the Academy* 3, no. 4: 643–651.

Daugherty, Timothy K., and Elizabeth W. Carter. 1997. "Assessment of Outcome-Focused Library Instruction in Psychology." *Journal of Instructional Psychology* 24, no. 1: 29–34.

———. 1998. "Library Instruction and Psychology—A Cooperative Effort." *Technical Services Quarterly* 16, no. 1: 33–41.

Hutchins, Elizabeth O., and Bonnie S. Sherman. 2001. "Information Literacy and Psychological Science: A Case Study of Collaboration." In *Library User Education: Powerful Learning, Powerful Partnerships*, pp. 183–193, edited by Barbara I. Dewey. Lanham, MD: Scarecrow Press.

Keller, John M. 1987. "Strategies for Stimulating the Motivation to Learn." *Performance and Instruction* 26, no. 8 (October): 1–7.

Landrum, R. Eric, and Diana M. Muench. 1994. "Assessing Students' Library Skills and Knowledge: The Library Research Strategies Questionnaire." *Psychological Reports* 75, no. 3 part 2: 1619–1628.

Leong, Frederick T. L., and James T. Austin, eds. 1996. "Using a Library Effectively." *The Psychology Research Handbook.* Thousand Oaks, CA: Sage.

Meho, Lokman, and Helen R. Tibbo. 2003. "Modeling the Information-Seeking Behavior of Social Scientists: Ellis's Study Revisited." *Journal of the American Society for Information Science and Technology* 54, no. 6: 570–587.

Merriam, Joyce, Ross T. LaBaugh, and Nancy E. Butterfield. 1992. "Library Instruction for Psychology Majors: Minimum Training Guidelines." *Teaching of Psychology* 19, no. 1: 34–36.

Nolan, Anne Cerstvik, and Marilyn P. Whitmore. 1992. "An Awareness Program for Tests and Measurement." *Research Strategies* 10 (Winter): 44–48.

Paglia, Alison, and Annie Donahue. 2003. "Collaboration Works: Integrating Information Competencies into the Psychology Curricula." *Reference Services Review* 31, no. 4: 320–328.

Persson, Dorothy, and Carlette Washington-Hoagland. 2003. *Library Use: Handbook for Psychology.* 3rd ed. Washington, DC: American Psychological Association.

———. 2004. "PSYCINFO Tutorial: A Viable Instructional Alternative." *Reference and User Services Quarterly* 44, no. 1: 69–77.

Rockman, Ilene F. 2004. *Integrating Information Literacy into the Higher Education Curriculum: Practical Models for Transformation.* San Francisco: Jossey-Bass.

Still, Julie. 1990. "A Boring Approach to Library Research: 'Boring's Mother-in-Law' as an Introduction to Psychology Sources." *Research Strategies* 8 (Spring): 85–89.

Sutton, Ellen D., et al. 1995. "Bibliographic Instruction in Psychology: A Review of the Literature." *Reference Services Review* 23, no. 3: 13–22+.

Thaxton, Lyn. 1985. "Dissemination and Use of Information by Psychology Faculty and Graduate Students: Implications for Bibliographic Instruction." *Research Strategies* 3 (Summer): 116–124.

————. 1987. "Conceptual Frameworks for Bibliographic Instruction in Psychology." In *Conceptual Frameworks for Bibliographic Instruction: Theory into Practice*, edited by Mary Reichel and Mary Ann Ramey. Littleton, CO: Libraries Unlimited.

————. 2002. "Information Dissemination and Library Instruction in Psychology Revisited: 'Plus ça Change . . .'" *Behavioral and Social Sciences Librarian* 21, no. 1: 1–14.

Thaxton, Lyn, Mary Beth Faccioli, and Anne Page Mosby. 2004. "Leveraging Collaboration for Information Literacy in Psychology." *Reference Services Review* 32, no. 2: 185–189.

12

Science

Gregg Sapp

Introduction

Recent surveys of the scientific achievement of students at all levels and the basic science literacy of the general population reveal that the American public lags behind many other nations in its understanding of science. Increasingly, scientific and technological issues affect everyone in American society, as consumers and citizens. Basic science literacy is thus a prerequisite to making informed decisions. While the general concept of information literacy is prevalent in library literature and practice, the more specific concept of science literacy has received far less attention. This chapter describes the conception and development of a librarian-taught, core curriculum course in science information literacy at the University at Albany, State University of New York (SUNY). Attention is given to how the course provides essential skills such as searching, retrieving, evaluating, and using information resources, but within the context of how scientific information resources are both similar to and different from others. Case studies illustrate concepts such as the scientific method, the transfer of scientific information from technical to popular literature, and the necessity for ethical conduct in the sciences. Finally, I suggest opportunities for course-integrated instruction.

The Importance of Science in Modern Society

Toward the end of his life, the celebrated science writer Issac Asimov was asked why he invested so much time and effort interpreting sometimes arcane principles of science and technology to a generally nonscientific public. His answer, paraphrased, was "Because science is too important to be left to the scientists." His point is that, in today's world, a scientifically literate public is essential to an informed, enlightened democracy. Thomas F. Gieryn observes, "Science and society are best seen as co-constructed: each has been built up with the other, in an endlessly recursive process. The interchanges between science and society are so thick and deep that finding a line to separate one from the other may be impossible" (Gieryn, 2005). To some, who tend to see science as esoteric and isolated from daily life, this may not seem intuitive. Still, today more than ever, science and technology impinge upon our daily lives in myriad ways, from the gadgets that we use, to the telecommunication and computer networks that keep us in touch with one another, to the decisions we make as citizens and consumers, to the way our elected representatives allocate funds for various projects, and even in some of the ethical issues raised when science pushes against social norms. Science is indeed too important to be left in the hands of a few.

There are, however, many concerns about how well the public understands science. Stephanie Pace Marshall, Judith A. Scheppler, and Michael J. Palmisano observe:

> The twenty-first century finds science progressing at a rate that increasingly outpaces the wisdom necessary for using newfound knowledge for public good. This raises critical questions concerning essential understandings of science for all citizens. National security, economic viability, and health and welfare of families and communities all require increasingly deeper levels of understanding of science. Can public education foster science literacy for all? (Marshall, Scheppler, and Palmisano, 2002)

While this question may be unanswerable regarding the future, there is evidence that the educational system has failed to meet this challenge in the past and that deficiencies exist in the present.

Every couple of years the National Center for Educational Statistics (NCES) and the National Science Foundation (NSF) compare the science achievements of American elementary, middle, and high school students to those in other countries. In a survey conducted as part of the NCES's Third International Mathematics and Science Study (TIMSS), U.S. twelfth graders scored seventeenth out of twenty-one nations in general science knowledge (National Center for Education Statistics, 1998). In a more focused survey, U.S. senior high school students ranked last in physics and mathematics on standardized tests administered to students in ten North American and European countries (NSF, 2002). Finally, it is notable that according to the NCES's 2000 science "report card," the average scores of high school seniors declined between 1996 and 2000 (NCES, 2001).

Many of these students are coming to American colleges and universities. Can these students become scientifically literate?

Science Information Literacy

There are myriad definitions and elucidations of what science literacy means. Consider a few:

> Scientific Literacy is the capacity to use scientific knowledge, to identify questions and to draw evidence-based conclusions in order to understand and help make decisions about the natural world and the changes made to it through human activity. (Organization for Economic Cooperation and Development, 2001)

> Science literacy is an active understanding of scientific methods and of the social, economic, and cultural roles of science as they are conveyed through various media and it is thus built upon an ability to acquire, update, and use relevant information about science. (Sapp, 1992)

> The scientifically literate person accurately applies appropriate science concepts, principles, laws, and theories in interacting with his universe. (Rubba and Anderson, 1978)

> In a word, to become scientifically literate is to become an effective citizen. (Shortland, 1988)

While other descriptions of science literacy include such elements as core competencies and an understanding of scientific methodology, the most common and unifying aspect of any definition is that science literacy is a practical, applied aptitude.

Within the communities of scientists and science educators, there have been a variety of projects and initiatives aimed at improving science literacy and the public understanding of science. Perhaps the most ambitious is the American Association for the Advancement of Science's (AAAS) "Project 2061" (AAAS, 2005). The project's title refers to the year of the next return of Halley's Comet, but, more than that, it means that science literacy is an ongoing goal to which the association is committed in the long term. Aimed at improving science literacy by reforming science education, the project's first major publication, *Science for All Americans* (Rutherford and Ahlgren, 1990), provided substantive information on the knowledge base and nature of research in the major scientific disciplines, but it also included a set of recommendations for what students should understand and be able to do in mathematics, science, and technology. This report led to the publication of *Benchmarks for Science Literacy: A Tool for Curriculum Reform* (AAAS, 1994), which set out a pathway toward achieving defined learning goals for elementary and secondary school students. In implementing the recommendations of these documents, several other reports, articles, and other publications have been generated. For example, several professional scientific societies, such as the American Chemical Society (ACS), have mounted tiered presentations of science information resources, based on professionally chosen benchmarks (ACS, 2005).

The National Academy of Sciences (NAS) developed another set of benchmarks. Their National Science Education Standards "present a vision of a scientifically literate populace. The standards outline what students need to know, understand, and be able to do to be scientifically literate at different grade levels. They describe an educational system in which all students demonstrate high levels of performance, in which teachers are empowered to make the decisions essential for effective learning, in which interlocking communities of teachers and students are focused on learning science, and in which supportive educational programs and systems nurture achievement" (National Research Council, 1995). These standards address teaching, professional development, assessment, content, programs, and education systems. In this case, as with the AAAS benchmarks, the NAS sees the goal of improving science education and thus long-term science literacy as a process that can be guided by establishing a framework of standards (Good, Cummins, and Lyon, 1999).

The science community's concern with science literacy and its emphasis on setting standards reflects similar concerns in the library community regarding information literacy. In its most pithy expression, information literacy is defined as a set of abilities requiring individuals to "recognize when information is needed and have the ability to locate, evaluate, and use effectively the needed information" (American Library Association, 1989). Pioneered by the Instruction Section (IS) of the Association of College and Research Libraries (ACRL), the concept of information literacy is buttressed by a set of standards and guidelines in areas involving the nature and extent of, access to, evaluation of, and ethical issues about information, as well supported by a "toolkit" with suggestions as to how they might be implemented (ACRL, 2005; ACRL, IS Research and Scholarship Committee, 2005). ACRL founded its Institute for Information Literacy to provide programmatic support in these areas. Finally, the common concerns and methodologies of the science and library communities come together under the umbrella concept of science information literacy. In May 2005, ACRL's Science and Technology Section (STS) published its own set of standards for science and technology literacy (ACRL, STS, 2005). While based largely upon ACRL's general information literacy standards, the science and technology standards recognize distinct needs for those seeking to achieve and maintain science literacy, such as the need to keep up-to-date with rapidly changing developments and to seek the most recent, relevant information.

Thus a scientifically literate person is invariably an information-literate person. Since these two skill sets are coterminous, they can be taught simultaneously, with reference to a combination of the standards set down for both fields. Librarians at the University at Albany's Science Library aimed to teach this kind of science information literacy in a credit-bearing course, which I describe in this chapter.

How to Follow Science through Society: A Course at the University at Albany, SUNY

Located in the state capital, the University at Albany is one of four "University Centers" in the State University of New York (SUNY) system. Established in

1844, the University at Albany provides undergraduate and graduate education, research, and public service and engages 17,000 students in nine schools and colleges across three campuses. Its libraries rank in the top 100 of Association of Research Libraries members and house over 2 million volumes in a central University Library and two branches, the Science Library and the Dewey Graduate Library for Public Affairs and Policy.

In 1998, the University at Albany, SUNY revised its general education program. Within the category of "Communication and Reasoning Competencies," information literacy became a core component of the institution's general education requirement. The learning objectives are that students be able to:

1   Locate, evaluate, synthesize, and use information from a variety of sources
2   Understand and use basic research techniques
3   Understand the various ways in which information is organized and structured
4   Understand the ethical issues involved in accessing and using information

Students can satisfy this requirement by taking various courses, including two that are offered by the University Libraries and taught by library faculty. The university has offered a 200-level Information Literacy course since 2000. This is a one-credit course, seven weeks in duration, meeting one day a week for two hours a week, and taught in seven or eight sections, twice during the fall and spring semesters. Class size is limited to twenty-three, which is the capacity of its electronic classroom. Due to enrollment caps, sections of this course are almost always full.

The Science Library opened in 1999; it was the first newly constructed academic building on campus in thirty years. Librarians and staff of the Science Library articulated their desire to establish its identity as a "teaching" library, where learning was an interactive process. Hence, the idea of developing a specialized course in science information literacy quickly emerged. The head of the library wrote and submitted a course proposal, which gained the endorsement of the university's undergraduate academic council. After approval, the Science Library hired an instruction librarian, who, along with the head of the Science Library, began teaching the course in 2003. We used the same basic structure as the general information literacy course regarding number of credits, class length, and so forth. The content and some of the objectives of this course, however, were quite different.

The catalog title for the course was simply Science Information Literacy, but the subtitle listed on the course syllabus suggested what it was really about: How to Follow Science through Society (see Appendix). Understanding the social relevance of science and being able to find appropriate information on topics of public interest, so often cited as a defining feature of science literacy, were central to the purpose of this course. That emphasis is also underscored in the course description:

> Using case studies and examples from scientific, technical, and medical literatures, this course will introduce students to the basic principles and processes of finding, organizing, using, producing, and evaluating

information resources in all media and formats. Students will learn about information flow in the sciences, at all levels of presentation, and how to access, search, and retrieve information in a variety of formats. They will learn to formulate effective searching on electronic databases and the Internet, and how to evaluate the quality of the information that they retrieve. They will become familiar with the practical, social, and ethical issues relating to the use of information, with special emphasis on the role of scientific information in an increasingly technological society.[1]

The instructors modeled the design, structure, and content of the course as much as possible upon benchmarks and standards from both professional scientific and library associations. For example, information literacy standards addressing the nature and extent of information were illustrated with reference to the volume of information produced in the sciences, the diversity of formats in which it is disseminated, how it travels from primary to secondary and tertiary levels, and that even more information exists in the form of grey literature. Standards pertaining to the evaluation of information were covered in many ways, with reference to the workings of the peer review system but also with examples of how scientific information can be variously interpreted, in some ways that convey dubious authority. In particular, one example is Stephen Jay Gould and Niles Eldredge's theory of "punctuated equilibrium." Students and instructors discuss the myriad ways in which this theory has been presented and interpreted, from the scholarly literature, to secondary sources of reliable authority, to the popular press, including newspapers, tabloids, religious literature, and even cartoons. Students are asked to decide whether they trust an information source and to explain why.

Finally, benchmarks cited from the scientific associations are also built into the course. We examine the "scientific method," emphasizing its checks and balances. Likewise, we expose students to specific topics, such as:

- Science versus pseudo-science
- Fraud and ethical issues in scientific research
- The importance of "numeracy" to decision making based on probabilities (for instance, how likely you are to win the lottery as compared to getting struck by lightning)

We use case studies throughout the course to illustrate key points and stimulate discussion.[2] Episodes from the history of science as well as more recent events are presented within the context of elaborating a benchmarked theme. For example, when discussing ethics in scientific research, we present a case study on the "delicate arrangement" struck between Charles Darwin and Alfred Russel Wallace, which raises several pertinent points. Briefly, Wallace, a largely unknown naturalist who independently proposed a theory of evolution by natural selection, wrote a draft on the subject, submitted it to Darwin for his commentary, and asked him to forward it for publication if he considered it worthy. Darwin was stunned to realize that Wallace's theory was in fact his own, which he had formulated years before but never published. He realized that if Wallace (who was far away, doing field work in Malaysia) published immediately, he alone would be credited with the discovery. What were Darwin's ethical options? Was the ultimate resolution fair, whereby both men published in the same journal but Darwin's draft letters were placed in the first position? This case not only raises ethical questions, but also reinforces the importance of priority in science, its competitive nature, and how affluence can influence how science is conducted and information is released (Darwin was rich and well connected; Wallace was comparatively isolated and nearly a pauper). These issues are as real today as in Darwin's age.

Another case study of local interest further demonstrates how economic interests can affect science and how good research and accurate data do not necessarily lead to "proof." A major concern about the health of the Hudson River is related to the presence of polychlorinated biphenyls (PCBs) in a stretch ranging downriver from Hudson Falls to just north of Albany. From the late 1940s until 1977, the General Electric Company legally discharged into the Hudson as much as 1.3 million pounds of PCBs, which are used in the production of electric capacitors. PCBs have been linked to increased risk of cancer in humans and have multiple impacts upon fish and wildlife. As early as 1984, the U.S. Environmental Protection Agency proposed removing the PCBs by dredging the sediment on the bottom of the river. Under the terms of the plan, the company would bear the enormous costs of dredging the river. Opponents to the proposal argue that the consequences of dredging might create even greater dangers than any current risks, because buried PCBs might be disturbed by the dredging. Further, they argue, PCB levels have been in decline in recent years, apparently because of the river's natural cleaning processes. Both sides agree on many things. The river is in fact slowly cleaning itself. The precise parts-per-million concentrations at various locations in the sediment are known. No one, including the public, scientists, and government officials, knows the exact health risks or what level of concentration is safe. Both sides look at the same data but come to different conclusions. How do you balance the known costs with the potential risks?

The primary assignment for students is to compile an annotated bibliography on some subject of current interest in the sciences. We teach basic search skills and principles of information organization, which students put to use when researching their bibliographies. Popular topics for bibliographies are fairly predictable, according to what might be in the news at a given time. Current examples of popular topics are stem cell research, global warming, and biological terrorism. Some students choose to tackle more difficult, theoretical, or even obscure subjects, some of which scientists themselves hotly debate, such as the origin of language, evolutionary psychology, the proof of Fermat's Last Theorem, and the possible existence of multiple universes. The bibliographies must include ten citations, with various options for mixing and matching publication types and formats, but they must include at least three primary sources, three secondary sources, and one tertiary source. Virtually any format is acceptable—monograph or periodical, newspapers, microformats, audiovisual materials, interviews with subject specialists—but a minimum of four different formats must be included, and also four online and four print (although this is negotiable if a relevant source is available in both formats). On the last day of class, each student must give a five-minute presentation on his or her topic.

Other than the annotated bibliography, grades are based on weekly homework assignments, class participation (class participation is very important, especially in discussion of cases), and a final take-home examination. The final exam consists of multiple choice and short answer questions, with a longer essay asking to describe each stage of the publishing cycle, from the origin of an idea through primary publishing, review, and incorporation in reference sources. Extra credit is offered for extracurricular activities, such as attendance at a science colloquium or a science-related public event.

When the course was first proposed, we anticipated that most students taking it would be science majors. In fact, the classes were much more academically heterogeneous, with about half coming from science disciplines (mainly biological science) and the rest from the humanities and social sciences. This is encouraging because it suggests that the nonscience students, who have the option of taking the general information literacy course, either overtly or intuitively understand the importance of science literacy—that it is, indeed, "too important to be left up to the scientists."

Possible Future Directions

The steps in creating a science information literacy course or for incorporating its principles into an existing curriculum include:

- Consider how science information literacy can complement the library's current instructional services.
- Examine the benchmarks and translate them into learning objectives. State these explicitly in the syllabus and reinforce them in class.
- Create an instructional context focusing on local or topical science issues.
- Develop active learning exercises and case studies to illustrate key points and stimulate discussion.
- Take advantage of local scientists to teach or serve as guest lecturers, resource persons, or in other supportive roles.
- Have a plan for evaluating the course that includes student feedback.

As librarians gain experience teaching science information literacy and research into how and under what circumstances the public acquires scientific and technical information, a number of possibilities present themselves. Two that we are exploring at the University at Albany are the following:

1   An advanced course in science literacy. Any course in science information literacy is implicitly also a course in the sociology of science, since social forces affect how science is created, made public, and used, and even in some cases what kinds of research are done and not done.

Troy Sadler used the word *socioscientific* to describe this phenomenon, and, echoing a theme prevalent throughout this chapter, he stressed that moral and ethical concerns are foundations of science literacy as they pertain to decision making (Sadler, 2004). In that regard, an advanced course in science information literacy might study the ways information travels through society and how it is used by different constituencies. Students would examine where politicians and public servants get their scientific information. It might be interesting to deconstruct a work of primary scientific information as different groups interpret and then recapitulate it, or to follow how information is presented as it is reconfigured for different audiences. The university could offer such a course at an upper-division undergraduate or graduate level, and invite partnerships with other departments, from all disciplines (Pollack, 2001).

2   Emphasis on science literacy in traditional course-integrated instruction. Library collaboration is possible with instructors from a wide variety of other disciplines, and is most commonly manifested as course-integrated instruction.

For example, Cecelia Brown and Lee R. Krumholz describe an initiative to integrate information literacy into an upper-division microbiology class, and assess its results via a survey (Brown and Krumholz, 2002). Unfortunately, the results were not especially encouraging, inasmuch as the authors had anticipated measurable improvement in the students' information-seeking abilities, but "this perceived enhancement was not reflected in a significantly improved ability to use information." Their project, though, was based upon the fairly standard model of in-class library instruction, where the instructors were given just two classes to impart their advice about search skills and information literacy concepts and then retreated back to the library hoping they had made an impact. This form of in-class instruction will remain important, but most librarians are aware of its limitations.

Perhaps a more rigorous form of course-integrated instruction would be more seamless and have a more positive result—not just episodic, one-shot presentations on skills and resources to a class, but a kind of integration whereby information literacy instruction integration permeates a subject course from beginning to end. In the updated "Research Agenda for Library Instruction and Information Literacy," one of the three assessment categories listed is "transferability." The concept is that skills learned in a one-credit course in science information literacy can be transferred to and applied in a subject-specific course. If these skills can be transferred to suit the content of that course, then they can likewise be taught within the context of that course. If, for instance, a Biology 101 course teaches evolutionary theory, then perhaps the case study of the "delicate arrangement" could be integrated into the instruction, and presented in a way not only to honor the biological content but also to elucidate some basic principles of the ethics of information use. Certainly, such a course might also cover scientific methodology and communication, and lessons could include training in searching databases and evaluating information. In this situation, a student could "kill two birds with one stone," meeting both an information literacy and a science general education requirement. By contrast, at institutions where information literacy is not included among general education requirements, students could still learn those skills without having to take an elective and do so in a way that enhances the content of the course. This is an area where partnerships could flourish, and it merits further investigation.

In summary, because science information literacy is so important, it is worth offering on its own virtues, but librarians and teaching faculty should consider alternatives for instilling its skills and values into students. Nobody should be science-illiterate.

Notes

1. The course syllabus can be viewed at http://library.albany.edu/science/syllabus_option.htm. It is updated every semester.

2. For more information on various uses of case studies in teaching science information literacy, see the University at Buffalo's "The Case Method of Teaching Science," http://ublib.buffalo.edu/libraries/projects/cases/teaching/teaching.html (accessed June 1, 2005).

Bibliography

American Association for the Advancement of Science (AAAS). *About Project 2061.* www.project2061.org/about/default.htm (accessed June 1, 2005).

———. 1994. *Benchmarks for Science Literacy: A Tool for Curriculum Reform.* New York: Oxford University Press.

American Chemical Society (ACS). *Chemistry.Org—Educators and Students.* www.chemistry.org/portal/a/c/s/1/educatorsandstudents.html (accessed June 20, 2005).

American Library Association. Presidential Committee on Information Literacy. 1989. *Final Report.* Chicago: American Library Association. www.ala.org/ala/acrl/acrlpubs/whitepapers/presidential.htm (accessed June 1, 2005).

Association of College and Research Libraries (ACRL). *Information Literacy.* www.ala.org/ala/acrl/acrlissues/acrlinfolit/informationliteracy.htm (accessed June 1, 2005).

Association of College and Research Libraries (ACRL). Instruction Section (IS), Research and Scholarship Committee. *Research Agenda for Library Instruction and Information Literacy.* www.ala.org/ala/acrlbucket/is/iscommittees/webpages/research/researchagendalibrary.htm (accessed June 1, 2005).

Association of College and Research Libraries (ACRL). Science and Technology Section (STS). 2005. "Information Literacy Standards for Science and Technology." *College and Research Libraries News* 66: 381–388. www.ala.org/ala/acrl/acrlstandards/infolitscitech.htm (accessed June 1, 2005).

Brown, Cecelia, and Lee R. Krumholz. 2002. "Integrating Information Literacy into the Science Curriculum." *College and Research Libraries* 63: 111–123.

Gieryn, Thomas F. 2005. "Introduction: Science and Society." In *Science, Technology, and Society: An Encyclopedia,* pp. ix–xviii, edited by Sal Restivo. New York: Oxford University Press.

Good, Ron, Catherine Cummins, and Gary Lyon. 1999. *The Nature of Science Assessment Based on Benchmarks and Standards*. Washington, DC: Educational Resources Information Center (ERIC document ED 442 644).

Marshall, Stephanie Pace, Judith A. Scheppler, and Michael J. Palmisano. 2002. "Introduction." In *Science Literacy for the Twenty-First Century*, pp. 15–19. Amherst, NY: Prometheus Books.

National Center for Education Statistics (NCES). 1998. *A Study of U.S. Twelfth Grade Mathematics and Science Achievement in the International Context, 1998*. www.nces.ed .gov/pubs98/twelfth/#executivesummary. Note: This finding comes with the disclaimer that it contains a 95 percent plus or minus confidence level (accessed June 1, 2005).

———. 2001. National Assessment of Educational Progress. *Science: The Nation's Report Card, 2001*. http://nces.ed.gov/nationsreportcard/science/results/natscalescore.asp (accessed June 1, 2005).

National Research Council. 1995. *National Science Education Standards, 1995*. www .nap.edu/readingroom/books/nses/html/ (accessed June 1, 2005).

National Science Foundation (NSF). 2002. *Science and Engineering Indicators 2002*. www.nsf.gov/sbe/srs/seind02/c0/fig00-06.htm (accessed June 1, 2005).

Organization for Economic Cooperation and Development. 2001. Program for International Student Assessment. "OECD PISA Provides International Comparative Data on Schooling Outcomes." www.oecd.org/document/8/0,2340,en_2649_34515_ 2675400_1_1_1_1,00.html (accessed June 1, 2005).

Pollack, Robert. 2001. "Some Practical Suggestions for Teaching Science in the Liberal Arts." *Annals of the New York Academy of Sciences* 935: 275–281.

Rubba, Peter A., and Hans O. Anderson. 1978. "Development of an Instrument to Assess Secondary School Students' Understanding of the Nature of Scientific Knowledge." *Science Education* 62: 449–458.

Rutherford, F. James, and Andrew Ahlgren. 1990. *Science for All Americans*. New York: Oxford University Press.

Sadler, Troy. 2004. *Moral and Ethical Dimensions of Socioscientific Decision-Making as Integral Components of Scientific Literacy*. Washington, DC: Educational Resources Information Center. ERIC ED 481 210.

Sapp, Gregg. 1992. "Science Literacy: A Discussion and Information Based Definition." *College and Research Libraries* 53: 21–30.

Shortland, Michael. 1988. "Advocating Science: Literacy and Public Understanding." *Impact of Science on Society* 38, no. 4: 305–316.

Appendix: Syllabus for Information Literacy and the Sciences

UNL 206: Information Literacy and the Sciences:
How to Follow Science through Society

Course Description. This is a one-credit course, meeting one day a week for seven weeks. Each class is two hours long. Using case studies and examples from scientific, technical, and medical literatures, this course will introduce students to the basic principles and processes of finding, organizing, using, producing, and evaluating information resources in all media and formats. Students will learn about information flow in the sciences, at all levels of presentation, and how to access, search, and retrieve information in a variety of formats. They will learn to formulate effective searching on electronic databases and the Internet, and how to evaluate the quality of the information that they retrieve. They will become familiar with the practical, social, and ethical issues relating to the use of information, with special emphasis on the role of scientific information in an increasingly technological society.

Course Objectives and Competencies Expected. Ever-increasing access to information requires researchers to be able to critically assess and evaluate a variety of resources. Commensurate with these skills is the ability to utilize information responsibly and ethically. UNL 205 (206), in recognition of the fact that each discipline has its own method of inquiry, prepares students to traverse the information terrain by introducing them to library infrastructure, information architecture, basic research methodologies, and the practical use of reference materials, print and online, for the enhancement of their potential to develop mature research skills.

Upon Completion of This Course, a Student Should Be Able to:

- Understand how sci-tech information is created, distributed, and used
- Describe the variety of information sources and tools available
- Identify the source, authority, scope, and perspective of information resources
- Turn a research topic into a thesis statement
- Create a research strategy, including a plan for organizing information resources
- Apply a standard style guide to the compilation of an annotated bibliography
- Know how to write a topic statement and an annotation
- Discuss current issues related to information policy and their impacts upon individuals and communities
- Be able to follow and keep up with science and technology in society

General Education: Information Literacy. This course satisfies the Information Literacy General Education requirement and provides students with the unique opportunity to learn and practice research skills under the guidance of library faculty. The course will fulfill the learning objectives for Information Literacy courses in the following ways:

You will learn how to effectively access and evaluate a wide variety of information sources. Evaluation skills are a critical component of this course because they enable you to choose the highest quality and most appropriate kind of information for your needs. You will synthesize and use the information that you find throughout the course for your final projects.

Research tools and techniques vary from discipline to discipline. You will have an opportunity in this course to explore a variety of research techniques, while focusing on a particular field of interest.

Scholarly information production is organized and structured. Understanding this organization will increase your research abilities and options. Even information on the Web is found through tools which have their own structure. It is equally important to understand what is available through the Web and what is not, and how best to use these tools to find what is there.

There are a wide range of ethical and social issues connected with accessing and using information, from plagiarism to Internet security to the digital divide. We will examine these concepts from different perspectives. Student participation in the discussion of these topics is highly encouraged, not only to increase your exposure to different view-points, but also to empower you in your own decision-making processes.

Grading and Course Requirements. Grades are weighted as follows:

- 30%—class assignments
- 30%—annotated bibliography
- 15%—test
- 15%—class participation
- 10%—topic presentation

Research Project. Weekly assignments contribute toward the completion of a cumulative project, an annotated bibliography on a scientific or technical topic of your choice and approved by the instructors. Assignments are as follows:

- Week two—submit preliminary topic for approval.
- Week three—submit topic statement.
- Week four—submit two annotations from primary or scholarly sources.
- Week five—submit two annotations from secondary or popular sources, from any two different formats.
- Week six—submit one annotation from a reference or tertiary sources.
- Week seven—submit final annotated bibliography, deliver class presentations.

The completed annotated bibliography must contain a minimum of ten items. The types of information that must be included are:

- Primary or scholarly sources
- Secondary or popular sources
- Tertiary or reference sources

The bibliography must also include materials from a minimum of four different formats. The formats of information resources that are acceptable include: books, book chapters, reference sources in book format, print article from magazine, print article from newspaper, print article from a journal, full text article from a database, Internet articles, technical reports, government documents, audiovisual media, interviews with a library subject specialist. Other formats must be approved by the instructor. In addition to the seven required annotations, you must include three additional sources or formats.

Class One.

Introduction: Review of syllabus, class policies and procedures, grading and requirements for annotated bibliography.

Discussion: Information literacy in an age of science and technology. How information literacy skills apply to finding, using, and understanding scientific information. Definitions of *information* and *science literacy*.

Assignments:

1. Write a brief (one paragraph) description of how you would seek information on a topic given in class.
2. Assignment One.
3. Readings: "Information Anxiety," "Data Smog."

Class Two.

Discussion: Information-seeking behaviors. Information anxiety and information overload. Obstacles and difficulties in locating usable information in the sciences. How to assess the authority, scope, and level of scientific information resources.

Demonstration: Introduction to libraries' Web site, library catalogs, e-reserves. Science Library Web site.

Assignments:

1 Write final topic statement.
2 Assignment Two (Hands-on Library Web).
3 Readings: "The Scientific Attitude."

Class Three.

Lecture: Instructions for writing an annotation. Bibliographic style guides and citation formats. Conventions for footnotes and endnotes. How to transform an annotated bibliography into a thesis statement.

Discussion: How scientific research is created, reported, and communicated by and among scholars. Information flow in the sciences. Primary sources: the peer review process in scholarly communication. Case studies: "cold fusion" and the "Sokol affair."

Demonstration: Searching online databases for primary, scholarly scientific information sources. Libraries Web sites for "Subject Pages & Guides" in sciences and "databases and online journals." Search strategies, Boolean operators, fields, controlled vocabulary (examples from: Ebsco Academic, Applied Science and Technology Abstracts, others.)

Assignments:

1 Primary/scholarly sources assignment.
2 Electronic Databases worksheet.

Class Four.

Lecture and demonstration: Print and electronic reference sources—dictionaries, encyclopedias, handbooks, bibliographies, Libraries Web site "reference collection."

Discussion: The Web as an information tool. Evaluation of Web resources. Web search engines versus online databases.

Activity: Search the Web and present one site judged to be authoritative, and one that is less reliable. Discuss rationale.

Assignments:

1 Reference/secondary source assignment.
2 Worksheet comparing Internet and electronic database sources.
3 Readings: "Science as a Candle in the Dark," "How to Tell What Is Science from What Isn't"

Class Five.

Discussion: Techniques for translating science in popular media—print, electronic, and audiovisual. Assessing accuracy and authority. Science journalism and how science is represented in the news. Representing mathematics in nontechnical literature; the problem of "innumeracy." Science versus psuedo-science. What constitutes "proof" in science.

Case studies: "PCBs in the Hudson River" and "global warming."

Demonstration: Searching catalogs, databases, and the Internet for popular science information.

Activity: Analysis of examples of science as presented in various media.

Assignments:

1 Popular science source assignment.
2 Readings: "The Baltimore Affair," "Cold Fusion."

Class Six.

Discussion: Information ethics. Privacy issues. The "Digital Divide." Fair use and copyright. Plagiarism and citation conventions. Fraud and accountability in scientific research. How to recognize propagandistic and politicized scientific information.

Case studies: Reporting and taking responsibility for laboratory research. "Gallo files," the "Baltimore Affair," privately funded research reports, and so on.

Assignments:

1 Complete annotated bibliography.
2 Prepare for class presentation.

Class Seven.

Activity: Class presentations. Submit complete annotated bibliographies. Course evaluation and post-test. Final suggestions for "keeping up with science in society."

13

Agricultural Sciences and
Natural Resources

Allison V. Level

"When tillage begins, other arts follow. The farmers therefore are
the founders of human civilization."

Daniel Webster, "On Agriculture,"
January 13, 1840 (Kaplan, 2002)

Introduction

Agricultural sciences and natural resources encompass a wide subset of the
scientific and technical literature. In most land-grant universities, agricultural
subjects include animal science, soil science, plant pathology, crop science,
entomology, horticulture, food science, and agricultural economics. Related
subjects can include human nutrition, landscape architecture, biotechnology,
veterinary medicine, rural development, agricultural engineering, and food marketing. The natural resource subject areas include fisheries, wildlife biology,
range management, hydrology, forestry, and ecology. Related natural resource areas can include geology, atmospheric sciences, land use planning, and bioremedi-
ation. This chapter will focus on successful instruction strategies and frequently
used resources for the more general topics of agriculture, natural resources, and
ecology.

Almost everyone will need and use natural resources or agricultural information in some form throughout his or her life. General information may include reading the nutrition label on a box of cereal, locating hiking information for a summer vacation to the Grand Canyon, or understanding the meaning behind the 18-6-12 numbers on a bag of lawn fertilizer. Research and scientific information in the disciplines is more complex and requires more in-depth user education and resource tools. On a continuum, from general information needs to more specific needs, the user groups include undergraduates and the general public, graduate students, and cooperative extension personnel, along with faculty and research scientists.

As a subject librarian, you may have in-class face time with undergraduate students and some graduate students while faculty, cooperative extension agents, and even the general public may call, e-mail, set up appointments to meet with you, or use your subject-based Web pages. Planning for and succeeding with these varying types of user education settings take knowledge, time, and practice. Most users can be afflicted with or continually be obsessed by the FIF-FTP syndrome. "What?" you say. Find It Fast, Full-Text Preferably.

For undergraduate students, Google is usually the first stop on the information-seeking trail. As subject librarians, we have the challenge of providing other "trails of interest" and information maps that students will seek out and want to use. Sure, the phrase "agricultural information" produces about 350,000 hits on Google, but will the first fifteen write the paper? Probably not. The first hits match the search terms entered, but at what point can one characterize a list of Web hits as information? Hans Christian von Baeyer explains, "The effectiveness problem is related to the usefulness of information. There is a hint here that, unless information leads to significant consequences, it is not really information at all" (von Baeyer, 2004). Librarians need to help provide the connections and link users with meaningful information and resources.

Training undergraduates about the effectiveness and usefulness of information can be a challenge, but old habits die hard for faculty and researchers too. Many times experts in the field get comfortable with their tried-and-true ways of seeking information. Like the well-worn set of hiking boots, they are broken in, comfortable, and you know what to expect when you put them on. When libraries change vendors, when search interfaces are upgraded, and when faculty and researchers need to branch out into new topics of interest the "information trail" becomes overgrown or ends up leading the researcher out into an unfamiliar wilderness.

Forms of Communication and the Scholarly Information Process

The scientific communication process involves both informal and formal communication channels. Informal channels include e-mail messages, listservs, lab notebooks, phone conversations, and blogs. Characteristically they are difficult to retrieve, contain current information, and are only temporarily stored. Formal channels of communication are public, more likely to be permanently stored, retrievable, and widely disseminated or available. Products of a more formal communication channel are books, journal articles, conference proceedings, agricultural experiment station research reports, and government documents.

The scholarly information process is part of a more formal communication channel and involves many steps and individuals. Understanding the communication channels and scholarly information process is one aspect of the 2005 *Information Literacy Standards for Science and Technology*. The ALA/ACRL/STS task force identified desired learning outcomes, including that the student:

- Knows how scientific, technical and related information is formally and informally produced, organized and disseminated. Understands the flow of scientific information and the scientific information life cycle.
- Understands cultural differences in science-based knowledge systems and in the development of knowledge.
- Differentiates between primary and secondary sources, recognizing how their use and importance vary with each discipline.

(ALA, 2005: 381–382)

The Scholarly Information Process in Figure 13-1 provides a general outline to the process of information dissemination in the sciences, but students must also realize that not all scientific discoveries follow this model. It is important to teach this process, but you should also provide information about the importance of some non-peer-reviewed publications such as preprints and e-prints (Manuel, 2004).

Lesson Planning and Preparation

In the book *Blink*, Malcolm Gladwell presents research and information about decisions made in the time it takes to blink your eye, as evidence of our adaptive unconscious at work. Based on research by psychologist Nalini Ambady, Gladwell remarks, "A person watching a silent two-second video clip of a teacher he or she has never met will reach conclusions about how good that teacher is that are very similar to those of a student who has sat in the teacher's class for an entire semester" (Gladwell, 2005). First impressions count, in teaching and in life. The saying goes, "Don't judge a book by its cover," but when you are teaching about books and research, the first two seconds are crucial. Successful instruction begins with good lesson planning and preparation. Consider these points in your own planning:

- Start early in the semester and contact faculty you have taught for in previous semesters and set up teaching times with their classes. They will be glad to have the library research session in their syllabus and you will be glad to have the teaching lab reserved.
- Ask to see a copy of any research assignment for the class. Knowing what the students must cover is helpful in planning your lesson.

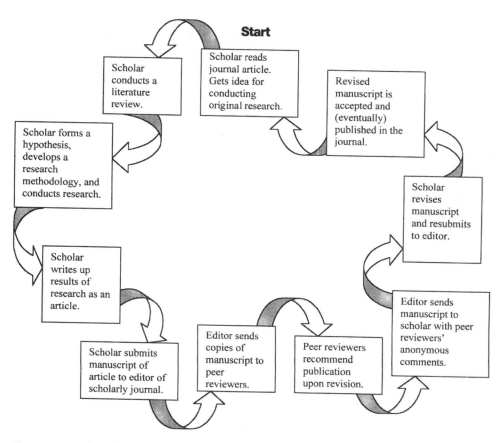

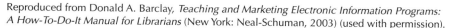

Figure 13-1   The Scholarly Information Process

Reproduced from Donald A. Barclay, *Teaching and Marketing Electronic Information Programs: A How-To-Do-It Manual for Librarians* (New York: Neal-Schuman, 2003) (used with permission).

- Find out if the faculty member has any favorite databases or reference books he or she wants to you cover when you teach.
- Scan for recent agriculture or natural resources topics in the news. Having several new and current topics will show students the importance of keeping up with current events. A focus on current events will connect learning with "real life" problems and situations.
- After you have outlined your lesson plan, practice all the database searches.
- Create an outline of your lesson, including how long you plan to spend on each topic. This will keep you from having to rush at the end of fifty minutes or less to get in the last of the information.
- Practice your timing and delivery. If you are new to teaching, plan ahead and book the teaching lab for a practice session. Stand in front and imagine the class, practice your searching examples and transitions, and consider what to do if the technology fails.
- Always have a back-up set of PowerPoint slides or screen shots you can use. Sure, you may need it only once a semester, but, like carrying an umbrella when it is not raining, being prepared is laudable.

What to Teach

Creating Examples for Instruction

Depending on your audience, teaching examples may be concise, showing the importance of keywords, subject headings, related words, and differences between library catalogs, general databases, and subject-specific databases.

If the example is, How can I find information about family farming, or what seems to be a decline in family farms, some sample keyword searches are:

- "family farm*" [this shows truncation with the * symbol and phrase searching with the quotation marks]
- (family farm* AND (decline* OR reduction)) [this illustrates Boolean logic]

In a library catalog, one result might be the book *The Fate of Family Farming: Variations on an American Idea* by Ronald Jager. If you look at the subject headings, you find:

Subject   Agriculture—United States.
               Family farms—United States.
               Agricultural productivity—United States.

When searching a multidisciplinary database using the keywords: family farm* the results often include records that provide other terms, such as:

Agriculture
family farms
farms, Small
farmers
farms

When searching a more agriculture specific database, the results provide terms such as:

- agricultural trade; family farms; farm size; small farms
- farm numbers; farm structure; trends
- family farms; farm income; finance; fiscal policy; inheritance of property; interest rates; property transfers; rent; succession

Effective Teaching Methods

Students in the sciences are interested in data, the experiment, the quantifiable pieces of the discipline. In agriculture and natural resources, the "ecosystem approach" of looking at a multitude of variables or impacts on a location, environment, or setting becomes important. This broader macro-lens view of a situation can be addressed by teaching not just the scientific journal literature but also encouraging students, especially those new to a discipline, to use handbooks, guides, or encyclopedias.

Figure 13-2   Sample Assignment: Information-Seeking Interview

Student Assignment: Conduct an Information-Seeking Interview. Select a Specialist in Agriculture, Natural Resources, or Science Policy to interview in person or via the telephone. Talk with this person about his or her information needs and the ways they receive and share information.

If you are new to campus or if you are looking to strengthen the instruction program in a discipline, then target a class, department, or faculty member to work with and focus your instruction efforts. This will allow you to get a "foot in the door" and build from there. When in the classroom, remember that starting strong is important:

- Get fired up—show spunk and enthusiasm. Use the first two seconds to your advantage and capture the attention of the class with your introduction. "Hi, I am . . . and my official title is reference librarian but if I could, I would change that to information detective."
- Ask questions to the class and encourage responses. "How many of you know the title of the book or author you need when you begin your research? Well, I don't, either. Usually I begin with 'I have a question about . . . '"
- Reward comments and questions with responses like, "That is a very good question." Then give the answer so everyone can hear both the question and the response.

Discovery learning is another way of student engagement. Students explore a topic in advance of class or use outside learning combined with in-class techniques (Jacobson and Xu, 2004). This type of learning situation works better if you teach a class over an entire semester, or if you work cooperatively with discipline-based faculty. Students are often surprised to find out how specialists use informal and formal channels of communication. They also learn that researchers rely on specific databases, journal table of contents (TOC) alerts, and the importance of professional societies. Figure 13-2 shows an assignment for which students interview a working professional about his or her information-seeking habits.

Best Resources for Agriculture and Natural Resources

General and technically specific reference and research resources exist for all the subject areas covered by agriculture and natural resources. For librarians new to the discipline or for nonscience librarians wanting to brush up on resources, the book *Using the Agricultural, Environmental, and Food Literature* by Barbara S. Hutchinson and Antoinette Paris Greider is an excellent start. Greider opens with an introduction to the literature and general sources. The remaining fifteen chapters, each written by a librarian or specialist, focus on specific areas such as animal science and livestock production, environmental sciences and natural resources, field crops, soil science, grey literature, and extension resources. The chapters list and recommend indexes, databases, bibliographies, encyclopedias, and government documents. There are handbooks and manuals, proceedings, statistical sources, and a list of the core journals for the subject areas. Some key societies and society publications are also mentioned.

As a starting point for general agricultural sciences and natural resources, it is important to cover the best and the basics. As in other scientific disciplines, journal articles, conference proceedings, society publications, and databases are key. Government reports and information from sources such as the U.S. Department of Agriculture (USDA) or the National Agricultural Library (NAL) should be incorporated into a lesson plan. For this chapter, selected databases, journals, and Web sites are given in the following lists. More detailed information can be found in *Using the Agricultural, Environmental, and Food Literature* and other books on information resources in the natural resources and agriculture.

Databases

- *AGRICOLA*. agricola.nal.usda.gov/. 1970– . Beltsville, MD: U.S. National Agricultural Library (NAL). This database includes records for items added to the National Agricultural Library collection. It is strong on USDA publications and also includes journal articles and book chapters. In the summer of 2005, NAL announced they will be re-scoping *AGRICOLA*, so the indexing and content may change.
- *AGRIS*. www.fao.org/agris. 1975– . Rome: AGRIS Coordinating Centre. *AGRIS* covers worldwide literature on all aspects of agriculture. The records are provided by intergovernmental centers and include journal articles and grey literature.
- *CAB Abstracts*. www.cabi-publishing.org/CABI. 1973– . Wallingford, UK: CABI. This database includes worldwide coverage of information on agriculture, veterinary medicine, forestry, entomology, and biology. The contents include journal articles, books, conference proceedings, and other publications. In 2005, CABI launched the *CAB Abstracts Archive*, which covers 1900–1973.
- *CRIS*. cris.csrees.usda.gov/. 1975– . Beltsville, MD: USDA Cooperative State Research, Education and Extension Service. The Current Research Information System (CRIS) is the USDA reporting and documentation outlet for publicly supported research in agriculture, forestry, food, and nutrition. This is a good source for information about research supported by USDA research-grant programs and state agricultural experiment stations, land-grant universities, and others.
- *Web of Science*. www.isiknowledge.com. 1945– . Philadelphia, PA: Institute for Scientific Information. This database provides online access to the ISI citation indexes, including the *Science Citation Index*. It provides weekly updated current indexing and abstracting to the key scholarly research journals in agriculture, natural resources, ecology, and other scientific disciplines.

Although *Web of Science* includes subject areas broader than just agriculture and natural resources, the important journals in these disciplines are included.

Journals

Scientific journals are important sources of current research information. More detailed lists of journals in specific agriculture and natural resource disciplines can be found in the Hutchinson and Greider book. Societies, associations, and scientific publishers provide the bulk of key journals. Currently there are a few open access journals in the agriculture and natural resources area, but not as many as in medicine, physics, or other scientific disciplines. For this chapter, a list of 150 core journals is provided on the CD-ROM accompanying this book (item 13-1 on the CD-ROM).

Web Resources

There is an abundance of Web resources in the agricultural sciences; the following is a short list of core sites. The descriptions are taken from the respective Web sites.

- *AgNIC, the Agriculture Network Information Center.* www.agnic.org. AgNIC is a voluntary partnership bringing you selected, quality agricultural, environmental, and food information and resources.
- *ATTRA—National Sustainable Agriculture Information Service.* www.attra.org. Provides information and other technical assistance to farmers, ranchers, extension agents, educators, and others involved in sustainable agriculture in the United States.
- *The Food and Agriculture Organization of the United Nations.* www.fao.org. FAO acts as a neutral forum where all nations meet as equals to negotiate agreements and debate policy.
- *National Agricultural Law Center.* www.nationalaglawcenter.org. The National AgLaw Center is the only agricultural and food law research and information facility that is independent, national in scope, and directly connected to the national agricultural information network.
- *National Agricultural Library.* www.nal.usda.gov. One of four National Libraries in the United States, NAL offers search facilities and gateways to agricultural information.
- *World Agricultural Information Centre Portal.* www.fao.org/waicent. This site provides essential documents, statistics, maps, and multimedia resources.

Integrating Resources for an Information Ecology

"Like a biological ecology, an information ecology is marked by strong interrelationships and dependencies among its different parts. The parts of an information ecology may be as different from each other as the sand, sunlight, saltwater, and starfish of a marine ecology, but they are as closely bound together" (Nardi and O'Day, 1999). In an academic setting, librarians work with a variety of individuals and groups who have some common interests but are often at opposite ends of a knowledge continuum. On one side are the undergraduates, who are new to a discipline. They need more information on how scientists communicate, which societies and associations are most important, and differences between popular journals, trade journals, and scholarly or society publications. Graduate students and faculty understand the discipline but need help with grey literature, government reports or documents, citation searching, complex statistical information, or geographic information systems (GIS) data.

Information services to these and other users involves providing Web pages, online tutorials, and PDF documents combining screen shot images and instruction for navigating complex databases or Web sites. In class instruction, information sessions on citation searching, setting up tables of contents or search alerts, or new features of a database may also be helpful. Anticipating and providing value-added information resources on "hot topics" for your constituents are important, such as the fall 2005 research focus on the bird flu (Avian influenza). Familiarize yourself with subject-based information sources, including journals, handbooks, Web sites, databases, books, government documents, cooperative extension reports, and other items, and then build an information ecology that fits the current needs of the students and researchers you serve.

Trends and Technologies for Future Instruction in Agriculture and Natural Resources

One trend of no surprise to anyone now working in the sciences is the growth of open access journals. The number of articles available, distribution, peer review process, access, and use of open access will continue to grow. In a 2004 survey by the Science Advisory Board, "almost 80% of the 1,400 respondents stated that limited access to full-text documents was the most annoying aspect of online literature searches" (Science Advisory Board, 2004). Open access will not provide access to all pertinent information, but it will offer a viable model that is distinct from traditional publishing routes. Librarians and researchers are justified in supporting open access publications. Even so, the ranking and value of open access journal articles at the time of tenure will continue to be a local issue with broader implications.

Further development of cooperative models of information creation and dissemination will continue. One such model is eXtension, a program of the Extension Committee on Organization and Policy (ECOP) of the National Association of State Universities and Land-Grant Colleges (NASULGC), with funding from the U.S. Department of Agriculture (USDA) Cooperative State Research, Education and Extension Service (CSREES). The mission of eXtension is "to advance the science and practice of engagement and outreach of land-grant colleges and universities to the people of the states they serve" (eXtension, 2005).

In a speech on biocomplexity, Dr. Rita Colwell mentioned learning new things about biology from a very unlikely source:

> Congressman George Brown of the House Science Committee and a long-time friend of science, made an astute observation in the commencement address he delivered at UCLA in 1994. He said to the graduates: Not unlike the way diverse cells in a multicellular biological organism signal their activity and thus coordinate their behavior with unlike cells to ensure the survival of the organism, we as citizens need to do the same. We can learn our place and function in the larger community only by signaling—by explaining ourselves. For the science community, this signaling is more than just biochemical—it means reaching across disciplines. It will take biologists, ecologists, physical scientists, computer scientists, engineers and surely those in the behavioral sciences to understand the signals for survivability. (Colwell, 1998)

Successful instruction in agriculture and natural resources will include signaling to researchers, farmers, students, cooperative extension agents, and others that librarians are in the know and can help them navigate the communication channels for scientific research. This communication and cooperation have been at the heart of the success of the AgNIC Alliance. AgNIC is a multifaceted collaboration of partnerships between land grant universities, nonprofit organizations, and cooperative extension and other agencies, and "the results of these partnerships are rich, cost-effective collections of essential information and services offered to users around the globe" (Gardner et al., 2002).

Conclusion

Agriculture and natural resource librarians can position themselves to be an important resource for students, generalists, and specialists. If we work correctly, we can become a keystone species in the ecology of our campuses. "We believe that information ecologies have keystone species too, although their contributions may be invisible at first glance. We see keystone species in information ecologies as those people, whose special contributions stitch together people, tools and practices, filling gaps and helping the whole enterprise to run well. In general, we find that keystone species are often people who translate, localize and otherwise create necessary bridges" (O'Day and Nardi, 2003).

The 2005 ALA/ACRL/STS *Information Literacy Standards for Science and Technology* will help librarians relate discipline-specific information to general information literacy standards and performance indicators. Much needs to be done in this area in the upcoming years, and if many librarians take a piece of the information literacy puzzle, then we can all work together to complete an important picture for the future direction of agriculture and natural resources instruction.

Bibliography

American Library Association (ALA). 2005. ACRL/STS Task Force on Information Literacy for Science and Technology. "Information Literacy Standards for Science and Technology." *C&RL News* (May): 381–388.

Barclay, Donald A. 2003. *Teaching and Marketing Electronic Information Literacy Programs: A How-to-Do-It Manual for Librarians*. New York: Neal-Schuman.

Colwell, Rita. 1998. "Balancing the Biocomplexity of the Planet's Living Systems: A Twenty-first Century Task for Science." *Bioscience* 48, no. 10 (October): 786–787.

eXtension. 2005. *Welcome to eXtension*. http://intranet.extension.org/index.php?module=articles&func=display&ptid=9&aid=22 (accessed July 14, 2005).

Gardner, Melanie, Jean Gilbertson, Barbara Hutchinson, Tim Lynch, Janet McCue, and Amy Paster. 2002. "Partnering for Improved Access to Agricultural Information: The Agriculture Network Information Center (AgNIC) Initiative." *ARL Bimonthly Report* 223 (August): 5–10.

Gladwell, Malcolm. 2005. *Blink: The Power of Thinking without Thinking*. New York: Little, Brown.

Hutchinson, Barbara S., and Antoinette Paris Greider, eds. 2002. *Using the Agricultural, Environmental, and Food Literature*. New York: Marcel Dekker.

Jacobson, Trudi E., and Lijuan Xu. 2004. *Motivating Students in Information Literacy Classes*. New York: Neal-Schuman.

Kaplan, Justin, ed. 2002. *Bartlett's Familiar Quotations: A Collection of Passages, Phrases, and Proverbs Traced to Their Sources in Ancient and Modern Literature*. Boston, MA: Little, Brown.

Manuel, Kate. 2004. "Generic and Discipline-Specific Information Literacy Competencies: The Case of the Sciences." *Science and Technology Libraries* 24, no. 3: 279–308.

Nardi, Bonnie A., and Vicki L. O'Day. 1999. *Information Ecologies: Using Technology with Heart*. Cambridge, MA: MIT Press.

O'Day, Vicki L., and Bonnie A. Nardi. 2003. "An Ecological Perspective on Digital Libraries." In *Digital Library Use: Social Practice in Design and Evaluation*, pp. 65–84, edited by Ann Peterson Bishop, Nancy A. Van House, and Barbara P. Buttenfield. Cambridge, MA: MIT Press.

Science Advisory Board. 2004. *Scientists Frustrated with Limited Access to Full-Text Documents*. www.scienceboard.net/community/news/news.214.html (accessed July 14, 2005).

Von Baeyer, Hans Christian. 2004. *Information: The New Language of Science*. Cambridge, MA: Harvard University Press.

14

Hospitality and Gaming

Cory Tucker

Introduction

The hospitality and gaming industry is rapidly growing and evolving, stimulated by rising disposable incomes throughout the developed world, more tolerant attitudes toward gambling, and governments' desire for new revenue sources. The $10 trillion worldwide industry called hospitality—travel, tourism, lodging, catering, restaurants, resorts, time-shares, cruises, and more—is riding a strong wave of global economic growth. Many Asian nations have seen exponential expansion of their hospitality enterprises. In the United States the hospitality and tourism industry is one of the fastest-growing industries. According to the National Restaurant Association, the food service industry employs more than 11.3 million workers, making the food service industry one of the leading generators of job growth in the United States. Hotel-keeping ranks seventh among service industries in the United States, coming only after such giants as public transportation and restaurant management. There are approximately 51,000 hotels in the United States with a total of 3.9 million rooms. The lodging industry employs 1.16 million people and directly supplies nearly 7.6 million jobs. In recent years the number of hospitality programs in higher education has grown tremendously to keep pace with this fast-growing industry.

Information literacy concepts and skills help students to think critically and aid their preparation for higher-level jobs in hospitality industries and peripheral sectors. Many hospitality programs have started to offer distance learning classes. For distance learning students, information literacy has added importance, because getting access to resources is often difficult for them.

Hospitality and gaming is a challenging arena due to the subject's broad scope and the information needs of faculty and students working in the discipline. At the University of Nevada, Las Vegas (UNLV), hospitality encompasses the following subjects:

- hotel administration
- gaming management
- food and beverage
- tourism
- event and meetings management
- recreation and leisure
- golf management
- sports management

Most of the curriculum and research in hospitality and gaming are directly related to the business discipline. What makes the hospitality and gaming curriculum special is its focus on a rapidly evolving and growing industry. Students in the field of hospitality range from undergraduate to graduate students. Degrees are offered at the bachelor's, master's, and doctoral levels. Students and faculty in hospitality and gaming exhibit research behavior that is similar to that of library patrons in the broader arena of business. For instance, they can be more demanding and time sensitive and have higher expectations than the typical library patron. Users prefer electronic resources, exhibit traits of urgency, and typically need the very latest information. Although an academic background in business is helpful to librarians supporting such a program, a librarian without this background can learn to support various business disciplines, including hospitality and gaming. This chapter will help you prepare to do just that.

Literature Review

Although several published articles discuss hospitality and gaming management's information sources, this chapter is the first published overview of library and information literacy instruction for the discipline. There are, however, several pertinent articles on instruction for business students. An article by Daniel P. Rutledge and Alicia Maehler discusses the impact of bibliographic instruction for improving research skills of undergraduates in business (Rutledge and Maehler, 2003). The instruction resulted in improved student performance on a course research project. Another article by Judd Vaughan, Betty Tims, Lucy Farrow, and Jeffery Periatt evaluates a library instruction component of an undergraduate introduction to business course in terms of its goals, content, format, and instructional effectiveness (Vaughan et al., 2004). Ann M. Feigen et al., discuss a model wherein information literacy competencies were targeted as outcomes in an undergraduate business curriculum (Feigen et al., 2002). Arthur H. Sterngold and Janet M. Hurlbert discuss a six-week project in a marketing strategy course incorporating library workshops, student-instructor conferences, and use of assignments to develop students' information literacy skills and prepare them to succeed in today's knowledge-based economy (Sterngold and Hurlbert, 1998). Julie O'Keeffe describes research strategies to help business students locate basic sources for company and industry data (O'Keeffe, 1998). Such basic information often consists of locating stock and financial information for a specific company. More complex information includes things such as company histories, plans affecting a company's viability, or trends in an industry to which the company must respond. O'Keeffe's strategy proceeds from relatively simple to more advanced types of information and research techniques, introducing new sources as necessary to answer more complex questions. I prefer this strategy because it helps students understand the sources, content, and organization of relevant business information sources. Hawes (1994) describes the growth of the information society and concludes that business schools need to do more to promote students' information literacy.

Several other articles discuss information sources for hospitality and gaming. Susan C. Awe, Kathleen Keating, and David G. Schwartz compiled an annotated resource list of gaming industry resources, covering Web sites, portals, and print resources, encompassing statistics, regulations, history, and industry trends (Awe et al., 2002). An article by Diane Zabel lists key Web sites for lodging, gaming, restaurants, food services, and tourism (Zabel, 2003). There are also two pertinent articles by Leslie E. Cummings and Thomas R. Mirkovich. The first of these is a guide to the literature of commercial gaming, including history, law and regulation, and resources on related economic, societal, and cultural topics (Cummings and Mirkovich, 1997/1998a). Their second article is a literature guide to key books, periodicals, and other resources for studying and teaching the business of gaming (Cummings and Mirkovich, 1997/1998b).

Getting Information to Faculty and Students: The Basics

Like most information users today, students and faculty prefer access to online, full-text resources. They want to access their information from their offices, computer labs on campus, and their residence or workplace. Library and information literacy instruction must address these user preferences in order to be relevant. To keep abreast of new sources and the library's means of delivery, faculty may request instruction sessions for themselves and for graduate students who teach. In these instruction sessions, faculty and graduate students expect to learn about:

- The library collection and its available resources
- Better searching techniques
- Full-text availability and the means to retrieve it
- Library services for faculty and graduate students
- Library reference and instructional support for students

The librarian should tailor instruction sessions to address specific assignments and the broader needs of the curriculum. Instruction sessions should generally demonstrate how to:

- Conduct a literature review in hospitality and gaming–related information
- Locate company information
- Locate industry information
- Locate market research–related information (e.g., about customers and competitors)

Lesson Planning and Preparation

Effective collaboration between the librarian and faculty is perhaps the most important aspect of planning and preparation for these instruction sessions. Hospitality and gaming encompasses a broad range of subjects, including economics, law, management, and marketing, making it essential that the librarian meet with faculty and understand their particular course-related goals. Information in this industry comes from diverse sources, and information produced by the industry often predominates over scholarly sources. Students must learn to read critically and distinguish between typical public relations hyperbole and more objective perspectives. You should obtain course syllabi, identify course objectives, and understand the associated assignments. Choose topics or subjects to demonstrate that are relevant to what the students are researching. This will grab their attention and keep them focused during the session. Next, select the most appropriate information resources to demonstrate. Depending on the amount of class time you have, selecting the resources to demonstrate can be tricky. Most class periods last either fifty or seventy-five minutes. Further, if you allow hands-on time for the students to get familiar with a database or publication, you will have less time to lecture to the class. Finally, become familiar with the scope and functionality of each resource you plan to demonstrate—if anything, you must *overlearn* the databases and other sources in order to be optimally effective.

Best Resources

Many of the same philosophies and principles in business are used in hospitality and gaming, and faculty and students use a lot of basic business resources to conduct their research. Much information related to hospitality and gaming is distributed by trade or professional organizations, whose publications and other information products can be very expensive. In addition, the format in which the information is delivered can be difficult to manage. Some information, especially annual reports, is delivered in PDF format through Web sites or e-mail. For libraries wishing to collect printed copies of these reports, there are associated binding and workload costs.

Research in hospitality and gaming at UNLV generally involves locating two types of information, namely, primary sources about companies and industries and secondary sources about them (e.g., articles and books). Students most often need to gather information about industry-related issues or trends from articles and books (i.e., secondary sources). Both primary sources and a special group of secondary sources provide information about company finances and industry trends. The key sources in both of these categories are in the following lists, as are the most important reference sources. The accompanying CD-ROM includes a list of periodicals and trade associations in hospitality and gaming (see file 14-1 on the CD-ROM).

Sources for Locating Articles and Books

- *ABI/Inform Global* by ProQuest Information and Learning. www.proquest.com. This resource covers the business side of hospitality and gaming. The database includes over 1,800 of the leading U.S. and international business and management journals with over 900 full-text titles from 1987 to the present. Subjects covered include advertising, marketing, economics, human resources, finance, taxation, and computers. *ABI/Inform Global* also includes information on over 60,000 companies. Business faculty, including those in hospitality and gaming, favor this database.

- *Business Source Premier.* EBSCO Information Services. www.ebsco.com/home. This database is another recommended option for the business aspect of hospitality and gaming. This database contains approximately 3,298 full-text scholarly journals and business periodicals covering management, economics, finance, accounting, international business, and much more. It includes country economic reports from the *Economist Intelligence Unit, Global Insight, ICON Group,* and *CountryWatch.* The database also contains more than 5,000 company profiles and 1,600 industry reports from Reuters' *Datamonitor.*

- *Digital Dissertations.* ProQuest Information and Learning. www.proquest.com. This database contains over 1.5 million entries, providing citations to North American and European dissertations from 1861 forward, with abstracts from 1980 forward. It also provides citations and abstracts for theses from 1988 forward. Faculty and graduate students are the primary users of dissertations.

- *Factiva.* ProQuest Information and Learning. www.proquest.com. This database is a great resource for timely information. It includes the full text of all editions of the *Wall Street Journal* and *Barron's,* three months of the *New York Times,* and 8,000 other serial publications, 20,000 company reports, and 8,500 business Web sites selected by *Factiva's* editors.

- *Hospitality and Tourism Index.* EBSCO Information Services. www.ebsco .com/home. This relatively new bibliographic database covers both scholarly research and industry news in every area of hospitality and tourism. It combines *Articles in Hospitality and Tourism* (AHT) and the *Lodging, Restaurant & Tourism Index.* Subject areas covered include hotel management, food service and beverage management, travel and tourism, event management, gaming, international cuisine, law, and market trends.

- *LeisureTourism.* CABI Publishing. www.leisuretourism.com. This database is comprised of citations and abstracts selected from *CAB Abstracts.* The database provides international coverage of literature in the areas of leisure, recreation, sport, tourism and hospitality activities, facilities, products, and services.

- *LexisNexis Academic.* LexisNexis. www.lexisnexis.com/academic. The Business section of *LexisNexis Academic* includes business news journals, company financial information, industry and market news, and U.S. Securities and Exchange Commission filings and reports.
- *SBRNet.* Sports Business Research Network. www.sbrnet.com. *SBRNet* focuses on the sporting goods and sports marketing industry. The site features market research and industry news covering all facets of the industry including sports equipment sales, sports participation, sports broadcasting, sports sponsorship, and sports marketing. This database is useful for students in sports management, recreation, and leisure.

Sources for Company, Industry, and Market Information

- *Datamonitor Business Information Center.* Reuters. www.reuters.com. This resource includes over 10,000 U.S. and international public and private company profiles, 2,500 industry profiles, and 100 country profiles. The company profiles include company and business description, history, key employees, products and services, competitors, company view, locations, and subsidiaries. A SWOT analysis (i.e., strengths, weaknesses, opportunities, and threats) is provided for the 500 largest companies. Industry profiles include an overview, segmentation, competitive landscape, leading companies, and forecasts. Each country profile provides a description of the economic performance and GDP, assessment of potential for development, and detailed market and industry analysis of the business environment.
- *Global Market Information Database.* Euromonitor International. www.euromonitor.com. This integrated online information system covers over 350 markets in 207 countries. Information is accessible in four modules: statistics (quantitative data and forecasts on consumer lifestyles, retailing, countries, and consumer markets), analysis (in-depth market analysis reports), companies (profiles of leading companies, including financial data, market share, and brand information) and sources (data providers by specific subject area). Statistical data go back as far as 1977 (although most series start in 1990) and are forecast to 2015.
- *MarketResearch.com Academic.* MarketResearch.com. http://academic.marketresearch.com. This resource includes market profiles from Kalorama Information, Packaged Facts, and Specialists in Business Information (SBI) covering industries including consumer goods, food and beverages, demographics, healthcare, technology, media, manufacturing, and others. Reports include extensive background information, forecasts and analyses on the topic, statistics, charts, graphs, and tables.
- *Mergent Online.* Mergent. www.mergent.com. *Mergent* contains financial information and current news on public companies traded in the United

States. Annual reports, performance information, EDGAR (SEC) filings, and timely articles for over 13,000 corporations are provided.

- *Mintel Consumer Intelligence*. Mintel International Group. www.mintel.com. A newcomer to academic markets, *Mintel* includes market research reports for industries in Europe, the United Kingdom, and the United States. Reports cover a variety of sectors including consumer goods, travel and tourism, financial industry, Internet industry, retail, and food and drink. Reports discuss market drivers, market size and trends, market segmentation, supply structure, advertising and promotion, retail distribution, consumer characteristics, and forecasts. Includes Mintel's Travel & Tourism Analyst and Country Reports.

- *North American Industry Classification System* (NAICS). www.census.gov/epcd/www/naics.html. Freely available. The NAICS has replaced the U.S. Standard Industrial Classification (SIC) system. The NAICS was developed jointly by the United States, Canada, and Mexico to provide new comparability in statistics about business activity across North America.

- *Standard & Poor's NetAdvantage* by Standard & Poor's. www2.standardandpoors.com. *NetAdvantage* supplies full-text access to ten core Standard and Poor's investor information sources: *Bond Guide, Corporation Records, Dividend Record, Earnings Guide, Industry Surveys, Mutual Fund Reports, Outlook, Register of Corporations, Stock Guide*, and *Stock Reports*. The *Industry Surveys* are very detailed, identifying trends and comparing company performance.

- *Standard Industrial Classification* (SIC). www.osha.gov/pls/imis/sicsearch.html. Freely available. The SIC system has been replaced by the NAICS. Some information resources still use SIC codes.

Encyclopedias, Handbooks, and Key Reference Materials

- American Hotel and Lodging Association. 2005. *Directory of Hotel and Lodging Companies*. Washington, DC: American Hotel Association Directory Corp. 720 pp. This directory lists hotel and lodging companies that own, manage, develop, or franchise properties worldwide, as well as referral groups and real estate investment trusts.

- *Casino City's Global Gaming Almanac*. 2005. Newton, MA: Casino City Press. ISBN: 1-931732-29-9. This almanac provides market, financial, legal, and regulatory information about land-based and online gambling in 250 regions and jurisdictions around the globe.

- *Casino City's North American Gaming Almanac*. 2005. Newton, MA: Casino City Press. ISBN: 1-931732-33-7. This almanac provides executive summaries of North American gaming markets, including the United States, Canada, and the Caribbean. For each region, a market overview is provided with overall market statistics along with a breakdown by state or province. It contains detailed reviews of gaming markets in each area including market size, overall revenue per gaming type, legal environment, and statistics such as number of gaming locations by gaming type, number of gaming machines, and number of table games.

- Miller, Richard K. 2005. *Entertainment, Cultural and Leisure Market Research Handbook*. Norcross, GA: Richard K. Miller and Associates. 554 pp. ISBN: 1-57783-042-3. This handbook provides current statistics and data on types of media and advertising including print, television, and radio. Also profiles leading media companies.
- Miller, Richard K. 2005. *Restaurant and Foodservice Research Handbook*. Norcross, GA: Richard K. Miller and Associates. 405 pp. ISBN: 1-57783-047-4. This detailed source provides current and projected market opportunities in the restaurant and food service industry. Every market sector in the dining and food service business is included. Other topics include what Americans eat, city-by-city analysis, full-service dining, quick-service restaurants, take-out and home-meal replacement, catering, contract food service, hotel restaurants, malls and retail locations, concessionaires, bars and taverns, on-board meals, travel and business dining, holiday dining, food festivals, unique restaurant concepts, management issues, e-commerce, technology, entertainment, and demographics.
- Miller, Richard K. 2005. *Travel and Leisure Market Research Handbook*. Norcross, GA: Richard K. Miller and Associates. 650 pp. ISBN: 1-57783-051-2. This handbook covers all aspects of travel and leisure including hotels, casinos, recreation activities, and travel spending. It also includes consumer expenditure statistics for all fifty states and major cities.
- PKF Consulting Corp. 2005. *Trends in the Hotel Industry*. San Francisco, CA: Hospitality Asset Advisors International. 120 pp. An annual report on the industry developed from over 5,000 annual income statements from hotels and motels across the United States. Information is presented by type, geographic location, rate, and size categories and provides detailed analyses of revenues, expenses, and profits.
- Plunkett's Research Ltd. 2005. *Plunkett's Airline, Hotel and Travel Industry Almanac*. Houston, TX: Plunkett's Research. 468 pp. ISBN: 1-593290-09-1. Plunkett's almanac covers trends, statistics, and market research focusing on hotels, hospitality, developers, resorts, tourists, business travel, leisure travel, airlines, discount airlines, cruise ships and cruise lines, passenger railroads, consolidators, travel agents and agencies, online booking and Internet travel research, consolidation, and profiles of leading companies.
- Walker, Terri C. 2005. *Casino and Gaming Market Research Handbook*. Newton, MA: Casino City Press. ISBN: 0-9720522-7-5. The handbook covers current issues in the gaming industry such as the economy, global unrest, U.S. and international markets, lotteries, riverboats, and land-based casinos and the increasing trend by states to expand gaming to generate revenue.

Library of Congress Subject Headings

The rapidly changing nature of hospitality and gaming notwithstanding, the library online catalog is an important resource. The following are recommended Library of Congress subject headings related to the industry:

Bed and Breakfast Accommodations
Casinos
Congresses and Conventions
Cookery
Food Service
Gambling
Health Resorts
Hospitality Industry
Hotel Housekeeping
Hotel Management
Hotels
Meetings
Motels
Resorts
Restaurant Management
Restaurants
Special Events
Tourism
Travel
Travelers

What to Teach

Once you are familiar with these information sources, you are ready to teach library instruction sessions in hospitality and gaming. First, introduce and demonstrate the three key periodical databases for hospitality and gaming: *Hospitality and Tourism Index*, *LeisureTourism*, and *ABI/Inform*. If time permits, you may want to demonstrate *Business Source Premier*, although it has the same interface as *Hospitality and Tourism Index* and a brief mention of its scope is adequate. After the demonstrations, give students five to ten minutes of hands-on time. During this time, you can circulate around the room and answer any questions. If student workstations are not available, you may want to offer individual or group sessions in an office or lab (provide telephone numbers and e-mail addresses so students and faculty can contact you). Alternatively, you can invite one or more students to the front of the class to conduct searches while you gently coach them.

Next, cover how to retrieve company- and industry-related information. You should distinguish between different types of companies, such as public or private and independent versus subsidiaries or otherwise-affiliated companies. Much more information is available about publicly held companies than for private companies. Ownership of a company and its status either as a parent or subsidiary are also important for locating information. Information about a subsidiary is often available only in information sources about or published by its parent company. The following list describes three basic categories of business information and provides examples of information sources associated with each.

- *Company-related information.* This includes company history, financial data sources, SEC filings, stock information, company products, rankings, and philanthropic activities. In the area of SEC filings, the librarian should identify and describe both annual and 10-K reports (a public company files a 10-K within 90 days after the end of its fiscal year). These are the two most detailed information sources available for companies. Show students how to locate several different annual and 10-K reports and company information from secondary sources. Two key databases to demonstrate for company information are *Mergent Online* (encompassing 10-K reports, annual reports, and secondary sources such as recent news) and *Datamonitor's Business Information Center* (whose secondary sources include company reports produced by Datamonitor and news from various sources).

- *Industry-related sources.* Industry-related information identifies trends in products and services and compares the performance of companies in a single industry or in related industries. Some industry information sources have their own categories or classification systems and organize industries into relatively broad groups, while other resources use the U.S. government's Standard Industrial Classification (SIC), the North American Industry Classification System (NAICS), or both. Researchers may find it helpful to create a list of keywords, including broad and specific terms, synonyms, and related words. For example, someone looking for information on the beer industry might create a list of keywords such as Alcoholic Beverages or Brewing Industry. The librarian should also explain the SIC and NAICS classifications and how to use them to find information about industries, companies, and individual business establishments.

- *Overviews, statistics, comparative financial ratios, and company rankings. Standard & Poor's NetAdvantage* and *Mergent Online*, both aimed at investors, are key sources for these types of industry-related information. Trade associations and regulatory agencies compile a vast amount of statistics and other information that may not be readily available in other resources. Trade associations also produce industry-specific publications, such as trade magazines and journals. Many trade publications are available in *Business Source Premier* and *ABI/Inform Global*. Libraries often subscribe to trade publications, so searching the online catalog by title or name of the association can be useful. Trade associations usually have a lot of useful information available on their Web sites. Companies must also comply with government regulations applicable to their industries. For information on regulatory sources, such as the Code of Federal Regulations, state statutes, and administrative codes, refer to Chapter 16 in this book on legal information.

- *Market information.* Students in hospitality and gaming often need to conduct market research in order to estimate the demand for their products or services. Information sources used in market research include demographics (local, national, and international), consumer spending, and market share (i.e., sales of competing products). Students may want demographic data in order to identify potential customers, their consumption behaviors, and buying habits. Planning a good advertising campaign is closely related to market research. It is important for market researchers to know how much certain companies (including competitors) spend on advertising in each of the dominant formats (print, Internet, television, radio). Three of the best databases for market research are *Global Market Information Database*, *Mintel*, and *MarketResearch Academic*. *Mintel* is the best database to use for demographic and market research information. *Mintel* provides detailed analyses on various sectors of the hospitality and travel industries. It also incorporates demographic statistics from the Simmons Market Research Bureau. *Mintel* and the *Global Market Information Database* provide excellent analyses and data on consumer spending and product sales.

Librarians should cover the following points when demonstrating each online resource:

- Content—the types of information in the resource (citations, abstracts, full text, statistical data)
- How it is organized
- How to search for and view information (including using link resolvers, if applicable)
- How to export information (saving to an external device or one's own computer; e-mailing)

I have described a general approach to teaching research techniques and information sources pertinent to hospitality and gaming. The topics and resources you emphasize will vary depending on the academic level of the class. The following lists contain some recommended sequences of instruction for different academic levels.

For lower-level undergraduate classes:

- Introduce students to the online catalog.
- Demonstrate key article databases: *Hospitality and Tourism Index* and *ABI/Inform Global*.
- Discuss company- and industry-related information: *Standard & Poor's NetAdvantage*.

For upper-level undergraduate and graduate classes:

- Concentrate on locating journal articles: *Hospitality and Tourism Index*, *LeisureTourism*, *ABI/Inform Global*, *Business Source Premier*. If the class needs scholarly research, supplement your coverage of the article databases with *Digital Dissertations*.
- Discuss company and industry-related information in more depth: *Standard & Poor's NetAdvantage* (spend lots of time on the "Industry References" section of *Standard & Poor's* "Industry Survey"), *Datamonitor*, *Mergent*, and *Global Market Information Database*.

Emerging Trends and Technologies

Several trends will have an impact on instruction and library support for hospitality and gaming in the future. One of these is the increasing availability of full-text information, both in online databases and free sources. Magazine and journal publishers in hospitality and gaming are slightly behind in the race to create journals full text in electronic format. This has a direct impact on users and the libraries that serve them. For example, the best resource for students and faculty in this area is *Hospitality and Tourism Index*, which does not provide full-text access. Currently there is poor online availability of both scholarly and trade periodicals in hospitality and gaming. So, although this discipline is a little behind in providing online access, we can expect that full-text access to periodicals will increase, particularly as online aggregators like ProQuest and EBSCO expand their coverage into these areas.

The second trend involves the format of company- and industry-related information. To reduce publishing costs, some associations and companies disseminate their reports via e-mail in PDF format. Some associations allow downloading of complete reports from their Web site. Libraries wishing to collect such reports need to decide the best means for doing so, for example, by printing the reports and adding them to the tangible collection, capturing a copy of the file, or linking to an external resource, or by cataloging them versus providing access on subject-related pages on the library Web site.

Conclusion

Research in hospitality and gaming is focused on business and social factors associated with the industry, which presents special challenges for an instructional librarian. As in any subject area, librarians should gain mastery in using key information resources, build relationships with faculty, and develop strong collections to serve faculty and students. Finally, librarians should emphasize appropriate information literacy concepts in every instruction session; doing so will help students to focus their research and think critically about the research process.

Bibliography

Awe, Susan C., Kathleen Keating, and David G. Schwartz. 2002. "Studies in Chance: A Selective Guide to Gaming Industry Resources." *Reference Services Review* 30, no. 2: 169–175.

Cummings, Leslie E., and Thomas R. Mirkovich. 1997–1998b. "The Business of Gaming a Literature Guide." *Journal of Hospitality and Tourism Education* 9, no. 4: 28–35.

———. 1997–1998a. "Foundation Gaming Resources: History, Law, Economics and Social Issues." *Journal of Hospitality and Tourism Education* 9, no. 4: 21–27.

Fiegen, Ann M., Bennett Cherry, and Kathleen Watson. 2002. "Reflections on Collaboration: Learning Outcomes and Information Literacy Assessment in the Business Curriculum." *Reference Services Review* 30, no. 4: 307–318.

Hawes, Douglass K. 1994. "Information Literacy and the Business Schools." *Journal of Education for Business* (September/October): 54–61.

O'Keeffe, Julie. 1998. "One Step at a Time: A Framework for Introducing Business Students to Basic Sources of Company and Industry Data." *Research Strategies* 16, no. 1: 71–77.

Rutledge, Daniel P., and Alicia Maehler. 2003. "An Assessment of Library Education Contributions to Business Student Learning: A Case Study." *Journal of Business and Finance Librarianship* 9, no. 1: 3–19.

Sterngold, Arthur H., and Janet M. Hurlbert. 1998. "Information Literacy and the Marketing Curriculum: A Multidimensional Definition and Practical Application." *Journal of Marketing Education* 20, no. 3: 244–249.

Vaughan, Judd, Betty Tims, Lucy Farrow, and Jeffery Periatt. 2004. "Evaluation and Assessment of a Library Instruction Component of an Introduction to Business Course: A Continuous Process." *Reference Services Review* 32, no. 3: 274–283.

Zabel, Diane. 2003. "The Best of the Web: Hospitality and Tourism Web Sites." *Journal of Business and Finance Librarianship* 8, no. 3/4: 167–179.

15

International Marketing Paired with Web Delivery

Patrick Ragains

Introduction

The European Union, Central American Free Trade Agreement, and other modern trade regimes aside, cross-border marketing and business are hardly new developments in the world. Evidence predating the earliest recorded histories shows ancient societies' use of foreign goods. Likewise, merchants have always sought foreign markets for their goods and services. Jared Diamond, in his book *Collapse: How Societies Choose to Succeed or Fail*, identifies international trade and foreign relations as critical factors in the growth and decline of societies (Diamond, 2005). Foreign trade is characterized today by complex business, legal, political, and cultural factors and is more significant in our lives than ever before.

Business students attending many colleges and universities gain exposure to international marketing in at least one course in their undergraduate studies, most often at the senior level. Business faculty expect their students to gather and use information for specific purposes, but few faculty assign the highest importance to the development of research skills among their students. A gap can easily exist between faculty's expectations for student performance and students' ability to find the information needed to complete their assignments competently, especially in a multifaceted course like international marketing. Library skills learned for freshman English, social science, humanities, and even other business courses may leave students unprepared to identify, locate, and use information from the wide range of sources associated with international business. Skilled librarians can help bridge this gap in a number of ways.

This chapter outlines a strategy for supporting international marketing courses at the undergraduate and graduate level. I describe a number of teaching techniques and a selection of information sources to support student assignments. Considering the wide range of business, legal, political, and cultural issues that set international marketing apart from the rest of the business curriculum, there is perhaps a special role for librarians to play in assisting students in such courses. Since today's students greatly prefer to use Web-based information, the means of delivery can be just as important as the sources. Most students in senior-level and graduate-level business programs are well focused and willing to seek guidance from their instructors and librarians, but they are busy and have little inclination to spend time completing optional instructional exercises, developing an individualized search strategy, mapping concepts, or performing other activities not clearly related to completing their required assignments. Nevertheless, it is important for such students to understand enough about information sources within the scope of international marketing to be able, once they enter the workplace, to understand and competently perform the tasks simulated earlier in their coursework.

Typical marketing assignments mirror common scenarios in the business world, where success can depend heavily upon gathering pertinent information, analyzing it, and rapidly deciding which elements to use and which to ignore. Research skills may have added importance in international business courses, since the need to negotiate unfamiliar legal, cultural, and other environments increases the complexity of the undertaking. Further, international business often involves more chance than do simpler domestic businesses, making it even more important to have mastery over the information pertinent to one's venture.

I suggest delivering as much content as possible to such students via a course-related Web page. Although I typically use a one-shot session to introduce these students to key sources, services, and search strategies, the Web page is the primary support mechanism. The Web page should include key sources students need to complete their marketing plans, cultural overviews, and research into topics such as ethical aspects of globalization, communication in intercultural settings, and bribery in the business cultures of various countries.

Of course, using a library Web page as an instructional tool is not limited to marketing or business classes. Librarians can adopt basic elements of this Web page design to support courses in many other subjects. You can use this model effectively in a number of situations. It works well when:

- The number or complexity of sources the students will need exceeds what you can present in the class time available to you.
- You have just established a new relationship with a faculty member who has asked for your instructional assistance. A well-constructed library Web page that supports a course will create a positive first impression and can become a

medium for long-term collaboration. Above all, it shows your commitment to assisting the instructor's students with their information needs. That is the bottom line of a library's instructional support role.

- The students whom you will assist meet at a remote site. The instructor may meet with them via interactive instructional television (IITV) or may travel to meet with the class for some or all of their scheduled sessions. A Web page including links to key sources and promoting navigability throughout your library's Web site will reduce the disadvantages these students may perceive due to their remote setting. Ideally, you will also meet with the class, either in person or via IITV, to discuss their needs with them, recommend sources and search techniques, and orient them to the page.

- A faculty member wants instructional support but is not willing to devote class time for you to meet with students. Although this is near the bottom of my list of favored instructional scenarios, providing a course-related Web page conveys a positive image of your library's instructional services. It is an effective entry-level strategy, since a great Web page can lead a reluctant faculty member to schedule a one-shot session or other face time for you and his or her classes in the future.

Literature Review

Literature from the field of academic librarianship supports a number of concepts that are pertinent but not limited to supporting business instruction. These points include familiarity with the aims of the instructional programs you serve; the perceived benefits of contact with students in specific courses beyond a one-shot classroom session; briefing library public service staff concerning students' course-related needs that may generate reserve requests, reference questions, and other items that require the library staff's attention; and benefits of the librarian's familiarity with the pertinent subject matter and its information sources. Some of these points are unrelated to classroom teaching effectiveness, but all are important for providing the best possible service. D. F. Kohl and L. A. Wilson stress that librarians should teach relevant search strategies rather than simply teaching about sources (Kohl and Wilson, 1986). This is certainly just as true today as it was before the Internet gained its pervasive presence in education. Martha Cooney and Lorene Hiris expand on this point, noting the value of holding a follow-up library workshop to coach students as they search databases, which is best held at a point in the semester when students are more familiar with the subject matter and better prepared to identify keywords, concepts, and interrelationships (Cooney and Hiris, 2003). In a discussion of support for online business courses offered to remote students, Mary G. Fraser, Shari Buxbaum, and Amy Blair note the importance of assisting faculty with identifying information sources (including articles in licensed electronic journals), providing reference assistance in more than one mode (in person, e-mail, chat), and acting as a copyright liaison concerning online course readings (Fraser, Buxbaum, and Blair, 2002). The present author's article on course-related library Web pages advocates specific teaching strategies and design elements that display resources to students in a manner that is easy for them to understand and facilitates use of the library site (Ragains, 2001). All of this points to a role that blends collaboration and service in support of business instruction, extending substantially beyond a one-shot session.

A review of studies written by business educators proves useful in understanding the goals of their curricula and in determining how to support instruction. Surveys conducted over the last decade indicate that business educators consider understanding foreign cultures to be the most important factor to teach in an international marketing course. Pyung E. Han found that faculty approached this goal by assigning students to conduct a cultural analysis of their target country or region (Han, 2004). Such an analysis is a key component of the environmental scan that is characteristic of many marketing assignments. David M. Andrus, Jay Laughlin, and Wayne Norvell found that, after cultural fluency, faculty considered the most important aspects of international marketing to teach in their courses to be competition among businesses and strategic planning (Andrus, Laughlin, and Norvell, 1995). William J. Lundstrom and Steven D. White found that business faculty wanted their international marketing students to gain "a portfolio of strategic, marketing, and international skills that can be applied as a global manager" (Lundstrom and White, 1997). Business community (i.e., nonacademic) respondents to the same survey emphasized the importance of human relations and competency in researching "customer expectations, positioning, channels, pricing, product development and decision-making tools" (Lundstrom and White, 1997). Students themselves recognize the growing importance of international marketing, but report that they feel inadequately prepared for a related career. This may indicate a need for change in the curriculum, most likely to give students more exposure to intercultural issues, in addition to greater emphasis on planning and understanding one's competitors (Turley and Shannon, 1999). Finally, Bernd Simon, Parissa Haghirian, and Bodo Schlegelmilch found that the quality of information technology used in international marketing courses influenced students' perceptions of instructional effectiveness (Simon, Haghirian, and Schlegelmilch, 2003). The cases studied involved video links, although it seems reasonable that students would react similarly to library-related technology associated with a course, particularly if it includes a Web interface designed specifically for their course.

Instructional Goals Reflected in Course Assignments

The Marketing Plan

Students assigned to develop an international marketing plan must apply the marketing and management concepts emphasized in their previous business courses in addition to new ideas presented in the international marketing course. In this way the course serves as a capstone for a portion of the business curriculum. Typical features of an international marketing plan are:

- A statement of goals and objectives.
- Analysis of current and projected market and revenue share for one's product or service. What are the leading companies and how much of the consumer market has each captured? What is a reasonable goal for a new company entering and competing for business in the same market?
- A promotional campaign. How will consumers learn about and be encouraged to buy the product or service?
- An implementation plan. Does the plan take legal and business requirements into account? Does it recognize cultural characteristics? Is it flexible, to better withstand changes in one's business environment?
- Audit control. How will the managers measure the plan's effectiveness and adjust its implementation if necessary?

The segments of the plan related to market and revenue share and implementation are most strongly related to information gathering and use. As with any course, you should solicit and gather this sort of information from the instructor, so you will be certain that your Web page and class presentation will be on target.

Understanding Broad Issues Pertinent to International Business and Marketing

International marketing students gain exposure to a range of issues related to cross-border business ventures, including free trade (also known as globalization) versus protectionism, cultural fluency, and business or social norms particular to one's market. Course instructors may assign position papers or debates around these topics. Students' grades for such issue-oriented assignments depend significantly upon gathering, reading, and citing reputable information sources. Clearly, you should assist students by demonstrating relevant searches in your library catalog and in article databases such as *Business Source Premier*, *ABI/Inform Global*, and news sources including *LexisNexis Academic* and *Global Newsbank*, each described in the following section.

Information Pertinent to International Marketing

The business of international marketing encompasses importing, exporting, freight forwarding, labor issues, transportation, and legal matters. International entrepreneurs must possess or acquire an adequate understanding of pertinent cultural issues, the market for their product or service, the competition, how to advertise and promote the product effectively, legal and regulatory issues, logistics, advertising, and other aspects of bringing the product to market. Government and business-produced information directly addresses these needs. Scholarly and professional literature is useful for planning and in business education, but is much less important than government and business information. Scholarly information has a role in international marketing education when students explore controversial issues such as foreign business ethics or the effects of globalization, but instruction librarians must realize that scholarly information reflects upon business matters from a distance.

Entrepreneurs or other business practitioners discover information about international marketing in many ways, including the news media, the Web, and contacts with others in business. State-funded trade promotion and small business development centers, field offices of the U.S. Department of Commerce's International Trade Administration, and private contractors who provide business counseling and training are all important sources of information. These sources provide practical advice, assistance with loan applications, and often a necessary reality check for novices hoping to launch a small business. Below are sources of information pertinent to international marketing, including general resources directed at the business community and scholarly sources.

General Information

Each of the following print and online sources includes more than one type of information supporting international marketing:

- *Exporters' Encyclopaedia.* Annual. New York: Dun and Bradstreet International. This annual compendium includes information on export markets, communications, transportation, and information sources and services. The companion looseleaf *Fact File* provides updated information.
- *GovCon: Government Contractor Resource Center.* www.govcon.com. This site lists current foreign business opportunities and other business leads.
- *International Trade Administration: Trade Information Center.* www.ita.doc.gov. This is the U.S. Department of Commerce's free site for promoting international trade, including sections on manufacturing and services, market access, importing, and more.
- *Internationalist: Center for International Business Information.* www.internationalist.com/business. This source is a gateway to many other sites providing information ranging from investment to translation services.
- *STAT-USA.* www.stat-usa.gov. This subscription database presents a comprehensive collection of data and information produced by the U.S. Department of Commerce. Among the sources included are current trade leads, exchange rates, and guides to doing business in various countries.
- *Tradeport.* http://tradeport.org. A free Web site with content similar to that found in *STAT-USA.*
- *TSNN.com: The Ultimate Tradeshow Resource.* www.tsnn.com. A commercial site listing trade shows worldwide, including contact information.
- *U.S. Bureau of Customs and Border Protection.* www.cbp.gov. This site presents information on current trade issues, duty rates, business forms, and more.
- *U.S. Department of Agriculture: Foreign Agricultural Service.* www.fas.usda.gov. This Web site includes trade leads and export information for agricultural producers.

- *U.S. Department of State—Business Center.* www.state.gov/business. This site presents information about countries, business opportunities, travel, trade policies, and more.

Country Information

- *CulturGrams.* http://online.culturegrams.com. A licensed database produced for educational institutions, providing brief but useful overviews of most countries of the world, including history, customs, lifestyles, and government.
- *Direction of Trade Statistics. Yearbook.* 1981– . This publication of the International Monetary Fund includes data for most countries in the world on the value of imports from and exports to their most important trading partners. Summary data are also included for the world, industrial countries, and developing countries. Also available as a quarterly publication and online via subscription at www.imfstatistics.org.
- *Europa World Year Book Online.* www.europaworld.com. This subscription source provides detailed political and economic overviews of over 250 countries and territories.
- *Global Market Information Database* (GMID). www.gmid.euromonitor.com. This commercial database includes demographic and economic statistics, including consumer lifestyles, and retailing for over 200 countries. GMID also includes company and product-related reports and market analysis reports for over 350 markets. The database provider originally produced this information for business, rather than academic, markets.
- *Main Economic Indicators.* Available in print and online from SourceOECD; also available from several online aggregators. This monthly statistical publication provides a wide range of indicators on recent economic developments in the twenty-nine Organization for Economic Cooperation and Development (OECD) member countries and ten nonmembers.
- *Monthly Statistics of International Trade.* Available in print and online from SourceOECD and several online aggregators. This publication is a reliable and up-to-date source of statistics on international trade of Organization for Economic Cooperation and Development (OECD) countries. Data are presented by economic groupings, countries, and regions.
- *National Trade Estimate on Foreign Trade Barriers.* www.ustr.gov. This annual publication of the U.S. Trade Representative describes trade barriers in most countries.
- *OECD Economic Surveys.* Available in print and online from SourceOECD and several online aggregators. These publications are detailed annual surveys of individual countries (OECD members and other emerging national economies).
- *Tariff Information by Country.* www.ita.doc.gov/td/tic/tariff/country_tariff_info.htm. This free site presents current tariff information, compiled by the U.S. Department of Commerce's International Trade Administration.

- *USA Trade Online.* www.usatradeonline.gov. A subscription database providing monetary value of imports and exports to and from the United States by Harmonized Tariff Schedule (HS) commodity codes, trading partner country, or customs port. *USA Trade Online* includes limited data for quantity of imports and exports. The data cover 1994 through the latest statistical month.
- *World Economic Outlook.* www.imf.org. A Web gateway to statistics and reports from the International Monetary Fund, including national Gross Domestic Products and other measures.
- *World Factbook.* www.odci.gov/cia/publications/factbook/index.html; also available in print. This annual publication of the U.S. Central Intelligence Agency provides brief background information on countries and their people. Online maps are included.

Sources for Articles

- *ABI/Inform Global.* www.proquest.com. This database has strong brand recognition among business faculty. It covers scholarly journals and industry trade publications, mostly full text.
- *Business Source Premier* (EBSCOHost). http://search.epnet.com. This database provides the full text of many academic and professional journals and business trade publications, including a large number covering foreign markets.
- *Business and Industry.* http://newfirstsearch.oclc.org/dbname=BusIndustry. This FirstSearch database covers over 1,200 trade magazines, newsletters, business press publications, and international business dailies from 1994 to the present.

Intercultural Communication

As already mentioned, business people and academics consider cultural knowledge of one's target market as critically important for anyone entering into international business. There are many good recent books on cross-cultural business communication. A search strategy to use in your library catalog follows:

- Search the Library of Congress Subject Heading **Intercultural communication**
- Limit by the keyword **Business**
- Sort by date

The following are several good books on cross-cultural business communication:

- Gesteland, Richard R. 1999. *Cross-Cultural Business Behavior: Marketing, Negotiating, and Managing across Cultures.* Copenhagen: Copenhagen Business School Press.
- Thomas, David C., and Kerr Inkson. 2004. *Cultural Intelligence: People Skills for Global Business.* San Francisco: Berrett-Koehler.

- Walker, Danielle Medina, Thomas Walker, and Joerg Schmitz. 2003. *Doing Business Internationally: The Guide to Cross-Cultural Success.* New York: McGraw-Hill.

Also, good e-books on intercultural business communication are available from *Books24×7*, an online vendor of business and computer-related titles. You can link e-books from your course Web page and electronic reserve listings.

Planning Your Presentation and Preparing the Web Interface

The main benefit of a course-related library Web page is to make the information sources pertinent to course assignments readily available to students. My own library uses a template for subject Web pages, which I use in a modified form for course-related pages. This is a very good model for several reasons:

- The template prominently displays licensed databases pertinent to the broad subject or course.
- Free Web sites related to the subject may be listed on the Web page in a separate section below licensed databases.
- The top banner on the page includes links to the library catalog and key points on the library Web site, thereby making the page an effective point of entry for most library services.
- Below the top banner are links that perform various functions. On the course page shown here, some links include anchors to various parts of the page, another links to reserve listings, another to a bibliography of additional sources related to international business, and one to a list of locally based international freight forwarders and brokers.
- The sidebar on the left side of the page includes a link describing procedures for off-campus use of licensed online sources and defines some icons that appear next to database and site names. The sidebar also lists both the course instructor's name and my own, with each name hyperlinked to his or her own e-mail address. Finally, we list update information on this area of the page.

Figure 15-1 shows a version of the Web page I use to support international marketing courses at the University of Nevada, Reno. I have shortened the page for display here and included it on the CD-ROM accompanying this book (open the folder named 15-1).

What to Teach

As I noted in the introduction to this chapter, basic library skills do not fully address information needs for international marketing. Nevertheless, some elements of the baseline orientation described in Chapter 1 are appropriate for these students. These include a quick orientation to the library Web site and requirements for off-campus access. The library catalog is less important for international marketing assignments, so it may not be necessary for you to discuss or demonstrate it.

University of Nevada, Reno Libraries   Search | Site Map | HELP

Catalog | Subjects | Databases | Reserves | Journals | News | eBooks | Reference

MKT 456/656: International Marketing

Off-Campus Access

UNR access

📄 - full text available

● - Open Access

Other Subjects

Contact the course instructor
Dr. Kyung-il Ghymn

Please direct questions about this page to Patrick Ragains

Updated 26 August 2005

- UNR's Best Online Resources for International Marketing
- Reserve Readings for MKT 456/656
- Selected World Wide Web Sources for International Marketing

- Download a library guide for MGRS 456/656 in Microsoft Word format
- Port of Reno information, including a list of brokers

UNR's Best Online Resources for International Marketing

- Business Source Premier (EBSCOHost) 📄

  About 3,050 full-text scholarly publications, plus abstracts for 3,850+ journals, in management, economics, finance, accounting, international business, and more. Also includes country economic reports and profiles for 5,000 large companies. 1965- present for selected titles.

- Associations Unlimited 📄

  Directory of more than 154,000 detailed listings for international, national, state, and regional organizations. Information for more than 300,000 nonprofit organizations.

- Business & Industry 📄

  Indexes over 1200 trade magazines, newsletters, business press and international business dailies. Use to find both US and international information on companies, industries, products and markets. Covers 1994 to present.

Figure 15-1   Course-Related Library Web Page for International Marketing

After covering these points, you should introduce and demonstrate sources based on their relevance to assignments or themes in the course, such as:

- Information sources for countries
- Demographic and social characteristics
- Pertinent legal and business information
- Debatable or controversial issues related to globalization and international business ventures

For each theme, choose appropriate sources from the section of this chapter titled "Information Pertinent to International Marketing." You should make clear transitions from one topic to the next. For instance, tell students, "Now, we're going to look at resources that you can use for your marketing plans," and "these sources will help you understand business practices in your target country." Additionally, stress that different search and retrieval techniques are needed to use different kinds of sources. The students may be used to searching *Business Source Premiere* for articles, but *GMID, USA Trade Online*, and other statistical databases require users to make a series of selections before they can display a customized table. Likewise, a gateway like *STAT-USA* and other similar subscription-based or free sites resemble many retail and corporate Web sites. In order to get the most out of these sites, users should employ some of the techniques outlined in Chapter 1 for examining a Web site (e.g., scan the home page for links to major topics; look for the site map and a site search tool).

If you have more time than a one-shot and a well-developed relationship with the course instructor, you might assign students to compile an annotated bibliography or literature review related to the broad topics mentioned previously. Mark Emmons discusses these in more detail in Chapter 3. These types of assignments, in addition to position papers and debates, encourage careful reading, analysis, and, ultimately, better understanding of the subject matter. Another option is to help students get comfortable using particular resources by holding lab workshops outside class time for them to practice using the *Global Market Information Database*, *USA Trade Online*, or other relatively complex sources.

Follow-up: What to Do after the Session

One-shot instruction has its limitations, and, whenever possible, you should continue your involvement after your session. First, make yourself available to students for the duration of the course. Make sure you have adequately informed your colleagues in the library concerning the course and expected student requests for information. Extend your eyes and ears by consulting with other library staff who assist them. Revise the Web page and other tools to ensure they meet students' needs. Be sure to notify the course instructor of any such changes. In my own case, I routinely check external links on the course-related library Web page, but also added to it by selecting both print and electronic books on international marketing and cross-cultural communication for course reserve, then placed a link on the page to the reserve listing. I also added links to locally based export brokers and freight forwarders. It is also important for you to keep learning about the subjects you support. You can learn more about international marketing and improve your presentations by meeting business people involved in the field, including local International Trade Administration staff situated in many metropolitan areas.

One of the biggest challenges I have encountered in supporting international marketing instruction has been identifying appropriate sources for import statistics by country for specific products and brands. It is also difficult to identify foreign market share for companies and their products. The compilation *World Market Share Reporter* and articles in industry trade magazines (many available in *ABI-Inform Global* and *Business Source Premier*) are often the best sources for these kinds of information. Different points of emphasis may emerge from one term to the next. These can reflect new points the instructor has discussed in class. In one semester, students may ask for more market share–related information, while in the next semester, they may have more questions about statistical sources or business communication. Students count on you and other library reference staff to guide them effectively, so be sure that you and your colleagues are familiar with the resources and are prepared to help them.

Trends and Technologies for Future Instruction in International Marketing

Web-based information sources have their pitfalls, and business-related sites are no exception. For instance, the federal and other government entities use the Web to communicate their values, and one result is that new political appointees replace their predecessor's agency site without advance notice to users. Further, many business-related sites require users to register to gain full access to site information, after which the site managers will send advertising e-mail to registrants (and typically will also sell their registrant's information to other marketers). This practice raises legitimate privacy concerns. Perhaps more important, since information content on the free Web is limited, this raises the question of how students will fare moving from school into the business world, where they will not have access to many subscription-based sources. This situation is only partially mitigated by federal depository libraries, which have free access to *STAT-USA* (although many depositories pay for site-wide licenses not covered by the depository-level access).

Another point to consider is the use of information resources when an international marketing class at your institution is linked with a class in another country. Several reported instances of such partnering emphasize the value of students' exposure to other cultures (Fish et al., 1998; Simon, Haghirian, and Schlegelmilch, 2003). This has been done via IITV, but webcams could easily replace older technology for this purpose. In such cases one must assume that different information resources would be available to students and faculty at the partner site. Qualitative differences in available licensed sources in two collaborating classes might result in notable differences in student performance at the two sites. Librarians supporting courses using this more "global" approach should discuss this issue with faculty.

Assessment

Formative assessment is perhaps most typical for this type of instructional support. Naturally, the course instructor's repeat invitations and adoption by other faculty indicate success on the librarian's part. Course instructors and students have little time to give structured feedback and most of the information you receive is likely to be anecdotal. As such, your success depends on meaningful involvement: communication with the course instructor; developing the Web page, bibliography, and other support tools (and improving them continuously); communicating with students effectively both in class and after your session with them; and involving other library public service staff in the follow-up effort.

Summative assessment might involve your department or division head observing you teach, reviewing your Web page, or reviewing students' and faculty's completed satisfaction surveys, if these are used in your library. A more robust assessment might involve direct attention from your business school, perhaps with some significant discussion of the library's instructional support role in the school's accreditation report.

Conclusion

This chapter emphasizes the importance of understanding course and program goals, closely followed by the need to be familiar with the real-world environments simulated in business courses. Librarians who establish and maintain contact with faculty and business practitioners will be well prepared to offer the best library-based instructional support, primarily by using the Web to bring course-related information within easy reach of students.

Bibliography

Andrus, David M., Jay Laughlin, and Wayne Norvell. 1995. "Internationalizing the Marketing Curriculum: A Profile of the International Marketing Course." *Marketing Education Review* 5, no. 2: 9–18.

Cooney, Martha, and Lorene Hiris. 2003. "Integrating Information Literacy and Its Assessment into a Graduate Business Course: A Collaborative Framework." *Research Strategies* 19: 213–232.

Diamond, Jared. 2005. *Collapse: How Societies Choose to Succeed or Fail*. New York: Viking.

Fish, Kelly E., Carlos Ruy Martinez, Roberto J. Santillan, and Jeff D. Brazell. 1998. "International Marketing Internet in the Classroom (IMIC): A Global Approach to the Group Case Method." *Marketing Education Review* 8, no. 2: 75–82.

Fraser, Mary G., Shari Buxbaum, and Amy Blair. 2002. "The Library and the Development of Online Courses." *Journal of Business and Finance Librarianship* 7, no. 2/3: 47–59.

Han, Pyung E. 2004. "The International Dimensions of Functional Business Courses." *American Business Review* 22, no. 1: 56–61.

Kohl, David F., and Lizabeth A. Wilson. 1986. "Effectiveness of Course-Integrated Bibliographic Instruction in Improving Coursework." *RQ* 26, no. 2: 206–211.

Lundstrom, William J., and Steven D. White. 1997. "A Gap Analysis of Professional and Academic Perceptions of the Importance of International Marketing Curriculum Content and Research Areas." *Journal of Marketing Education* 19, no. 2: 16–25.

MKT 456/656: International Marketing. www.library.unr.edu/instruction/courses/mkt/mkt 456.html (accessed September 22, 2005).

Ragains, Patrick. 2001. "A Primer on Developing and Using Course-Related Library Web Pages." *Research Strategies* 18: 85–93.

Simon, Bernd, Parissa Haghirian, and Bodo Schlegelmilch. 2003. "Enriching Global Marketing Education with Virtual Classrooms: An Effectiveness Study." *Marketing Education Review* 13, no. 3: 27–39.

Turley, L. W., and J. Richard Shannon. 1999. "The International Marketing Curriculum: Views from Students." *Journal of Marketing Education* 21, no. 3: 175–180.

PART IV

Teaching Special Topics in Information Literacy

The final part of this manual will give you a basic familiarity with legal, patent, and government information and help you prepare to teach pertinent research skills to students and coworkers. These topics often stand apart from librarians' normal subject liaison responsibilities. Legal research is often a component of practice-based education, such as in business, public administration, education, and nursing. Students in these and other programs need court decisions, statutes, administrative rules and regulations, executive orders, and other legal information related to their area of study, yet often lack convenient access to a good law library. In Chapter 16, Duncan Aldrich shows how to retrieve much of this information from free Web-based sources. Government documents collections are multidisciplinary, yet their organization is often arcane, making special efforts necessary to identify information not covered in other databases, indexes, and bibliographies. Susie Skarl outlines a comprehensive government information training program in Chapter 17. Familiarity with patents uncovers a universe of information largely unavailable elsewhere and promotes an increased appreciation of scientific and technological innovation in the modern world. Engineers, artists, historians, and amateur genealogists are among those interested in patents. In Chapter 18, the closing chapter, Brian Carpenter describes how U.S. patents are organized and discusses pertinent teaching techniques.

Other topics not included here deserve similar treatment in the literature of library and information literacy instruction. These include statistical data sources and wider coverage of legal information (e.g., foreign and international sources).

Indeed, these and other topics are candidates for coverage in a subsequent edition of this manual.

Practice the research and teaching techniques described in these final chapters and integrate them into your teaching, whether you are responsible for freshman-level instruction, subject-specific instruction for upper-division undergraduates and graduate students, or staff training. Doing so will ultimately open the eyes of your students and other researchers to wider horizons of information and give them more tools to deepen their own scholarship.

16

Legal Research for Non-Law Students

Duncan Aldrich

Introduction

In our sociopolitical environment there is a continuous tension between our lives and the rules that society imposes. Speed limits are easy to exceed, neighbors are often eager to bring lawsuits for seemingly trivial encounters, excessive partying can lead to a night in the drunk-tank, or worse, to an arrest for DUI. On a less personal level, businesses operate in a setting rife with laws and regulations intended to establish fair practices, to protect the environment, to create guidelines and review processes for regulating the safety of drugs and the quality of food, and so on.

Unfortunately, many students know or remember very little about how laws are made and cases judged and even less about information resources associated with the courts. This chapter examines four types of legal research for which you may often be tapped to improve students' understanding of the legal system. For each of the four areas I will introduce basic concepts and definitions, describe information resources generated as laws are made and cases judged, and suggest instruction scenarios you may fold into your class plans.

The target audience for this chapter is librarians who need to master (or refresh) concepts underlying the legal process and acquaint themselves with information resources associated with legal research. Our targeted classroom is the undergraduate course needing some background in legal research but that is specifically not a law-related class.

Assumptions and Limitations

Optimally, your classroom will have personal computers (PCs) on which all students can actively engage in the instruction or a smart classroom having an instructor's PC connected to an overhead projector. Prior to our current media-enriched learning environment, instructors out of necessity distributed handouts and then guided their students through the information therein. This approach was cumbersome and often boring, both for students and instructors. Accordingly, I have migrated my presentations from handouts to simple Web pages or PowerPoint in order to mix in some visual stimulation. Unless your institution absolutely cannot support tools like PowerPoint and Web pages, use them. For those of you who are not familiar with HTML scripting, I recommend PowerPoint as a viable and more easily mastered alternative.

Since many of you will not have access to law library collections, I have focused my discussion on materials that are freely accessible on the Web. Our use of resources for examples is limited to a handful of very useful Web sites such as the Library of Congress's *Thomas*, the U.S. Government Printing Office's *GPO Access*, Cornell University Law School's *LII: Law Information Institute*, and several academic and commercial sites that provide useful tutorials and user guides. Because these sites tend to have content going back only into the late 1980s, our focus is on cases and legislation that have occurred over the past two decades.

I must note up front that there are limitations associated with these Web resources that you can minimize by using *Westlaw*, *LexisNexis*, Congressional Quarterly's *CQ Electronic Library*, and other subscription-based services. In fact, I use *LexisNexis* extensively in instruction and recommend that those of you with access to subscription-based legal resources use them in classroom situations when your emphasis is on legal processes and information content. Subscription-based legal information services usually require less time for nuts-and-bolts training and offer a significantly larger and more powerful array of search tools. The obvious drawback to using campus-licensed subscriptions for law-related research is that many of your students will not have ready access to these resources in their post-college lives. Hence they may derive more benefit from legal research instruction based on resources that are freely available on the Web.

Types of Legal Research

The types of legal research instruction expected of you will vary noticeably across institutions. For instance, if your college has an interdisciplinary program on the environment, you may receive requests to instruct students on finding legal documentation underlying environmental policies. If you work in a location that has a large immigrant population (either legal or illegal), you may find yourself providing instruction on immigration laws and regulations.

This chapter focuses exclusively on four commonly requested types of legal research required in undergraduate, nonlaw classes:

- Laws and statutes
- Legislative histories
- The regulatory process
- Court cases and case law

Often complicating legal instruction is the division of government into four levels:

- U.S. federal
- State
- Local (city or county)
- International

Given space constraints, we will concentrate on legal processes and information from the federal government. With fifty states and countless local jurisdictions, it is impossible to cover all resources and research methodologies, although I will point out some similarities between the state, local, and federal legal systems. Any thorough discussion of international legal research for librarians awaits future discussion—even a brief introduction to international law would easily fill a chapter on its own. The *International Law* pages on the United Nations' Web site provide an excellent starting point for insights into the international legal system. Also, I omit examination of specialized legal research topics such as tax, business, and intellectual property law. Of course, these topics are of potential interest in an undergraduate curriculum. Many valuable Web sites offer information on each of these legal research topics, such as *Hieros Gamos Legal Directories* for intellectual property and tax law and the "Business Law" section of *Business.gov* for business law.

Preliminaries to Instruction

Effective instruction requires that you engage in dialogue (phone, e-mail, or in person) with course instructors to reach a clear understanding of their expectations. These points are covered elsewhere in this book. Of course, you must know the class topic and legal materials to cover. You should expect to dedicate at least one third of your class time to walking students through search interface basics and search strategies. Although students are generally familiar with Web search tools, the search interfaces on the free Web sites I suggest vary substantially from one another, so it is important for you to familiarize students with the nuances of each. Additionally, each Web site is likely to have some less-than-obvious functionality, so learning such tricks will greatly enhance student success.

Mastering the content and technical peculiarities of these Web sites requires a considerable time investment on your part as instructor. The scope of this chapter does not allow discussion of the obscure or arcane functionalities found in *Thomas, GPO Access*, and the other resources used as examples. Though a few

Web site navigation tips are included in instruction scenarios, you are on your own to figure out the vagaries of the sites you use for class. Be sure you have them figured out before your class! Getting caught underprepared in the classroom can be horribly embarrassing.

There are several key publications that provide clear and concise information you may wish to review to get up to speed on legislative and legal research:

- *Finding the Law*, 11th ed. Includes sections on statutes, legislative histories, administrative law, and case law (Berring and Edinger, 1999).
- *How Our Laws Are Made*. A U.S. House of Representatives publication, this short volume provides a concise yet very complete discussion of the legislative process. For years distributed in paper, this item is now available on the Web (House, current).
- *Introduction to United States Government Information Sources*, 6th ed. The chapter "Legislative Branch Information Sources" reviews the legislative process, legislative histories, publication of laws, and presidential actions. The chapter "Administrative Law" provides an excellent overview of the regulatory process and administrative decisions. Regardless of which edition you use, this is an excellent starting point (Morehead, 1999).

Laws and Statutes: Basics

In the U.S. federal government the words *act*, *law*, and *statute* are essentially synonymous. They are directives passed by Congress and signed into law by the president. The terms *act* and *law* may be used interchangeably, although *act* sometimes is used to refer to a bill passed by Congress but not yet signed in to law. *Statute* specifically refers to published laws as opposed to England's unwritten common law. In most U.S. states, laws are passed by state legislatures and signed by the state's governor. At the local level, laws are passed by town or county councils or boards and are often referred to as ordinances.

At the federal level and in most states, laws passed by the legislature and signed by the president or governor are first published individually as *slip laws*. At the end of each Congress the federal slip laws are republished in chronological order in bound volumes published in paper as the *United States Statutes at Large*, and available as *Public Laws* on GPO Access. Approximately every seven years all statutes currently in effect are organized by subject into the multivolume set *United States Code*. In legal jargon this subject organization is referred to as codified law. Most states have a similar pattern for publications of laws, including slip laws, published collections of statutes in chronological order, and periodic codification, for example, the *Nevada Revised Statutes* (Nevada Legislative Counsel Bureau).

What to Teach

Your two major objectives for instruction regarding laws are to familiarize students with basic definitions and then to expose them to resources with which they can identify and retrieve them. Be aware that this instruction scenario can be adapted to most state laws and many local ordinances, depending on whether the jurisdiction publishes their laws to the Web. Two excellent Web sites linking to legal information for all states and territories are *FindLaw* (www.findlaw.com/11state gov/) and Cornell's *LII* (www.law.cornell.edu/states/listing.html). Although Seattle Public Library's Municipal Codes Online (www.spl.org/default.asp?pageID= collection_municodes) is a starting point for local government codes, you will need to consult Google or other Web search engines to verify the availability of these materials on the Web.

One obvious method for heightening student engagement for this and all other legal research topics is to use captivating props. For instance, in classes at the University of Nevada, I frequently use Public Law 107-89 as a sample federal statute and Nevada Revised Statutes (NRS) 201.358 to exemplify a chapter of codified law. Public Law 107-89 stipulates that Yucca Mountain, Nevada, will be the national repository for high-level nuclear waste and NRS 201.358 is the section of Nevada codified law making it illegal for HIV-positive prostitutes—whether practicing their trade legally or otherwise—to engage in sexual activity.

Depending on the expectations of the course instructor, you may have students look for preselected laws or have them use keywords to locate laws on a given subject. A word of warning regarding keyword searches. I have learned the hard way that having students come up with their own topic can lead to chaos in the classroom, particularly when there are no laws using the keywords they select. Consequently, when having students do keyword or subject searches, you should consider feeding them a canned topic.

In class, have your students use the Library of Congress's *Thomas* to locate and retrieve specific laws by public law number or, alternatively, do a keyword search to identify laws by topic (do both if you have sufficient time). *Thomas* works best using a known public law number, as you will readily see when you navigate from the *Thomas* homepage to its Public Laws page. To retrieve and display a known public law simply highlight the year it was passed and select the public law number in the Range of Public Laws window. Scroll to the entry for the public law you want and click either the Text or PDF link. For recent laws, the text that displays is the final copy of the bill that Congress passed and the president signed into law which, by definition, is a public law. For older laws, the text of the actual public law is displayed.

Thomas was not well designed to do keyword searches for identifying laws by topic. Users may perform subject searches, however, from the Bills, Resolutions search page. On that page, click the Search Multiple Congresses link, select the Congress or Congresses in which you are interested, enter your search terms, then click the Enrolled Bills Sent to the President radio button.

This completes your basic instruction on public laws. But note that the bill text screen includes links to many associated legislative documents. You are perfectly positioned to begin instruction on legislative histories as described in the following section.

Legislative Histories

It is surprising how little students remember from their high school government classes and the extent to which library instruction is merely a recital of the steps involved in a bill becoming a law. In a sound byte, the legislative process is:

1 A bill is introduced by a member of Congress (only members are permitted to introduce legislation).
2 The bill is assigned to one or more committees, and the committee may or may not take action on the bill (those that are not acted on "die in committee").
3 Committees may or may not hold hearings on the bill (hearings are held on most major legislation, though the USA PATRIOT Act was a surprising exception).
4 The committee may or may not report the bill to the floor for consideration.
5 Legislators may or may not amend it.
6 Legislators may or may not pass it.
7 If the bill is passed in both chambers, action may be needed to reconcile differing versions (with one chamber accepting the other's version or a conference committee negotiating a single version).
8 The enrolled bill may or may not be approved by the president.
9 A presidential veto may or may not be overridden by Congress.

Legislative histories trace the journey of laws from introduction as bill through the presidential signature into law. Bill tracking is identical to legislative history but follows all introduced bills rather than only those ultimately passed into law.

Legislative Documentation

The first documentation generated in the legislative process is the original text of bills as introduced. In the federal government, bills can be introduced in either the Senate or the House of Representatives. Most bills experience some changes or amendments in their passage through Congress. The first place where bill language may change is during the committee mark-up process, wherein bill language is modified in light of hearings and other considerations of the committee. Next the bill text may be amended during the floor debate in either chamber of Congress (i.e., the House or Senate). Changes often are made near the end of the legislative process when differences between similar bills passed in the House and Senate are reconciled. The final version, when passed by both houses, is called the *enrolled* version of the bill. Of course many bills die in Congress or are vetoed by the president and are never enacted into law.

While the text of enrolled bills represents the actual letter of the law and is useful for a verbatim review of the proposed legislation, other publications generated during the legislative process provide the researcher with greater insight into the political and policy ramifications of the legislation. For example, transcripts, summaries, or minutes of legislative committee hearings record the perspectives of professional witnesses invited to give testimony on the bill. Such hearings are a valuable source for review of information congressional committees collected while considering bills, and also for researchers interested in examining the position of experts on particular policy topics, such as members of Mothers Against Drunk Driving (MADD) contributing their opinion on blood alcohol levels and vehicle operation. Congressional committee hearings are published as verbatim transcripts of the hearing sessions. State legislative committee hearings are generally published as meeting minutes or summaries.

Committee reports accompany bills that committees transmit to the floor for consideration and vote. These often discuss the history of previous legislation and include sections with titles like "Need for This Legislation." These sections provide the most concise statements of underlying policy issues and insight into the legislature's purpose or intent in passing legislation when statutory language is unclear. During instruction sessions I usually note that committees base their reports on committee hearings, just as students base their final papers on data they accumulate through their research. Congressional committee hearings and reports are available in many federal depository libraries and online, although only selectively, on *GPO Access*.

Full transcripts of floor debates in the U.S. Congress are published in the *Congressional Record* (*GPO Access*). Most states publish minutes or summaries of legislative debates. Students will find comments made on the floor a rich source for gleaning the stance legislators took on particular issues. Reported votes in the legislature will likewise provide insight into how individual legislators and party groups stood on particular issues.

The final element in a legislative history is comments the president, governor, or another chief executive makes upon signing a bill into law. At the federal level any comments will be published in the *Weekly Compilation of Presidential Documents* (*GPO Access*). Finding such comments for most other levels of government, if any are available, usually involves researching local news services likely to report on state and local politics.

What to Teach

Your primary instructional objectives concerning the legislative process should be to describe the documentation generated as a bill wends its way through a legislature and to demonstrate methods for discovering and retrieving that documentation. However, all too often you will find that the instructor expects you to explain in detail the trail a bill takes through Congress. Consult with the course instructor to determine the appropriate level of detail to convey to the class.

To introduce students to legislative documentation, have them use the strategies previously discussed for retrieving public laws on *Thomas*. Three separate strategies can be used to search for legislative histories. The simplest is to select the public law number on *Thomas*'s Public Laws template. The second technique is to search by subject keyword on the Search Bill Summary & Status template. The third and recommended approach is to query the Search Bill Summary & Status by bill number option. Note that to toggle between Word/Phrase and Bill Number searches you must click the drop-down menu under Enter Search. Beginning with the bill number reinforces the perception that legislation is introduced as a bill and finalized as a statute.

By retrieving and selecting a bill, you have completed the search-related component of your instruction. You can now discuss documentation related to your bill. After a quick review of the text of the bill, click on Bill Summary & Status from the links at the top of the bill page. Next, select All Congressional Actions, which pulls up the full history of the bill, including the date of introduction, committee actions, amendments, passage in both chambers, enrollment, and presidential signing. For most bills considered since 1989, links are provided to the full text of reports and congressional debates and to selected hearings. Have your students pull up a report and direct them to such interesting sections as background and purpose for legislation and invest a few minutes explaining that hearings, reports, and debates are useful in research on any social, political, health, environmental, economic, or other issue having a basis in government policy.

Thomas's Multi-Congress Search option available from the Bills, Resolutions is useful when you are unsure of the Congressional session to search for your desired bill or if you need to search similar bills introduced in more than one session. Using a Word/Phrase search here and checking the Enrolled Bill Sent to the President radio button will provide you a list of bills that Congress has passed and sent to the president for signature. Since the president does not sign all enrolled bills, however, you must review Congressional Actions to determine if your bill was signed into law or not.

Finally, consult the *Weekly Compilation of Presidential Documents* on GPO Access to retrieve comments the president made upon signing the act into law. From the *Weekly Compilation* homepage, link to Search. On the Search screen, highlight the appropriate year and enter your keywords. To narrow your search, include the month the president signed the act. Be aware that presidents do not comment on all acts they sign. Whether the president comments or not, the *Weekly Compilation* lists all signings.

Administrative Regulations

If statutes are directives that tend to paint a big picture, they leave it to executive agencies to establish the details in regulations. Executive departments and agencies ultimately report to a chief executive, such as a president or a governor. These offices are responsible for executing laws within their jurisdiction (federal, state, or local). To do so, they promulgate administrative regulations. The authority empowering agencies to establish regulations is written in the language of statutes or executive orders. Regulations are rules having the weight of law.

Basic Regulatory Process

Federal agencies have established procedures for adopting regulations which are generally referred to as the rulemaking process. The process starts with the enactment of laws or presidential orders instructing or authorizing agencies to establish one or more regulations. Publication of a preliminary draft of the regulation as a proposed rule in the *Federal Register* initiates a period during which the public (including individuals, institutions, and interest groups) may comment on the draft. After the comment period has ended, regulations are usually redrafted, finalized, and formally published in the *Federal Register* as a final rule, and then later codified in the *Code of Federal Regulations* (CFR; GPO Access), an annually updated subject compilation. This process of draft, comment period, and adoption for regulations is similar in states. State regulations are often referred to as administrative codes, which acknowledge the executive branch (administrative) origins of the regulations.

What to Teach

Your main objectives in instruction regarding regulations are to describe the process by which regulations are established, to identify publications generated in that process, and to illustrate the relationship between statutes and regulations. Each of these objectives is most easily met using the excellent functionality of subscription-based online services. As before, the steps outlined here incorporate only freely available online resources. This assures that virtually all instructors will have access to the Web sites discussed in this chapter.

REGULATIONS.gov is a recently launched federal Web site that posts all proposed federal regulations that are open for public comment. It is an excellent starting point for examining the regulatory process and associated documentation. Have your students link to *REGULATIONS.gov* and note that they can browse the site by topic, by agency, or by a listing of proposed regulations posted that day, or that they can search using keywords. Also point out that only regulations currently open for comment are posted to the site; once the comment period has closed, the item is no longer accessible on *REGULATIONS.gov*.

I recommend that your class explore *REGULATIONS.gov* either by a specific federal agency or by keywords that reflect the course subject matter, such as using the keywords **nuclear waste** or **Yucca Mountain** to check whether there are any pending regulations pertaining to the proposed nuclear waste repository at Yucca Mountain, Nevada. In fact, while searching the keyword index when I was writing this chapter, I found one open regulation regarding proposed specifications for casks that will be used for storing nuclear waste materials (70 FR 29931).

When reviewing items they identify on *REGULATIONS.gov*, students should note that each entry includes a citation for the *CFR* section that the proposal would change or add and links to both PDF and TXT copies of the *Federal Register* notice on *GPO Access* and to a form on which interested parties can submit comments. To demonstrate how they can compare the proposed regulations to existing wording in *CFR* sections, have your students navigate to the Regulations by Topic page, then on that page find the *CFR* title (broad subjects including agriculture, commerce, and protection of the environment) noted in their proposed regulation using their browser's Edit/Find function. Clicking on the *CFR* title links them to a table for that title from which they can navigate to the section they are seeking.

As already mentioned, older regulations are outside the scope of *REGULATIONS.gov*. To research older regulations, walk your students through the *CFR* or *Federal Register* (both on *GPO Access*). Whether researching older regulations or using *REGULATIONS.gov*, have your students pull up and scan *Federal Register* pages to review the cross-references to federal statutes, executive orders, and the *CFR*. As an interesting example for a political science or business class, have students use *GPO Access* to locate the *Federal Register* notice concerning global terrorism sanctions (68 *FR* 34196). A review of this item reveals that it establishes Part 594 in *CFR* Title 31 and that it is authorized under Executive Order 13224. Among other points, this illustrates that agencies may propose and establish regulations as a result of executive orders (i.e., not only Congressional legislation).

Switching from the *Federal Register* to the *CFR*, have the class search either for 31 *CFR* 594 or for the keyword phrase **global terrorism sanctions**. On the page of search results, have them look for the phrase **global terrorism** using their browsers' Edit/Find function. Looking at the item Global Terrorism Sanctions Regulations, you will find at the end of the table of contents a reference back to 68 *FR* 34196, to EO 13224, and to various other statutes authorizing the establishment of these regulations.

Court Cases and Case Law

A case is an action that is cause for a criminal trial, lawsuit, or reported court decision. Opinions are the written decisions or rulings of federal and state appellate judges and certain other special federal courts. Cases are important in legal research for a number of reasons, including their ability to set precedents for future legal arguments and judicial decisions. Research in cases and case law ranges from the relatively simple task of identifying specific cases to the much more complex assessment of the impact of specific cases on subsequent court opinions. Some high-profile criminal cases are of great interest, such as the Chicago Seven, O. J. Simpson, and Michael Jackson cases, particularly to journalism students.

In undergraduate-level coursework, however, it is usually precedent-setting opinions of higher courts, such as the U.S. Supreme Court, that substantially impact social policy that are the target of most student researchers. Most adult Americans are familiar with the precedents set by such benchmark cases as *Brown v. Board of Education*, *Griswold v. Connecticut*, and *Roe v. Wade*. We are less aware that hundreds of cases are regularly cited in court for their legal precedence, and thousands are cited in court as attorneys argue their points. Decisions in precedent-setting cases often establish the underpinnings for major social and cultural policies, such as racial segregation versus integration and right-to-life versus choice.

Case Law Basics

In the United States there is a remarkable array of court jurisdictions, ranging from traffic courts to municipal courts, county courts, state courts, state appellate courts, state supreme courts, federal district courts, federal courts of appeals, and finally the U.S. Supreme Court. Add to this mix local justices of the peace and various special courts such as the U.S. Bankruptcy and Federal Claims courts, and the variety and volume of cases become mind-boggling.

A rule of thumb is that other than the appellate, supreme, and specialized courts, each court hears cases involving laws passed at their level of government. Municipal courts hear infractions of city ordinances, state courts try cases involving state laws, and federal courts adjudicate on federal law. Cases go before appellate and supreme courts only after they have already been tried in a lower court. These appellate courts generally publish opinions on a case, as opposed to lower courts, where juries and judges typically find for or against defendants rather than issuing precedent-setting decisions.

Perhaps more remarkable is that there is another entire court system to administer regulatory law. Administrative courts, set up in government agencies, hear cases and issue opinions regarding the infringement of regulations issued by their agencies. For instance, the Environmental Protection Agency's Office of Administrative Law Judges has responsibility for hearing cases involving the Clean Air and Water acts, among others. I am aware of few if any requests for training undergraduates pertaining to administrative decisions. If a faculty member asks you to discuss administrative decisions, you should review the section for *United States Federal Law* on the Rutgers Web site (http://law-library.rutgers.edu/ilg/usfedlaw .php) for insights into administrative law.

What to Teach

There are dozens of available instructional approaches regarding tools used in researching cases and case law in this tangle of a judicial system. The three examples we will focus on here are the simple requirement for students to locate known cases by case name or citation, the somewhat more complicated assignment to identify cases by subject keyword, and the far more complicated process of tracking the impact of specific cases on subsequent court opinions.

For all instruction on searching for case opinions, use either Cornell University's *LII: Legal Information Institute* or *FindLaw.com.* While both sites have their pros and cons, I generally find *LII* preferable for instruction owing to its more intuitive search interface and results display. Both have collections of landmark Supreme Court cases. Users can find some state supreme court cases from free Web services, but availability of state lower court and local cases is extremely limited other than through expensive, top-end online subscriptions. At best, you can use the free Web resources I recommend to demonstrate the nature of court opinions, but I do not recommended them as exhaustive legal research tools. Students desiring to use such resources should be directed to licensed online services or local law libraries.

On *LII* it is easy to find and retrieve cases by either case name or subject keyword. Your main instructional goal here should be to make students aware of the scope of *LII* and similar sites and these sites' applicability to their research, rather than to train them in specific search techniques. If the instructor does not identify a specific case to locate, you may choose *Griswold v. Connecticut* as an interesting example. This 1965 case, which threw out Connecticut's law prohibiting the use of birth control, was monumental at that time and has had substantial impact on subsequent legal decisions, including *Roe v. Wade*.

The search phrase "Griswold v. Connecticut" currently retrieves 114 results. Have students browse through the first dozen or so and note that those entitled "Griswold v. Connecticut" have various subtitles, including Opinion, Concurrence, Dissent, and Syllabus. View the Opinion, note its case citation (381 U.S. 479 for *Griswold v. Connecticut*), and scroll through the document. Take a couple of minutes to scan the introductory sentences and observe that hyperlinks are provided to the many other cases cited in this opinion. Next, pull up the Concurrence, Dissent, and Syllabus links to get a sense of these documents. Explain to students that the purpose of a dissenting opinion is to officially publish an opinion disagreeing with the majority, that concurring opinions are made by judges who agree with the majority opinion but wish to state an additional or differing explanation for reaching that decision, and that a syllabus is merely a brief case summary.

Keyword searching in *LII* is straightforward, although the results are cumbersome and often hard to work with. For example, the keyword phrase **birth control** returns 142 cases. Without examining each item in this set of results it is not possible to determine their relative value to the researcher. This leads me to caution students that keyword searching generally is not a recommended strategy for approaching case law research, due to the typically ambiguous search results. One must usually know of one or more relevant case citations at the outset in order to conduct effective research in case law. I describe this below.

Tracing the impact of cases on subsequent decisions is usually approached using subscription-based legal reference tools (paper or online) published by *Shepard's*, a resource that lists cases and identifies which subsequent cases referred to each case. Alternatively, I will illustrate a process for tracing the impact of cases on subsequent case law using freely available Web resources which do not include the sophisticated indexing available in *Shepard's*. Hence, students will not get the full grasp of "Shepardizing," though they will have exposure to a modestly effective method for discovering the impact of selected cases.

On *LII*, have the class search for a U.S. Supreme Court opinion using its citation (381 U.S. 479). I recommend searching on the citation rather than the case name because the citation format is standardized and displays uniformly across opinions, whereas case names may or may not be mentioned. The search results will include the various opinions, dissents, and other materials for the case cited, and will also present a list of subsequent Supreme Court opinions referring to the case they have searched.

Have your students peruse this list and choose an opinion to review. In most cases there are many references linking to other court opinions, so it is difficult to hone in on the reference to the case you are searching. Have students use their browsers' Edit/Find function to locate the pertinent reference by dropping down the Edit window, clicking on Find (or using the Windows shortcut Ctrl-F), and keying in their citation (e.g., 381 U.S. 479). This enables them to find the reference in the opinion and verify that the present case refers back to their citation. Remember, the list of Supreme Court opinions is not exhaustive. *LII*'s collection of opinions is limited to complete coverage since 1991 with selected major cases prior to 1991.

To reinforce the concept of legal precedence, have your students return to the *LII* homepage and navigate to the Other Federal Court Opinions search template. Under U.S. Courts, select Search All Circuit Court Opinions on the Internet and have your students search using the case number segment of their citation (in our case, 479). This type of search helps to minimize problems related to inconsistent display of citations in the circuit court opinions available through *LII*. There will be some irrelevant items in the search results, but this is a reasonably effective strategy for locating circuit court opinions referring to your case. Now tell your students to pick an opinion to peruse and locate the reference to their cases using the Edit/Find function. Having thus compiled lists of Supreme Court and federal circuit court opinions, your students have a rich set of materials in support of their research—although I remind you that this approach would be insufficient for the exhaustive research that legal practitioners do, which requires tools such as Shepardizing and West's key system of subject classification.

Conclusion

You can use the instruction suggestions I have outlined either individually or together to meet your students' needs. These examples require varying amounts of time, which is one crucial thing to consider when you plan a session. For example, although you could spend fifteen to twenty minutes explaining legal basics, more often you may find yourself needing a full class session to cover legislative histories, or an instructor may ask you to teach a class that identifies both laws and regulations on a particular topic. Depending on the degree of detail the professor expects, some instruction plans will require more than one class session. As a rule of thumb you should suggest to the professor that you create a follow-up assignment. Then, either you or the professor can review the assignment during a subsequent class meeting or have students hand the assignment in to one of you.

Bibliography

Administrative Office of the U.S. Courts. *U.S. Courts.* www.uscourts.gov (accessed November 20, 2005).

Berring, Robert C., and Elizabeth A. Edinger. 1999. *Finding the Law.* 11th ed. St. Paul, MN: West Group.

Congressional Quarterly. *CQ Electronic Library.* http://library.cqpress.com/index.php (accessed November 20, 2005).

Cornell University Law School. *LII: Legal Information Institute.* www.law.cornell.edu (accessed November 20, 2005).

Georgetown University Law Library. *Legislative History Research.* www.ll.georgetown .edu/guides/legislative_history.cfm (accessed November 20, 2005).

Hieros Gamos Legal Directories. www.hg.org (accessed November 20, 2005).

LAW.COM. *Law.com Dictionary.* http://dictionary.law.com (accessed November 20, 2005).

LexisNexis. *LexisNexis Academic.* http://web.lexis-nexis.com/universe/ (accessed November 20, 2005).

Morehead, Joseph. 1999. *Introduction to United States Government Information Sources.* 6th ed. Englewood, CO: Libraries Unlimited.

Nevada Legislative Counsel Bureau. *Nevada Law Library.* www.leg.state.nv.us/law1.cfm (accessed November 20, 2005).

REGULATIONS.gov. www.regulations.gov (accessed November 20, 2005).

Rutgers, the State University of New Jersey. *United States Federal Law.* http://law-library.rutgers.edu/ilg/usfedlaw.php (accessed November 20, 2005).

Thomson FindLaw. *FindLaw.* www.findlaw.com/casecode/supreme.html (accessed November 20, 2005).

Thomson West. *Westlaw.* www.Westlaw.com (accessed November 20, 2005).

United Nations. *International Law.* www.un.org/law (accessed November 20, 2005).

U.S. Congress, House of Representatives. *How Our Laws Are Made.* http://thomas.loc .gov/home/lawsmade.toc.html (accessed November 20, 2005).

U.S. Congress, Library of Congress. *Thomas.* http://Thomas.loc.gov (accessed November 20, 2005).

U.S. Courts, District of Idaho. *Glossary of Legal Terms.* www.id.uscourts.gov/glossary.htm (accessed November 20, 2005).

U.S. Government Printing Office. *GPO Access.* www.gpoaccess.gov (accessed November 20, 2005).

University of California, Irvine Libraries. *From Idea to Law: The Federal Legislative Process.* http://tutorial.lib.uci.edu/public_policy/ (accessed November 20, 2005).

17

Government Information Research

Susie A. Skarl

Introduction

Prior to the mid-1990s, much government information lay outside the mainstream of library catalogs and core indexes and, consequently, was greatly underutilized. Finding government information required negotiating cumbersome search tools, specialized indexes, and separate call number systems. By the end of the 1990s, government information had become more accessible on the World Wide Web. Although the Internet has made searching and finding government information less taxing for patrons, most still require instruction from library staff in order to satisfy their needs in the best possible manner. Concurrent with this rapid transition from print to electronic government information, many government documents reference desks have been merged into general reference service points. Therefore, the need for staff instruction and guidance in government resources has gained in importance. This chapter focuses on lesson plans, instruction techniques, outreach activities, and assessment activities that will acquaint you and increase your comfort level with government information resources. I offer training approaches you can use to familiarize both colleagues and library users with print and electronic resources. The CD-ROM accompanying this book includes several government information–related handouts and PowerPoint presentations to use as training tools (see items 17-1, 17-2, and 17-3 on the CD-ROM).

I emphasize staff training for two reasons. First, government information is multi-disciplinary, making it useful in most library reference settings. However, reference staff often lack regular contact with government information, hence the desirability of in-service training to help them gain skill in answering patrons' questions and guiding them through the maze of government publications and resources. Second, pending changes in the Federal Depository Library Program (FDLP) will likely de-emphasize tangible depository collections. FDLP stakeholders, including librarians, administrators, and Government Printing Office (GPO) managers, are anticipating a reduction in the number of depository libraries. Thus it is necessary for the current generation of government publications librarians to educate other library service providers concerning the content and means of retrieving this information (Seavey, 2005). These developments are mirrored in the publishing and dissemination of international, foreign, state, and local government information as well.

The Scope of Government Information

U.S. federal government information and public documents encompass nearly every subject area. Whether a patron needs information about a recent law passed by Congress, transcripts of a hearing from decades ago, current health information, crime statistics, or information about a NASA space mission, it is likely that an entity of the U.S. government has published something on it. For over 100 years, such publications have been distributed through a system of federal depositories, mainly situated in public, academic libraries across the country (Mann and McDevitt, 2003).

Government publications are often "the best kept secret" in a library (Hutto, 2004). Many depository libraries have housed government documents in a separate section from their other books and periodicals. Most have shelved their U.S. documents according to Superintendent of Documents classification (SuDoc), unlike the rest of the library collection, which is typically organized under the Library of Congress or Dewey Decimal classification system. At best there were only a select few persons in each library who knew the ins and outs of government publications and could help users find them. All of this began to change near the end of the twentieth century, first with the Internet, then with the point-and-click technology of the World Wide Web. Web publishing was eagerly embraced by national, state, and local governments eager to get their information to the masses in a cost-effective manner (Mann and McDevitt, 2003). At the Patent and Trademark Depository Library Program's annual training seminar in April 2005, the GPO's Judy Russell announced that, for the first three months of the year, 93 percent of items distributed through the Federal Depository Library Program were available on the Web.[1] This migration is precipitating change in many libraries. Many federal depository personnel, functions, and services are being merged into general reference departments in their host libraries (Cox and Skarl, 2004). More important, every library today can have a respectable virtual collection of federal government information. Libraries must implement effective practices to deliver this virtual collection to users.

Training Library Staff

Any government information training program for staff should provide background information on how documents are received and processed, an overview of the FDLP, and a sampling of patron needs and the types of questions they asked (Farrell, 2002). To meet the challenge of keeping colleagues informed of the rapid changes and updates in government information resources, education and training of staff should be integrated into existing staff training programs; announcing new resources to reference staff; and alerting staff to new databases or Web sites (Farrell, 2002; Rawan and Cox, 1995; Taylor and Schmidt, 2001). Rawan and Cox also note that trainers should emphasize answering questions, solving problems, and allowing hands-on practice with sources, with less emphasis on lecturing (1995).

In an introductory government information training session for colleagues, begin with brief overviews of the FDLP and your state's depository program. A ninety-minute training session should include a brief history of the programs and cover how these collections are organized, focusing on the Superintendent of Documents (SuDoc) classification system and the Swank (state) or other state systems for classifying state government publications.

Following this introduction, staff should gain familiarity with the most important tools used to find government information in print and online formats. Discuss and distribute common reference books such as:

- *Statistical Abstract of the United States*
- *City and County Data Book*
- Your state's statutes and administrative code

For an active learning activity, break the participants into groups and give them a reference question using a specific source. For example, using the *Statistical Abstract of the United States*, ask one group to find approximately how many people are covered by health insurance in the United States. Using the *City and County Data Book*, ask another group to name the top five cities in the United States with the highest Asian population in 2000.

You can provide a good introduction to government resources available online with an overview and hands-on time with *GPO Access* (www.gpoaccess.gov), *Firstgov.gov* (www.firstgov.gov), and *Google Uncle Sam* (www.google.com/uncle sam). Demonstrate *Google's* "Advanced Search" and limit your search to the .gov domain. Another good exercise is to give two groups the same question to search on two different sites. If you want to know what the U.S. government has published on Attention Deficit Disorder (ADD), have one group search for the term on *Firstgov.gov*, and the other group search on *Google Uncle Sam*. Ask participants to discuss the search strategies they used on various sites and to summarize what they found (e.g., research studies, consumer health-oriented publications, and statistical information). In addition to federal Web sites, provide an overview of related resources found on state, county, and local government sites (including online statutes, administrative codes, and school district policies).

Federal, state, and local governments collect and publish statistics on a wide variety of social, economic, and environmental topics. *Fedstats.gov* (www.fed stats.gov) is perhaps the best government statistical portal, providing links to official statistics collected and published by more than 100 federal agencies. It is relatively easy for novice searchers to use, in part because they do not have to know in advance which agency produces the statistics they want. *Fedstats.gov* also provides links to data on states, cities, counties, and Congressional districts, data access tools, and various online statistical reference sources. Some practice questions to try on *Fedstats.gov* are:

- At midyear 2003, how many inmates were held in the nation's local jails?
- Find the number of live births to 15- to 19-year-olds in 2002.
- Find the number of marriages in the United States in 2002.

Other sources you may want to cover in your first training session include the U.S. Census Bureau Web site (www.census.gov), its *American FactFinder* (AFF) component, the *AFF* tutorial (http://factfinder.census.gov/home/en/epss/tutorials .html), and *Thomas* (http://thomas.loc.gov; covered in the chapter on teaching legal research to nonlaw students).

A sixty- or ninety-minute session would typically allow you to cover three to five Web gateways or subject categories. As such, do not expect all attendees to feel completely at ease with government-related questions after this session. Remind them of some applications for social science-, science-, health-, and public policy-related questions and encourage them to consult with you and other knowledgeable staff when they feel the need to do so. Your supportiveness can be just as important to your colleagues as gaining new knowledge to use in reference encounters.

Follow-up training will help reinforce topics you introduced earlier, give staff an opportunity to ask questions, and allow you to cover more topics and sources. Once you have laid the groundwork, it will be appropriate to offer more sessions, each covering a single subject or resource in greater depth. Possibilities include federal, state, and local legislation, ordinances and codes, the U.S. Census Bureau and *American FactFinder* Web sites, health information, and a more detailed look at government statistics. Consult regularly with your colleagues to identify other government-related subjects that would benefit them and library users.

If your library subscribes to commercial databases that include government information, you should focus on them in staff training. Some of these databases are:

- *Academic Search Premier*. http://search.epnet.com. This aggregator database includes full-text access to U.S. federal government periodicals, such as *Environmental Health Perspectives*, *Joint Force Quarterly*, and *Public Health Reports*.
- *CQ.com*. www.cq.com. A news and analysis service that tracks legislation before Congress and alerts users to late-breaking news.
- *CQ Electronic Library*. http://library.cqpress.com. This database contains full-text articles on a comprehensive range of public policy topics in three

components: CQ *Public Affairs Collection*, CQ *Researcher*, and CQ *Weekly*. A fourth component, the CQ *Voting and Elections Collection*, presents national election statistics.

- *LexisNexis Congressional*. http://web.lexis-nexis.com/congcomp. This database provides access to congressional publications, including hearings, reports, prints, documents, hot topics, bills, laws, regulations, and legislative histories.
- *LexisNexis Primary Sources in U.S. Presidential History*. www.lexisnexis.com/academic/luniv/hist. This database provides the full text of both primary and secondary sources related to U.S. presidential history. In addition to autobiographies, case law, and statutes, the database includes speeches, government publications, and photographs.
- *PAIS International*. Available from several vendors; FirstSearch version available at http://newfirstsearch.oclc.org. *PAIS* includes citations to and limited full text of books, government reports, proceedings, and journal articles on public policy and the social sciences in general. The FirstSearch version of *PAIS* works with link resolvers.

Along with federal and state sources, an introduction to international and intergovernmental publications would be beneficial to library reference staff. Such familiarity will assist service pool members in library instruction and reference consultations in the subject areas of political science, history, geography, and international business. For example, H. M. Sheehy and D. Cheney developed an Introduction to Research in International Relations course to focus on the intergovernmental organizations and selected resources related to international relations from the U.S. government, Canada, and the United Kingdom (1997). In a workshop such as this, you can explore the structure and function of each government and organization, in addition to the way in which a government or organization's activities are controlled by its departments or its member states.

Some online sources and databases to highlight when discussing international resources include:

- *LexisNexis Statistical*. This source provides access to statistics produced by the U.S. government, major international intergovernmental organizations, professional and trade organizations, commercial publishers, independent research organizations, state government agencies, and universities. It is comprised of three indexes: the American Statistics Index (ASI), Index to International Statistics (IIS), and Statistical Resources Index (SRI).
- Northwestern University. *Foreign Governments*. www.library.northwestern.edu/govpub/resource/internat/foreign.html. This Web site provides links to foreign national governments.
- Northwestern University. *International Governmental Organizations*. www.library.northwestern.edu/govpub/resource/internat/igo.html. This gateway is a comprehensive list of links to intergovernmental organizations (IGOs).
- *Official Documents System of the United Nations* (ODS). http://documents.un.org. ODS covers all types of UN documentation from 1993 to the present in several different languages.

- *UNBIS* (United Nations Bibliographic Information System). http://unbisnet .un.org. *UNBIS* is an official catalog of UN documents and publications, in addition to commercial publications and other non-UN sources.

In addition to training sessions or seminars, which allow you to expose your colleagues to a baseline of government-related knowledge and information-finding skills, it is beneficial to provide them with periodic updates on new sources and services. Some examples include:

- Government information in the news. An excellent example of this is *New Mexico News Plus*, a Web-based service of the New Mexico State Library that is updated daily and provides access to government reports, legislation, federal court decisions, statistics, and regulations mentioned in the news (www.stlib.state.nm.us).
- Legislative information (especially when your state legislature is in session).
- New department and agency Web sites. These commonly appear after new federal and state executives take office.
- Environmental agency sites with new impact statements.
- Patents, trademarks, and copyrights.

Workshops, your own one-on-one contacts, and service alerts will encourage staff to integrate government resources into their routine searching strategies when assisting or instructing patrons and help them keep abreast of new sources. Listservs such as GOVDOC-L, PTDLA-L, and INTLDOC and mailings from the UN Depository Program often list new reports on popular topics. You can forward these messages to your coworkers, mention them in discussions, and link to the pertinent reports on your library Web site.

Liaison Activities with Subject Specialists

One of the most successful ways to integrate government publications into the mainstream of your library's instructional program is to consult regularly with your library's subject specialists. There are several benefits when you alert subject librarians to government resources specific to their areas of interest. Not only will you help them increase their knowledge about the most up-to-date government resources in their fields, but you will also prepare them to introduce these resources to their user groups. If you are a government information specialist and also have subject or departmental liaison responsibilities, make your own efforts a model for your colleagues.

There are so many government resources online that you should maintain an up-to-date gateway on your library's Web site, linking to the most pertinent information for your users. When you do this, patrons and your coworkers will come to rely on your Web pages and consider you a trusted resource for their government information needs. You may find it useful to collaborate with subject specialists when designing and adding content to your Web pages. Doing so will make them more knowledgeable concerning government information in their specialties, and they will be more likely to introduce and promote these resources to their users. For example, it would be mutually beneficial to meet with your library's health sciences specialist to discuss health-related government resources, including the following topics:

- Online databases, including *PubMed* (linked from www.ncbi.nlm.nih.gov)
- Consumer health information on *MedlinePlus*: http://medlineplus.gov
- Statistics from the National Center for Health Statistics at www.cdc.gov/nchs/default.htm

Collaborating with Subject Specialists in Instruction Activities

It is especially valuable for government information librarians to collaborate with subject specialists when planning and delivering instruction. C. LaGuardia and colleagues, D. J. Morganti and F. C. Buckalew, and C. Daniels and D. Jurena argue that successful team teaching will benefit instruction librarians by exposing them to more information resources (both licensed and free), new teaching perspectives, and techniques, by building confidence and aiding classroom management in labs (Daniels and Jurena, 1997; LaGuardia et al., 1993; Morganti and Buckalew, 1991). For example, in a graduate construction engineering course, an engineering librarian and government documents librarian can introduce students to engineering research databases, such as *Compendex*, *Scopus*, *ScienceDirect*, and *INSPEC*, and then present government resources focusing on construction and housing. The following are some related U.S. government sources:

- *American FactFinder*: www.census.gov
- *Census Bureau Housing Topics*: www.census.gov/hhes/www/housing.html
- *Construction Statistics*: www.census.gov/const/www
- *National Institute for Occupational Safety and Health* (NIOSH): www.cdc.gov/niosh/topics/construction/default.html
- *Science.gov*: www.science.gov

Faculty and Graduate Seminars and Brown Bag Lunch Discussions

Many academic libraries promote library resources by offering faculty or graduate seminars or informal brown bag discussions about library resources. If your library offers these kinds of events for users, suggest presenting a seminar focusing on a specific government resource or topic. This type of seminar not only provides an opportunity to teach the faculty about a specific government resource, but also allows you to introduce yourself to faculty, promote the library's print and online resources, offer individual research consultations, and suggest pertinent government-related instruction sessions for their students.

A seminar on the U.S. Census Bureau and *American FactFinder* Web sites may interest faculty and graduate students in several departments, including education, social sciences, business, and engineering. In a sixty-minute session, you can give a brief overview of information on the sites and show attendees how to construct and retrieve demographic profiles for local geographic areas, including your state, county, municipalities, census tracts, block groups, and zip codes. After they retrieve a table, tell participants to click on *FactFinder*'s Data Sets icon to find more related data. Provide participants with handouts or links that give definitions and summarize what other types of data can be found on the census Web site. For example, you may want to highlight some of the following:

- *About the Data*: An overview of Census Bureau data, censuses, and surveys, with links to the Decennial Census, American Community Survey, Economic Census, Population Estimates Program, Population Projections, and more.
- *Data Sets*: Access to all data in *American FactFinder*, including Decennial Census, American Community Survey, Economic Census and Surveys, and Population Estimates Data.
- *Fact Sheet*: Easy access to data for the United States, states, counties, cities, towns, and zip codes
- *Maps & Geography*: *American FactFinder* (AFF) has two tools for creating, viewing, printing, and downloading maps:
  - Reference Maps: A tool to view the boundaries of census geographies, such as counties, cities and towns, urban areas, congressional districts, census tracts, census blocks, and more.
  - Thematic Maps: A tool to view geographic patterns in census data. Thematic Maps are available for Census 2000, the 1990 Census, the Economic Census, and the Population Estimates program.
- *Reference Shelf*: Includes links to population reports and publications, data and statistics, and Census Bureau resources.
- *Subjects A to Z*: Essentially a public site map to census information.
- *Tools*: Includes links to data extraction tools, such as data sets; state and county quick facts; the Census Bureau's *DataFerret*; and several other resources.

Working with Teaching Faculty

In today's electronic information environment, librarians and instructional faculty have new opportunities to teach students to find government materials and incorporate them into their research. Data and full-text documents are now available from most federal Web sites. This type of collaboration can create teaching alliances to aid students in finding electronic government information (Asher et al., 2002). As with any other library instruction "one-shot" session, you should meet with the faculty member in advance to plan the session. Discuss the Web sites, primary sources, and government and licensed databases you are considering for the class. This sort of consultation helps you build a relationship with a member of the teaching faculty and provides another opportunity to promote pertinent government-related resources.

What to Teach

J. A. Downie suggests that government information specialists examine their library's instruction program to find teaching opportunities focused on student assignments (Downie, 2004). Although academic librarians have some opportunities to include government information in instruction and encourage their use by students, pertinent government information is frequently omitted from library orientations (Downie, 2004). Once students are aware of government sources and learn some search skills and strategies to find them, they will discover additional materials that can help them with future assignments.

How can students benefit most from government information instruction in a one-shot session? P. Ragains states that students will benefit most from such lessons if instruction on the use of relevant information and search techniques is integrated meaningfully into course assignments and if follow-up assistance is available from course instructors or librarians (Ragains, 1995). S. Anthes notes that in order to hold the participants' attention, instructors need to show enthusiasm about the documents collection, focus on a particular class assignment or information need, and concentrate on key concepts (Anthes, 1993). This will be more effective and less confusing than trying to include everything. The most important points for students to learn are that the government publishes information relevant to their needs and that the information is freely accessible to them. Since users and staff often see documents as different or difficult compared to other library collections, it helps to stress the online and free aspects first, and then introduce students to the print documents collection.

Mainstreaming Government Information in Instruction

The following scenarios show how to introduce students to government information resources in a library session that is not specifically focused on government resources:

- Comparing primary and secondary sources. Many English and Communication faculty ask librarians to teach students the difference between primary and secondary sources. To illustrate this point, break the students into groups comparing primary and secondary sources. Examples of primary sources include Congressional hearings, census data, and the *Weekly Compilation of Presidential Documents.*
- Authoritativeness. Government Web sites are excellent examples when instructors request a demonstration of authoritative, comprehensive, current, and accurate sites. Choose from among Web sites providing statistics in health, education, and crime, expert testimony. Showing government research reports, such as those on the recent prisoner abuse scandals in Iraq, will bring home the point of authority when examining a Web site.
- Courses focusing on college majors or careers. Introduce students to the *Occupational Outlook Handbook* at www.bls.gov/oco.

Presenting Government Information to Students "On Demand"

As mentioned previously, history and particular social science courses often have a clear connection with government-produced information, and assignments in these fields often call for use of such sources. Following are two examples to use in political science courses:

- In a freshman-level Introduction to American Politics course, students have been assigned to research a proposed constitutional amendment. Present and allow hands-on practice with the U.S. Constitution (www.house.gov/Constitution/Constitution.html) and your state's constitution. Walk them through a search for legislative histories on *Thomas*. See Chapter 16 and item 17-3 on the CD-ROM for sample lessons using *Thomas*.
- In an upper-division undergraduate course on focusing on public policy (which could be offered to nursing, education, social work, criminal justice, or political science students), show pertinent government sources and give an overview of the organization of government publications. Give demonstrations and allow students to practice using your library's online catalog, government information Web site, and any pertinent commercial databases your library may license, such as *LexisNexis Congressional* or *PAIS International*. If government publications are listed in your library catalog, you can easily show how to find government, scholarly, and popular publications on the same topic. Critical thinking comes into play when you ask students to consider the different perspectives characteristic of information sources based on authorship and target audience, even when the publications are on a single subject. The same is true when you discuss search results from multi-subject databases like *Academic Search Premier* or *PAIS*.

Graduate-level library instruction usually involves smaller groups of students with specific research interests. When meeting with graduate students it is often best to present sources in more depth than you would for undergraduates and to discuss advanced search strategies. You may choose the same sources you would present to undergraduates, but discuss them in a more detailed manner, for example, explaining the usefulness of particular information sources in professional practice. Graduate students are typically well motivated and on the watch for resources and services they can use for their own benefit. They are more likely than undergraduates to tell you what they want and let you know when they are not getting it. By forcing you to dig more deeply into your own knowledge base, meeting with such groups also sharpens your own reference and instruction skills.

Assessment

Many government information librarians focus on outreach and instruction efforts to increase the exposure of colleagues, teaching faculty, and students to the rich resources found in government publications. How well are we doing? What are our library users learning? J. A. Downie encourages librarians to assess instruction

---

Figure 17-1   Government Information Staff Training Workshop: Practice Questions

1   Search the Library Catalog for the following title: *Supporting Families in Transition: A Guide to Expanding Health Coverage in the Post-Welfare Reform World.*
    What is its SuDoc number?
    What agency issued this document?

2   A patron needs the following information about Nevada Senator John Ensign:
    a. His birth date
    b. Besides being a senator, what Ensign's other profession is
    c. The phone number of his Washington office
    Please list your search strategy and information sources you used to find the answer.

3   This month, the federal government introduced a Web site that compares detailed information about Medicaid- and Medicare-certified nursing homes in the country. What is the URL of this new Web site? What federal department is associated with this Web site?
    Please list your search strategy and the information sources you used to find the answer.

4   A patron has the following call number: Co29-C54-C73/9:C76x/1992-1996. Just from the call number, can you tell what level of government published it? Can you tell if it is a monograph or a serial? Try to answer without looking at the publication. Find the publication on the shelf to see if you are right. What is it?

5   A patron comes in saying she heard about a controversy over the train tracks in Reno and that the Nevada Supreme Court recently made a ruling about it. She wants to find the ruling.

6   Can you find the Nevada Supreme Court opinions in the catalog? (Hint: you may have to try a keyword search). What is the call number for the Nevada Supreme Court opinions? Is there another way to find the opinions besides going to the shelf? Try to find the opinion your patron is looking for and give a one-sentence summary of the court's decision.

7   Go to the Clark County, Nevada, Web site. Find the Elections Department page. How would you find out which county commission district you are in and who your commissioner is? Find out and write the answer below.

---

efforts by analyzing reshelving statistics, Web logs, and citation lists from papers, in addition to putting counters on Web pages and asking the reference staff to record their use of government sources before and after training (Downie, 2004). Similarly, Barclay states that there are typically four methods of collecting information to evaluate the effectiveness of instruction: anecdote, survey, test, and evidence of use (Barclay, 1993).

Figure 17-1 is a "homework" assignment to give staff after an introductory session on government information. This assignment would cover many of the federal, state, and local sources discussed at the training session and would give colleagues an opportunity to become more familiar with the sources by solving a patron's research question. You can modify this worksheet to fit your library and use it as an outcomes assessment tool.

Figure 17-2 is an example of a short online survey to give students after an instructional workshop. When designing a feedback survey such as the following, you will have to consider how you would like to collect the survey results. If you have a relatively small amount of results to analyze, the completed surveys could go directly to an e-mail address and you could calculate the results manually. For surveys with a larger response rate, you may want to use a database such as *Microsoft Access* or *MySQL* to analyze the results.

Emerging Trends for Government Information Instruction

A survey of instruction-related literature published since the early 1990s shows that government information librarians have made substantial progress in alerting colleagues and library users to government resources. To strengthen your own promotion efforts, consider the following:

- Work directly with teaching faculty to develop pertinent assignments and guides incorporating government information. For suggestions, see Chapter 2 of this book, which covers collaborating with faculty.
- Work with your library's instruction department to create an online tutorial focusing specifically on government resources.
- Create a monthly or quarterly e-mail or online newsletter for colleagues, teaching faculty, and library users that will announce new government resources. An RSS feed (an acronym for both "Rich Site Summary" and "Really Simple Syndication") from your library catalog can alert them to new

---

Figure 17-2   Political Science 320: Online Feedback Form

Please take a few moments to give us some comments about your library instruction session.

1. Who was your instructor?

2. Rate the effectiveness of the instructor who taught your class in terms of good organization and clear presentation.
   _____Excellent
   _____Good
   _____Fair
   _____Poor

3. Your class included an introduction and hands-on time with various government information resources. Please rate the overall value of learning about government information. Will it help you with your research assignment for this class?
   _____Excellent
   _____Good
   _____Fair
   _____Poor

4. Should library instruction with an emphasis on government information continue to be included as part of this class?
   _____Yes
   _____No

In the space below, please let us know how the library instruction workshop can be improved.

Thank you for taking the time to complete our survey.

Figure 17-3   Usability Test for "Gateway to Government Information" Workshop

Indicate your class standing:

Freshman   Sophomore   Junior   Senior   Graduate student

Usability Test Questions

1   Locate the Libraries' "Gateway to Government Information" Web site.

2   Where would you go to download 2004 U.S. tax forms?

3   Who are the senators for the state of Nevada?

4   You are thinking about majoring in hotel administration, and you would like to find out about working conditions and salaries in the hospitality or casino/gaming industry. Where can you find this information?

5   Many government publications in the library can be checked out. Where do you go in the library to check them out?

6   You are doing a report on agriculture and need statistics on agriculture in the United States. Where can you find these statistics?

7   You need some basic information on the Supreme Court. Where can find out about the Supreme Court?

8   You are doing research on ethnic minorities and need population figures for ethnic groups in the United States. Where would you go to find this information?

9   You need to do a speech on the federal government. Where can you find basic information about the federal government and its divisions and agencies?

10   You need to do a persuasive speech on a current issue, and your instructor has assigned you the topic of gay marriage. Where would you go to find government information about this topic?

11   Find the text of the Americans with Disabilities Act. Write its citation below.

Post-Test Interview Questions

1   If you could say one thing to the people working on this Web site, what would it be?

2   What did you find especially good about the Libraries' Government Information Web site?

3   What did you find frustrating about the Libraries' Government Information Web site?

4   Are you currently using any sites or search engines to find government information?

5   How would you prefer to learn about changes or enhancements to the Libraries' Web site?

6   Do you have any other comments about the Government Information Web site?

---

acquisitions by library department or branch, in particular subjects, or within other parameters.

- Work with other government document librarians in your city, state, or region to offer instruction, training, and outreach activities. An event such as a "Government Information Training Day" is an excellent way to teach, promote, and highlight federal, state, and local government resources to library staff.

- Conduct periodic usability testing with library users on your government resources Web pages. Usability testing assesses how easy your target audience finds the site to use, understand, and navigate. As user needs change, so must the site. Considering users' reactions to your library site will help the organization be more responsive to their needs (Cobus, Dent, and Ondrusek, 2005). Figure 17-3 is a sample usability test for the government information suite of pages on an academic library Web site.

Conclusion

The World Wide Web has given the public unprecedented access to government information. Government information specialists must continue their efforts to familiarize users with the wide range of resources available. By collaborating with library instruction and subject librarians and pursuing outreach and liaison activities with faculty members, government information can be integrated into the mainstream of library reference instruction services. Increased awareness of these resources will enrich the experience of students and other users we serve.

Note

1. Judith C. Russell, Address delivered at the Patent & Trademark Depository Library Program Training Seminar, Alexandria, Virginia, April 7, 2005.

Bibliography

Anthes, S. 1993. "Outreach, Promotion, and Bibliographic Instruction." In *Management of Government Information Resources in Libraries*, pp. 173–182, edited by D. H. Smith. Englewood, CO: Libraries Unlimited.

Asher, C., S. Knapp, and H. Yi. 2002. "Effective Instruction Needed to Improve Students' Use of Government Documents." *Journal of Government Information* 29: 293–301.

Barclay, Donald. 1993. "Evaluating Library Instruction: Doing the Best You Can with What You Have." *RQ* 33: 195–202.

Cobus, L., V. F. Dent, and A. Ondrusek. 2005. "How Twenty-Eight Users Helped Redesign an Academic Web Site: A Usability Study." *Reference and User Services Quarterly* 44: 232–246.

Cox, J. L., and S. A. Skarl. 2004. "Government Information Education and Training: A Selected Annotated Bibliography." *Reference Services Review* 32: 313–319.

Daniels, C., and D. Jurena. 1997. "Two Heads Are Better Than One: Team Teaching in the Information Age." Paper presented at the Annual Meeting of the Nebraska Library Association. ERIC ED 410978.

Downie, J. A. 2004. "The Current Information Literacy Instruction for Government Documents." Pt. 1. *DttP* 32: 36–39.

———. 2004. "The Current Information Literacy Instruction for Government Documents." Pt. 2. *DttP* 32: 17, 20–22.

Farrell, M. P. 2002. "Training for Documents Reference in a Merged Reference Center." *DttP* 28: 11–16.

Hoover, D. 2002. *Sociology 101—Census 2000: Collecting Census Data from the Web.* http://library.hunter.cuny.edu/dhoover/soc/soc1.html (accessed August 14, 2005).

Hutto, D. 2004. "Teaching about Government Information: Introduction." *Dttp* 32: 14.

LaGuardia, C., A. Griego, M. Hopper, L. Melendez, and C. Oka. 1993. "Learning to Instruct on the Job: Team-Teaching Library Skills." *Reference Librarian* 40: 53–62.

Mann, W., and T. R. McDevitt, eds. 2003. *Government Publications Unmasked: Teaching Government Resources in the 21st Century*. Pittsburgh: Library Instruction Publications.

Morganti, D. J., and F. C. Burckalew. 1991. "The Benefits of Team Teaching." *Research Strategies* 9: 195–197.

Ragains, P. 1995. "The Legislative/Regulatory Process and BI: A Course-Integrated Unit." *Research Strategies* 13: 116–121.

Rawan, A. R., and J. L. Cox. 1995. "Government Publications Integration and Training." *Journal of Government Information* 22: 253–266.

Seavey, C. A. 2005. "Documents to the People: Musings on the Past and Future of Government Information." *American Libraries* 36, no. 7: 42–44.

Sheehy, H. M., and D. Cheney. 1997. "Government Information and Library Instruction: A Means to an End." *Journal of Government Information* 24: 313–330.

Swank, Raynard. 1944. "A Classification for State, Country, and Municipal Documents." *Special Libraries* 35, no. 4: 116–120.

Taylor, Suzanne N., and Fred C. Schmidt. 2001. "Reference Services and Federal Documents: Current Status and Issues." *Colorado Libraries* 27, no. 2: 21–24.

18

Patent Research

Brian B. Carpenter

Introduction

It is fitting to conclude this book on information literacy instruction with a discussion of patents and the techniques for finding them. Inventors often have a substantial economic stake in understanding information sources for patents and intellectual property. More broadly, society also has a stake in supporting technological innovation in fields ranging from simple household products to lifesaving medicines. In this chapter I describe basic strategies and methods for teaching students, inventors, and researchers how to research patents issued in the United States. For many of these methods I have built upon ideas and strategies put forth by patent examiners employed in the U.S. Patent and Trademark Office (USPTO), staff in the USPTO Patent and Trademark Depository Library (PTDL) Program Office, and my own coworkers.[1] Patent searching techniques developed in the PTDL community over the last two decades have been documented in only a few publications (Hitchcock, 2000; Wherry, 1995). Library public service providers do not need a background in the sciences or engineering processes in order to provide competent instruction in patent searching. All that matters is a willingness to show people how to use the research resources supplied by the USPTO and related information.

What Are Patents?

A patent for an invention is a property right issued to the inventor by the USPTO. Generally, the term of a new patent is twenty years from the date on which the application for the patent was filed in the United States. The patent grant confers "the right to exclude others from making, using, offering for sale, or selling" the invention in the United States or "importing" the invention into the United States. The USPTO may grant patents for "any new and useful process, machine, manufacture, or composition of matter, or any new and useful improvement thereof." Other general criteria for patentability are "nonobviousness"; that is, the invention must be "sufficiently different from what has been used or described before that it may be said to be nonobvious to a person having ordinary skill in the area of technology related to the invention," and must not be "useful solely in the utilization of special nuclear material or atomic energy in an atomic weapon" (42 U.S.C. 2181 (a)).

There are three types of patents:

- *Utility patents* may be granted to anyone who invents or discovers any new and useful process, machine, article of manufacture, or composition of matter, or any new and useful improvement thereof.
- *Design patents* may be granted to anyone who invents a new, original, and ornamental design for an article of manufacture.
- *Plant patents* may be granted to anyone who invents or discovers and asexually reproduces any distinct and new variety of plant (USPTO, *General Information Concerning Patents*, 2005).

A patent search, also known as a prior art search, is a search for one or more patented inventions. Why is patent searching important? The first, if not always most obvious, answer is to gather information necessary to avoid infringing on someone else's patented invention. Patent law states that a person cannot get a patent on someone else's invention. Also, once an invention is given patent protection, it cannot be patented ever again. Inventors must be aware of all existing inventions that may be very similar or practically identical to their own. Second, the search is a good way to learn about other competing inventions that are already on the market—a patent search is a normal component of product research and development. Finally, inventors and others often must know who owns existing innovations or has the right to manufacture them. All of this information can be found in a patent document. In order to receive patent protection for a device, design, or plant, an inventor must fully disclose all information about it. But patents are not just important to students or independent inventors; manufacturers sometimes find that specifications for machine parts can be found only in the text of a patent, chemists find that variations for chemical innovations can be found in a patent, and historians often find that a patent provides the only documentation of particular technological innovations. How does one take this wealth of information and present it as an organized body of information that people can research, whatever their purpose? That is what I will attempt to explain in this chapter. You should freely take any methods discussed here and build on them. That is what teaching is all about in our profession: building on each other's research and experience so the general public can benefit.

Using the USPTO's Seven-Step Strategy

Frequently, inventors, researchers, and students try to do a prior art search themselves and find too many patents to read, find no patents on an invention similar to what they would like to patent, or find several patents on inventions similar to theirs but suspect that more patents exist than those that they have found.

As is true of most disciplines, there are some baseline concepts and information sources underlying all research involving U.S. patents. The baseline for patent searchers is the Seven-Step Strategy, as explained in Figure 18-1. A preliminary search is possible by this method, which was developed for general use in the early 1990s by Marie Moisdon and several staff of the Patent and Trademark Depository Library Program Office. Patent examiners have used this model for much longer. The strategy has been revised and modified to reflect changes in information technology, but the steps remain basically the same.

As you can see, the Seven-Step Strategy focuses on information sources. But how can an inventor get into the proper mindset to execute the strategy? Over a period of several years, Mary Moisdon and USPTO staff members Michael White and Tom Turner, working with several USPTO examiners, created a checklist of sorts which poses five basic questions:

1 What does my invention do? What is the essential function of the invention?
2 What is the end result? What is the essential effect or product resulting from the invention?
3 What is it made of?
4 What is it used for?
5 What are some common and technical terms that can be used to describe the invention?

By answering these questions, an inventor will be better prepared to identify the proper U.S. patent classification to use in a search.

Once a person has broken down an invention into its component parts and identified some descriptive words, it is easier to determine which classification it might fall into. That is when to proceed with the Seven-Step Strategy. I offer the following tips for you to use when teaching the strategy to individuals or groups.

Step 1: Search the Index to the U.S. Patent Classification

The *Index to the U.S. Patent Classification* is available at www.uspto.gov/web/ patents/classification/uspcindex/indextouspc.htm. It is an alphabetical list of nouns, adjectives, and adverbs showing the associated class or subclass that describes the function, effect, structure, end product, or use of a category of inventions. The

Figure 18-1   Seven-Step Strategy for Searching U.S. Patents on the Web

1   Search the *Index to the U.S. Patent Classification*. Begin with this alphabetical subject index to the *Manual of Classification*. Look for common terms describing the invention and its function, effect, end product, structure, and use. Note the class and subclass numbers associated with the terms you select.

2   Search the *Manual of Classification*. Locate class and subclass numbers in the *Manual of Classification*. Note where the terms fall within the U.S. Patent Classification System. Scan the entire class schedule, paying attention to the dot indent. Revise your search strategy as needed.

3   Search the *Classification Definitions*. Read the definitions to establish the scope of classes and subclasses relevant to the search. The definitions include important search notes and suggestions for further searching.

4   Browse titles and abstracts of patents and applications. Check if you are on the right path. First, retrieve and browse through titles of patents and published applications in the given class and subclass. If the patents you find do not reflect your own invention or idea, redirect your search: search on new keywords, retrieve lists of patents and published applications, note their class and subclass numbers, and go back to Step 2. USPTO databases on the Web include the full text of patents from 1976 to the current week and images (searchable only by class or number) from 1790 to the current week, plus published applications from 2001 to the present.

5   Retrieve all patents and applications with your desired subclasses. Once you have identified the relevant classes and subclasses, obtain a list of all patent numbers granted from 1790 to the present and all published applications from 2001 to the present for every class and subclass to be searched.

6   Read the front page of each patent and application retrieved. Check the patents and applications for exemplary claim(s) and a representative drawing for all patents on the list(s) to eliminate patents unrelated to your invention.

7   Retrieve complete patent documents. After you have eliminated patents and applications unrelated to your invention, read the complete text and examine drawing(s) of the most closely related documents to determine how different they are from your invention.

Adapted from www.uspto.gov/web/offices/ac/ido/ptdl/step7.htm (USPTO).

important thing to keep in mind is that one cannot just go to the index and always find one's type of invention listed. Using a computerized emergency vehicle developed by Texas A&M's Texas Engineering Extension Service (TEEX) as an example, we can logically think of specific keywords such as **patrol car**, **police car**, or **computerized police car**. But in its broadest sense, the car is simply a vehicle, just like a boat, a plane, a submarine, a train, or a truck. Figure 18-2 shows how to use the Find feature of a Web browser to locate a keyword or phrase in the index.

Step 2: Search the Manual of Classification

Once a patent searcher has used the *Index to the U.S. Patent Classification* to identify the broad categories related to an invention, then it is on to the next step. The Web-based version of the manual is available at www.uspto.gov/web/patents/classification. Clicking on the hyperlinked class or subclass listed next to

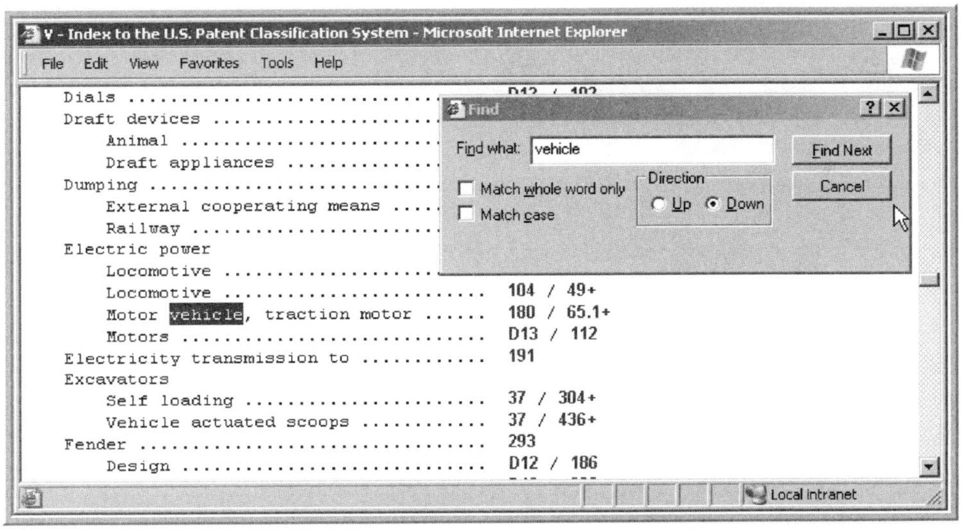

Figure 18-2 The *Index to the U.S. Patent Classification*

the desired word or phrase moves the user into the *Manual of Classification*. The *Manual of Classification* is a hierarchical list of categories of technology and design, arranged from the least to most detailed categories. Reading entries in the *Manual of Classification*, you will likely guess that different kinds of inventions can be classified under one classification number. Patent examiners point out the reason for this: although inventions may look very different or even have different names, if they perform the same function or the same end result is achieved, then they are classified in the same category. Computerized emergency vehicles are classified under class 701—Data Processing Vehicles, Navigation and Relative Location, as shown in Figure 18-3.

Understanding the Manual of Classification

The U.S. patent classification system is used to describe inventions according to the type of device, process, function, or design. Patent classification follows a hierarchical arrangement, similar to an outline used to write a term paper. Each indented subclass heading further qualifies the heading under which it is indented. This means that each subclass includes all characteristics of superior subclasses in the hierarchy. Patent information users must understand this hierarchical arrangement in order to conduct a successful search. Figure 18-4 shows the classification schedule for electronic games.

Step 3: Search the Classification Definitions

The classification tools on the USPTO Web site allow the searcher to move directly from the *Manual of Classification* to the *Classification Definitions*, which provides the most detailed information about what technologies or designs are

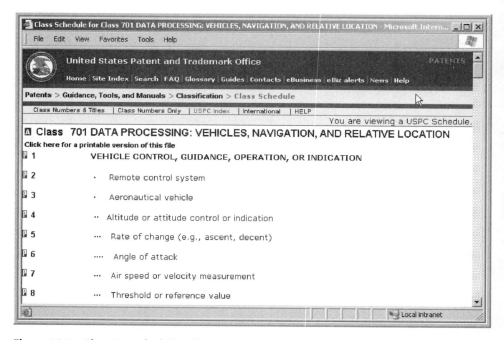

Figure 18-3   The *Manual of Classification*

included in each patent subclass. The *Classification Definitions* provides short narrative definitions of an invention category in terms that both a lawyer and someone familiar with that technology can understand. As with the *Index to the U.S. Patent Classification* and *Manual of Classification*, it is important to remember these definitions are purposely broad so they can cover a large number of similar inventions. For instance, Figure 18-5 shows a typically broad patent subclass definition, this one encompassing the game of football (Class 473, Subclass 470).

Someone who knows a lot about football would readily understand this definition. For one just learning about the game, it might be more difficult to understand the definition and how it relates to their invention. Yet even knowledgeable inventors may need help interpreting the definitions. In such cases, you should encourage inventors to talk with either an attorney or a local inventor group that has strong ties to the legal community. In states where a prohibition against unauthorized practice of law (UPL) is enforced, you certainly should do so.

Step 4: Browse Titles and Abstracts of Patents and Applications

Once a patent researcher has read relevant definitions and has selected an appropriate class and subclass for an invention, the hyperlinked red and white icon labeled *p* for patent leads to a list of all patented inventions in that patent subclass. The date range covered encompasses 1790 through the most recent week. Inventors, library staff who assist them, and other patent information users must realize that once an invention is patented, it cannot be patented again. This is stated more succinctly in Title 35, section 102 of the *United States Code*, which spells out

Figure 18-4   How to Read Class and Subclass Listings in the *Manual of Classification*

Class

463   AMUSEMENT DEVICES: GAMES

Subclass

No.   Title

1   INCLUDING MEANS FOR PROCESSING ELECTRONIC DATA (E.G.,
      COMPUTER/VIDEO GAME, ETC.)
2   In a game including a simulated projectile (e.g., bullet, missile, ball, puck, etc.)
3   Paddle-type game (e.g., pinball, tennis, baseball, golf, hockey, etc.)
4   Simulated court game or athletic event (e.g., soccer, basketball, etc.)
5   Simulated projector with diverse interactive target
6   In a race game
7   In a game requiring an element of a participant's physical skill or ability (e.g.,
      hand-eye coordination, reflex, etc.)
8   Martial-art type (e.g., boxing, fencing, wrestling, etc.)
9   In a game requiring strategy or problem solving by a participant (e.g., problem
      eliciting response, puzzle, etc.)
10   With chance element or event (e.g., backgammon, Scrabble, etc.)
11   Card- or tile-type (e.g., bridge, dominoes, etc.)
12   Ultimate outcome dependent upon summation of plural card or tile values (e.g.,
      blackjack, etc.)
13   Ultimate outcome dependent upon relative odds of a card or tile combination
      (e.g., poker, etc.)
14   Chess- or checker-type

In the preceding example, Subclass 4 is read as:

AMUSEMENT DEVICES: GAMES

1   INCLUDING MEANS FOR PROCESSING ELECTRONIC DATA
2   In a game including a simulated projectile (e.g., bullet, missile, ball, puck, etc.)
4   Simulated court game or athletic event (e.g., soccer, basketball, etc.)

Subclass 13 is read as:

AMUSEMENT DEVICES: GAMES

1   INCLUDING MEANS FOR PROCESSING ELECTRONIC DATA
9   In a game requiring strategy or problem solving by a participant (e.g., problem
      eliciting response, puzzle, etc.)
10   With chance element or event (e.g., backgammon, Scrabble, etc.)
11   Card- or tile-type (e.g., bridge, dominoes, etc.)
13   Ultimate outcome dependent upon relative odds of a card or tile combination
      (e.g., poker, etc.)

Subclass 14 is read as:

AMUSEMENT DEVICES: GAMES

1   INCLUDING MEANS FOR PROCESSING ELECTRONIC DATA
9   In a game requiring strategy or problem solving by a participant (e.g., problem
      eliciting response, puzzle, etc.)
14   Chess- or checker-type

Figure 18-5 Classification Definition of U.S. Patent Class 473, Subclass 470

For game using goal or target for projectile (e.g., football, rugby, etc.):

This subclass is indented under **subclass 465**. Playing field or court game wherein the game or sport is played on a playing area having either a defined structure associated therewith or having a compartment, subarea, or section located thereon over or within which the players do not normally move; which defined structure or compartment, etc. constitutes a point of aim for, and which is intended to indicate the correctness of aim of, a game projectile when propelled thereat by a player, so that whenever, in accordance with the rules defined for the game or sport, the projectile hits, enters, or passes through the structure or compartment, etc., the score of a player or team is incremented, or when a specified number of projectiles assigned to a player or team hits, enters, or passes through the structure or compartment, etc., the game ends for at least that player or team.

the requirements for novelty. Figure 18-6 shows partial results of a classification search on the USPTO Web site. Note the search syntax shown in the upper left region of the screen (CCL/701/36), which refers to the current classification of inventions under Class 701, Subclass 36.

When a list of related inventions is presented on the screen, searchers will notice that inventions in a single patent subclass will have different titles. This is true even though the inventions may have similar functions, results, end products, structure, or use. Inventors, their agents, or attorneys choose the titles of

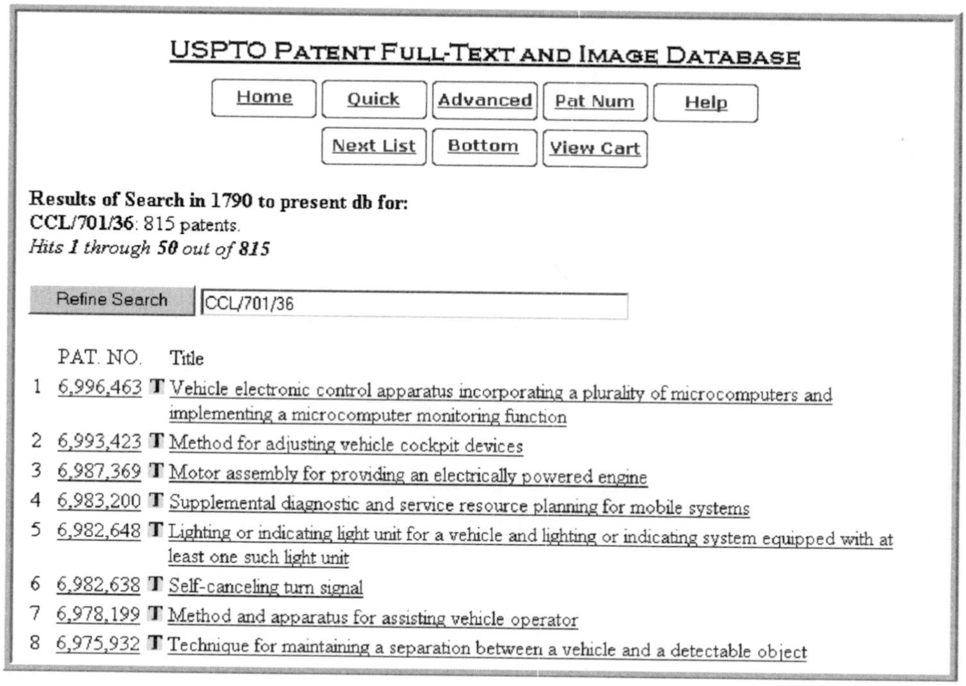
USPTO PATENT FULL-TEXT AND IMAGE DATABASE

Home | Quick | Advanced | Pat Num | Help

Next List | Bottom | View Cart

Results of Search in 1790 to present db for:
CCL/701/36: 815 patents.
*Hits **1** through **50** out of **815***

Refine Search | CCL/701/36

	PAT. NO.		Title
1	6,996,463	T	Vehicle electronic control apparatus incorporating a plurality of microcomputers and implementing a microcomputer monitoring function
2	6,993,423	T	Method for adjusting vehicle cockpit devices
3	6,987,369	T	Motor assembly for providing an electrically powered engine
4	6,983,200	T	Supplemental diagnostic and service resource planning for mobile systems
5	6,982,648	T	Lighting or indicating light unit for a vehicle and lighting or indicating system equipped with at least one such light unit
6	6,982,638	T	Self-canceling turn signal
7	6,978,199	T	Method and apparatus for assisting vehicle operator
8	6,975,932	T	Technique for maintaining a separation between a vehicle and a detectable object

Figure 18-6 Patent Number and Title List

This list is hyperlinked from classification definitions at www.uspto.gov.

their own inventions, and such a title does not have to adhere to any strict format. It can be a spelled-out acronym, a chemical formula name, a technical name describing the product's function, or a legalistic title used to describe it. This is one of the main reasons that keyword searching any database of U.S. patent information yields inferior results when compared to a classification search.

Step 5: Retrieve All Patents and Applications with Your Desired Subclasses

A patent searcher may perform this step in the search process at the same time as Step 4 (Browse Patent Titles and Abstracts). However, identifying the correct subclasses is a recursive and relatively open-ended process. Searchers should continuously evaluate the adequacy of their search when viewing results. This may lead the searcher to select and search on subclasses other than those first chosen. The searcher should continue this process until satisfied that the patents retrieved reflect his or her interest as closely as possible.

Step 6: Read the Front Page of Each Patent and Application Retrieved

The next step is to read the text sections of the patent. The text of every U.S. patent issued since 1976 is available in hypertext markup language (html) on the USPTO Web site. Scanned images of all patents are also available and may be displayed with a Web browser plug-in for Tagged Image File Format (TIFF) files. For any patents issued before 1976, users must rely on the scanned images, since no text display is available. A text display shows all words and other textual information in a patent, including the patent number, its title, date issued, names of all associated inventors, classifications, name of the USPTO examiner handling the case, references, abstract, specifications, and claims.

All patent searchers must know that the classifications shown on a patent are the original classifications assigned at the time of the patent's issue. This assigned or issued number never changes on the face of the granted patent. However, as classifications are redefined and new ones are added to reflect developing technology, patents will be retrievable under their new "current classifications" (CCL). The field of search on the front page summarizes research done by the patent examiner to determine any and all related classes and subclasses for a particular invention. Inventors should do similar searches when they are doing their own research. They must discover any patented inventions that might sink their own prospective application.

The References Cited in a patent is a list of patents and other information sources that the examiner found to be closely related to the present invention and comprise a short technological history of the invention. This list is significant to patent researchers since it may list other related inventions that might invalidate a new application. Figure 18-7 shows a References Cited list from a patent's text display on the USPTO Web site.

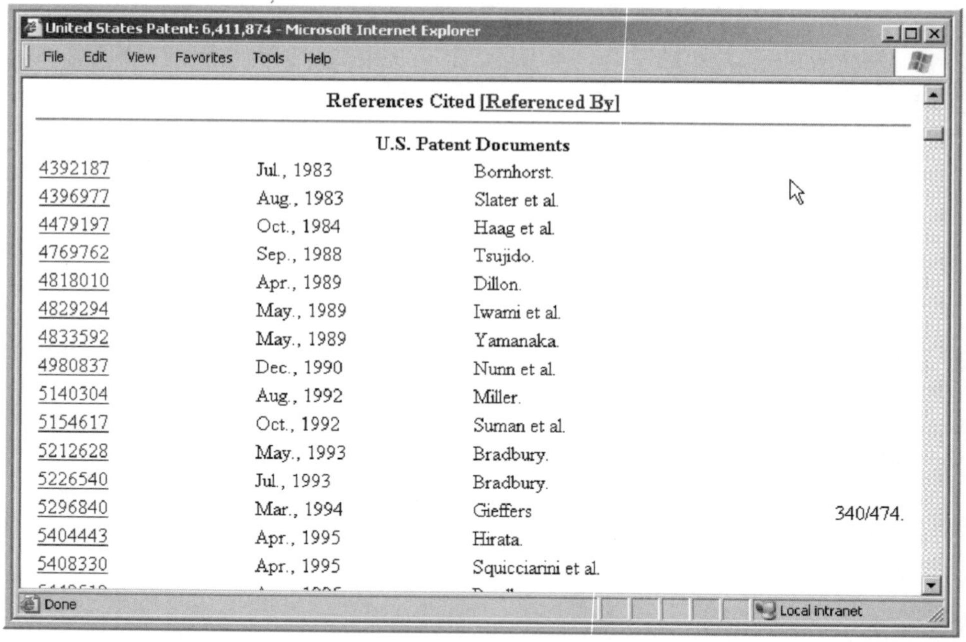

4392187	Jul., 1983	Bornhorst.	
4396977	Aug., 1983	Slater et al.	
4479197	Oct., 1984	Haag et al.	
4769762	Sep., 1988	Tsujido.	
4818010	Apr., 1989	Dillon.	
4829294	May., 1989	Iwami et al.	
4833592	May., 1989	Yamanaka.	
4980837	Dec., 1990	Nunn et al.	
5140304	Aug., 1992	Miller.	
5154617	Oct., 1992	Suman et al.	
5212628	May., 1993	Bradbury.	
5226540	Jul., 1993	Bradbury.	
5296840	Mar., 1994	Gieffers	340/474.
5404443	Apr., 1995	Hirata.	
5408330	Apr., 1995	Squicciarini et al.	

Figure 18-7 A Patent's References Cited List

Note that U.S. patent numbers are hyperlinked to facilitate retrieval.

Using these resources on the USPTO site, an independent inventor or researcher can learn how classification hierarchies work and do a preliminary search for any existing technology that might kill a planned patent application.

The remaining text in the patent includes an abstract, statement of any government interest, background, summary, object, summary and detailed description of the invention, description of the drawings, examples, any pertinent tables or charts, and, finally, the claims. Claims are the inventor's claim to originality, or patentability of an invention. Each claim refers directly to a class or subclass designation listed on the front page of the patent. Figure 18-8 shows the claims for one of our earlier examples, a computerized emergency response vehicle.

Step 7: Retrieve Complete Patent Documents

The next step is to view scanned images of the most relevant patents. If the user is using the USPTO public Web site, these are available from the button labeled Image. From the pubWEST database (currently available only in patent and trademark depository libraries and to the USPTO's examiners), they need only click on the desired patent in the list of patents provided. In either platform, scanned images of patents appear in their respective viewers. All images of patents in the USPTO database are provided in TIFF. Users must obtain a Web browser plug-in in order to view these image files. Links to several free browser plug-ins are available on the USPTO site, and your library and instructional workstations should have one installed to facilitate training and the needs of

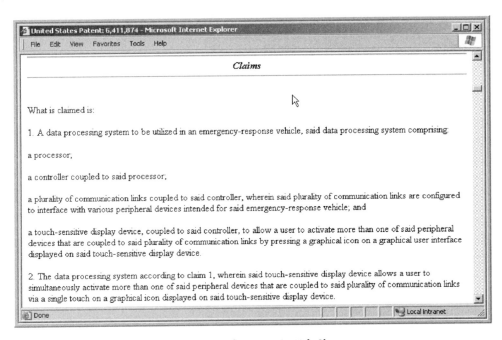

Figure 18-8   Patent Claims as Shown on the USPTO Web Site

end users. Patent images appear in a separate frame in the Web browser that allows the user to view the front page, just the drawings, just the specifications, or just the claims. Scanned patents can be printed or downloaded from the USPTO Web site, depending on the functionality of the plug-in (some allow only one page at a time to be printed). Figure 18-9 shows a patent image on the USPTO site.

In pubWEST, the image viewer is integrated into the platform and does not have to be downloaded separately. When a pubWEST user selects the button to view the image, the screen splits so that the text of the patent appears on the left side of the screen and the TIFF image appears on the right side of the screen. With pubWEST, images can be printed one page at a time, a selected number of pages can be printed, or the entire patent can be printed. Figure 18-10 shows pubWEST's image display.

Cassis®: A Good Offline Patent Database and Search Resource

During the course of researching a patent, a student or researcher may be unable to get access to the Web. *Cassis®* is an offline, DVD-ROM–based family of patent and trademark databases produced by the USPTO. *Cassis®* can serve as limited substitute for the Web interfaces mentioned above. *Cassis®* stands for Classification and Search Support Information System. Like pubWEST and the USPTO public site, *Cassis®* can be searched by keyword, including title, inventor name, city, state, and country, but works best when searched by classification. *Cassis®* is comprised of several different databases, which are the following:

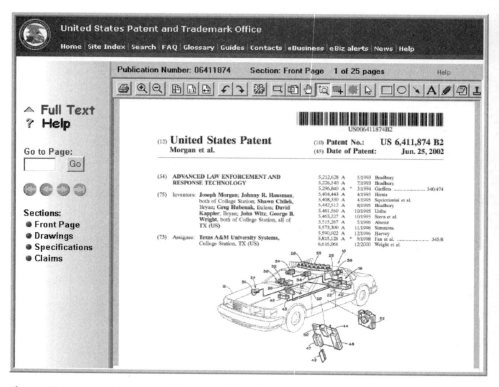

Figure 18-9   Patent Image on USPTO Public Web Site

- *Patents ASSIST.* Includes classification tools (*Index to the U.S. Patent Classification*, *Manual of Classification*, and definitions), *Manual of Patent Examining Procedure*, a directory of registered patent attorneys and agents, directory of USPTO contacts, and more.
- *Patents BIB.* Covers 1969 to present. Displays bibliographic data and, for selected years, abstracts.

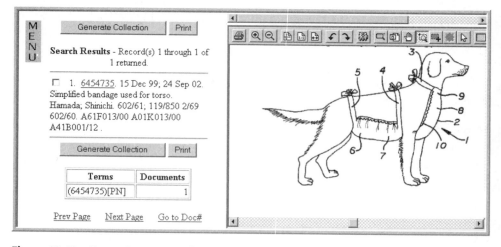

Figure 18-10   Patent Image on pubWEST

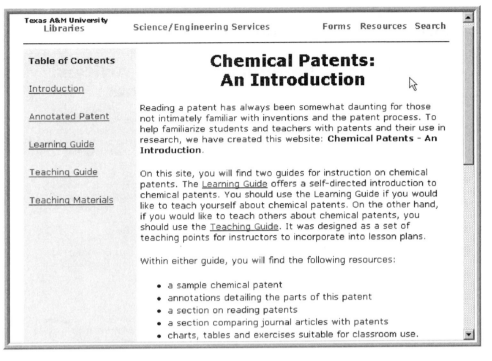

Figure 18-11 *Chemical Patents* Home Page

- *Patents CLASS.* Covers 1790 to present. Allows retrieval of patent numbers by class and subclass and retrieval of class and subclass data by patent number.
- *Patents & Trademarks ASSIGN.* Shows current assignees.
- *Trademarks BIB.* Shows bibliographic data for pending and registered trademarks.

Most of these databases are available on the USPTO Web site, but the functionality of the bibliographic and classification databases is much more suitable in a DVD-ROM environment, because of the data's complexity and level of detail. At some point in the future it might be possible to move these specialized resources in a Web format, but even then, people are likely to want a portable resource they can search offline. *Cassis®* or some future variant of that resource seems the best bet as that offline database.

Chemical Patents: A Web-Based Teaching Aid

Training guides can make it easier for students and researchers to understand how patents work and why they are important. *Chemical Patents: An Introduction* is a Web-based guide showing the similarities of patents to journal literature in the field of chemistry (see Figure 18-11). It is available at http://lib-oldweb .tamu.edu/se/chempat (Texas A&M University Libraries, 2003). This guide has three objectives: to help chemistry researchers (1) identify the parts of a patent,

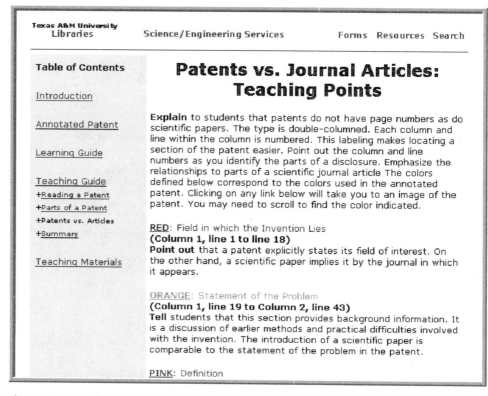

Figure 18-12   *Chemical Patents* Teaching Points

(2) compare and contrast patents to journal articles, and (3) recognize patents as primary literature and acknowledge their importance to the chemical industry. This self-directed guide allows users to advance at their own pace.

The *Chemical Patents* guide begins by identifying the different types of information on the front page of a patent, including the patent number, classification, and the references cited. The second section is titled "Patents vs. Journal Articles: Learning Points." This page identifies and explains the field of interest, background information or the "statement of the problem," the initial and detailed definitions of the invention, object of the invention (the benefits it provides), examples of end products from a chemical patent, and the claims (aspects of the invention that are new and therefore patentable). Each part of the patent is color-coded in order to catch users' attention. The third section presents ten questions designed to help the user better understand chemical patents. The fourth part compares scientific journal articles to patents—for example, a patent number is analogous to an article citation; the inventor is the same as an author.

Figure 18-12 shows *Chemical Patents'* teaching points. This section is almost identical to *Chemical Patents'* homepage in scope and format, but it is aimed at teachers and professors and goes into more detail than does the learning guide. For example, the "Reading a Patent" section gives advice on how to teach students about the importance of patents. The "Review Exercises" section includes the answers. Finally, in addition to the patent and article comparison chart, the teacher's guide includes a PowerPoint version.

Assisting Historical Researchers

Some instructors have more of a historical interest in technology. That is, they want students to consider technological innovations as indicators of past societal trends and interests or as precursors to social change. Individuals may also contact your library and request information about an older relative's invention or about a manufactured device in their possession (old inventions often turn up in archaeological surveys of military, mining, and other settlement sites). *LexisNexis Academic* (http://web.lexis-nexis.com/universe) allows keyword searching of utility patents issued before 1976 and is a good tool for historical researchers, since the USPTO site allows full-text searching only as far back as 1976. *LexisNexis Academic* includes text of utility patents beginning in 1790, design patents from December 7, 1976, and plant patents from December 14, 1976. The following sources list many kinds of inventions and their creators:

- *The Art of Invention.* http://artofinvention.tripod.com.
- Casey, Susan. 1997. *Women Invent: Two Centuries of Discoveries That Have Shaped Our World.* Chicago: Chicago Review Press.
- *Collection of Historical and Interesting U.S. Patents: In Celebration of Our Nation's Bicentennial.* 1976. Washington, DC: USPTO. Microfilm (available in Patent and Trademark Depository libraries).
- de Vries, Leonard, and Ilonka van Amstel. 1991 (reprint). *Victorian Inventions.* London: J. Murray.
- *Delphion's Gallery of Historic Patents.* www.delphion.com/historic.
- *Inductees of the National Inventors Hall of Fame.* Annual. Akron, OH: National Inventors Hall of Fame Foundation.
- Leggett, Mortimer Dormer. 2000 (reprint). *Subject-Matter Index of Patents for Inventors Issued by the United States Patent Office from 1790 to 1873, Inclusive.* North Stratford, NH: Ayer Co. Publishers. Reprint of the 1874 ed. published by the U.S. Government Printing Office, Washington, DC. 3 vol. 1874 ed. (also reproduced in *Executive Branch Documents,* 1790–1909, C.I.S. Microfiche).
- Philbin, Tom. 2003. *The 100 Greatest Inventions of All Time: A Ranking Past and Present.* New York: Citadel Press.
- Van Dulken, Stephen. 2000. *Inventing the 20th Century: 100 Inventions That Shaped the World: From the Airplane to the Zipper.* Washington Square: New York University Press.

Practical Aspects of Assisting Inventors and Other Patent Researchers

When science and engineering faculty assign their students to conduct patent searches, they often want them to find either a patent for an invention close to their own field of expertise (e.g., chemistry, mechanical engineering) or something related to their students' coursework. As discussed throughout this book, the best way to begin planning an instruction session is simply to call the professor and ask what he or she has in mind. For instance, a horticulture professor may be especially interested in the Plant Variety Protection Act, genetic engineering, and plant patents. Based on such a discussion, you should be able to select two or three patents to show as examples to the class.

If you work in a setting in which you provide group instruction in patent searching and related topics, you probably spend even more time assisting individual inventors or others who wish to conduct a patent search. Most of your walk-in patrons who may wish to do this have probably never used the USPTO databases before. When teaching people in your service area, you must take care not to perform the person's search yourself or offer anything more than general advice. Doing so is known as Unauthorized Practice of Law (UPL). The best way to avoid UPL and still provide good training is to use a generic concept that most people can easily understand. Two examples I have used are a train anti-collision system incorporating a global positioning system (GPS) component and the computerized emergency vehicle developed at Texas A&M University. Another technique to prevent unauthorized practice of law is to search on a technology that the student or inventor can identify with but at the same time is deliberately different from his or her exact innovation (e.g., searching for a type of toy, mechanical device, or design that is different from the inventor's) (Arant and Carpenter, 1999; Banicki, 2003).

When training either groups or individuals, you may show a search that will retrieve a patent issued to a local inventor or assigned to a local company. This will tend to capture your students' attention because it connects with something that is already familiar. Whatever type of technology or design you search is less important than showing patrons how to discover and search on the proper patent classifications. By far, searching by classification yields the best results when searching prior art.

Always provide novice searchers with handouts explaining the material you present. The reason for this is twofold. First, few people can memorize the Seven-Step Strategy and then successfully do a search by themselves. Handouts will remind them of the steps to follow. Second, a handout gives the person something concrete for the time spent in a learning situation. During the years I worked in a PTDL and Partnership library, I always felt it was important to provide easy-to-understand guides that would empower inventors and students to do their initial searches on their own. Once they felt they had exhausted all avenues themselves, they could come back to a PTDL, review the concepts, ask questions, and learn about other patent resources and strategies. Of course, if an inventor decides to consult with a patent attorney or agent instead, that is fine too. Teaching them how to "fish for themselves" keeps you from falling into that gray area of practicing law. Further, we must realize that inventors themselves are the real experts on their device or other creation. Once an inventor has the resources for a proper search and knows how to use them, he or she can do a much more effective search than any library reference staff could ever do for him or her.

S. R. Ranganathan's fourth law of library science tells us to "save the time of the reader" (Ranganathan, 1957). From this, we can understand the need to provide reference and instruction for our users in ways that meet their needs and do not place any undue demands on their time. Patent researchers do not want to sit for hours on end learning how to research. At best, they want learn in about an hour or less how to do a prior art search (at worst, they want you to do the search for them). The first hurdle is convincing them that a comprehensive patent search takes longer than an hour or two. Some patent examiners say that a search takes an average of ten hours but that the amount of time needed varies greatly depending on the complexity of the technology. For instance, one may expect to complete a prior art search for board games in less time than for electrical circuits, software, or drugs. Using the USPTO's Seven-Step Strategy as a model, you should be able to tell users about the proper sources to use, how to use them, how to formulate a search strategy, and some tips and tricks that might help expand their search, all in about forty-five to sixty minutes. This amount of time is a good fit for many group instruction settings. When you assist individual users who do not have that much time, you can usually cover the classification tools and initial search (Steps 1–4) in fifteen to twenty minutes. If the person is going to use the USPTO public Web site, tell him or her how to get the image viewer and to check back with you when they have questions.

Also tell your audience you are only showing them how to do a preliminary search on their innovation. To do an exhaustive search, a person needs to search not only U.S. and international patent databases but also technical and trade journals in that field of invention, any existing theses or dissertations, and any published workshops or proceedings. Researchers can do some of this on their own, but to identify all the resources that need to be checked requires consultation with a professional patent searcher, a USPTO patent examiner, or either a PTDL or PTDL Partnership representative. The USPTO is beginning to release search templates on its Web site, describing recommended sources and techniques for performing thorough prior art searches in various technologies. These recommended templates go far beyond searching U.S. patents and, as such, should provide valuable guidance to inventors and other patent researchers (USPTO, *Patents Search Templates*, 2005). Services of a Partnership Library become especially important when the researcher needs to learn about USPTO filing requirements, training sessions on how to do a good preliminary search, and how to use some of the more specialized databases (USPTO, PTDL Partnership Libraries, 2005).

Emerging Trends

"The only thing constant is change." Yes, it is a trite expression, but so true. In the early 1990s none of us could imagine going to a workstation, sitting down and connecting to a massive database, and being able to do a decent preliminary U.S. patent search by ourselves (i.e., without having to make a payment to an online provider). Even more fantastic is the ability to search foreign patent databases, most at no charge. Some of the better known of these databases include those of Japan, the World Intellectual Property Office, and the European Patent Office (EPO). The EPO database, also known as *esp@cenet*, contains patent documents in portable document format (PDF) from all EPO member states, including the United States and Japan, from the 1920s to the present. It allows researchers to do a patent search for similar inventions across a large number of countries and a broad range of years. *Esp@cenet* is available at www.european-patent-office.org/espacenet/info/access.htm. In the near future, users may see improvements in the speed and precision of resources such as *esp@cenet*, which could enable them to perform robust classification searches across different national patent systems.

Conclusion

The information presented here should give library personnel who do not specialize in patent searching enough knowledge to teach various audiences how to do a preliminary search. Intellectual property reference service is a specialty, but it is certainly approachable by generalist library reference service providers. That said, you should freely consult with trained patent and trademark depository librarians when you are unable to answer a question or run out of good ideas—they are a skilled, unbiased, and free resource who can support the interests both of inventors and historical patent researchers. A directory of PTDLs is available on the USPTO Web site at www.uspto.gov/go/ptdl/ptdlib_1.html. You should also consider purchasing reference and circulating copies of *Patent It Yourself* by David Pressman (Nolo Press), which is revised annually. This book and Nolo's other self-help legal guides explain intellectual property matters in everyday language.

Again, I invite readers to build upon what I have presented here and always remember to give credit where credit is due, for we all learn pieces for our great methods or search strategies from someone else. Fresh perspectives can add to our collective knowledge, all for the benefit of our users.

Note

1. I wish to acknowledge a number of fellow librarians, scientists, computing specialists, USPTO patent examiners, and Patent and Trademark Depository Library Program staff who have aided my understanding of patents and search techniques. These include Kathryn Taylor, Marie Moisdon, Don Kelly, Charles Rademaker, Douglas Salser, Harold Smith, Michael White, Tom Turner, Mary Ellen Teasdale, Dean Poppell, Brian Quigley, and Dr. Michael Rosynek.

Bibliography

Arant, Wendi, and Brian Carpenter. 1999. "Where Is the Line? Legal Reference Service and the Unauthorized Practice of Law (UPL)—Some Guides That Might Help." *Reference and User Services Quarterly* 38 (Spring): 235–239.

Banicki, Cynthia A. 2003. "A Librarian's Guide to Legal Reference Assistance." Presentation at the 26th Annual Patent and Trademark Depository Library Training Seminar, March 16–21.

Hitchcock, David. 2000. *Patent Searching Made Easy: How to Do Patent Searches on the Internet and in the Library*. 2nd ed. Berkeley, CA: Nolo Press.

Ranganathan, S. R. 1957. *The Five Laws of Library Science*. London: Blunt and Sons.

Texas A&M University Libraries. 2003. *Chemical Patents: An Introduction*. http://lib-oldweb.tamu.edu/se/chempat (accessed November 14, 2005).

U.S. Patent and Trademark Office (USPTO). 2005. *General Information Concerning Patents*. www.uspto.gov/web/offices/pac/doc/general/index.html (accessed November 16, 2005).

———. 2005. *USPTO Patents Search Templates*. www.uspto.gov/web/patents/searchtemplates (accessed November 13, 2005).

———. 2005. *PTDL Partnership Libraries*. www.uspto.gov/go/ptdl/partinfo.htm (accessed November 15, 2005).

Wherry, Timothy Lee. 1995. *Patent Searching for Librarians and Inventors*. Chicago: American Library Association.

Index

About the Editor and Contributors

Patrick Ragains is Business and Government Information Librarian at the University of Nevada, Reno. He holds an MLS from the University of Arizona (1987) and an MA in History from Northern Arizona University (1984). He has published articles in *Journal of Government Information, portal: Libraries & the Academy*, and *Research Strategies*, two of which were recognized by the American Library Association's (ALA) Library Instruction Round Table (LIRT) as among the best twenty articles on library instruction published in 1995 and 2001. He is former chair of the Association of College and Research Libraries (ACRL) Research Committee and is active in the ACRL Instruction Section.

Tina M. Adams is Reference Librarian at Northern Arizona University. She holds an MA degree in Library and Information Science from the University of South Florida (2001). She has published articles in *College and Research Libraries* and *Journal of Library Administration* and has presented at international, national, and local meetings and conferences. She is a member of ALA/ACRL.

Duncan Aldrich is Dataworks Coordinator at the University of Nevada, Reno Libraries. He received an MA in comparative frontier studies from the University of Oklahoma (1977) and an MLIS from the University of Oklahoma (1985). Mr. Aldrich has published articles in the *Journal of Government Information*, in *Government Information Quarterly*, in *College and Research Libraries*, and in the *Chronicles of Oklahoma*. He also has published several book chapters. He is active in ALA/GODORT, of which he is past chair (1993–1994). He has also worked as a consultant to the U.S. Government Printing Office and served two terms on the Depository Library Council to the Public Printer of the United States.

Neal Baker is Information Technology and Reference Librarian at Earlham College. He has an MA in Film Studies from the University of Iowa (1993) and an MA in Library and Information Science from the University of Iowa (1995). His articles on film and science fiction literature have appeared in such peer-reviewed serials as *Contemporary French Civilization*, *Journal of the Fantastic in the Arts*, and *Extrapolation*. He is a Field Bibliographer for the *MLA International Bibliography* and has published book chapters in *Into Darkness Peering: Race and Color in the Fantastic* and *Best Practices in Library Instruction in the First Year*.

Brian B. Carpenter is a freelance writer living in Hendersonville, Tennessee. He was formerly Associate Professor at Texas A&M University Libraries and spent two years (1992–1994) as a Fellowship Librarian at the Patent and Trademark Depository Library Program Office, USPTO. He has published numerous articles and delivered many presentations on patents and intellectual property.

Jean S. Caspers is Reference and Instruction Librarian at Linfield College in McMinnville, Oregon. She holds an MLS from the University of Arizona (1989). Ms. Caspers has published articles in *College and Research Libraries*, *FID Review*, *Journal of Library Administration*, *Reference Librarian*, and *Research Strategies*. She has also published chapters in *Teaching Information Retrieval and Evaluation Skills to Education Students and Practitioners: A Casebook of Applications* (Chicago: ALA, 1995), *The Collaborative Imperative* (ACRL, 2000), *Reference Librarians at the Gateway* (Haworth, 2000), and *Off-Campus Library Services* (Haworth, 2001). She is active in the ACRL, having chaired several key committees since 1995.

Mark Emmons is Coordinator of Information Literacy and Instruction Services at the University of New Mexico Libraries. He holds an MLS from the University of California, Los Angeles (1990). He is author of the book, *Film and Television: A Guide to the Reference Literature* (Libraries Unlimited, 2006). Mr. Emmons has published articles in *College and Research Libraries*, *Library HI TECH*, and *Public Services Quarterly*. He is active in the ALA/ACRL Instruction Section, having chaired the Instruction Section's Planning and Teaching Methods Committees, and has served as president of New Mexico Academic and Research Librarians.

R. Sean Evans is Reference Librarian at Northern Arizona University. He holds an MA in Information Resources and Library Science from the University of Arizona (2000) and an MA in History and Political Science from Northern Arizona University (1981). He recently published an article in *Journal of Library Administration*. Mr. Evans has presented at a wide array of conferences on topics including distance education, federal documents issues, and the USA PATRIOT Act.

Alexander Gyamfi is Reference and Instruction Librarian in the Science Library at University at Albany, SUNY. He holds three advanced degrees from the University at Albany, SUNY: an MA in Africana Studies (1996), MLS (2000), and PhD in Educational Administration (2003). He has recently published an article in the journal *Information Development*.

Peggy Keeran is an Associate Professor and Arts and Humanities Reference Librarian at Penrose Library, University of Denver. In 1984 she received her MLIS and an MA in Art History from the University of California, Berkeley. She has published articles in *The Reference Librarian*, *Research Strategies*, and *Art Documentation*, has co-authored a book titled *Literary Research and the Romantic Era: Strategies and Sources*, and is co-editor for the forthcoming Scarecrow series *Literary Research: Strategies and Sources*. She has served on the Executive Board for ARLIS/NA as the West Regional Representative, as chair and as secretary/treasurer for the local ARLIS/Mountain West chapter, and as a member of ALA's Wilson Indexes Committee.

Joel D. Kitchens is Reference Librarian and Associate Professor at Texas A&M University. He holds an MLS (1996) and MA in History (1992), both from the University of Alabama. He is a former member of the Bibliographies and Indexes Committee of ALA's Reference and User Services Association (RUSA) History Section and has published articles on history and library-related issues in *The Journal of Academic Librarianship*, *Research Strategies*, *The Alabama Review*, and *Library Collections, Acquisitions and Technical Services*.

Allison V. Level is the Natural Resources and Agriculture Librarian at Colorado State University (CSU) Libraries. She has an MEd in Higher Education Administration and Student Personnel from Kent State University (1985), and her MLS is from Emporia State University (1990). Her publications appear in *Library Management*, *Journal of Women and Minorities in Science and Engineering*, *Reference Services Review*, *Collection Building*, *Colorado Libraries*, *Journal of Agricultural and Food Information*, and *Issues in Science and Technology Librarianship*. She authored a chapter in the book *Designs for Active Learning*. Level is a member of the Executive Council for the U.S. Agricultural Information Network (USAIN) and is the CSU representative to the Agriculture Network Information Center (AgNIC) Coordinating Committee. She is a member of ALA/ACRL and has served on the ACRL's Instruction Section Research and Scholarship Committee and Science and Technology Section, serving on many committees and also as the Science and Technology Section Chair.

Ann Roselle is Library Director at Phoenix College. She holds an MA in Sociology (1989) and MS in Information and Library Science (1991). She has published articles in *Government Information Quarterly*, *Journal of Academic Librarianship*, *Journal of Government Information*, *Library and Information Science Research*, *Library Review*, and *Research Strategies* and a chapter in *Encyclopedia of Library and Information Science* (Vol. 65). She is former president of the Northwest Government Information Network (2000–2001); Secretary of the Embassy Relations Committee, subgroup of the ALA Presidential Advisory Council (1997–1998); and Secretary of the Professional Development Subcommittee of the Botswana Library Association (1994–1995).

Gregg Sapp is Head of the Science Library at the University at Albany, SUNY. He received an MLS from the University of Washington and an MEd from Montana State University. He has published peer-reviewed articles in *College and Research Libraries*, *Science and Technology Libraries*, and issues in *Scientific and Technical Libraries*. He is the author of *Library Journal*'s annual review article, "Best Scientific and Technical Books for General Readers." He has also written several books, including *Building a Popular Science Library Collection* (Greenwood Press, 1995) and *A Brief History of the Future of Libraries* (Scarecrow Press, 2002).

Nonny Schlotzhauer is Social Sciences Librarian at the Pennsylvania State University. He holds an MLS from the University of Pittsburgh (1991). He has published articles in *Behavior and Social Sciences Librarian*, *UN Journal*, and *Regional Development Dialogue*. He is a member of ALA/ACRL and the International Federation of Library Associations (IFLA).

Susie A. Skarl is Urban Studies Librarian at University of Nevada, Las Vegas (UNLV) Libraries. Prior to this position, she was Federal Depository Librarian at UNLV. She obtained her master's degree in Library Science (MLS) from Kent State University in 1999. She has published articles in *Reference Services Review* and *Library Hi Tech*. She is active in the ALA (RUSA) and ACRL Instruction Section.

Cory Tucker is the Business Librarian at the University of Nevada, Las Vegas. He received his MLS from the University of South Florida in 2001. He has published articles in *Reference Services Review*, *Library Hi-Tech*, and the *Journal of Business and Finance Librarianship* and is a member of the ALA and ACRL.

Janelle M. Zauha is Associate Professor and Reference Team Leader in the Libraries of Montana State University—Bozeman. She holds an MA in Library and Information Science from the University of Iowa (1993) and an MA in Literature from Clark University (Worcester, MA, 1989). She has published chapters in

Continuing Professional Development—Preparing for New Roles in Libraries: A Voyage of Discovery, Sixth World Conference on Continuing Professional Development and Workplace Learning for the Library and Information Professions (Munich: Saur, 2005), and has contributed articles to *PNLA Quarterly, Public Libraries, Acquisitions Librarian, Internet Reference Services Quarterly,* and *Collection Building.* She is active in ALA, ACRL, and the Montana Library Association and has served as president of the Pacific Northwest Library Association (PNLA) in 2004–2005.

DATE DUE
